Autism Spectrum Disorder: Neuromodulation, Neurofeedback and Sensory Integration Approaches to Research and Treatment

Edited by

Estate M. Sokhadze

and

Manuel F. Casanova

Foundation for Neurofeedback and Neuromodulation Research

Foundation for Neurofeedback and Neuromodulation Research
1715-K S. Rutherford Blvd. #200
Murfreesboro, TN 37130
www.theFNNR.org

Editors: Estate (Tato) M. Sokhadze and Manuel F. Casanova (University of South Carolina School of Medicine-Greenville, Greenville, SC)
Layout Design & Graphics: Cynthia Powers
Copy Editor: Jon Frederick
Cover Art: Trent Altman (trentsstudio.com)
Correspondence: Admin@theFNNR.org

Autism Spectrum Disorder: Neuromodulation, Neurofeedback and Sensory Integration Approaches to Research and Treatment

Publishers: Foundation for Neurofeedback & Neuromodulation Research (FNNR) and BMED Press, Murfreesboro, TN & Corpus Christi, TX

ISBN: 978-0-9978194-4-1

Contents

Preface

Manuel F. Casanova and Estate M. Sokhadze

University of South Carolina School of Medicine-Greenville, Greenville, SC

Luigi Galvani's accidental discovery in 1780 that a dead animal's muscles could twitch, if stimulated by an electrical spark, engendered the idea of "animal electricity." Nerves were more than tubes filled with fluid; they were conduits for electrical current. Science stood in opposition to religion as it rapidly eroded the foundation of vitalism. In a macabre leap of faith, Galvani's nephew, Giovanni Aldini, progressed from frog legs to attempts at the reanimation of criminals. He would wait by the guillotine to collect the fresh specimens provided by decapitation and then pass a current through their mouth and ears so as to provoke facial grimacing. Reports of such efforts inspired Mary Shelley to write Frankenstein, the sapient creature whose vitality and life force originated from a burst of electricity; a force that presumably breached life and death. The experiments sparked a debate as to the existence of an intrinsic source of animal electricity and whether it was phenomenologically identical to other natural phenomena. During this transformative time period, Benjamin Franklin (1752) showed that lightning was electrical in nature. He also helped explain the behavior of the Leyden jar, an early capacitor, as a storage device of electric charge. Indeed, Benjamin Franklin introduce the term Leyden battery to describe the grouping together of several Leyden jars. Shortly afterwards, Alessandro Volta combined zinc and copper discs in an acidic solution to provide a pile wherein the number of cells influenced the shock they produced. Contrary to the Leyden jar, the voltaic pile was able to deliver continuous electric current to a circuit.

Until the introduction of the dynamo in the 1870s, the electrical industry was powered by batteries.

The initial attempts at electrotherapy used electric baths and Oudin coils (an autotransformer) as means of delivering high voltages at low current levels to patients. The availability of portable devices powered by batteries allowed for a more moderate and controlled intervention. However, these improvised machines were soon adapted so that the low voltages produced by batteries were stepped up by transformers thus shocking those patients that held the electrodes in their hands or had them applied somewhere else on their bodies. The machines looked impressive and complex enough to generate a placebo effect. Electrotherapy was soon the object of wild theoretical assertions and a quack cure for a vast variety of conditions. Among these, Radionics was the brainchild of Albert Abrams, a physician, who claimed to diagnose the ills of patients without meeting them in person. A sample derived from a patient (e.g., hair, blood, or handwritten note) was attached to a machine that allowed a measure of its "energy frequency." It was Dr. Abrams belief that disease was caused by unhealthy frequencies and that they could be countered by healthy ones. The American Medical Association went on to describe Abrams as the "dean of gadget quacks" (Barrett, 2012).

One of the many imitators of Abrams was Royal Raymond Rife, an American inventor, who claimed to have visualized microbes with a specially designed optical microscope. He believed that these pathogens were the cause of cancer and themselves could be destroyed by applying a beam ray of destructive resonant frequencies. Several deaths have resulted from the use of Rife devices and its fraudulent claims.

In the midst of these controversial claims, in the 1930's, electroconvulsive therapy (ECT) was introduced to medical practice as a way of treating mental disorders. Drugs inducing convulsions had already been used in medical practice.

The electric current passing through the brain induced a seizure lasting 30 to 60 seconds. At the beginning, patients were not given anesthesia and high levels of current were used. However, the technique was steadily modified, and side effects were avoided. It is presently used under anesthesia in patients with severe major depression, bipolar disorder or schizophrenia who have not responded to other treatments.

By altering the action of nerve cells, ECT started the modern era of neuromodulation which now spans non-invasive (e.g., transcranial magnetic stimulation) and invasive techniques (e.g., deep brain stimulation). Most of these techniques are thought to act by altering natural biological mechanisms and seem to find a place in multidisciplinary treatment settings when use of other interventions (e.g., drugs) may lead to the development of tolerance, addiction or adverse side effects. Moreover, neuromodulation seems to be a promising treatment for some neurodevelopmental disorders. Many of these conditions are recognized as complex or multifactorial disorders which are not tied to a single genetic cause. Neurodevelopmental disorders are likely polygenic in origin and their expression is dependent on lifestyle and environmental factors. Indeed, the nature of multifactorial disorders makes them difficult to treat. Drugs may target only one neurochemical system, when many different ones may be affected. Treatment is also compounded by the heterogeneity of clinical manifestations among affected patients. Multifactorial conditions in this regard call for individualized or precision interventions for homogenous subgroups within what otherwise may be described as a spectrum of disorders.

Autism spectrum disorder (ASD) is a multifactorial condition of unknown origin. A triple hit hypothesis postulates the necessity of the combined influences of a genetic risk factor, environmental exigencies and a vulnerable time period of brain development (Casanova, 2007). Symptoms suggest that it is a gray matter disease of generalized spread throughout the cerebral cortex while the presence of seizures indicates an imbalance in its excitatory to inhibitory bias. EEG and threshold studies of vibrotactile sensation elucidate this shift in the excitatory/inhibitory bias as a defect of lateral inhibition. The suggested pathology can be targeted by neuromodulation techniques while simultaneously providing for putative severity dependent outcome measures.

Transcranial magnetic stimulation (TMS) was the first neuromodulation technique used in ASD that targeted core pathological processes (Sokhadze et al., 2009). Until that moment in time, therapeutic attempts in autism had been symptomatic and, in the case of drugs, had severe side effects. Several hundred patients have now been treated in this way with significant improvements in behavior. Synergism has now been reported when combining this technique with neurofeedback (Sokhadze et al., 2014). Given the high comorbidity between autism and attention deficit/hyperactivity disorder (ADHD) it will be useful to explore whether any benefit accrued to neurofeedback is primarily evident in this subgroup of patients.

In this book several researchers report their results using rTMS in autism. Gomez et al. expand on several of their clinical trials and summarize the status of the field while Casanova et al. review some of their rTMS work as related to gamma oscillations. In complementary fashion, Ni and Huang review the use of patterned theta burst TMS application in autism and report clinical results of their own trial. Given the preliminary success of neuromodulation in ASD, the reader may consider it wise to think about other techniques of brain activity entrainment and, indeed, Casanova et al. propose using sympathetic (passive) resonance as a potential method of altering brain waves and behavioral states in autism.

More recently, low constant current stimulation has been introduced as a way of altering the resting membrane potential of neurons. The simplicity, accessibility, and low risk of using a battery powered device have instigated a vast amount of research. Studies are now focusing on its putative effects in autism. Preliminary results show improvements in both behavioral and cognitive symptoms. Parmar et al. review the application of transcranial direct current stimulation (tDCS) in their chapter. Future research will focus on standardizing protocols, defining the most appropriate outcome measures and assessing its long-term efficacy.

Electroencephalographic (EEG) biofeedback (i.e., neurofeedback) has more than 60 years of history steaming from the studies of Kamiya, Hardt, Green, Tansey, Sterman and other pioneers in late 60s and early 70s. Neurofeedback (NFB) has been recognized as a suitable tool for modulating neural plasticity (reviewed in Kamiya, 2011). By operant conditioning of EEG, NFB provides an effective way to train electrophysiological activity of the targeted cortical topography. Neurofeedback training is considered as one of the most effective and salient treatments for children with attention deficit hyperactivity (ADHD). The clinical efficacy of using NFB for ADHD treatments was reviewed and discussed in several meta-analyses of randomized clinical trials (Arns et al., 2009, 2013, 2014; Hurt et al., 2014). Considering that NFB has gained significant support as an effective treatment for ADHD, some attempts have been made to transfer this ADHD neurotherapy technique to treat core symptoms of ASD. Still, the question remains unanswered as to whether present day protocols that have been shown to be efficacious in ADHD are also effective for ASD.

Several papers reviewed application of neurofeedback for ASD treatment and many of them provide evidence that some of the core symptoms of autism can be improved by using neurofeedback training (Coben, 2013; Jarusiewicz, 2002; Kouijzer et al., 2009, 2013; Linden & Gunkelman, 2013; Wang et al., 2016). Most of them used suppression of theta at fronto-central or central sites, enhancement of low beta (13–21 Hz, sometimes 13–18 Hz) sub-band, or enhancement of sensory-motor rhythm (SMR, 12–15 Hz) at the central sites (C3, Cz, C4). Another line of treatment based on neurofeedback focuses on mu-rhythm training (Pineda et al., 2014). Some protocols use quantitative EEG-guided and coherence measures (Coben, 2013; Linden & Gunkelman, 2013). Our group's approach included neurofeedback training at the prefrontal topography, specifically at the midline prefrontal site. This selection of cortical topography was determined by prior studies on EEG gamma rhythm in children with autism showing alterations of evoked and induced gamma oscillations during attention tests demonstrating notable changes at frontal topographies (Sokhadze et al., 2009). In our pilot study (Wang et al., 2016) using 40 Hz gamma power upregulation we found that theta-to-beta ratio showed a significant linear decrease over 18 sessions of neurofeedback. The positive effects of neurofeedback training further were manifested by improvement in the aberrant behavior scores. In a pilot study presently underway we have compared outcomes of 18 versus 24 versus 36 sessions of neurofeedback using three different NFB training protocol in children with autism and two or three sessions per week. More data on application of neurofeedback in ASD treatment can be found in the chapter by Barterian et al.

We decided to include sensory integration approaches in this book because sensory abnormalities are typical of autism spectrum disorder. Sensory stimuli cause inappropriate responses with some ASD individuals exhibiting over-stimulation, others showing under-stimulation, and some exhibiting both conditions at various times. These sensory challenges may result in some forms of the unusual behaviors that are present in autism (O'Connor, 2012). Many treatments and interventions have focused on methods to reduce the abnormalities of sensory processing in autism. Sensory integration intervention is the most commonly implemented therapy by occupational therapists for children with ASD and is one of the most commonly requested types of occupational therapy treatments in general (Goin-Kochel et al., 2007). In a chapter by Schoen et al. the authors describe their approaches to sensory integration in children with ASD.

A variety of interventions directed at reducing sound sensitivity and related auditory problems are currently used by practitioners and parents, with positive results reported in many cases. The Berard method of auditory integration training (AIT) is of particular interest for several reasons. There are some research studies that provide behavioral and some physiological data to document efficacy (Berard & Brockett, 2011; Rimland & Edelson, 1994). The Berard AIT program is based on a theory that the use of electronically modulated, and on occasion, selectively filtered music, retrains the ear and auditory system to work properly. More detailed insight about Berard AIT is described in the chapter by Brockett.

According to several recent theories sensory processing abnormalities may play an important role in impairments of perception, cognition, and behavior noted in individuals with autism. Among these sensory abnormalities, visual distortion may force autistic individuals to rely on peripheral vision, develop strabismus, and manifest "stereotypic behaviors." In a chapter by Kaplan and Kotsamanidis-Burg, the authors review visual processing abnormalities typical for autism and visuomotor training and therapy based on wearing prism lenses and an intensive course of visual therapy. The chapter is followed by a pilot experimental study conducted by Sokhadze et al. using Kaplan's method of behavioral visual therapy.

The book is concluded by a series of cases studies where rTMS, neurofeedback, and sensory integration therapies (AIT, prism lenses-based therapy) are used in combination. Despite increased awareness about autism and increased prevalence of autism in the USA and worldwide, there is relatively little information available about the basics of core clinical symptoms, behavioral features of autism spectrum disorder, and standards for diagnosis and treatment. This is one of the main reasons we decided to include two chapters devoted to a clinician's perspective on diagnosis and treatment of ASD. One more chapter is devoted to questions related to genetic risks of autism. Another chapter by Sokhadze et al. reviews the role of autonomic nervous system dysfunctions in autism.

This book was initially planned as a collection of studies devoted to neuromodulation methods in autism research and treatment. However, it ended up with a wider scope, as understanding autism spectrum disorder is not possible without addressing numerous important clinical and neurodevelopmental facets of the disorder. Even though it was technically impossible to cover all past and current approaches to neuromodulation, neurofeedback and sensory integration therapies in autism, we hope that this book will serve as a useful contribution to the literature on this topic.

References

Arns, M., Conners, C. K., & Kraemer, H. C. (2013). A decade of EEG theta/beta ratio research in ADHD: A meta-analysis. *Journal of Attention Disorders, 17*(5), 374–383.

Arns, M., Heinrich, H., & Strehl, U. (2014). Evaluation of neurofeedback in ADHD: The long and winding road. *Biological Psychology, 95*, 108–115.

Arns, M., de Ridder, S., Strehl, U., Breteler, M., & Coenen, A. (2009). Efficacy of neurofeedback treatment in ADHD: The effects on inattention, impulsivity and hyperactivity: A meta-analysis. *Clinical EEG and Neuroscience, 40*(3), 180–189.

Barrett, S. (2012). Rife machine operator sued. Quackwatch. Retrieved from https://www.quackwatch.org/04ConsumerEducation/News/rife.html

Berard, G., & Brockett, S. (2011). *Hearing equals behavior: Updated and expanded.* Manchester Center, VT: ShiresPress Press.

Casanova, M. F. (2007). The neuropathology of autism. *Brain Pathology, 19*(4), 422–433.

Coben, R. (2013). Neurofeedback for autistic disorders: Emerging empirical evidence. In M. F. Casanova, A. S. El-Baz, & J. S. Suri (Eds.), *Imaging the brain in autism* (pp. 107–133). New York, NY: Springer.

Goin-Kochel, R. P., Myers, B. J., & Mackintosh, V. H. (2007). Parental reports on the use of treatments and therapies for children with autism spectrum disorders. *Research in Autism Spectrum Disorders, 1*(3), 195–209.

Hurt, E., Arnold, L. E., & Lofthouse, N. (2014). Quantitative EEG neurofeedback for the treatment of pediatric attention-deficit/hyperactivity disorder, autism spectrum disorders, learning disorders, and epilepsy. *Child and Adolescent Psychiatric Clinics of North America, 23*(3), 465–486.

Jarusiewicz, B. (2002). Efficacy of neurofeedback for children in the autistic spectrum. A pilot study. *Journal of Neurotherapy, 6*(4), 39–49. Kamiya, J. (2011). The first communications about operant conditioning of the EEG. *Journal of Neurotherapy, 15*(1), 65-73

Kouijzer, M. E., van Schie, H. T., Gerrits, B. J., Buitelaar, J. K., & de Moor, J. M. (2013). Is EEG-biofeedback an effective treatment in autism spectrum disorders? A randomized controlled trial. *Applied Psychophysiology and Biofeedback, 38*(1), 17–28.

Kouijzer, M. E. J., de Moor, J. M. H., Gerrits, B. J. L., Congedo, M., & van Schie, H. T. (2009). Neurofeedback improves executive functioning in children with autism spectrum disorders. *Research in Autism Spectrum Disorders, 3*(1), 145–162.

Linden, M., & Gunkelman, J. (2013). QEEG-guided neurofeedback for autism: Clinical observations and outcomes. In M. F. Casanova, A. S. El-Baz & J. S. Suri (Eds.), *Imaging the brain in autism* (pp. 45–60). New York, NY: Springer.

O'Connor, K. (2012). Auditory processing in autism spectrum disorder: A review. *Neuroscience and Biobehavioral Reviews, 36*(2), 836–854.

Pineda, J. A., Carrasco, K., Datko, M., Pillen, S., & Schalles, M. (2014). Neurofeedback training produces normalization in behavioural and electrophysiological measures of high-functioning autism. *Philosophical Transactions of the Royal Society of London. Series B, Biological Sciences, 369*(1644), 20130183.

Rimland, B., & Edelson, S. (1994). The effects of auditory integration training on autism. *Journal of Speech-Language Pathology, 3*(2), 16–24.

Sokhadze, E. M., El-Baz, A., Baruth, J., Mathai, G., Sears, L., & Casanova, M. F. (2009). Effects of low frequency repetitive transcranial magnetic stimulation (rTMS) on gamma frequency oscillations and event-related potentials during processing of illusory figures in autism. *Journal of Autism and Developmental Disorders, 39*(4), 619–634.

Sokhadze, E. M., El-Baz, A. S., Tasman, A., Sears, L. L., Wang, Y., Lamina, E. V., & Casanova M. F. (2014). Neuromodulation integrating rTMS and neurofeedback for the treatment of autism spectrum disorder: An exploratory study. *Applied Psychophysiology and Biofeedback, 39*(3–4), 237–257.

Thompson, L., Thompson, M., & Reid, A. (2010). Functional neuroanatomy and the rationale for using EEG biofeedback for clients with Asperger's syndrome. *Applied Psychophysiology and Biofeedback, 35*(1), 39–61.

Wang, Y., Sokhadze, E. M., El-Baz, A. S., Li, X., Sears, L., Casanova, M. F., & Tasman, A. (2016). Relative power of specific EEG bands and their ratios during neurofeedback training in children with autism spectrum disorder. *Frontiers in Human Neuroscience, 9*, 723.

1

Introduction to Autism Spectrum Disorder

Grace Mathai Kuravackel and Lonnie L. Sears
University of Louisville, School of Medicine, Louisville, KY

Autism spectrum disorder (ASD) is a developmental disorder that presents with atypical language and social behavior, along with restrictive and repetitive behaviors and unusual interests (American Psychiatric Association [APA], 2013). Prior to 1980 (APA, 1980), ASD symptoms were considered to be representative of early onset schizophrenia (APA, 1952, 1968). The fourth revision of the DSM categorized the symptoms of ASD into three distinct pervasive developmental disorders (PDDs): autism, PPD–not otherwise specified, and Asperger syndrome (APA, 1994). The classification of the PDDs did not change with the DSM IV–text revision (APA, 2000). With the fifth edition of the DSM, the three PDDs are collapsed into one diagnostic disorder, ASD. The diagnosis of Asperger syndrome and PDD–not otherwise specified are no longer given in the DSM-5. The new DSM-5 diagnostic disorder ASD has two main criteria: (A) persistent social communication and social interaction deficits and (B) restricted, repetitive patterns of behavior, interests, or activities.

Based on DSM-IV criteria, the prevalence of ASD in the United States is estimated to have increased from 1 in 10,000 people in the 1990s (Rutter, 2007) to 1 in 68 people (about 4.7 million) in 2014, with a 4:1 male to female prevalence (Baio et al., 2014). Widening the Autism Spectrum in the DSM-IV to include Asperger syndrome increased the supports for ASD and the diagnostic surveillance in health and educational care.

Table 1.1.
DSM 5 criteria for Autism Spectrum Disorder

Criteria A

- Social-emotional reciprocity.
- Nonverbal communicative behaviors used for social interaction.
- Developing, maintaining, and understanding relationships.

Criteria B

- Stereotyped or repetitive movements, use of objects, or speech.
- Insistence on sameness, inflexible adherence to routines, or ritualized patterns of verbal or nonverbal behavior.
- Highly restricted, fixated interests that are abnormal in intensity or focus.
- Hyper- or hyporeactivity to sensory input or unusual sensory environment interest.

Criteria C

- Symptoms were present in early developmental period.

Criteria D

- Symptoms correlate with clinically significant impairments in social or occupational functioning.

Criteria E

- Impairments are not better explained by intellectual disability or global developmental delay.

Specifiers

- With or without intellectual impairment.
- With or without language impairment.
- Any associated or known medical or genetic condition.
- Any associated neurodevelopmental, mental or behavioral disorder.

Severity Rating

Level 1: Requires support.

Level 2: Requires substantial support.

Level 3: Requires very substantial support.

Note. Adapted criteria for Autism Spectrum Disorder in the Diagnostic and Statistical Manual for Mental Disorders, (DSM-V©). American Psychiatric Association (2013).

It also improved ASD awareness, which helps explain the increasing ASD prevalence (Baio et al., 2014; Fombonne, 2009; Rutter, 2007).

Diagnostic Screeners for ASD

Primary care providers screen children for ASDs between the ages of 18 and 24 months based on American Academy of Pediatrics (AAP) guidelines (Council on Children with Disabilities, 2006; Johnson & Myers, 2007). Numerous screening tools specific to ASD symptoms are available (Council on Children with Disabilities, 2006; Gardner, 2012; Zwaigenbaum, 2011). A commonly used tool is the Modified Checklist for Autism in Toddlers Revised Form (Herlihy et al., 2014; Robins et al., 2014).

The Childhood Autism Rating Scale (CARS; Schopler, Reichler, & Renner, 1988) is one of the most widely researched rating scales for evaluating clinical behaviors of autism (Lord & Corsello, 2005). The CARS-original version (CARS; Schopler et al., 1988) is now referred to as the CARS2-Standard Version (CARS2-ST) and includes updated field trial data. The CARS2-ST continues to be used with children under the age of 6 and individuals of any age with less developed verbal skills and IQ scores less than 80. The CARS2-High Functioning Version (CARS2-HF) was added to assess individuals with estimated overall IQ scores of 80 or higher who are verbally fluent and 6 years of age or older. Research indicates that CARS2 continues to be an appropriate diagnostic tool for individuals referred for an ASD evaluation across the lifespan when using the DSM-5 criteria (Dawkins, Meyer, & Van Bourgondien, 2016).

Another ASD-specific screening questionnaire that is widely used in clinical practice as well as in research is the Social Responsiveness Scale (SRS; Constantino & Gruber, 2012). The

SRS consists of 65 items that can be scored in 15 minutes by a parent or teacher. One of the advantages of the SRS is that it has been designed to assess social impairment associated with ASD as rated by multiple informants on a Likert response scale. Therefore, the SRS is considered suitable to capture autistic characteristics in varying degrees and to provide a severity index of autistic social impairment (Constantino & Gruber, 2012).

Importance of Referral for Diagnostic Evaluations

Primary care providers refer children for expert diagnostic evaluations if they appear to be at risk for ASD, based on this preliminary screening tool. Some absolute "red flags" that should prompt referral for further diagnostic evaluation for ASD are not babbling or gesturing (pointing or waving "bye-bye") by 12 months. These red flags are consistent with the social communication and restricted and repetitive behavior hallmarks of ASD. Ideally, timely referral for children with positive ASD screening results to both a developmental clinic for further diagnostic evaluations and referral to community early intervention program should occur simultaneously (Gardner, 2012; Johnson C. & Myers, 2007; Manning-Courtney et al., 2013).

There are no medical markers to definitively diagnose ASD. Reliable detecting of ASD involves comprehensive developmental screening of multiple areas of functioning, and ASD specific screening, which is superior to clinician observation alone (Daniels & Mandell, 2013; Guevara et al., 2013; Miller et al., 2011). The presentation of ASD can range from a child who is nonverbal and unlikely to make social initiations, to a child who is verbally fluent, but overly reliant on previously learned scripts of speech and social behavior. Because of this variability in symptom presentation and severity, diagnostic decision-making can be a complex process with no singular algorithm specific to the diagnosis of ASD. In a clinical sense this has meant that no one behavior, such as responding to name or joint attention, excludes a diagnosis of ASD. For example, though responding to name and joint attention are important characteristics of ASD in toddlers, by older preschool many children with ASD may be competent in these behaviors. A child who will follow a point and respond to their name as a toddler can still merit a diagnosis of ASD if he or she does not seek to share enjoyment with others, smile responsively except during intense physical activity, show much interest in their siblings or same-age peers and use language to answer questions and make socially-directed comments (Johnson N., Burkett, Reinhold & Bultas, 2016).

Very often other variables such as cognitive functioning and age can complicate the diagnosis of ASD. Specific behaviors that are considered to be red flags are dependent on developmental factors associated with language and age and require caregiver report whether that is elicited through questionnaires or interviews (Bishop, Richler & Lord, 2006; Richler, Bishop, Kleinke & Lord, 2007; Sigman & McGovern, 2005). To address these challenges, the National Research Council Committee on Educational Interventions for Children with Autism (2001) advised that each child suspected of having ASD have an evaluation that incorporates the following standards: the assessment of multiple areas of functioning including adaptive skills, an appreciation that variability in performance and ability is common in autism, and the use of a developmental perspective when assessing behavior and synthesizing results.

The Diagnostic Process

It is particularly important to differentiate ASD from other developmental disorders. The inclusion of standardized cognitive, adaptive and developmental testing, as well as an assessment of language, when administered by experienced professionals will help in this differentiation. Important information regarding overall level of ability and functioning in verbal and nonverbal areas will help tease out important factors that support an ASD diagnosis. The separation of verbal and nonverbal estimates of functioning is particularly important because many children with ASD may show stronger nonverbal skills than one might expect from their language level or play. Standardized scores from a skilled examiner allow the clinician to consider questions such as: can intellectual disability and/or language delay explain the difficulties in social interaction? Given this level of ability, are observed difficulties in communication and social behavior above and beyond what would be expected? And finally does the level of social ability fall short of what is expected given cognitive or language ability? (Huerta & Lord, 2012).

"Multidisciplinary" should be interpreted to mean that multiple areas of functioning should be considered during a diagnostic evaluation and is completed by clinicians with extensive experience in the standardized testing of children with ASD. In addition to covering multiple domains, diagnostic evaluations should consider information from multiple sources. A comprehensive evaluation must, at minimum, include a parent interview and an observational assessment of the child's current functioning by an experienced clinician in a context in which social-communicative behavior and play or peer interaction can be observed. For the diagnosis of ASD, diagnostic specificity is much worse if only one or the other is performed (Huerta & Lord, 2012).

Diagnostic Instruments for ASD

The National Research Council Committee on Educational Interventions for Children with Autism (2001) clearly indicates that best practice diagnostic tools should assess social functioning in a developmental context and should take into account the variability of behavior across settings. Following these criteria, a useful child testing tool in autism evaluations continues to be the Autism Diagnostic Observational Schedule (ADOS- Lord, Rutter, DiLavore, & Risi, 1999). Recent revisions to the ADOS have improved its accuracy and expanded its clinical utility to include an indicator of severity.

The revised version of the ADOS known as ADOS-2 (Luyster et al., 2009) has included a toddler version which enables clinicians to use this version for younger children starting at 12 months. Other reliable screening tools for Autism in Toddlers and Young Children (STAT) Stone, Coonrod & Ousley, 2000) and the Communication and Symbolic Behavior Scales (CSBS: Wetherby, Allen, Cleary, Kublin, & Goldstein, 2002) are also recommended for use in young children. These instruments are considered to be more valuable in their utility as they are standardized in their administration and coding, which ensures more reliable assessment of complex social behaviors (Lord et al., 2000).

The ADI-R has been established as a useful diagnostic tool in the assessment of ASD. This is a parent interview and more recently the ADI-R has been extended to include toddler versions of the diagnostic algorithm (Kim & Lord, 2010). One drawback is that the ADI-R is a lengthy instrument that requires significant training. Alternative, reliable methods of collecting parent report are needed. Currently, the use of the Social Communication Questionnaire (SCQ: Rutter, Bailey, Berument et al., 2003) in conjunction with the ADOS appears to be a reasonable replacement when it is not possible to do an ADI (Corsello et al., 2007).

The Importance of Diagnostic Evaluations

Formal diagnostic testing is important for a number of reasons. As mentioned earlier although ASD is considered to have genetic and neurobiological underpinnings, there are no accurate biologically-based tests. As a result, the diagnosis of ASD is one based on patterns of behavior and symptoms (DSM 5). Estimates of functioning in key domains can also provide important prognostic information about the course of autism symptoms. For example, nonverbal cognitive skills at age 2 predict verbal ability at age 5 (Thurm et al., 2007). Poor adaptive skills coupled with repetitive behaviors at 2 also predict more behavioral difficulties in older children with ASD; using any words at 2 and having more expressive language at 3 are predictors of more positive social outcomes (Anderson, Oti, Lord, & Welch, 2009). Finally, even when diagnostic certainty is high, formal diagnostic assessment can contribute to treatment planning. The results obtained from a diagnostic evaluation can shed light on the function of behaviors and identify both "near" and "eventual" treatment targets, thereby increasing the utility of interventions (Huerta & Lord, 2012).

Importance of Early Intervention

The ultimate goal of early detection and screening is to ensure that children with autism spectrum disorder (ASD) can access evidence-based interventions to provide the best opportunity for optimal development and outcomes (Zwaigenbaum et al., 2009). With the growing evidence that ASD can be diagnosed accurately before 2 years of age (Guthrie, Swineford, Nottke, & Wetherby, 2013) the second year of life has been reported to be a particularly critical developmental period for children with ASD, for various reasons. The second year is a dynamic period of brain growth, during which increases in brain volume and atypical connectivity associated with ASD first emerge (Lewis et al., 2014) but also a time of substantial neural plasticity providing greater potential to alter developmental course (Dawson, 2008).

Intervention approaches for children aged <2 to 3 years need to be developmentally appropriate and should take into consideration their dependence on experiential learning, their natural environments and occur within social interactions in the context of day to day caregiving (Zwaigenbaum et al., 2009). Recommendations for early intervention from the working group (Zwaigenbaum et al., 2015) who reviewed literature in this area include (a) Current best practices for interventions for children aged <3 years with suspected or confirmed ASD should include a combination of developmental and behavioral approaches and begin as early as possible. (b) Current best practices for children aged <3 years with suspected or confirmed

ASD should have active involvement of families and/or caregivers as part of the intervention. (c) Interventions should enhance developmental progress and improve functioning related to both the core and associated features of ASD, including social communication, emotional/behavioral regulation, and adaptive behaviors. (d) Intervention services should consider the sociocultural beliefs of the family and family dynamics and supports, as well as economic capability, in terms of both the delivery and assessment of factors that moderate outcomes.

Two comprehensive intervention programs (Early Start Denver Model [ESDM; Rogers et al., 2012] and the UCLA/ Lovaas model) are examples of evidence-based approaches in early intervention which have shown significantly improved outcomes relative to comparison groups after therapeutic durations of 8 weeks to 2 to 3 years. These types of programs are referred to as Naturalistic Developmental Behavioral Intervention (NDBI: Schreibman et al., 2015) based on incorporating strengths of developmental and behavioral approaches.

Comorbidity in Autism Spectrum Disorders

Autism comorbidity is characterized by an overlap of autism with psychiatric, genetic and neurological conditions (Rice, Schendel, Cunniff, & Doernberg, 2015). Recent studies show major subgroupings within ASD with a prevalence rate of 77.5% seizure rate in the first group; gastrointestinal disorders (prevalence 24.3%) and auditory disorders and infections (prevalence 87.8%) in the second group, and the third was characterized by psychiatric disorders with a prevalence rate of 33.0% (Doshi-Velez, Ge, & Kohane, 2014). With regard to psychiatric disorders, attention deficit and hyperactivity disorder (ADHD) has a weighted mean prevalence of 48% (Frias, Palma, & Farriols, 2015). In recent studies, those who met criteria for ASD on DSM 5, had co-occurring obsessive compulsive disorder at 61.4%; eating behavior problems at 35.7% and anxiety at 8.8% (Romero et al., 2016). ASD and intellectual disability (ID) co-occur frequently, and symptoms of autism, particularly language delays, stereotypies, and self-injury, increase as the severity of ID increases (Wing & Gould, 1979). Recent studies have found that 55 % of their sample of children with ASD had an intellectual disability (i.e., IQ <70), 17 % had below average intellectual functioning (i.e., IQ ranging from 70 to 85), 28 %

had average intellectual functioning, and 3 % had above average intellectual functioning (Charman et al., 2011).

High Functioning ASD and Treatment Approaches

Individuals diagnosed with ASD and have normative cognitive function and better developed verbal abilities are often referred to as high functioning ASD. Many individuals on the higher end of the autism spectrum may have difficulties associated with executive functioning skills involving attending, planning and organizational abilities. Further difficulties include initiating, maintaining reciprocal conversations, managing social situations, heavy reliance on routines, hyper focus on certain topics and tendency toward anxiety and depression.

Executive Skills Training

One of the cognitive impairments proposed to underlie the symptoms of ASD is executive dysfunction (Happé & Ronald, 2008; Hill, 2004; Russell, 1997). Pennington and Ozonoff (1996) identified five overlapping executive functioning domains: (1) inhibition, the ability to suppress a certain behavior or to ignore distracting information; (2) cognitive flexibility (or set-shifting), the ability to shift between different thoughts or actions; (3) generativity (or fluency), the ability to generate novel ideas; (4) working memory, the ability to hold certain information active while performing a task; and (5) planning, the ability to look ahead before starting to perform a task.

To assist individuals on the spectrum to be more independent in managing their time, tasks and materials, visuals and organizational supports are used to help them understand the meaning and importance of organization, develop an awareness of what necessary organizational supports are necessary for them and help them develop an individualized organization system that works for them (Coyne, 1996).

Social Skills Training

Review of literature indicates that certain goals are necessary for social skills training. These have been identified as increasing social motivation and initiations, improvement of appropriate social responding, reduction of interfering behaviors and promotion of skill generalization (Rao, Beidel & Murray, 2008; Williams White, Koenig & Scahill, 2007). Effective interventions are predominantly based on social learning theory and involve framing complex social conventions as rules that can be learned through modelling age-appropriate social interaction skills, role plays or teaching social scripts for common situations, and successively practicing social interaction with a clinician or within a group setting. Differential reinforcement of response attempts and positive behaviors are utilized to facilitate generalization.

Cognitive Behavior Therapy

Individuals with autism spectrum disorders (ASD) may exhibit significantly more anxiety than do individuals in the population at large (Bellini, 2004; Kim, Szatmari, Bryson, Streiner, & Wilson, 2000). Cognitive behavior therapy (CBT) is considered the primary nonpharmacological treatment for anxiety and depression in typical individuals (Ollendick, King, & Chorpita, 2006). Attwood (2004) described how modifications to CBT might be accommodated for individuals with Asperger's disorder. His suggestions include six components: (1) assessment of mood disorder, (2) affective education, (3) cognitive restructuring, (4) stress management, (5) self-reflection, and (6) practice.

Visual aids and structured worksheets such as using multiple-choice questions may be superior to open-ended questions to minimize word retrieval during assessment. Additional assessment tools that may prove useful include charts to measure intensity of mood on a continuum and a picture dictionary to help young clients or those with more limited verbal repertoires to better define and describe the intensity of their emotions. In addition, compiling a list of antecedents unique to the ASD population could assist the individual to signal mood changes in maintaining a mood diary. Researchers have noted a 50% improvement rate which is consistent with other studies examining CBT for typical individuals (e.g., Walkup et al., 2008).

Conclusions and Future Directions

Identification of autism and recognition of its comorbidities is critical for initiating effective interventions to improve the lives of individuals and their families. Current best practices indicate that children identified by parents or professionals as being at risk for autism receive a thorough evaluation by a trained professional involving observational measures of social skills and repetitive behavior and a diagnostic interview with parents and caregivers. Difficulty accessing these services and challenges in the early diagnosis of autism require improved diagnostic approaches to identify persons at risk for autism so that effective intervention can begin. One of the most promising approaches is the use of biomarkers, such as described in following chapters, to improve our diagnostic capability and develop better measures to monitor intervention effects. Combining behavioral and biologic measures to diagnose autism will not only enhance identification and treatment strategies but also improve our understanding of the neurodevelopmental abnormalities in autism and related disorders.

References

American Psychiatric Association. (1952). *Diagnostic and statistical manual of mental disorders* (1st ed.). Washington, DC: Author.

American Psychiatric Association. (1968). *Diagnostic and statistical manual of mental disorders* (2nd ed.). Washington, DC: Author.

American Psychiatric Association. (1980). Diagnostic and statistical manual of mental disorders (3rd ed.). Washington, DC: Author.

American Psychiatric Association. (1994). *Diagnostic and statistical manual of mental disorders* (4th ed.). Washington, DC: Author.

American Psychiatric Association. (2000). *Diagnostic and statistical manual of mental disorders* (4th ed.). Washington, DC: Author.

American Psychiatric Association. (2013). *Diagnostic and statistical manual of mental disorders* (5th ed.). Arlington, VA: American Psychiatric Publishing.

Anderson, D. K., Oti, R., Lord, C., & Welch K. (2009). Patterns of growth in adaptive social abilities among children with autism spectrum disorder. *Journal of Abnormal Child Psychology, 37*(7), 1019-1034.

Attwood, T. (2004). Cognitive behaviour therapy for children and adults with Asperger's syndrome. *Behaviour Change, 21*(3), 147-161.

Baio, J., Wingate, M., Kirby, R. S., Pettygrove, S., Cunniff, C., Schulz, E., & Ghosh, T., et al. (2014). Prevalence of autism spectrum disorder among children aged 8 years -Autism and developmental disabilities monitoring network, 11 sites, United States, 2010. *Morbidity & Mortality Weekly Report, 63*(2), 1-21.

Bellini, S. (2004). Social skill deficits and anxiety in high-functioning adolescents with autism spectrum disorders. *Focus On Autism & Other Developmental Disabilities, 19*(2), 78-86.

Bishop, S. L., Richler, J., & Lord, C. (2006). Association between restricted and repetitive behaviors and nonverbal IQ in children with autism spectrum disorders. *Child Neuropsychology, 12*(4-5), 247-267.

Charman, T., Pickles, A., Simonoff, E., Chandler, S., Loucas, T., & Baird, G. (2011). IQ in children with autism spectrum disorders: Data from the special needs and autism project (SNAP). *Psychological Medicine, 41*(3), 619-627.

Constantino, J. N., & Gruber, C. P. (2012). *Social responsiveness scale* (2nd ed.) (SRS-2). Torrance, CA: Western Psychological Services.

Corsello, C., Hus, V., Pickles, A., Risi, S., Cook, E. H. Jr., Leventhal, B. L., & Lord, C. (2007). Between a ROC and a hard place: Decision making and making decisions about using the SCQ. *Journal of Child Psychology and Psychiatry, and Allied Disciplines, 48*(9), 932-940.

Council on children with disabilities. (2006). Identifying infants and young children with developmental disorders in the medical home: An algorithm for developmental surveillance and screening. *Pediatrics, 118*(1), 405-420.

Coyne, I. T. (1996). Parent participation: A concept analysis. *Journal of Midwifery & Women's Health, 23*(4), 733-740.

Daniels, A. M., & Mandell, D. (2013). Children's compliance with American Academy of Pediatrics well-child care visit guidelines and the early detection of autism. *Journal of Autism and Developmental Disorders, 43*(12), 2844-2854.

Dawkins, T., Meyer, A. T., & Van Bourgondien, M. E. (2016). The relationship between the childhood autism rating scale: Second edition and clinical diagnosis utilizing the DSM-IV-TR and the DSM-5. *Journal of Autism and Developmental Disorders, 46*(10), 3361-3368.

Dawson G. (2008). Early behavioral intervention, brain plasticity, and the prevention of autism spectrum disorder. *Development and Psychopathology, 20*(3), 775-803.

Doshi-Velez, F., Ge, Y., & Kohane, I. (2014). Comorbidity clusters in autism spectrum disorders: an electronic health record time-series analysis. *Pediatrics, 133*(1), e54-e63.

Fombonne, E. (2009). Epidemiology of pervasive developmental disorders. *Pediatric Research, 65*, 591-598.

Frias, A., Palma, C., & Farriols, N. (2015). Comorbidity in pediatric bipolar disorder: Prevalence, clinical impact, etiology and treatment. *Journal of Affective Disorders, 174*, 378-389.

Gardner, M. (2012). Finding what we're looking for: Evidence-based early identification and nursing care of young children at risk for autism spectrum disorders. In E. Giarelli & M. Gardner (Eds.), *Nursing of autism spectrum disorder: Evidence-based integrated care across the lifespan*. New York, NY: Springer.

Guevara, J. P., Gerdes, M., Localio, R., Yuanshung, V. H., Pinto-Martin, J., Minkovitz, C. S., ... Pati, S. (2013). Effectiveness of developmental screening in an urban setting. *Pediatrics, 131*(1), 30-37.

Guthrie, W., Swineford, L. B., Nottke, C., & Wetherby, A. M. (2013). Early diagnosis of autism spectrum disorder: Stability and change in clinical diagnosis and symptom presentation. *Journal of Child Psychology and Psychiatry, and Allied Disciplines, 54*(5), 582-590.

Happé, F., & Ronald, A. (2008). The 'fractionable autism triad': A review of evidence from behavioural, genetic, cognitive and neural research. *Neuropsychology Review, 18*(4), 287-304.

Herlihy, L. E., Brooks, B., Dumont-Mathieu, T., Barton, M. L., Fein, D., Chen, C. M., & Robins, D. L. (2014). Standardized screening facilitates timely diagnosis of autism spectrum disorders in a diverse sample of low-risk toddlers. *Journal of Developmental and Behavioral Pediatrics, 35*(2), 85-92.

Hill, E. L. (2004). Evaluating the theory of executive dysfunction in autism. *Developmental Review, 24*, 189-233.

Huerta, M., & Lord, C. (2012). Diagnostic evaluation of autism spectrum disorders. *Pediatric Clinics of North America, 59*(1), 103.

Johnson, C. P., & Myers, S. M. (2007). American Academy of Pediatrics Council on children with disabilities: Identification and evaluation of children with autism spectrum disorders. *Pediatrics, 120*, 1183-1215.

Johnson, N. L., Burkett, K., Reinhold, J., & Bultas, M. W. (2016). Translating research to practice for children with autism spectrum disorder: Part I: Definition, associated behaviors, prevalence, diagnostic process, and interventions. *Journal of Pediatric Health Care: Official Publication of National Association of Pediatric Nurse Associates & Practitioners, 30*(1), 15-26.

Kim, S. H., & Lord, C. (2010). Restricted and repetitive behaviors in toddlers and preschoolers with autism spectrum disorders based on the autism diagnostic observation schedule (ADOS). *Autism Research, 3*(4), 162-173.

Kim, J. A., Szatmari, P., Bryson, S. E., Streiner, D. L., & Wilson, F. J. (2000). The prevalence of anxiety and mood problems among children with autism and Asperger syndrome. *Autism, 4*(2), 117-132.

Lewis, J. D., Evans, A. C., Pruett, J. R., Botteron, K., Zwaigenbaum, L., Estes, A., ... Piven, J. (2014). Network inefficiencies in autism spectrum disorder at 24 months. *Translational Psychiatry, 4*, e388.

Lord, C., Rutter, M., DiLavore, P. C., & Risi, S. (1999). Autism Diagnostic Observation Schedule. Los Angeles, CA: Western Psychological Services.

Lord, C., Risi, S., Lambrecht, L., Cook E. H. Jr., Leventhal, B. L., DiLavore, P. C., ... Rutter, M. (2000). The autism diagnostic observation schedule-generic: A standard measure of social and communication deficits associated with autism spectrum disorder. *Journal of Autism and Developmental Disorders, 30*(3), 205-223.

Luyster, R., Gotham, K., Guthrie, W., Coffing, M., Petrak, R., Pierce, K., ... Lord, C. (2009). The Autism Diagnostic Observation Schedule-toddler module: A new module of a standardized diagnostic measure for autism spectrum disorders. *Journal of Autism and Developmental Disorders, 39*(9), 1305-1320.

Manning-Courtney, P., Murray, D., Currans, K., Johnson, H., Bing, N., Kroeger-Geoppinger, K., & Messerschmidt, T. (2013). Autism spectrum disorders. *Current Problems in Pediatric and Adolescent Health Care, 43*(1), 2-11.

Miller, J. S., Gabrielsen, T., Villalobos, M., Alleman, R., Wahmhoff, N., Carbone, P. S., & Segura, B. (2011). The each child study: Systematic screening for autism spectrum disorders in a pediatric setting. *Pediatrics, 127*(5), 866-871.

National research council committee on educational interventions for children with autism (2001). Committee on early intervention for children with autism. Goals for children with autism and their families. In C. Lord & J. McGee (Eds.), *Educating children with autism spectrum disorders: Report of the Committee on Early Intervention in Autism* (pp. 21-44). Washington, D.C: National Academy of Sciences.

Pennington, B. F., & Ozonoff, S. (1996). Executive functions and developmental psychopathology. *Journal of Child Psychology and Psychiatry, and Allied Disciplines, 37(*1), 51-87.

Rao, P. A., Beidel, D. C., & Murray, M. J. (2008). Social skills interventions for children with Asperger's syndrome or high-functioning autism: A review and recommendations. *Journal of Autism and Developmental Disorders, 38*(2), 353-361.

Rice, C., Schendel, D., Cunniff, C., & Doernberg, N. (2004, February). Public health monitoring of developmental disabilities with a focus on the autism spectrum disorders. In *American Journal of Medical Genetics Part C: Seminars in Medical Genetics* (Vol. 125, No. 1, pp. 22-27). Hoboken: Wiley Subscription Services, Inc., A Wiley Company.

Richler, J., Bishop, S. L., Kleinke, J. R., & Lord C. (2007). Restricted and repetitive behaviors in young children autism spectrum disorders. *Journal of Autism and Developmental Disorders, 37*(1),73-85.

Romero, M., Aguilar, J. M., Del-Rey-Mejías, Á., Mayoral, F., Rapado, M., Peciña, M., & ... Lara, J. P. (2016). Psychiatric comorbidities in autism spectrum disorder: A comparative study between DSM-IV-TR and DSM-5 diagnosis. *International Journal of Clinical and Health Psychology, 16*(3), 266-275.

Robins, D. L., Casagrande, K., Barton, M., Chen, C. M., Dumont-Mathieu, T., & Fein, D. (2014). Validation of the modified checklist for autism in toddlers, revised with follow-up (M-CHAT-R/F). *Pediatrics, 133*(1), 37-45.

Rogers, S. J., Estes, A., Lord, C., Vismara, L., Winter, J., Fitzpatrick, A., ... Dawson, G. (2012). Effects of a brief early start Denver model (ESDM)-based parent intervention on toddlers at risk for autism spectrum disorders: A randomized controlled trial. *Journal of American Academy of Child and Adolescent Psychiatry, 51*(10), 1052-1065.

Russell, J. (1997). *Autism as an executive disorder*. Oxford: Oxford University Press.

Rutter, M. (2007). Incidence of autism spectrum disorders: Changes over time and their meaning. *Acta Paediatrica, 94*(1), 2-15.

Rutter, M.; Bailey, A.; Berument, SK., et al. (2003). *Social communication questionnaire (SCQ)*. Los Angeles, CA: Western Psychological Services.

Schopler, E., Reichler, R. J., & Renner, B. R. (1988). *The childhood autism rating scale (CARS)*. Los Angeles: Western Psychological Services.

Schreibman, L., Dawson, G., Stahmer, A. C., Landa, R., Rogers, S. J., McGee, G. G., & ... Halladay, A. (2015). Naturalistic developmental behavioral interventions: Empirically validated treatments for autism spectrum disorder. *Journal of Autism and Developmental Disorders, 45*(8), 2411-2428.

Sigman, M., & McGovern, C. W. (2005). Improvement in cognitive and language skills from preschool to adolescence in autism. *Journal of Autism and Developmental Disorders, 35*(1), 15-23.

Stone, W. L., Coonrod, E. E., & Ousley, O. Y. (2000). Brief report: screening tool for autism in two-year-olds (STAT): Development and preliminary data. *Journal of Autism and Developmental Disorders, 30*(6), 607-612.

Thurm, A., Lord, C., Lee, L. C., & Newschaffer, C. (2007). Predictors of language acquisition in preschool children with autism spectrum disorders. *Journal of Autism and Developmental Disorders, 37*(9), 1721-1731.

Walkup, J. T., Albano, A. M., Piacentini, J., Birmaher, B., Compton, S. N., Sherrill, J. T., & ... Kendall, P. C. (2008). Cognitive behavioral therapy, sertraline, or a combination in childhood anxiety. *The New England Journal of Medicine, 359*(26), 2753-2766.

Wetherby, A., Allen, L., Cleary, J., Kublin, K., & Goldstein, H. (2002). Validity and reliability of the communication and symbolic behavior scales developmental profile with very young children. *Journal of Speech Language and Hearing Research, 45*(6), 1202-1218.

Williams White, S., Keonig, K., & Scahill, L. (2007). Social skills development in children with autism spectrum disorders: A review of the intervention research. *Journal of Autism and Developmental Disorders, 37*(10), 1858-1868.

Wing, L., & Gould, J. (1979). Severe impairments of social interaction and associated abnormalities in children: epidemiology and classification. *Journal of Autism and Developmental Disorders, 9*(1), 11-29.

Zwaigenbaum, L., Bryson, S., Lord, C., Rogers S, Carter A, Carver L, ... Yirmiya, N. (2009). Clinical assessment and management of toddlers with suspected autism spectrum disorder: Insights from studies of high-risk infants. *Pediatrics, 123*(5), 1383-1391.

Zwaigenbaum, L. (2011). Screening, risk, and early identification of autism spectrum disorders. In D. G. Amaral, G. Dawson, & D. Geschwind (Eds.), *Autism spectrum disorders* (pp. 75-89). New York, NY: Oxford University.

Zwaigenbaum, L., Bauman, M. L., Fein, D., Pierce, K., Buie, T., Davis, P. A., ... Wagner, S.(2015). Early screening of autism spectrum disorder: Recommendations for practice and research. *Pediatrics, 136*, S41-59.

2

Autism Spectrum Disorder: Treatment From the Developmental-Behavioral Pediatrics Perspective

Steven H. Ma, Darla H. McCain, and Desmond P. Kelly

Autism spectrum disorder (ASD) is a disability in neurodevelopment characterized by persistent impairments in reciprocal social communication and interaction and restricted, repetitive patterns of behavior, interests, or activities (American Psychiatric Association, 2013). Prevalence estimates for ASD vary depending upon population studied and methods of assessment. In 2012 ASD prevalence in the United States from the Autism Developmental Disabilities Monitoring (ADDM) Network was 14.6 per 1,000 (one in 68) among 8-year-old children with estimated prevalence by sex of 23.6 per 1,000 (one in 42) boys and 5.3 per 1,000 (one in 189) girls (Christensen et al., 2016). Children and adolescents with ASD require a family-centered, comprehensive management approach from a team of medical providers, therapists, educators, and community agencies who are able to collaborate to develop an individualized treatment plan that addresses the strengths and needs of the child and family. Developmental-Behavioral pediatricians have extensive training in diagnosing and managing ASD and co-occurring conditions as well as a deep understanding of the psychosocial aspects of working with families. The following will provide a diagnostic and therapeutic framework for children and adolescents with ASD from the perspective of the Developmental-Behavioral pediatric specialist.

Division of Developmental-Behavioral Pediatrics
Greenville Health System
Greenville, South Carolina, United States
Correspondence should be addressed to Steven H. Ma; sma@ghs.org.

Diagnostic Approach

ASD Diagnosis

Diagnosis of ASD is made by comprehensive evaluation, ideally through a multidisciplinary team approach, and includes a thorough history of symptoms across multiple settings with careful attention to Diagnostic and Statistical Manual of Mental Disorders, Fifth Edition (DSM-5) ASD criteria, physical exam, neurological exam, behavioral observations, hearing screening, direct assessment of the child's cognitive and adaptive development, and the use of a diagnostic measure specific to ASD to supplement informed clinical judgment (Volkmar et al., 2014). This comprehensive approach helps the team establish the diagnosis of ASD, determine etiology when possible, and identify co-occurring conditions and maladaptive behaviors that might interfere with treatment.

Etiology

Establishing a potential etiology may provide information about a child's prognosis and needed medical interventions and inform genetic counseling for future family planning. There is no known single cause for ASD, which is a highly heterogeneous disorder. Current epidemiological evidence points to a complex interplay between genetic predisposition and environmental factors (Grafodatskaya, Chung, Szatmari, & Weksberg, 2010). It is well known that ASD occurs with greater frequency among children with certain syndromes (e.g., fragile X, tuberous sclerosis complex) (Richards, Jones, Groves, Moss, & Oliver, 2015). During the medical evaluation, growth parameters should be reviewed and the child should be carefully examined for dysmorphic features and neurocutaneous stigmata. Additionally, a three-generation family history should be gathered with emphasis placed on neurobehavioral and neurodevelopmental disorders. Thorough genetics evaluation is estimated to yield an identified etiology in 30-40% of patients with ASD (Schaefer & Mendelsohn, 2013). As such, the American College of Medical Genetics and Genomics recommends that genetic testing be discussed with all patients and families with ASD, and if a specific syndromic diagnosis is suspected, proceed with targeted testing after appropriate genetic counseling. Routine evaluation for metabolic or mitochondrial disorders is not recommended but should be considered based on pertinent history and clinical symptomatology. Lastly, routine neuroimaging is also not recommended for children diagnosed with ASD in the absence of neuroregression or major neurologic abnormalities but should be considered for children with ASD and microcephaly.

Associated Conditions and Maladaptive Behaviors

During the initial evaluation for ASD and at subsequent follow-up visits, the clinician should identify conditions that co-occur with ASD so that appropriate treatment can be implemented. Co-occurring disorders, like intellectual disability and seizures, increase the functional impairment beyond the core ASD symptoms and can compound family stress. Maladaptive behaviors can also impair a child's functioning and will need to be addressed as they occur. While severe behaviors often take precedence during discussions with the family, the child's general health and well-being should also be addressed as some aspects of general health maintenance (e.g., dental care) can be more problematic in children with ASD compared to their typically-developing peers.

Global developmental delay and intellectual disability are often an associated finding in children identified with ASD. Data gathered from the Autism and Developmental Disabilities Monitoring Network in 2012 indicated that 31.6% of the children in this study were classified in the range of intellectual disability (IQ < 70 or examiner-reported intellectual disability) (Christensen et al., 2016). As noted above, the comprehensive evaluation for a child with ASD should include cognitive and adaptive assessments. This helps identify children with global developmental delay and intellectual disability and guides treatment recommendations for educational services.

Seizure disorder. Prevalence estimates for seizure disorder in individuals with ASD range from 5% to 46% (Spence & Schneider, 2009) with higher risk noted in those individuals with severe intellectual disability (Danielsson, I.C. Gillberg, Billstedt, Gillberg, & Olsson, 2005) and those with identified genetic disorders. Seizure onset typically has two peak times during childhood: between birth to 5 years and between 10 to 15 years (Parmeggiani et al., 2010). Children with ASD should be monitored for symptoms suggestive of seizures and EEG obtained and referral made to pediatric neurology when indicated.

Psychiatric disorders. Psychiatric disorders are common in children with ASD, including attention-deficit/hyperactivity disorder (ADHD), anxiety disorders, mood disorders, and Tourette's/tic disorder (Tsai, 2014), and many youth with ASD suffer from not one but multiple psychiatric comorbidities (Joshi et al., 2010; Simonoff et al., 2008). Diagnosing a psychiatric disorder in a child with ASD can be challenging due to the overlap of symptomatology between ASD and psychiatric disorders, particularly anxiety disorders. Concomitant intellectual disability and communication deficits can further complicate the diagnostic process. Despite these diagnostic challenges, it is imperative that mental health comorbidities be recognized and appropriate interventions be put in place to avoid further functional impairment for the child and social-emotional burden for the family.

Irritability and maladaptive behaviors. Children with ASD often suffer from significant irritability and maladaptive behaviors. Moderate to severe irritability has been estimated to occur in approximately 20% of children with ASD (Lecavalier,

2006) and can manifest as verbal and physical aggression, tantrums, and self-injurious behaviors. One of the most challenging maladaptive behaviors that children and adolescents and their families face is self-injurious behavior (SIB). SIB has been reported in up to 50% of young children with ASD, with approximately 15% of cases being categorized as severe (Baghdadli, Pascal, Grisi, & Aussilloux, 2003). SIB can manifest in a variety of forms, including head banging, biting, skin picking, and scratching. SIB can be persistent over time and result in minor, acute injuries or sometimes permanent damage. SIB can also interfere with development of appropriate adaptive skills. Children engaging in significant SIB should be evaluated for comorbid psychiatric disorders and undergo a functional behavioral assessment (FBA) to determine the behavioral function of the SIB so appropriate treatment can be implemented, which can include behavioral and/or pharmacological interventions depending on the case (Minshawi, Hurwitz, Morriss, & McDougle, 2015).

Pica. Children with ASD can engage in pica or repetitive mouthing or licking of nonfood items. These behaviors may increase a child's risk for lead exposure (Shannon & Graef, 1996) and may result in life-threatening complications, including intestinal blockages and tears. Children engaging in pica should be considered for periodic lead screening (Filipek et al., 2000) and behavioral intervention (Matson et al., 2013).

Aberrant feeding behavior and growth. Children with ASD are frequently reported to show highly-selective eating behavior (Bandini et al., 2010) with aversions to specific textures, colors, smells, or temperatures. Preferred foods tend to be calorically dense, nutrient-poor carbohydrates that may be easier to chew (e.g., snack crackers) compared to fruits, vegetables, and meats. High food selectivity can result in inadequate nutrient intake and may contribute to unhealthy weight status.

Children with ASD have been found to have a higher prevalence of overweight and obesity (Broder-Fingert, Brazauskas, Lindgren, Iannuzzi, & Van Cleave, 2014; de Vinck-Baroody et al., 2015; Egan, Dreyer, Odar, Beckwith, & Garrison, 2013; Hill, Zuckerman, & Fombonne, 2015). Clinicians need to monitor weight status and provide dietary recommendations, referring for nutritional counseling and weight management services when indicated.

Sleep problems. Sleep problems in children with ASD are very common and can be chronic in nature with children sleeping fewer hours and showing more frequent night awakenings than their typically-developing peers. A recent study suggested two thirds of children with ASD have chronic insomnia (Souders et al., 2017). Inadequate or poor quality sleep can have detrimental impacts on the child's cognitive, behavioral, and emotional functioning. Furthermore, sleep disruption in children negatively impacts their caregivers' sleep. It is therefore imperative that children with ASD be routinely screened and assessed for sleep disturbances during the initial evaluation and at follow-up visits (Malow et al., 2012). A thorough sleep history can be completed through parent interview, parent-report questionnaires, and sleep diaries. Initial treatment for sleep disturbance involves sleep education, environmental changes, behavioral interventions, and consideration of melatonin. Based on history and response to treatment, further evaluation by a sleep medicine specialist may be warranted.

Oral health problems. Oral health care is an important aspect of any child's overall health, and families are encouraged to establish a dental home; however, this can be a source of marked distress for the child with ASD as well as his/her caregivers. Parents of children with ASD have reported difficulty with almost all aspects of their child's oral care, including daily home oral care, oral care at the dentist, and accessing professional oral care (Stein, Polido, Najera, & Cermak, 2012). Children with ASD have been shown to exhibit significantly more uncooperative behaviors during routine dental cleanings and experience greater physiological and behavioral distress compared to their typically-developing peer group (Stein et al., 2014). Compounding these difficulties is limited access to oral health professionals who have experience working with children with special needs. Lastly, given the significant behavioral challenges and anxiety associated with visits to the dentist, children with ASD may require sedation, which results in additional financial burdens to families.

Compresensive Treatment Approach

Effective treatment of children with ASD requires a comprehensive management plan with clear treatment goals, optimal medical care, treatment of comorbidities, and coordination of effective therapies and strategies. The extent to which a child with ASD is affected varies widely and can change over time, as the child grows and develops. The management plan, therefore, should be iterative, growing and changing as the child transitions into adolescence and eventually adulthood. The majority of children with ASD have the ability to improve skills in their areas of difficulties with appropriate treatment.

Treatment Goals

Management of the child with ASD following diagnosis includes establishing realistic treatment goals and recommending effective therapies and strategies addressing these goals. Development of effective goals will take into account a child's individual profile of strengths and needs in the context of his/her family, being sensitive to the family's culture, ethnicity, religion, and other affiliations that might influence the family's health beliefs and practices. Intervention plans should target the following areas: communication, social skills, daily living skills, play and leisure skills, academic achievement, and interfering behaviors. Ultimately, the aim is to maximize functional independence and quality of life of the individual, promote socialization, and reduce interfering, maladaptive behaviors.

Behavioral Approach

Behavioral intervention is used to target the core symptoms of ASD as well as problematic behaviors and is the cornerstone of a comprehensive treatment plan. The most extensively studied behavioral intervention is Applied Behavior Analysis (ABA). ABA is founded on the principles of learning and motivation, and is used to increase and maintain desirable behaviors, reduce interfering maladaptive behaviors, teach new skills, and generalize behaviors. There are a variety of treatment models using ABA principles, including early intensive behavioral intervention (EIBI) and Pivotal Response Treatment (PRT). Research involving specific treatment models and their effectiveness is often mixed and fraught with methodological limitations (Maglione, Gans, Das, Timbie, & Kasari, 2012); however, individual, comprehensive ABA is considered a well-established, first-line treatment for children with ASD (Smith & Iadarola, 2015). Empirical evidence also suggests intensive behavioral interventions delivered early in life can improve developmental outcomes in children with ASD (Rogers & Vismara, 2008; Warren et al., 2011).

Educational Approach

Another important aspect of the comprehensive management of a child with ASD is guiding families on access to school services and supports. Children with ASD who show functional impairments are entitled to evaluations in their local school district as guaranteed in the United States under Public Law 101-476, the Individuals with Disabilities Education Act (IDEA). Based on these evaluations, children are considered for special education services in the school setting. For children 3-21 years of age, Autism is included as an educational category of disability under IDEA through which a child can receive specialized instruction after development of an individualized education plan (IEP). Children who do not require an IEP may qualify for educational accommodations under Section 504 of the Rehabilitation Act of 1973.

Within the school system, supports should be tailored to the individual student's needs with goals targeting verbal and nonverbal communication, behavior regulation, social skills, motor skills, and academic skills. Effective programming typically involves direct, explicit, and intensive instruction in the areas of needs and is provided by a team of educators collaborating with behavioral specialists and therapists, including speech-language pathologists and occupational therapists. To facilitate generalization of skills, collaboration with the family should also be an integral part of this process.

Several educational models have been developed to address the challenges that children with ASD face in the learning environment, one of which is the Treatment and Education of Autistic and related Communication Handicapped Children (TEACCH). This structured teaching approach works to enhance communication and social interaction and has shown positive effects for social functioning and maladaptive behavior (Virues-Ortega, Julio, & Pastor-Barriuso, 2013). Most educational programs for children with ASD found in the community are considered "eclectic" treatment approaches, combining ABA methods, TEACCH-based techniques, speech-language therapy, and sensory integration methods carried out by occupational therapists.

Psychopharmacologic Approach

Medication can be a useful adjunctive therapy to address medical or psychiatric comorbidities and provide symptom control to improve a child's day-to-day functioning and participation in behavioral interventions. Medications, however, do not target the core symptoms of ASD, and should be considered only after modifiable behavioral and environmental factors and medical problems have been appropriately addressed and/or excluded. Symptoms targeted for a medication trial often include: hyperactivity, inattention, impulsivity, aggression, self-injurious behavior, anxiety, obsessive-compulsive behaviors, tics, repetitive behaviors, depressive symptoms, and sleep dysfunction. Before starting medication, a careful review of the risks and benefits of medication should be discussed with the family and informed consent obtained. The family and physician should target specific symptoms and behaviors and set realistic goals for improvement.

Depending on the medication chosen, baseline laboratory studies and vital signs should be completed. Children with ASD can be more sensitive to medication effects and more likely to experience adverse effects than children without ASD (DeFilippis & Wagner, 2016). Medications should therefore be started at lower doses and titrated more slowly. Children receiving medication should participate in regular follow-up visits to assess treatment effectiveness and check for potential side effects so that dose adjustments or changes can be implemented. Negative or suboptimal response to medication should prompt careful review of any changes in the child's health or environment. Periodic trials off medication should be considered to establish whether the medication is still needed.

There are a variety of medications used to target symptoms in children with ASD, the best-studied of which are the atypical neuroleptics. Risperidone and aripiprazole have been approved by the United States Food and Drug Administration (US FDA) for the treatment of severe irritability associated with autism. Notable side effects of atypical neuroleptics include weight gain, sedation, and risk of extrapyramidal symptoms. Given the side effect profile, atypical neuroleptics should be used to treat significant irritability and problem behavior only in the context of safety concerns or changes in school or residential placement due to severity of problem behavior (McGuire et al., 2016).

Stimulant medications (Nickels et al., 2008) such as methylphenidate and mixed amphetamine salts, and non-stimulant medications, such as atomoxetine, can be important adjuncts to treatment by helping children improve focus and control impulsivity. Alpha-2-adrenergic agonists (e.g., guanfacine, clonidine) are also used to manage symptoms of inattention, hyperactivity, impulsivity, and irritability. When depression or comorbid anxiety is a significant component of the clinical picture, antidepressants or anxiolytics may be helpful.

Complementary and Alternative Medicine

Many interventions are promoted that purport to treat or even "cure" ASD. It is incumbent on clinicians to recognize that families will be exposed to much information regarding complementary and alternative medicine (CAM) treatment approaches and are likely to utilize at least some nonstandard treatments (Perrin et al., 2012). Clinicians should specifically inquire about the use of CAM to facilitate open discussion and foster continued partnership with the family during the treatment process. Discussion should include the quality of the evidence in current research and potential risks and benefits that include not only potential adverse physical effects but potential diversion from other evidence-based treatments and potential financial burdens of unproven treatments. When a family decides to try a CAM intervention, the physician should assist the family to identify appropriate target symptoms and develop a plan to monitor treatment effectiveness.

A common inquiry among families with a child with ASD pertains to nutritional/dietary interventions. Gluten-free diets are commonly used as an alternative therapy in children with

ASD with estimates in one study of 1 in 5 preschool-aged children with ASD ever having been placed on a gluten-free diet (Rubenstein et al., 2017). Currently, the level of evidence within scientific literature is limited and weak with regards to specific dietary interventions demonstrating improvement in target behaviors (Sathe, Andrews, McPheeters, & Warren, 2017). Certain restrictive diets, such as a diet devoid of artificial colors/dyes or gluten-free and/or casein-free diet, have not been shown to improve target behaviors across populations. Consuming a completely organic diet has also not been demonstrated to improve target behavior in children with ASD. However, some families believe strongly that a particular diet drastically improved their child's behaviors. Despite the lack of evidence base, if the family is able to support this dietary modification and the child is consuming the recommended vitamins and nutrients to support healthy growth, there is little reason to dissuade a family from making this type of intervention, providing they have a system for objectively measuring potential behavior changes.

Other nutritional interventions include dietary supplements, such as omega-3 and N-acetylcysteine, and more invasive treatments (e.g., methyl–B12 injections). Families should be made aware that supplement use is not subject to US FDA regulation; therefore, consistent, high quality supplements cannot be ensured. Regardless of the specific dietary intervention, it is crucial to have ongoing discussions with the family about the potential risks and benefits to the child with ASD and/or to the family.

Supporting Families

The patient and his/her family should be involved participants in the healthcare decision making process. The healthcare delivery team must seek to address not only the presenting medical problems, but also identify any additional factors that may limit or impact the implementation of a healthcare plan. For example, unaddressed career, housing, transportation, financial or insurance concerns may be impediments. It is equally important to ensure that the parents, caregivers, and siblings are supported in the context of the healthcare plan delivery. Interventions beneficial to the family might include: care coordination by a social worker to help the family get established with local community agencies; counseling regarding long-term planning goals, transition topics, and patient advocacy; and linking families with legal services.

Conclusion

ASD is a lifelong neurodevelopmental disorder with complex genetic and environmental underpinnings. The role of the Developmental-Behavioral pediatrician working with a child with ASD involves initial diagnosis of ASD and any associated comorbid disorders and maladaptive behaviors that might interfere with a child's progress. The Developmental-Behavioral pediatrician also provides ongoing medical, developmental, and behavioral guidance as the child transitions to adolescence and eventually to adulthood. The cornerstone of this long-term care is collaboration, building and fostering working relationships with the child's family and community service providers. Through this collaborative process, the family and team of providers can develop an individualized, comprehensive treatment plan that addresses the child's strengths and needs in the context of the family and the community, ultimately helping the child learn to function to his or her maximal potential.

References

American Psychiatric Association. (2013). *Diagnostic and statistical manual of mental disorders* (5th ed.). Washington, DC: Author.

Baghdadli, A., Pascal, C., Grisi, S., & Aussilloux, C. (2003). Risk factors for self-injurious behaviours among 222 young children with autistic disorders. *Journal of Intellectual Disability Research, 47*(8), 622–627.

Bandini, L. G., Anderson, S. E., Curtin, C., Cermak, S., Evans, E. W., Scampini, R., . . . Must, A. (2010). Food selectivity in children with autism spectrum disorders and typically developing children. *The Journal of Pediatrics, 157*(2), 259–264.

Broder-Fingert, S., Brazauskas, K., Lindgren, K., Iannuzzi, D., & Van Cleave, J. (2014). Prevalence of overweight and obesity in a large clinical sample of children with autism. *Academic Pediatrics, 14*(4), 408–414.

Christensen, D. L., Baio, J., Van Naarden Braun, K., Bilder, D., Charles, J., Constantino, J. N., . . . Yeargin-Allsopp, M. (2016). Prevalence and characteristics of autism spectrum disorder among children aged 8 years – Autism and Developmental Disabilities Monitoring Network, 11 Sites, United States, 2012. *Morbidity and Mortality Weekly Report, Surveillance Summaries (Washington, D.C.:2002), 65*(3), 1–23.

Danielsson, S., Gillberg, I. C., Billstedt, E., Gillberg, C., & Olsson, I. (2005). Epilepsy in young adults with autism: A prospective population-based follow-up study of 120 individuals diagnosed in childhood. *Epilepsia, 46*(6), 918–923.

DeFilippis, M., & Wagner, K. D. (2016). Treatment of autism spectrum disorder in children and adolescents. *Psychopharmacology Bulletin, 46*(2), 18–41.

de Vinck-Baroody, O., Shui, A., Macklin, E.A., Hyman, S. L., Leventhal, J. M., & Weitzman, C. (2015). Overweight and obesity in a sample of children with autism spectrum disorder. *Academic Pediatrics, 15*(4), 396–404.

Egan, A. M., Dreyer, M. L., Odar, C. C., Beckwith, M., & Garrison, C. B. (2013). Obesity in young children with autism spectrum disorders: Prevalence and associated factors. *Childhood Obesity, 9*(2), 125–131.

Filipek, P. A., Accardo, P. J., Ashwal, S., Baranek, G. T., Cook, E. H., Jr., Dawson, G., . . . Volkmar, F. R. (2000). Practice parameter: Screening and diagnosis of autism: Report of the Quality Standards Subcommittee of the American Academy of Neurology and the Child Neurology Society. *Neurology, 55*(4), 468–479.

Grafodatskaya, D., Chung, B., Szatmari, P., & Weksberg, R. (2010). Autism spectrum disorders and epigenetics. *Journal of the American Academy of Child & Adolescent Psychiatry, 49*(8), 794–809.

Hill, A. P., Zuckerman, K. E., & Fombonne, E. (2015). Obesity and autism. *Pediatrics, 136*(6), 1051–1061.

Joshi, G., Petty, C., Wozniak, J., Henin, A., Fried, R., Galdo, M., . . . Biederman, J. (2010). The heavy burden of psychiatric comorbidity in youth with autism spectrum disorders: A large comparative study of a psychiatrically referred population. *Journal of Autism and Developmental Disorders, 40*(11), 1361–1370.

Lecavalier, L. (2006). Behavioral and emotional problems in young people with pervasive developmental disorders: Relative prevalence, effects of subject characteristics, and empirical classification. *Journal of Autism and Developmental Disorders, 36*(8), 1101–1114.

Maglione, M. A., Gans, D., Das, L., Timbie, J., & Kasari, C. (2012). Nonmedical interventions for children with ASD: Recommended guidelines and further research needs. *Pediatrics, 130,* S169-178.

Malow, B. A., Byars, K., Johnson, K., Weiss, S., Bernal, P., Goldman, S. E., . . . Glaze, D. G. (2012). A practice pathway for the identification, evaluation, and management of insomnia in children and adolescents with autism spectrum disorders. *Pediatrics, 130,* S106-124.

Matson, J. L., Hattier, M. A., Belva, B., & Matson, M. L. (2013). Pica in persons with developmental disabilities: Approaches to treatment. *Research in Developmental Disabilities, 34*(9), 2564–2571.

McGuire, K., Fung, L.K., Hagopian, L., Vasa, R.A., Mahajan, R., Bernal, P., . . . Whitaker, A. H. (2016). Irritability and problem behavior in autism spectrum disorder: A practice pathway for pediatric primary care. *Pediatrics, 137,* S136-148.

Minshawi, N. F., Hurwitz, S., Morriss, D., & McDougle, C. J. (2015). Multidisciplinary assessment and treatment of self-injurious behavior in autism spectrum disorder and intellectual disability: Integration of psychological and biological theory and approach. *Journal of Autism and Developmental Disorders, 45*(6), 1541–1568.

Nickels, K. C., Katusic, S. K., Colligan, R. C., Weaver, A. L., Voight, R. G., & Barbaresi, W. J. (2008). Stimulant medication treatment of target behaviors in children with autism: A population-based study. *Journal of Developmental & Behavioral Pediatrics, 29*(2), 75–81.

Parmeggiani, A., Barcia, G., Posar, A., Raimondi, E., Santucci, M., & Scaduto, M. C. (2010). Epilepsy and EEG paroxysmal abnormalities in autism spectrum disorders. *Brain & Development, 32*(9), 783–789.

Perrin, J. M., Coury, D. L., Hyman, S. L., Cole, L., Reynolds, A. M., & Clemons, T. (2012). Complementary and alternative medicine use in a large pediatric autism sample. *Pediatrics, 130,* S77-182.

Richards, C., Jones, C., Groves, L., Moss, J., & Oliver, C. (2015). Prevalence of autism spectrum disorder phenomenology in genetic disorders: A systematic review and meta-analysis. *The Lancet Psychiatry, 2*(10), 909–916.

Rogers, S. J., & Vismara, L. A. (2008). Evidence-based comprehensive treatments for early autism. *Journal of Clinical Child & Adolescent Psychology, 37*(1), 8–38.

Rubenstein, E., Schieve, L., Bradley, C., DiGuiseppi, C., Moody, E., Thomas, K., & Daniels, J. (2017). The prevalence of gluten free diet use among preschool children with autism spectrum disorder. *Autism Research, 11*(1), 185-193.

Sathe, N., Andrews, J. C., McPheeters, M. L., & Warren, Z. E. (2017). Nutritional and dietary interventions for autism spectrum disorder: A systematic review. *Pediatrics, 139*(6), 1-8.

Schaefer, G. B., & Mendelsohn, N. J. (2013). Clinical genetics evaluation in identifying the etiology of autism spectrum disorders: 2013 guideline revisions. *Genetics in Medicine: Official Journal of the American College of Medical Genetics*, *15*(5), 399-407.

Shannon, M., & Graef, J. W. (1996). Lead intoxication in children with pervasive developmental disorders. *Journal of Toxicology: Clinical Toxicology*, *34*(2), 177–181.

Simonoff, E., Pickles, A., Charman, T., Chandler, S., Loucas, T., & Baird, G. (2008). Psychiatric disorders in children with autism spectrum disorders: Prevalence, comorbidity, and associated factors in a population-derived sample. *Journal of the American Academy of Child & Adolescent Psychiatry*, *47*(8), 921–929.

Smith, T., & Iadarola, S. (2015). Evidence base update for autism spectrum disorder. *Journal of Clinical Child & Adolescent Psychology*, *44*(6), 897–922.

Souders, M. C., Zavodny, S., Eriksen, W., Sinko, R., Connell, J., Kerns, C., . . . Pinto-Martin, J. (2017). Sleep in children with autism spectrum disorder. *Current Psychiatry Reports*, *19*(6), 34.

Spence, S. J., & Schneider, M. T. (2009). The role of epilepsy and epileptiform EEGs in autism spectrum disorders. *Pediatric Research*, *65*(6), 599–606.

Stein, L. I., Lane, C. J., Williams, M. E., Dawson, M. E., Polido, J. C., & Cermak, S. A. (2014). Physiological and behavioral stress and anxiety in children with autism spectrum disorders during routine oral care. *BioMed Research International*, *2014*, 694876.

Stein, L. I., Polido, J. C., Najera, S. O., & Cermak, S. A. (2012). Oral care experiences and challenges in children with autism spectrum disorders. *Pediatric Dentistry*, *34*(5), 387–391. Retrieved from http://www.aapd.org

Tsai, L. Y. (2014). Prevalence of comorbid psychiatric disorders in children and adolescents with autism spectrum disorder. *Journal of Experimental and Clinical Medicine*, 6(6), 179–186.

Virues-Ortega, J., Julio, F. M., & Pastor-Barriuso, R. (2013). The TEACCH program for children and adults with autism: A meta-analysis of intervention studies. *Clinical Psychology Review*, 33(8), 940–953.

Volkmar, F., Siegel, M., Woodbury-Smith, M., King, B., McCracken, J., & State, M. (2014). Practice parameter for the assessment and treatment of children and adolescents with autism spectrum disorder. *Journal of the American Academy of Child and Adolescent Psychiatry*, 53(2), 237-257.

Warren, Z., McPheeters, M. L., Sathe, N., Foss-Feig, J. H., Glasser, A., & Veenstra-Vanderweele, J. (2011). A systematic review of early intensive intervention for autism spectrum disorders. *Pediatrics*, 127(5), e1303-1311.

3

The Evolution of Autism Risk Genes

Emily L. Casanova & Manuel F. Casanova

The vast majority of major effect genes that underlie autism risk are syndromically-associated (Casanova E., Sharp, Chakraborty, Sumi, & Casanova M., 2016). However, some of these genes are also linked with idiopathic cases, albeit in association with less deleterious mutation types (Alvarez-Mora et al., 2016, for example; Karimi, Kamali, Mousavi, & Karahmadi, 2017, for review). The majority of idiopathic cases, however, do not appear to be associated with rare genetic variations, suggesting that common polygenic risk factors and environmental exigencies lie at the root of most cases of autism (Klei et al., 2012). As autism is a complex phenotype, its genetic background mirrors that trend, encompassing rare major/minor and common minor effect variants (Berg & Geschwind, 2012).

Genetics work to date indicates significant functional enrichment patterns amongst major effect genes in autism. For instance, a number of studies have reported that epigenetic and synaptic genes are common targets for mutation in the condition (Casanova et al., 2016; De Rubeis et al., 2014; Iossifov et al., 2014; Pinto et al., 2014). Of the epigenetic regulators, chromatin-related and transcription genes are overrepresented in particular and exhibit especially high penetrance for the autism phenotype (Casanova et al., 2016; De Rubeis et al., 2014). Meanwhile, synaptic gene mutations target all functional

University of South Carolina School of Medicine-Greenville, Greenville, SC, US forms, from structural synaptic components to enzymes to chemical messengers (Casanova et al., 2016).

Evolution According to Gene Class

Ongoing research by our laboratory has described a unique feature landscape characteristic of autism risk genes, which suggests that even within the genome "form ever follows function" (Casanova E., Switala, & Casanova M., 2017a; Sullivan, 1896; Williams, Casanova M., Switala, Li, Qiu, 2013). In particular, we have found that autism risk genes tend to:

1. be exceptionally long, primarily reflective of long introns (previously reported by King et al., 2013);
2. produce larger, more complex proteins;
3. contain greater absolute transposable (mobile) element content within their introns;
4. contain more absolute and relative conserved noncoding elements (CNE) within their introns;
5. produce more transcript variants;
6. are comparatively mutation intolerant (low allelic variability).

Many of these features share a strong interrelationship with one another. Sometimes, this may be due to actual structural overlap. For instance, transposons are known to have donated significant CNE content to the genome; therefore, it is little surprise that their respective numbers tend to correspond (Feschotte, 2008). However, in the case of low mutation tolerance and long gene size, the latter—contrary to expectation—is associated with lower mutation rates in part due to the effects long introns have on topoisomerase I activity, reducing the occurrence of transcription-associated mutations (Niu & Yang, 2011). In addition, mutations within long genes, which are often integral to embryonic development, are strongly selected against when they do occur, suggesting that as a functional class they are indeed comparatively "intolerant" (Han et al., 2017; Sironi et al., 2005). Recent research suggests that this intolerance is partly rooted in epigenomic patterns particular to long genes, which promote haploinsufficiency when mutations occur, resulting in autosomal dominant disease patterns (Han et al., 2017). Interestingly, autosomal dominant inheritance patterns are overrepresented in syndromic forms of autism as discussed in Casanova et al. (2016).

Although the presence of introns may reduce the rate of mutagenesis, it is clear that a primary function of the intron is to house noncoding elements that underlie the regulatory complexity of gene expression (Ludwig, 2002). They contain elements that may affect expression at numerous levels, including transcription, polyadenylation, mRNA export, translation, and mRNA decay (Nott, Meislin, & Moore, 2003). To illustrate these effects, Nott et al. designed mammalian constructs that contained intron 6 from the human *triose phosphate isomerase* (*TPI*) gene at two positions within the *Renilla* luciferase open reading frame. They found that not only did this intron promote mRNA accumulation, it also improved translational yield. Meanwhile, large-scale studies have found that across mammalian species, when conserved intron losses occur they are usually extremely small (< 150 bp) and almost exclusively target housekeeping genes, which are constitutively expressed and rely on comparatively fewer CNE than other gene types (Casanova et al., 2017; Coulombe-Huntington & Majewski, 2006).

Much of organismal diversity appears to be the result not of alterations to the exome but to the progressive elaboration of the regulome (Levine & Tijan, 2003). As mentioned earlier much of that regulome has been derived from the insertion and retention of transposable elements, most of which are now transpositionally extinct within the human genome. Interestingly, these once-mobile elements also create genomic instability due to their repetitive content, which promotes slippage, double stranded breaks, and other replication errors (Bose, Hermetz, Conneely, & Rudd, 2014; Robberecht, Voet, Esteki, Nowakowska, & Vermeesch, 2013). This is especially the case with intronic *Alu* elements, which promote exceptionally high rates of translocation when DSBs are introduced adjacent to identical elements (Elliott, Richardson, & Jasin, 2005). Interestingly, the breakpoints of copy number variations, a mutational variant overrepresented in conditions like autism and schizophrenia, often overlap *Alu* and *LINE1* sequences in humans (Robberecht et al., 2013).

Primates, *Alu*'s, & Autism Risk Genes

Alu elements are an especially interesting type of retrotransposon, composing over 10% of the human genome and, in particular, are well represented in autism risk genes (Casanova et al., 2017a). They are a nonautonomous form of short interspersed element (SINE) that is dependent on the enzymatic machinery produced by *LINE1* elements in order to retrotranspose. In this way, they are said to "piggyback" the *LINE1*s.

Unlike the *mammalian-wide interspersed repeat* (*MIR*) elements (a type of ancient SINE that is common to all extant mammals), *Alu* elements are comparatively young and are particular to primates, having evolved around the time of the early primate radiation ≤ 65 million years ago (mya), shortly after the Cretaceous-Paleogene (K-Pg) extinction (Kriegs, Churakov, Jurka, Brosius, & Schmitz, 2007). *AluJ*s are the oldest subfamily, yet the succeeding subfamily, *AluS*, which proliferated roughly 40 mya, is by far the most successful *Alu* element in the primate lineage, with over 650,000 retained insertions—more than twice as many as the *AluJ* and *AluY* subfamilies combined (Deininger, 2011).

Although they target similar sequence sites within the genome as their distantly-related autonomous cousins, the LINEs, *Alu*'s are preferentially retained in gene-rich regions (i.e., Giemsa negative bands) while *LINE1*s are mostly relegated to the heterochromatin (Kazazian, 2011). In part, this may be due to size differences: *LINE1*s measure thousands of base pairs in length while *Alu*'s only several hundred, making the latter's insertion into gene-rich regions potentially less deleterious.

However, *Alu*'s preferential retention in Giemsa negative bands likewise suggests they have been exapted within the primate lineage for the purposes of gene regulation and, on rare occasion, exonization. For example, circular RNAs (circRNA) are a stable circular form of RNA that is abundant in the eukaryotic genome. They are derived primarily from exonic and intronic sequences, whose borders in the human genome often contain complementary (i.e., inverted) *Alu* elements (Jeck et al., 2013). According to Qu et al. (2015), these circRNAs function as "microRNA sponges, regulators of splicing and transcription, and modifiers of parental gene expression" (p. 141). Given the regulatory and transcriptional complexity of long genes, it is likely that a significant portion of *Alu* insertions have been readily co-opted in these genes within the primate lineage.

Another key example of *Alu* exaptation is nuclear hormone response elements (HRE). Researchers have found that a significant number of HRE have been derived from *Alu* elements, including targets of the estrogen, thyroid, and retinoic acid receptors (Babich et al., 1999). The evolution of apes has been characterized by significant sexual dimorphism in terms of body mass, canine tooth size, fur, and skin. This dimorphism was apparently even more exaggerated in extinct apes and may in part have been driven by the rapid expansion of *Alu* repeat insertions and their co-option as HRE (Plavcan, 2002).

Given the sex-skewed nature of autism, these *Alu*-derived HRE (which may be overrepresented in autism risk genes given their high *Alu* content) may also play a significant role in the 4:1 male-to-female diagnostic ratio. In support of this, the autism transcriptome exhibits a male-typic pattern, suggesting that autism risk genes are indeed expressed differently between the sexes (Werling, Parikshak, & Geschwind, 2016). However, to what extent *Alu*-derived HREs may be responsible for this skewing and thus Female Protective Effect is unknown, but is a prime area for further study (Constantino, 2016).

Why have we focused so heavily on Alu elements at the expense of other genomic repeats? The fact that a subset of cephalically-enriched developmental genes has experienced a rapid evolution since the primate radiation is intriguing. Increases in encephalization appear to have occurred numerous times within different simian lineages, suggesting an element of convergent evolution and a potentially hereditary mechanism underlying that propensity (Phillips, 2008). *Alu* elements are prime candidates as drivers of some of those changes, many now functioning as enhancers that have been under accelerated evolution in humans compared to chimpanzee (Capra et al., 2013a; Su et al., 2014). Although we no longer see high *Alu* insertion rates as once occurred in earlier primates, *Alu*-derived noncoding elements in brain-enriched genes seem to be major targets of recent and ongoing evolution in hominins.

Table 3.1
Phyletic Branches, Ranks, and Approximate Ages of Last Common Ancestor Used to Calculate Differences Between Autism Risk and Randomized Control Genes

Phyletic Branches	Approximate Age of Last Common Ancestor
Fungi (#1)	1,500 mya
Chordates (#2)	600 mya
Bilateria (#3)	525 mya
Vertebrates (#4)	500 mya
Cartilaginous fish (#5)	450 mya
Bony vertebrates (#6)	415 mya
Amniotes (#7)	300 mya
Marsupials and placental mammals (#8)	160 mya
Laurasiatherian mammals (#9)	90 mya
Primates (#10)	65 mya
Old world primates (#11)	25 mya

The Evolutionary Age of Autism Risk Genes

The feature landscape of genes tends to vary by evolutionary age. Ancient eukaryotic genes, common to all extant eukaryotes today, are relatively mutation intolerant and produce longer amino acid sequences than their younger counterparts (Albá & Castresana, 2005). Because these features are reminiscent of those previously reported in autism risk genes, it begs the question: Are autism genes more ancient than most?

Utilizing a list of high-risk autism genes compiled from Casanova et al. (Casanova, E., Gerstner, Sharp, Casanova, M., & Feltus, 2017b) and the SFARI gene database (syndromic, categories 1-3; N = *154*), we compared the average age of these risk genes to a randomized list of 100 control genes. The oldest eukaryotic phyletic branch for each gene was derived using

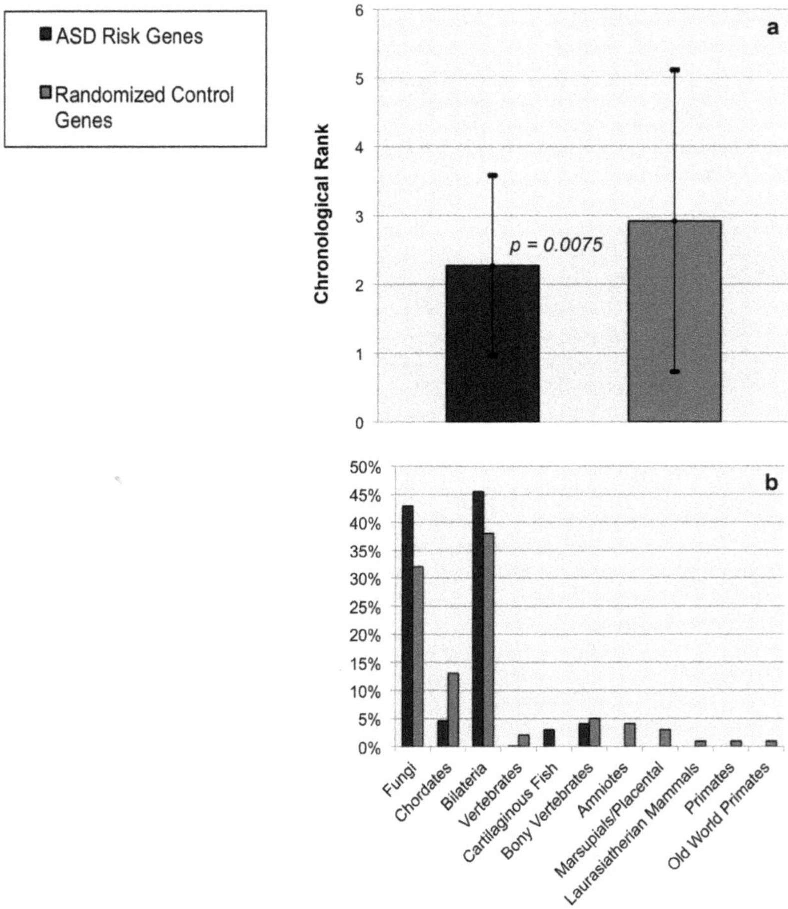

Figure 3.1. (a) Group differences in chronological ranking between autism risk and randomized control genes. Bars indicate standard deviations. See Table 3.1 for rank definitions. (b) Percentage of genes by group per phyletic branch.

Ensembl's "Gene Tree" feature. (Three risk genes were removed from our list because they had no Gene Tree data.) The literature was then searched for a rough estimate of the last common ancestor (LCA) between that branch and the human lineage, and then each category was chronologically ranked for statistical comparison (heteroscedastic student's *t*-test; see Table 3.1).

We have found that, as their structural features would predict, autism risk genes tend to be more ancient than other genes in the human genome—most either shared with our LCA with fungi (and perhaps even with protists or prokaryotes) or the early bilaterians, ranging from 525–1,500 million years in age ($p = 0.0075$). This suggests that, indeed, the feature landscape of autism risk genes is partly due to their evolutionary age and the variable constraints that apply to these different classes of genes.

Interestingly, older genes tend to have more physical interactions, are enriched in a wider variety of tissues, and interact with and are regulated by more genes, suggesting that they tend to be foundational to a wider variety of cellular networks (Capra et al., 2013b). By extension, it is possible that the network complexity of autism risk genes is greater than most and their loss-of-function or impairment may lead to far-reaching effects across tissues, resulting in high mutation intolerance. In support of this we find that syndromic forms of autism with intellectual disability (ID) are more likely to present with multiple congenital anomalies than other genetic forms of ID, indicating they regulate developmental processes across a variety of tissue types (Casanova et al., 2017b).

We have not addressed in this chapter whether older genes in general tend to house high transposable element (and thus *Alu*) content. However, for those ancient genes that are tissue- and stage-specific and not constitutively expressed (i.e., not housekeeping genes), they would indeed fit the stereotype. We can, however, state that autism risk genes in particular, whose roots are comparatively ancient, are enriched in transposable elements. What's more, not only are these elements points of genomic instability, they themselves are additional targets for genetic variation in autism and other neurodevelopmental conditions (Takata, Ionita-Laza, Gogos, Xu, & Karayiorgou, 2016).

Summary

The evolution of autism risk genes has ancient roots, some having arisen more than 1.5 billion years ago during the early reign of single-celled eukaryotes. Meanwhile, others genes are common to bilaterians, animals which are bilaterally symmetrical, containing identifiable anterior, posterior, dorsal, and ventral regions of the body. In addition to having a head (sensory organs and ganglia/brain), most bilaterians house a coelom or body cavity that holds the digestive tract and other viscera, linking evolutionary developments of the brain and gut. These genes evolved more than half-a-million years ago.

Autism risk genes, for reasons not entirely understood, maintain a common feature landscape: they are large and may contain vast intronic expanses; their introns house extensive transposable element and regulatory content; they produce numerous transcripts and large, presumably complex proteins; and they, like other genes of their age, are relatively mutation intolerant. In turn, this mutation intolerance may be the result of lower mutation rates due to the effects long introns have on topoisomerase I activity, but it may also flow from their propensity for haploinsufficiency and the foundational roles these genes play in cellular networks.

In particular, the foundational nature of autism risk genes implies not only their far-reaching effects across tissue types, it also suggests a means by which many different mutations via overlapping redundant networks can collapse onto a common phenotype such as autism. Whether this is the case remains to be seen, but it is a testable hypothesis with the data currently

References

Albá, M. M., & Castresana, J. (2005). Inverse relationship between evolutionary rate and age of mammalian genes. *Molecular Biology and Evolution, 22*, 589–606.

Alvarez-Mora, M. I., Calvo Escalona, R., Puig Navarro, O., Madrigal, I., Quintela, I., Amigo, J., ... Rodriguez-Revenga, L. (2016). Comprehensive molecular testing in patients with high functioning autism spectrum disorder. *Mutation Research, 784–785*, 46–52.

Babich, V., Aksenov, N., Alexeenko, V., Oei, S. L., Buchlow, G., & Tomilin, N. (1999). Association of some potential hormone response elements in human genes with the *Alu* family repeats. *Gene, 239*, 341–349.

Berg, J. M., & Geschwind, D. H. (2012). Autism genetics: Searching for specificity and convergence. *Genome Biology, 13*, 247.

Bose, P., Hermetz, K. E., Conneely, K. N., & Rudd, M. K. (2014). Tandem repeats and G-rich sequences are enriched at human CNV breakpoints. *PLoSOne, 9*, e101607.

Capra, J. A., Erwin, G. D., McKinsey, G., Rubenstein, J. L., & Pollard, K. S. (2013a). Many human accelerated regions are developmental enhancers. *Philosophical Transactions of the Royal Society, B, 368*, 20130025

Capra, J. A., Stolzer, M., Durand, D., & Pollard, K. S. (2013b). How old is my gene? *Trends in Genetics, 29*, 659–668.

Casanova, E. L., Sharp, J. L., Chakraborty, H., Sumi, N. S., & Casanova, M. F. (2016). Genes with high penetrance for syndromic and non-syndromic autism typically function within the nucleus and regulate gene expression. *Molecular Autism, 7*, 18.

Casanova, E. L., Switala, A. E., & Casanova, M. F. (2017a). The feature landscape of autism risk genes indicates their enrichment in developmental regulation. *International Meeting for Autism Research (IMFAR)*, San Francisco, California, May 11, 2017.

Casanova, E. L., Gerstner, Z., Sharp, J. L., Casanova, M. F., & Feltus, F. A. (2017b). Widespread genotype-phenotype correlations in intellectual disability. *bioRxiv*, 220608.

Constantino, J. N. (2016). Data from the Baby Siblings Research Consortium confirm and specify the nature of the female protective effect in autism: A commentary on Messinger et al.

Molecular Autism, 7, 32.
Coulombe-Huntington, J., & Majewski, J. (2006). Characterization of intron loss events in mammals. *Genome Research, 17*, 23–32.
Deininger, P. (2011). *Alu* elements: Know the SINEs. *Genome Biology, 12*, 236.
De Rubeis, S., He, X., Goldberg, A. P., Poultney, C. S., Samocha, K., Cicek, A. E., ... Buxbaum, J. D. (2014). Synaptic, transcriptional and chromatin genes disrupted in autism. *Nature, 515*(7526), 209–215.
Elliott, B., Richardson, C., & Jasin, M. (2005). Chromosomal translocation mechanisms at intronic *Alu* elements in mammalian cells. *Molecular Cell, 17*, 885–894.
Feschotte, C. (2008). Transposable elements and the evolution of regulatory networks. *Nature Reviews Genetics, 9*, 397.
Han, X., Chen, S., Flynn, E. D., Qu, S., Wintner, D., & Shen, Y. (2017). Distinct epigenomic patterns are associated with haploinsufficiency and predict risk genes of developmental disorders. *bioRxiv*, 205849.
Iossifov, I., O'Roak, B. J., Sanders, S. J., Ronemus, M., Krumm, N., Levy, D., ... Wigler, M. (2014). The contribution of de novo coding mutations to autism spectrum disorder. *Nature, 515*(7526), 216–221.
Jeck, W. R., Sorrentino, J. A., Wang, K., Slevin, M. K., Burd, C. E., Liu, J., ... Sharpless, N. E. (2013). Circular RNAs are abundant, conserved, and associated with *ALU* repeats. *RNA, 19*, 141–157.
Karimi, P., Kamali, E., Mousavi, S. M., & Karahmadi, M. (2017). Environmental factors influencing the risk of autism. *Journal of Research in Medical Sciences, 22*, 27.
Kazazian, H. H. Jr. (2011). *Mobile DNA: Finding treasure in junk.* New Jersey: FT Press.
King, I. F., Yandava, C. N., Mabb, A. M., Hsiao, J. S., Huang, H. S., Pearson, B. L., ... Zylka, M. J. (2013). Topoisomerases facilitate transcription of long genes linked to autism. *Nature, 501*, 58.
Klei, L., Sanders, S. J., Murtha, M. T., Hus, V., Lowe, J. K., Willsey, A. J., ... Devlin, B. (2012). Common genetic variants, acting additively, are a major source of risk for autism. *Molecular Autism, 3*, 9.
Kriegs, J. O., Churakov, G., Jurka, J., Brosius, J., & Schmitz, J. (2007). Evolutionary history of 7SL RNA-derived SINEs in supraprimates. *Trends in Genetics, 23*, 158–161.
Levine, M., & Tijan, R. (2003). Transcription regulation and animal diversity. *Nature, 424*, 147–151.
Ludwig, M. Z. (2002). Functional evolution of noncoding DNA. *Current Opinion in Genetics & Development, 12*, 634–639.
Niu, D.-K., & Yang, Y.-F. (2011). Why eukaryotic cells use introns

to enhance gene expression: Splicing reduces transcription-associated mutagenesis by inhibiting topoisomerase I cutting activity. *Biology Direct, 6*, 24.

Nott, A., Meislin, S. H., & Moore, M. J. (2003). A quantitative analysis of intron effects on mammalian gene expression. *RNA, 9*, 607–617.

Phillips, K. (2008). Big brains arose twice in higher primates. *American Academy for the Advancement of Science (AAAS): EurekAlert!* July 9. Retrieved from: https://www.eurekalert.org/pub_releases/2008-07/amon-bba070908.php

Pinto, D., Delaby, E., Merico, D., Barbosa, M., Merikangas, A., Klei, L., ... Scherer, S. W. (2014). Convergence of genes and cellular pathways dysregulated in autism spectrum disorders. *American Journal of Human Genetics, 94*, 677–694.

Plavcan, M. J. (2002). Sexual dimorphism in primate evolution. *American Journal of Physical Anthropology, 116*, 25–53.

Qu, S., Yang, X., Li, X., Wang, J., Gao, Y., Shang, R., ... Li, H. (2015). Circular RNA: A new star of noncoding RNAs. *Cancer Letters, 365*, 141–148.

Robberecht, C., Voet, T., Esteki, M. Z., Nowakowska, B. A., & Vermeesch, J. R. (2013). Nonallelic homologous recombination between retrotransposable elements is a driver of de novo unbalanced translocations. *Genome Research, 23*, 411–418.

Sironi, M., Menozzi, G., Comi, G. P., Bresolin, N., Cagliani, R., & Pozzoli, U. (2005). Fixation of conserved sequences shapes human intron size and influences transposon-insertion dynamics. *Trends in Genetics, 21*, 484–488.

Su, M., Han, D., Boyd-Kirkup, J., Yu, X., & Han, J.-D. (2014). Evolution of *Alu* elements towards enhancers. *Cell Reports, 7*, 376–385.

Sullivan, L. H. (1896). The tall office building artistically considered. *Lippincott's Magazine, March* 403–409.

Takata, A., Ionita-Laza, I., Gogos, J. A., Xu, B., & Karayiorgou, M. (2016). De novo synonymous mutations in regulatory elements contribute to the genetic etiology of autism and schizophrenia. *Neuron, 89*, 940–947.

Werling, D. M., Parikshak, N. N., & Geschwind, D. H. (2016). Gene expression in human brain implicates sexually dimorphic pathways in autism spectrum disorders. *Nature Communications, 7*, 10717.

Williams, E. L., Casanova, M., Switala, A., Li, H., & Qiu, M. (2013). Transposable elements occur more frequently in autism-risk genes: Implications for the role of genomic instability in autism. *Translational Neuroscience, 42*, 172–202.

4

Autism, Transcranial Magnetic Stimulation and Gamma Frequencies

Manuel F. Casanova,[1,2] Estate M. Sokhadze,[1] Ioan Opris,[3] Xiaoli Li,[4] and Emily L. Casanova[1]

Autism or autism spectrum disorders (ASD), makes reference to a range of neurodevelopmental conditions presently defined by behavioral findings. The signs typically appear in early childhood and include difficulties in both establishing social relationships and in their ability to communicate with others. In addition, autistic individuals exhibit rigid and repetitive patterns of behavior, interests, and activities. Symptoms vary widely among affected individuals in regards to severity, onset, developmental skills and adaptive functions. Nearly three quarters of autistic individuals suffer from medical comorbidities including anxiety, depression, and attention deficit hyperactivity disorder. There is no single cause for autism and most people refer to it as a syndrome; a group of condition tied together by associated symptoms. The majority of cases are idiopathic in origin but approximately 10% have a recognized genetic anomaly (Glennon et al., 2017).

In autism, the presence of abnormalities of language, socialization, and executive functions suggests some type of

[1]Department of Biomedical Sciences, University of South Carolina School of Medicine Greenville
[2]Department of Pediatrics, Greenville Health System,
[3]Miami Project to Cure Paralysis, University of Miami Miller School of Medicine
[4]State Key Laboratory of Cognitive Neuroscience and Learning, Beijing Normal University
Correspondence should be addressed to Manuel F. Casanova; m0casa02@louisville.edu

dysfunction of the cerebral cortex. The large variety of symptoms, seizure types, and patterns of EEG abnormalities indicate that a significant span of the cerebral cortex is affected. The underlying deficit or pathology appears to provide for an excitatory/inhibitory imbalance that propitiate sensory abnormalities and seizures (Casanova et al., 2003). More specifically, there is no primary type of seizure in autism; generalized, complex partial (with or without generalization), and absence have all been reported (Spence and Schneider, 2009). Cortical dysfunction appears to have its onset during brain development. In this way plastic brain changes and environmental influences promote adaptive modifications. The lack of numbness, weakness, spasticity, ataxia, gait disorder, visual loss, and disconnection syndromes suggests the absence of overt white matter pathology (Casanova, 2006; Filley, 2012). Although no abnormal development or destruction of white matter (myelin sheaths) has been reported in autism the organization and distribution of fibers may be altered (Aoki et al., 2017). Indeed, the corpus callosum appears to be relatively smaller than normal, cases of dysgenesis may be common, and the ratio of long projection to short arcuate fibers may be altered (Casanova et al., 2011; Lau et al., 2013).

There are no medications currently approved to treat autism spectrum disorders core symptoms. The lack of empirically validated options to manage ASD has led desperate parents to try almost any conceivable alternative treatment (Goodman, 2014). In a large study (n=578 children) approximately 40% of children with ASD were receiving some type of complementary/alternative treatment. The use of these treatments is increasing despite the fact that, according to the American Academy of Pediatrics, "scientific validation and support for many interventions is incomplete and disparate" (Levy & Hyman, 2003).

Recent studies suggest that Transcranial Magnetic Resonance (TMS) may offer a therapeutic avenue to ADS that targets core symptoms of the condition (Casanova et al., 2015; Oberman et al., 2015; 2016). TMS is a noninvasive procedure that uses magnetic fields to induce excitation or inhibition within targeted regions of the brain. Although experience is limited, meta-analysis of TMS studies in children indicate that it is a fairly safe technique (Krishnan, et al., 2015). However, until sufficient data regarding the safety of TMS becomes available, users should institute the same guidelines as in adults and are encouraged to screen for possible side effects on a session-by-session basis (Allen et al., 2017).

Neuropathology

A short review of the neuropathology of both non-idiopathic and idiopathic autism suggests the presence of a defect in neuronal migration (Casanova, 2007; 2014). Studies stemming from the Autism Atlas Study initially sponsored by the National Alliance for Autism Research (NAAR) have shown the presence of periventricular nodular heterotopias (candle gutterings), accumulations of neurons within the white matter, and cortical dysplasia in the majority of patients examined. (Casanova, 2007). Researchers have expanded on these findings in studies that attest to the presence of an increased number of neurons within the gray/white matter boundary as well as within the molecular cortical layer of ASD patients (Bailey et al., 1998; Avino & Hutsler, 2010; Hutsler & Casanova, 2015). The heterotopic findings are widespread including both cerebral hemispheres and cerebellum. Contrary to heterotopias of genetic causation, the abnormal cell islands in the brains of autistic individuals are sporadic and vary in their location among patients. The findings support a migratory defect of neuroblasts as they head towards the cerebral plate early during corticogenesis and immediately following the asymmetric division of periventricular germinal cells. The ensuing cortical abnormality is a dysplastic phenomenon characterized by minicolumnar abnormalities (Casanova et al., 2013; Opris & Casanova, 2014).

Minicolumns are modular units of both neurons and their projections formed by the gliophilic radial migration of neuroblasts as they make their way from the periventricular zone to the cortical plate. Once within the cortical plate these neuroblasts develop into pyramidal cell and establish a working relationship with inhibitory cells (interneurons). The working relationship between interneurons and pyramidal cells appears to be at fault in autism. More specifically, the resultant minicolumnopathy in ASD is characterized by a reduction of the peripheral neuropil space spanning all cortical laminae examined (Casanova et al., 2010). The peripheral neuropil space provides a "shower curtain of inhibition" to the minicolumns. Defects in this shower curtain of inhibition allow for information within the core of the minicolumns to be processed without the benefit of inhibitory modulation and to suffuse into adjacent minicolumns. The resultant cascade of excitation provides for a nonlinear amplification of signals (Casanova, 2007; Hutsler &e Casanova, 2016). When signals are processed in this environment the resulting stochastic resonance provides for magnification in noisy environments.

A possible therapeutic intervention for autism would be one that would strengthen the "shower curtain of inhibition" for minicolumns. Many of the inhibitory fibers within the peripheral neuropil space stand at ninety degrees to the surface of the cerebral cortex. Some of these fibers come from the horse tail projections of double bouquet cells that serve to frame the outer boundaries of the minicolumns. The multiple axonal projections stem from the same node or soma making their joint stimulation (e.g., TMS) easier than for a single projection with similar orientation (e.g., pyramidal cell apical dendrites or axons). In this regard, low frequency stimulation with TMS would take advantage of the geometrical orientation of these inhibitory elements. Higher frequencies would stimulate all cellular elements within a region of interest. Given that the majority of cells within the cerebral cortex are pyramidal, the overall effect of higher frequency stimulation would be excitation.

Transcranial Magnetic Stimulation

A metal that retains its attraction and repulsion characteristics over other metals is known as a permanent magnet. The ends of a bar magnet are called poles and the strength of the magnetic field is expressed as the density of magnetic flux lines traveling from its north to south pole. Ferromagnetic materials, like iron or nickel, are not themselves magnetic but acquire this property when they are in close proximity to a magnet. This material loses its magnetism as the magnetic field to which it is exposed disappears. Electromagnets, as well as ferromagnetic materials, are temporary magnets created by passing a current through a wire. Even though the conductor does not have magnetic poles, the flux lines still have directional orientation. Thus, when the wire is wound in a coil, the magnetic flux of each individual coil loop combines with those of its neighbors to produce an overall field pattern similar to that of a bar magnet.

The addition of a ferromagnetic core to an electromagnet concentrates the magnetic flux and increases the strength of the magnetic field. Although such a modification to the electromagnet increases its flux, the core concentrates and contains much of the magnetic field within itself. Thus, the end effect of adding a ferromagnetic core to an electromagnet is to reduce the effect of the magnetic field at a distance. This reduction is especially salient as the strength of the magnetic field varies inversely with the square of the distance. Since TMS tries to maximize its effects at a distance (i.e., needs to penetrate the brain) the coil may be wrapped around air or another material such as glass or Bakelite instead of a ferromagnetic metal. In this way, the coil is better able to expand its magnetic flux while simultaneously remaining free of losses associated with hysteresis and Eddy currents that occur within the ferromagnetic core. However, since compared to radio waves, TMS uses low frequency pulses these losses are minimal. As previously surmised, the real loss accrued to the use of air cores comes from a reduction in magnetic field strength. Research into iron cores for TMS has continued focusing on developing new ways to minimize power requirements and heat generation, with some models claiming improved penetration of the magnetic field (Epstein & Davey, 2002).

In order to provide physiological results TMS requires a magnetic field of 1-3 tesla; the same static magnetic field strength as used in magnetic resonance imaging (MRI). Ampere's Law states a relationship between current and magnetic field. In order to compensate for the loss in magnetic strength accrued to using an air core, TMS uses very high currents. Despite the low resistance of the wire the high current dissipates energy as heat much like the filament of an incandescent lightbulb (note: power equals current squared times resistance). The electrical resistance of the wire ultimately limits how much you can increase the magnetic field by varying its current. Different machines use proprietary methods for cooling their coils. Powdered cores in particular offer high resistivity and low hysteresis and eddy current losses

In TMS a bank of supercapacitors produces a pulse of very high current. Capacitors store energy as an electrostatic charge, can be charged quickly, and deliver very high power. Contrary to batteries which store their energy as a chemical reaction and whose lifetime is limited by discharge cycles, capacitors can discharge millions of times without losing their energy storage capacity. The electrical current generated this way is in the kiloampere (kA) range. As a matter of comparison, currents over 10 milliamperes (mA) are perceived as painful by the human body and currents between 100 and 200 mA can be lethal.

Coil geometry is of importance in determining the focality and depth of stimulation of a magnetic field. The aim for TMS is to stimulate a focal area of the brain without affecting adjacent regions. Reducing the distance between the poles of the electromagnet, diminishes the distance traveled by the magnetic flux. Air has a high reluctance or resistance to the flow of magnetic energy. The closer together you appose the ends of the magnet the stronger the field. These characteristics have led to designs of closed flat coils. The most commonly used designs are circular or have a figure of eight (double cone). Some attempts have been made at varying the coil design (H-type coil) in order to achieve deep penetration of the brain. Since magnetic field strength varies inversely with the square of the distance (*vide supra*) deep stimulation requires vastly stronger magnetic fields. Thus far such attempts have led to excessive superficial stimulation and to the unintended activation of large areas of the brain (Deng et al., 2014).

According to the Law of Faraday when the lines of flux cut the path of a conductor an electromagnetic force (EMF) or voltage is self-induced in the conductor. The value of the resultant voltage is proportional to the length of the conductor, the number of turns in the coil, the spacing between the turns, the number of layers of windings, the type of winding, the diameter of the coil, and the type of core material. Skin effect losses are minimal given the low frequencies used in TMS; however, parasitic capacitance between individual turns of the wire may change the behavior of the coil.

The expansion (and later collapse) of the magnetic field generated by the pulsed current from the capacitor generates the relative movement between the lines of flux and the wire of the coil. As long as the magnetic field is moving with respect to the conductor an induced voltage is generated. The fast rise of the pulse contributes to the strength of the magnetic field from the coil.

The principle by which TMS works is that of mutual inductance. This is what happens in the secondary coil of a transformer. As the pulsed current causes the magnetic field to expand and contract around the coil it induces current in other conductors exposed to the same. In this case, membrane bound, water filled projections act as conductors. Although water itself is a poor conductor it is a great ionic solvent. The dissolved ions in the cytoplasm make water an excellent conductor and the projection of cells thus act as wires. The closer the TMS coil is placed to the anatomical element of interest the larger the number of flux lines will cut through the same. Changes are maximum for those anatomical elements standing at ninety degrees to the magnetic field. Distance and orientation dictate the degree of flux linkage or coefficient of coupling between the involved elements.

In mutual induction, it is difficult or impossible to transfer the same amount of power from the primary coil to the secondary conductor (i.e., somatic projections). These two elements are physically separated and not ideally coupled. For TMS the amount of power applied far exceeds the amount found or used in normal physiology. In the end, stimulation follows an all or none type of pattern instead of the graded transmission encountered during information processing. The meaning of operating in the nonlinear portion of physiological response as well as the side effects of unwanted power dissipation should be the object of future TMS research.

Transcranial Magnetic Stimulation in Autism

The limited radiation of the TMS coil restricts its effectiveness to a small span of the cerebral cortex, which is approximately the size of a quarter. Since stimulation of multiple areas in a study design is impractical, the selection of a region of interest is of great importance when defining the experimental design of a trial. Until present, our group has performed 15 clinical trials of TMS in ASD for which several hundred patients were recruited. In all of these studies the dorsolateral prefrontal cortex (DLPC) was the targeted region of interest. A waitlist control group was used as patients could differentiate active *vs.* sham stimulation. Otherwise participants in the waitlist control group were offered the active treatment at the end of the study.

The DLPC is a recently evolved region of the human brain that has a long maturation period. It plays an important role in executive functions such as organizing, planning, and sustaining attention. Its role in executive functions places it at the interface of the action-specific perception cycle that characterize the ability of a person to react to environmental stimuli. Anatomically the DLPC lies in the second third of the middle frontal gyrus and can be located by Neuronavigation or approximated using standardized electrode placement for EEG (F3/F4). Many, but not all, autistic individuals have difficulties with executive function. The attendant dysfunction is one that can readily be targeted by TMS. In addition, normalizing the function of the DLPC has the added advantage of modulating a vast expanse of the cortex. The resulting functional or connectional diaschisis that happens when targeting the DLPC could provide benefits not imaginable when considering this region of interest in isolation.

Most studies of TMS in children have described few or no side effects. Among the side effects reported are an "itching" sensation around the nose, a tension-type headache, jaw twitching, and dizziness. These adverse effects have been considered mild and transient. In a recent meta-analysis by Krishnan et al. (2015) the data of 48 studies involving more than 513 patients were reviewed. The incidence of adverse effects was similar to that observed in adults. Krishnan et al. (2015) emphasized the scant literature outlining the need for longer treatment and follow up sessions. A review of the literature in ASD reached similar conclusions suggesting that TMS could offer a transformative approach to the treatment of autism (Oberman et al., 2015; 2016).

In ASD, successful outcomes have been operationalized according to behavioral improvements. Thus, although the interventions of different trials may have targeted cognitive skills in attention or executive functions the ultimate goal has been on how the patient's observable behavior allows them to integrate themselves into society. In this regard, most of the studies have used the same behavioral outcome measures: ABC, SRS, and RBS-R. These behavioral evaluations post-TMS have shown decreased irritability, hyperactivity, stereotyped behavior and compulsive behavior ratings. Other neuropsychological measures were meant to assess reaction time and response accuracy. In one study post rTMS reaction time to targets did not show any statistically significant difference but there was significant improvement in error percentage (Sokhadze et al., 2010). In addition, several studies have indirectly reported on the safety of rTMS based on autonomic dependent variables, i.e., R-R intervals, pNN50, NN50, SD R-R intervals, power of LF of HRV, LF/HF ratio, skin conductance level (Wang et al., 2016); and increased cardiac vagal control and reduced sympathetic arousal (considered as improvements) in ASD (Casanova et al., 2014).

Several studies have reported outcome measures of executive function in rTMS trials in ASD. According to Sokhadze and colleagues (2010, 2014) low-frequency rTMS minimizes early cortical responses to irrelevant stimuli. According to the latter authors, the improved selectivity in early cortical responses led to better stimulus differentiation at later-stage responses as evident by the P3b and P3a components (Sokhadze et al., 2010). The results of the study were further pursued when the same researchers examined post rTMS changes on error monitoring and correction function in autism (Sokhadze et al., 2012). The process of performance monitoring is an essential prerequisite for adaptively altering behavioral responses and making decisions for correction of behavior according to task demands. Executive function of behavioral performance monitoring comprises error detection and response conflict monitoring, functions that were measured in this study by their electrophysiological correlates: the fronto-central error-related negativity (ERN) and the error-related positivity (Pe). The results of the study showed significant post TMS differences in the response-locked ERP (ERN) as well as behavioral response monitoring measures indicative of improved error monitoring and correction.

Casanova and colleagues (2012) focused on later stage ERP indices of selective attention in an rTMS trial of ASD individuals. Selective attention is a component of working memory as it oversees decisions and regulates the ability to focus on task-relevant goals while excluding salient distracters. In this study the researchers found that rTMS resulted in significant improvement in both N200 and P300 components and a reduction in response errors, repetitive behavior, and irritability. Focused attention appears to show a significant linear improvement in response over 18 sessions of rTMS (Sokhadze et al., 2014). The authors also noted that the most pronounced improvements in ERP measures were observed closer to the site of stimulation, that is, at the frontal and fronto-central ROI (i.e., N100, P2d, N200, P3a components) as compared to posterior ROI (i.e., parietal and parieto-occipital P200, N200 and P3b).

Gamma Frequencies

Oscillations of pyramidal cells in minicolumns and across assemblies of minicolumns are maintained by networks of different species of interneurons. In this regard interneurons make a critical contribution to the generation of network oscillations and help synchronize the activity of pyramidal cells during transient brain states (Mann & Paulsen, 2007). Local excitatory-inhibitory interactions help shape neuronal representations of sensory, motor and cognitive variables, and produce local gamma-band oscillations (30-100 Hz) (Donner & Siegel, 2011). The excitatory-inhibitory bias caused by faulty pyramidal cell-interneuronal dyads provides a receptive scenario to gamma frequency abnormalities in autism.

The brain's limited long-range wiring cannot directly sustain coordinated activity across arbitrary cortical locations, but it can convey patterns of synchronous activity as oscillatory neuronal fluxes, represented by local field potentials measured by electroencephalography (EEG). Coordination of oscillations at varying interacting frequencies allows for relatively efficient and unconstrained segregation in varying forms and across hierarchical cortical levels. Disrupted patterns of coordinated oscillatory output in distributed minicolumnar networks might be associated with cortical "disconnection" in autism. More specifically, altered oscillatory activity in developing cortical circuits may contribute to impaired development of intra-areal and transcortical connections giving rise to a bias in short (e.g. arcuate) vs. long corticotectal projections (e.g., commissural fibers) (Casanova et al., 2006; Casanova et al., 2009).

Gamma activity reflects the ability of a certain class of inhibitory neurons, known as parvalbumin-expressing GABAergic interneurons (PEGIs), to coordinate the firing of their neural networks with a frequency of 30-80 Hz. Parvalbumin is a calcium-binding protein, and its expression in PEGIs allows a faster firing rate than other interneurons, due to a shorter period of hyperpolarization between action potentials (Kuznetsova and Deth, 2008). PEGIs begin to develop after about six months of age, in association with the onset of gamma synchrony and the capacity for attention (Csibra et al., 2000). However, their high firing rate is associated with a high level of ATP production and an associated high level of reactive oxygen species generation, implying a higher level of antioxidant demand. In animal models with low GSH synthesis, PEGIs fail to develop (Cabungcal et al., 2006), providing a link between antioxidant status and the capacity for gamma activity.

Gamma frequencies are closely associated with sensory processing, working memory, attention, and many other cognitive domains (Ward, 2003; Jensen et al., 2007). The pervasive nature of abnormalities ingrained in this oscillatory activity bears significant analogy to the cognitive deficits observed in autism. It is therefore unsurprising that gamma oscillations have been claimed to be directly related to the pathophysiology of autism (Sohal, 2012).

Previous studies by our group have used event-related potentials (ERPs) and induced gamma activity as outcome measures for repetitive low frequency transcranial magnetic stimulation (rTMS) in autism (Sokhadze et al., 2009; Baruth et al., 2010). The use of TMS was meant to increase the inhibitory tone of cellular elements surrounding the minicolumns of autistic individuals as a way of enhancing signal contrast. These studies used Kanizsa illusory figures in order to investigate the relative evoked gamma power before and after TMS stimulation to the DLPC in ASD and age-matched controls (Sokhadze et al., 2009; Baruth et al., 2010). At baseline evoked gamma activity was not discriminative of stimulus type in individuals with ASD, whereas in controls, early gamma power offered significant differentiation between target and non-target stimuli.

Following rTMS individuals with ASD showed significant improvement in discriminatory gamma activity between relevant and irrelevant visual stimuli.

In summary, small study sizes and variability in stimulation parameters and brain regions targeted limit the generalizability of TMS studies in autism spectrum disorders. Clinical data from previous safety studies and out own results reinforce the favorable safety profile of TMS use in children. Outcome measures in these trials indicate that TMS may improve behavioral manifestations of autism and core symptomatology (i.e., executive symptoms). Since not every ASD patient improves with therapy questions still remain as to how best define the responsive subgroup. Preliminary studies with gamma frequencies suggests that baseline tracings may help identify responders.

References

Allen CH, Kluger BM, Buard I. Safety of transcranial magnetic stimulation in children: a systematic review of the literature. *Pediatr Neurol* 68:3-17, 2017.

Aoki Y, Yoncheva YN, Chen B, Nath T, Sharp D, Lazar M, Velasco P, Miham MP, Di Martino A. Association of white matter structure with autism spectrum disorder and attention deficit/hyperactivity disorder. *JAMA Psychiatry* 74(11):1120—1128, 2017.

Avino TA, Hutsler JJ. Abnormal cell patterning at the cortical gray-white matter boundary in autism spectrum disorders. *Brain Res* 1360:138-146, 2010.

Bailey A, Luthert P, Dean A, Harding B, Janota I, Montgomery M, Rutter M, Lantos P. A clinicopathological study of autism. *Brain* 121:889-905, 1998.

Baruth JM, Casanova MF, El-Baz A, Horrell T, Mathai G, Sears L, Sokhadze E. Low-frequency repetitive transcranial magnetic stimulation (rTMS) modulates evoked-gamma frequency oscillations in autism spectrum disorder (ASD). *J Neurother* 14(3):179-194, 2010.

Cabungcal JH, Nicolas D, Kraftsik R, Cuénod M, Do KQ, Hornung JP. Glutathione deficit during development induces anomalies in the rat anterior cingulate GABAergic neurons: Relevance to schizophrenia. *Neurobiol Dis.* 2006 Jun;22(3):624-37.

Casanova MF. The neuropathology of autism. *Brain Pathol* 17(4):422-

33, 2007.

Casanova MF. The neuropathology of autism. In Fred Volkmar, Kevin Pelphrey, Rhea Paul, Sally Rogers (eds). *Handbook of Autism and Pervasive Developmental Disorders 4th edition*, ch. 21. Pp. 497-531, 2014.

Casanova MF, Buxhoeveden D, Gomez J: Disruption in the inhibitory architecture of the cell minicolumn: implications for autism. *The Neuroscientist*, 9(6):496-507, 2003.

Casanova MF, van Kooten IAJ, Switala AE, van Engeland H, Heinsen H, Steinbusch HWM, Hof PR, Trippe J, Stone J, Schmitz C. Minicolumnar abnormalities in autism. *Acta Neuropathologica* 112(3):287-303, 2006.

Casanova MF, Trippe J, Tillquist C, Switala A. Morphometric variability of minicolumns in the striate cortex of Homo sapiens, Macaca mulatta, and Pan troglodytes. *Journal of Anatomy* 214(2): 226-234, 2009.

Casanova MF, El-Baz A, Elnakib A, Switala AE, Williams EL, Williams DL, Minshew NJ, Conturo TE. Quantitative analysis of the shape of the corpus callosum in patients with autism and comparison individuals. *Autism* 15(2):223-38, 2011.

Casanova MF, El-Baz A, Vanbogaert E, Narahari P, Switala A. A topographic study of minicolumnar core width by lamina comparison between autistic subjects and controls: possible minicolumnar disruption due to an anatomical element in-common to multiple laminae. *Brain Pathol* 20:451–458, 2010.

Casanova MF, Baruth JM, El-Baz A, Tasman A, Sears L, Sokhadze E. Repetitive transcranial magnetic stimulation (rTMS) modulates event-related potential (ERP) indices of attention in autism. *Translational Neuroscience* 3(2): 2012.

Casanova MF, El-Baz AS, Kamat SS, Dombroski BA, Khalifa F, Elnakib A, Soliman A, Allison-McNutt A, Switala AE. Focal cortical dysplasias in autism spectrum disorders. *Acta Neuropathol Commun* 1:67, 2013.

Casanova MF, Hensley MK, Sokhadze EM, El-Baz AS, Wang Y, Li X, Sears L. Effects of weekly low-frequency rTMS on autonomic measures in children with autism spectrum disorders. *Frontiers in Human Neuroscience* 8(851), 2014

Casanova MF, Sokhadze E, Opris I, Wang Y, Li X Autism spectrum disorders: linking neuropathological findings to treatment with transcranial magnetic stimulation. *Acta Paediatr* 104(4):346-55, 2015.

Csibra G, Davis G, Spratling MW, Johnson MH. Gamma oscillations and object processing in the infant brain. *Science* 290(5496):1582-5, 2000.

Deng Z-D, Lisanby SH, Peterchev AV. Coil design considerations for deep transcranial magnetic stimulation. *Clin Neurophysiol*

125(6):1202-1212, 2014.
Donner TH, Siegel M. A framework for local cortical oscillation patterns. *Trends in Cognitive Sciences* 15(5):191-199, 2011.
Epstein CM, Davey KR. Iron-core coils for transcranial magnetic stimulation. *J Clin Neurophysiol* 19(4):376-81, 2002.
Filley CM. White matter dementia. *Ther Adv Neurol Disord* 5(5):267-277, 2012.
Glennon JM, Karmiloff-Smith A, Thomas MSC. Syndromic autism: progressing beyond current levels of description. *Review J of Autism Dev Disor* 4(4):321-327, 2017.
Goodman B. Alternative therapies widely used for autism. *Health Daily Reporter*. Retrieved from http://www.webmd.com/brain/autism/news/20140114/alternative-therapies-widely-used-for-autism#1
Hutsler JJ, Casanova MF. Cortical construction in autism spectrum disorder: columns, connectivity and the subplate. *Neuropathol Appl Neurobiol* 42(2):115-34, 2016.
Jensen O, Kaiser J, Lachaux JP. Human gamma0frequency oscillations associated with attention and memory. *Trends in Neurosci* 30(7):317-24, 2007.
Keita L, Mottron L, Dawson M, Bertone A. Atypical lateral connectivity: a neural basis for altered visuospatial processing in autism. *Biol Psy* 70(9):806-11, 2011.
Krishnan C, Santos L, Peterson MD, Ehinger M. Safety of noninvasive brain stimulation in children and adolescents. *Brain Stimul* 8(1):76-87, 2015.
Kuznetsova AY, Deth RC. A model for modulation of neuronal synchronization by D4 dopamine receptor-mediated phospholipid methylation. *J Comput Neurosci.* 2008 Jun;24(3):314-29.
Lau YC, Hinkley LB, Bukshpun P, Strominger ZA, Wakahiro MLJ, Baron-Cohen S, Allison C, Auyeung B, Jeremy RJ, Nagarajan SS, Shen EH, Marco EJ. Autism traits in individuals with agenesis of the corpus callous. *J Autism Dev Disord* 43(5):1106-1118, 2013.
Levy SE, Hyman SL. Use of complementary and alternative treatments for children with autistic spectrum disorders is increasing. *Pediatr Ann* 32(10)685-91, 2003.
Mann E.O. and Paulsen O. (2007) Role of GABAergic inhibition in hippocampal network oscillations. *Trends Neurosci.* 30:343-349.
Oberman LM, Enticott PG, Casanova MF, Rotenberg A, Pascual-Leone A, McCracken JT. Transcranial magnetic stimulation (TMS) therapy for autism: an international consensus conference held in conjunction with the international meeting for autism research on May 13th and 14th, 2014. *Front Hum Neurosci* Jan 6; 8:1034, 2015.
Oberman LM, Enticott PG, Casanova MF, Rotenberg A, Pascual-Leone A, McCracken JT. Transcranial magnetic stimulation in autism spectrum disorder: challenges, promise, and roadmap for

future research. *Autism Res* 9(2):184-203, 2016.

Opris I, Casanova MF. Prefrontal cortical minicolumn: from executive control to disrupted cognitive processing. *Brain* 137(7): 1863–1875, 2014.

Sohal VS. Insights into cortical oscillations arising from optogenetic studies. *Biol Psychiatry* 12(12):1039-1045, 2012.

Sokhadze EM, El-Baz A, Baruth J, Mathai G, Sears L, Casanova MF. Effects of low frequency repetitive transcranial magnetic stimulation (rTMS) on gamma frequency oscillations and event-related potentials during processing of illusory figures in autism. *J Autism Dev Disor* 39:619-634, 2009.

Sokhadze E, Baruth J, Tasman A, Mansoor M, Ramaswamy R, Sears L, Mathai G, El-Baz A, Casanova MF. Low-frequency repetitive transcranial magnetic stimulation (rTMS) affects event-related potential measures of novelty processing in autism. *Appl Psychophysiol Biofeedback* 35:147-161, 2010.

Sokhadze EM, Baruth JM, Sears L, Sokhadze GF, El-Baz AS, Casanova MF. Prefrontal neuromodulation using rTMS improves error monitoring and correction function in autism. *Appl Psychophysiol Biofeedback* 37:91-102, 2012

Sokhadze EM, El-Baz AS, Tasman A, Sears LL, Wang Y, Lamina EV, Casanova MF. Neuromodulation integrating rTMS and neurofeedback for the treatment of autism spectrum disorder: an exploratory study. *Appl Psycophysiol Biofeedback* 39:237-257, 2014.

Sokhadze EM, El-Baz AS, Sears LL, Opris I and Casanova MF. rTMS neuromodulation improves electrocortical functional measures of information processing and behavioral responses in autism. *Front. Syst. Neurosci.* 8:134, 2014.

Spence SJ, Schneider MT. The role of epilepsy and epileptiform EEGs in autism spectrum disorders. *Pediatr Res* 65(6):599-606, 2009.

Wang Y, Hensley MK, Tasman A, Sears L, Casanova MF, Sokhadze EM. Heart rate variability and skin conductance during repetitive TMS course in children with autism. *Applied Psychophysiology and Biofeedback* 40(3): 2015

Ward LM. Synchronous neural oscillations and cognitive processes. *Trends in Cognitive Sciences* 7(12):563-569, 2003.

5

Theta Burst Stimulation in Autism

Hsing-Chang Ni,[1] and Ying-Zu Huang[2,3]

Autism spectrum disorder (ASD) is a heterogeneous neurodevelopmental disorder characterized by early onset difficulties in social communication and repetitive, restricted behaviors and interests (Lai, Lombardo, & Baron-Cohen, 2014). The prevalence rate of ASD is around 1% in the world (Lai et al., 2014). Although the precise causes of ASD are unknown, several genetic and environmental risk factors have been proposed (Hallmayer et al., 2011). Previous studies found more than 100 genes were associated with ASD including several rare and specific candidate genes and de novo copy number variants or single nucleotide variations (Vorstman et al., 2017). Generally speaking, most of these genes are associated with synaptic function, cellular signal pathway and fundamental cell biological processes which play important roles in brain development (Krishnan et al., 2016). In the past decade, several MRI studies have demonstrated neurodevelopmental deviations in brain anatomy, function and connectivity across the lifespan in ASD (Ecker, Bookheimer, & Murphy, 2015).

Although the etiology and neural correlates in ASD have become clearer in recent years, the advances in the management of ASD have progressed slowly. Behavioral interventions

[1]Department of Psychiatry, Chang Gung Memorial Hospital at Linkou, Taipei, Taiwan
[2]Neuroscience Research Center and Department of Neurology, Chang Gung Memorial Hospital and Chang Gung University College of Medicine, Taoyuan City 333, Taiwan
[3]Institute of Cognitive Neuroscience, National Central University, Taoyuan City 320, Taiwan
Correspondence should be addressed to Hsing-Chang Ni at alanni@adm.cgmh.org.tw

such as applied behavioral interventions (Spreckley & Boyd, 2009), early intensive behavioral interventions (Eldevik et al., 2009) and naturalistic developmental behavioral interventions (Schreibman et al., 2015) are most commonly applied in clinical practice. Despite the positive effects of behavioral interventions, the benefits should be regarded conservatively because of methodological limitations and the lack of long-term follow up (Ospina et al., 2008). Besides, although risperidone and aripiprazole are approved to by the Food and Drug Administration in the States for treating patients with ASD, these drugs are used for improving associated symptoms such as irritability and hyperactivity but not for core deficits in ASD (Accordino, Kidd, Politte, Henry, & McDougle, 2016). Recently, some studies found biological interventions, such as oxytocin (Vanya, Szucs, Vetro, & Bartfai, 2017) and GABA modulation agents (Brondino et al., 2016), could be beneficial to ASD. However, the results remain inconsistent. Overall, there have been limited biological interventions to improve core symptoms of ASD so far.

In the past decades, transcranial non-invasive brain stimulation (NIBS), such as repetitive transcranial magnetic stimulation (rTMS), transcranial electrical stimulation (including tDCS: transcranial direct current stimulation, tACS: transcranial alternative current stimulation and tRNS: transcranial random noise stimulation) and paired associative stimulation, has been developed to modulate the conscious human brain and been widely used for investigating the physiology and pathophysiology of the central nerve system (Dayan, Censor, Buch, Sandrini, & Cohen, 2013). Moreover, seeing the ability of cortical modulation, NIBS protocols have been tried to treat a variety of neurological and psychiatric disorders, and, indeed shown clinical benefits in many clinical trials (Kuo, Paulus, & Nitsche, 2014; Poleszczyk, 2015). Among the trials, rTMS has had a great success in the management of major depressive disorder (McClintock et al., 2017). These known potentials in other disorders lead to the expectation of therapeutic benefits of NIBS on ASD, which has lacked efficient biological treatments so far.

Theta burst stimulation (TBS)

Transcranial magnetic stimulation (TMS) is a noninvasive technique to stimulate the human brain. By generating a briefly changing magnetic field penetrating through the intact scalp and skull, TMS is capable of inducing eddy currents to active cortical neuronal circuits. rTMS has been noticed to produce alterations in cortical excitability outlasting the stimulation for minutes to more than one hour (Y. Z. Huang et al., 2017). These effects are known to be modulated by drugs affecting N-methyl-D-aspartate (NMDA) receptors and calcium channels, which are critical for induction of synaptic plasticity (Y. Z. Huang, Chen, Rothwell, & Wen, 2007; Wankerl, Weise, Gentner, Rumpf, & Classen, 2010). Recordings of descending volleys evoked by TMS given to the primary motor cortex (M1) from the cervical epidural revealed that TMS directly activated the pyramidal neurons to generate a direct wave (D wave) and activated inputs through synapses onto the pyramidal neurons to generate indirect waves (I waves) to form a motor evoked potential (MEP). rTMS over M1 mainly changes I waves, instead of D waves (Di Lazzaro et al., 2010), suggesting the effect of rTMS is mainly on the synapses. Furthermore, the effects of rTMS interact with physical activity and motor learning following the rule of metaplasticity, which is a phenomenon describing how synaptic plasticity is altered by the history of synaptic activities (Y. Z. Huang, 2016; Y. Z. Huang, Rothwell, Edwards, & Chen, 2008; Jung & Ziemann, 2009; Ziemann, 2004). All these lines of evidence suggest that rTMS modulates the cortical excitability by altering the efficacy of synaptic transmission, leading to synaptic long-term potentiation (LTP) or long-term depression (LTD) that are bases of neuronal plasticity (Hoogendam, Ramakers, & Di Lazzaro, 2010; Y. Z. Huang et al., 2017). The ability to modulate the cortex through plasticity-like mechanisms leads to the expectation of therapeutic benefits of rTMS. Therefore, rTMS has been broadly applied for therapeutic purposes in several psychiatric and neurological disorders in the past decade (Chou, Hickey, Sundman, Song, & Chen, 2015; Slotema, Blom, Hoek, & Sommer, 2010). Among them, major depressive disorder is the first one to get the approval of therapeutic indication by the United States Food and Drug Administration in 2008. Traditionally, rTMS delivers regular pulses at a certain frequency and induces different directions of the after-effects according to the frequency of stimulation applied. In general, low-frequency (e.g. 0.9 or 1 Hz) stimulation has an inhibitory effect, while high-frequency (5 Hz or more) leads to excitatory effects (Klomjai, Katz, & Lackmy-Vallee, 2015).

In contrast, theta burst simulation, which was inspired by the firing pattern recorded from the hippocampus of animals, gives bursts of three TMS pulses at a frequency of 50 Hz every 200ms. TBS is capable of inducing excitatory and inhibitory after-effects by adjusting the pattern, instead of frequency, of stimulation (Y. Z. Huang, Edwards, Rounis, Bhatia, & Rothwell, 2005). Excitatory LTP-like effects are induced for up to 30 min when a 10-burst TBS train is given every 10 seconds for 20 times (intermittent TBS, iTBS). In contrast, a continuous uninterrupted TBS train for 20 or 40 seconds (continuous TBS, cTBS) leads to inhibitory LTD-like effects for 20 or 60 min. TBS produces after-effects similar to traditional rTMS in a much shorter stimulation duration with less total TMS pulses at a lower stimulus intensity (Y. W. Huang, Jeng, Tsai, Chen, & Wu, 2007; Y. Z. Huang et al., 2005; Y. Z. Huang, Rothwell, Chen, Lu, & Chuang, 2011). For instance, to induce an inhibitory effect for 20 min, 20 min of 1-Hz rTMS with1200 total pulses at 90% of active to rest motor threshold is required, while 20 sec of cTBS that contains 300 pulses at 80% AMT is good enough for generating a similar duration of inhibition (Pell, Roth, & Zangen, 2011).

Mechanism of TBS

Although both TBS and traditional rTMS changes I waves to have their effects on MEPs, they may work slightly differently according to the physiological studies with descending volleys recording. One-Hz frequency rTMS and cTBS both decrease the size of MEPs. However, low frequency rTMS protocol selectively suppresses the late I waves without changing the amplitude of the I1 wave, while cTBS suppresses mainly the I1 wave (Di Lazzaro & Rothwell, 2014). In contrast, iTBS enhances later I waves while 5-Hz rTMS enlarges both D and I-waves, although both facilitate the amplitude of MEPs (Di Lazzaro et al., 2008). In addition, TBS does not follow the "rule of frequency," which works well for traditional rTMS. The direction of the after-effects of TBS is modulated by changing the pattern, not frequency of stimulation.

Pharmacological studies revealed that the TBS-induced after-effects were blocked by pre-treating with memantine, an NMDA antagonist, and were modified by D-cycloserine, an NMDA agonist (Y. Z. Huang et al., 2007; Teo, Swayne, & Rothwell, 2007). An L-type voltage-gated Ca^{2+} channel antagonist, nimodipine, also had influence on the effect of TBS (Wankerl et al., 2010). According to the studies on animal brain slices, both LTP and LTD can be induced by activating NMDA receptors to trigger post-synaptic Ca^{2+} influx. Although it remains puzzling what governs the balance between LTP and LTD, the pattern of Ca^{2+} influx seems to be critical for judging the direction of induced plasticity. A sudden increase to high levels of Ca^{2+} favors LTP whereas prolonged and moderate levels of Ca^{2+} promote LTD (Kemp & Bashir, 2001; Malenka & Nicoll, 1999; Sheng & Kim, 2002; Yang, Tang, & Zucker, 1999). Hence, iTBS that triggers quick and short duration of

Ca^{2+} influxes induces LTP-like effects, while cTBS produces prolonged increase of Ca^{2+} level to cause LTP-like effects. This hypothesis is confirmed by a theoretical model that explains the pattern dependency of the after-effects of TBS (Y. Z. Huang et al., 2011). In addition to NMDA and calcium, other neurotransmitter systems such as glutamate (Moore, Cooper, & Spruston, 2009) and GABA (Stagg et al., 2009) are also involved in TBS-induced plasticity effects.

Furthermore, animal studies found that TBS on anesthetized rats modulates plasticity related markers, e.g. c-Fos, zif268 early gene expression, amounts of GAD67 (67 kD isoform of glutamate decarboxylase) and the calcium-binding proteins parvalbumin and calbindin (Aydin-Abidin, Trippe, Funke, Eysel, & Benali, 2008; Benali et al., 2011; Trippe, Mix, Aydin-Abidin, Funke, & Benali, 2009). These findings further confirm that plasticity mechanisms are involved in the mechanisms of TBS. A study on the 6-OHDA lesioned Parkinson's disease rat model revealed a reduced effect of iTBS and the amount of reduction was negatively correlated with the number of surviving functional dopamine cells, suggesting that dopamine is also an important neurotransmitter for plasticity, and is required for TBS to generate its after-effects (Hsieh et al., 2015). These findings further support that TBS modulates brain excitability though the mechanism of synaptic plasticity.

Other than the local effects occurring under the stimulation coil, several studies also demonstrated remote modulation effects of TBS over un-stimulated brain regions. For example, cTBS over the dorsal premotor area could suppress corticospinal excitability measured from the primary motor cortex (Y. Z. Huang, 2010; Y. Z. Huang et al., 2012; Y. Z. Huang et al., 2009). cTBS and iTBS over the lateral cerebellum were also shown to decrease and increase the amplitude of motor evoked potential (MEP) elicited from contralateral M1, respectively (Koch et al., 2008; Li Voti et al., 2014). The amplitude of ipsilateral

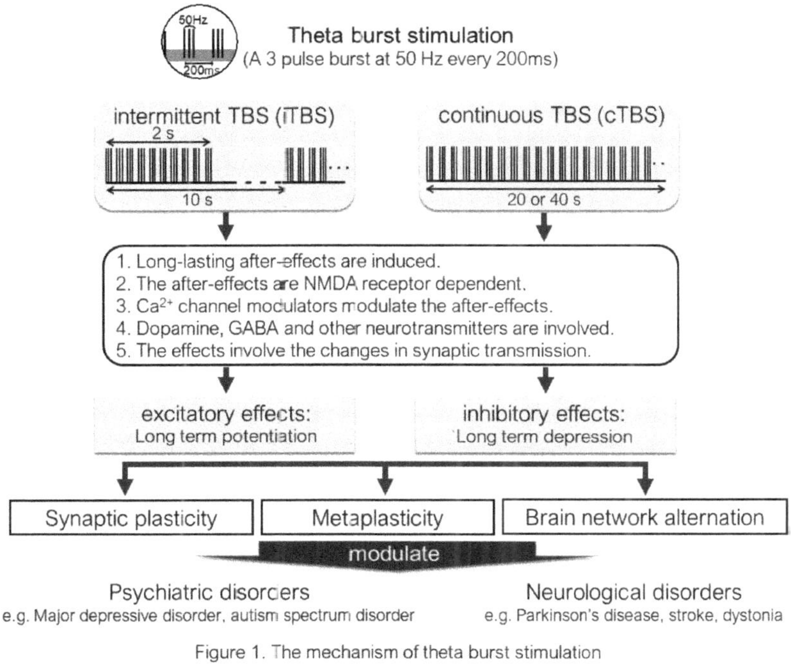

Figure 5.1. The mechanism of theta burst stimulation

and contralateral somatosensory evoked potential can also be modulated by TBS over the primary sensory regions (Jacobs et al., 2012; Katayama & Rothwell, 2007; Katayama, Suppa, & Rothwell, 2010).

TBS also alters the functional brain connectivity and default mode network connectivity. One recent article demonstrated that cTBS over the lateral cerebellum reduced the intrinsic functional connectivity between cerebellum and frontal/parietal cognitive regions (Rastogi et al., 2017). Another study found that cTBS over the precuneus selectively affected the resting state functional network from precuneus to the left temporal pole (Mancini et al., 2017). On the other hand, one report demonstrated that iTBS over the left inferior parietal lobe could increase distal GABA levels in the posteromedial default mode network areas. This effect was related to baseline fMRI connectivity between the affected regions and the TBS-targeted area (Vidal-Piñeiro et al., 2015). iTBS may also modulate the connectivity between right anterior insula and dorsolateral prefrontal cortex by the mediating effect from GABA and Glx (composite of glutamate and glutamine; Iwabuchi et al., 2017). A summary of mechanisms of TBS is illustrated in Figure 5.1.

TBS for assessing cortical dysfunction in ASD

Since TBS is efficient for assessing plasticity in the conscious human brain, TBS has been used to study the cortical dysfunction in ASD. In a pilot study, Oberman and colleagues (2010) investigated plasticity and metaplasticity using TBS and intra-cortical inhibition in two female adults with fragile X syndrome, five female adults with ASD and five neurotypical controls. She found that ASD participants showed abnormalities in plasticity and metaplasticity. The neurotypical controls showed no" carry-over" effect from day 1 to day 2 in their response to cTBS and iTBS. In contrast, the ASD group had excessive plasticity responses to both cTBS and iTBS on day 1, but attenuated responses on day 2 when an opposite protocol was applied on day 1, suggesting aberrant metaplasticity. In addition, high heterogeneity in intra-cortical inhibition tested by short interval intra-cortical inhibition (SICI) and long interval intra-cortical inhibition (LICI) was found in ASD as compared to controls, suggesting cortical dysfunction in ASD.

The same group further confirmed that the effect of TBS lasted significantly longer in the Asperger's syndrome (AS) group than in the control group in another study with a larger sample size (Oberman et al., 2012). In contrast to the controls whose average time to return to the baseline MEP value following cTBS was 35.5 minutes (SD = 13.2), it took 87 minutes (SD = 26.3) for the AS group to return to the baseline. As for the average time to return to the baseline following iTBS, it was 37.2 minute (SD = 35.3) for the controls and 77.8 minutes (SD = 31.3) in AS individuals. By setting 50 minutes as cut-off point, cTBS could be used as a diagnostic tool that has a sensitivity of 0.93 and specificity of 0.8.

Furthermore, a positive linear relationship between age and the duration of cortical modulation induced by TBS was found in male children and adolescents with ASD (Oberman, Pascual-Leone, & Rotenberg, 2014). Besides, one third of these young patients had a paradoxical facilitatory response to the inhibitory protocol (cTBS). However, in contrast to the prolonged plasticity reported by Oberman's group, abnormally reduced cortical plasticity was reported in a case-control pilot study showing reduced facilitatory after-effect at 20 min after iTBS in adolescents with ASD (Pedapati et al., 2016).

Therapeutic application of TBS in ASD

Several approaches have been tried to apply rTMS for treating ASD in the past few years. Sokhadze and Casanova have extensively investigated the therapeutic effects of different rTMS protocols over the dorsolateral prefrontal cortex (DLPFC) in ASD. In the study, they tried rTMS at different frequencies (0.5–5 Hz) over different locations (left, right and bilateral DLPFC) at different inter-session intervals (one to two sessions per week) to have different total numbers of sessions (1–18). As a result, low-frequency rTMS over the DLPFC improved the repetitive behaviors, modulated the executive functions and heart rate variability in ASD (Casanova et al., 2012; Sokhadze et al., 2009, 2010; Wang et al., 2016). However, none of these protocols improved the social deficits in ASD.

Later, Enticott and colleagues (2011; 2014) evaluated the therapeutic effect of the deep rTMS using an H-coil over the bilateral dorsomedial prefrontal cortex (dmPFC) in ASD. The H-coil was designed for stimulation of deeper brain regions. In comparison with the commonly used figure -eight coil that stimulates around 1.5 to 3 cm beneath the scalp, the estimated effective depth of H-coil is 4 to 5 cm over the lateral and medial frontal regions and 2 to 3 cm at the medial prefrontal regions (Roth, Amir, Levkovitz, & Zangen, 2007). In a prospective, double-blinded and placebo-controlled study, daily weekday treatment of 5 Hz deep rTMS over the bilateral dmPFC for 2 weeks was found to yield a reduction of social impairment based on the social relatedness subscale of the Ritvo Autism-Asperger Diagnostic Scale in adults with ASD. However, there was no significant finding in other behavioral outcome measurements, e.g. the Autism Spectrum Quotient, Interpersonal Reactivity Index and experimental mentalizing measures such as animations mentalizing test and reading the mind in the eyes test (Enticott et al., 2014). In addition to DLPFC and dmPFC, Broca's area has been stimulated in a double-blinded, multiple crossover and sham-controlled study in Asperger's syndrome (Fecteau, Agosta, Oberman, & Pascual-Leone, 2011). One session of 1 Hz rTMS over the left pars triangularis improved the naming skills, but the rTMS over the adjacent left opercularis lengthened name latency in participants with Asperger's syndrome. So far, there has been no golden protocol of rTMS over ASD so far. There are too many parameters need to adjust and test, since it is known that the effects of rTMS depend on several factors such as intensity of stimulation, frequency of stimulation, number of total sessions, frequency of sessions, stimulus locations and individual symptom severity (Rotenberg, 2014).

Similar to traditional rTMS, the therapeutic benefits of TBS have been applied in several neurological disorders, e.g. Parkinson's disease (Kishore et al., 2012), dystonia (Edwards, Huang, Mir, Rothwell, & Bhatia, 2006), Huntington's disease (Orth et al., 2010) and Gilles de la Tourette syndrome (Suppa et al., 2011), and in psychiatric disorders, including major depressive disorder (Bakker et al., 2015; Li et al., 2014), schizophrenia

(Eberle, Wildgruber, Wasserka, Fallgatter, & Plewnia, 2010) and obsessive-compulsive disorder (Wu et al., 2010).

However, the investigation of therapeutic effect of TBS on ASD has been quite limited so far. TBS is in fact considered more suitable than traditional rTMS for being a therapeutic protocol for ASD because of its shorter stimulation duration (TBS: 20–190 seconds; rTMS: 5–30 minutes; Pell et al., 2011). The advantages of shorter stimulation of TBS are very important in ASD. For example, patients with ASD are commonly comorbid with anxiety and attention-deficit hyperactivity disorder so that it is not easy for them to be compliant to rTMS for a long time. Besides, some patients with ASD have difficulties of hypersensitivity that also make long rTMS stimulation unbearable to them. If the patient feels uncomfortable in the first stimulation session, it is not easy to persuade them to come back again for the following stimulation courses.

In the first randomized, sham-controlled and cross-sectional TBS study, Ni and colleagues (2017) explored the impact of one session iTBS over the bilateral DLPFC and bilateral posterior superior temporal sulcus (pSTS) on the neuropsychological function and autistic behaviors in 19 adults with ASD. In this study, participants received iTBS over the bilateral DLPFC, bilateral pSTS and inion as sham control in three sessions in a randomized order with a 1-week interval. The behavioral outcomes were measured using the Yale-Brown Obsessive Compulsive Scale (Y-BOCS) and the social responsiveness scale (SRS) in both participants and their parents. The neuropsychological functions were measured using the Conner's Continuous Performance Test (CCPT) and the Wisconsin Card Sorting Test (WCST). As a result, iTBS over DLPFC significantly decreased the reaction time in the CCPT, but left the WCST remained unchanged. On the other hand, iTBS over bilateral pSTS marginally increased total errors in the WCST, but not altered the CCPT.

Interestingly, discrepancy was found between behavior outcomes reported by parents and patients themselves. In comparison to the sham session, parents reported a significant decrease in compulsive behaviors 8 hours and 2 days after pSTS session. However, the patients did not report similar improvement. In contrast, although patients reported marginal improvement in social communication 8 hours after pSTS session, such improvement was not observed from their parents. Similar inconsistency was also found in DLPFC session. Patients, but not parents, reported significant improvement in social communication 8 hours after the DLPFC session. However, patients and their parents both reported marginal improvement in social communication and autistic mannerism respectively 2 days after the DLPFC session.

Although there has been only a single-session pilot study with several limitations, including a limited sample size, inadequate measurement of neuropsychological function, the results are encouraging and suggestive for further investigation on the therapeutic effect of TBS on ASD.

Prospectives on TBS in ASD

Although TBS has shown potential benefits for patients with ASD, it is still in early stages and many more efforts are required. First, the ideal stimulation location remains unclear. Several brain regions, e.g. amygdala, somatosensory, temporal and prefrontal cortices, are known to be involved in the social brain network that could be critical for the function in ASD (Fernandez, Mollinedo-Gajate, & Peñagarikano, 2017), and may deserve further investigation for the therapeutic effect of TBS on ASD. Second, the optimal protocol for ASD is needed. Although it could be time consuming, the optimal timing (e.g. how frequent for one session of stimulation) and repetition (how many sessions for a complete treatment course) should be evaluated and decided. Third, the best neuronal state in response to TBS therapy is unknown. The effects of TBS are known to be affected by the neuronal state under the coil (Fang, Huang, Hwang, & Chen, 2014; Y. Z. Huang et al., 2017; Y. Z. Huang et al., 2008), and could be enhanced by adjusting the state (Li et al., 2016). Hence, the effect of TBS on ASD could be augmented by delivering TBS at the right neuronal state. Fourth, more objective outcome measures are required for assessing the improvements. In addition to the behavioral questionnaires reported by patients and their family, the outcomes may be evaluated in broader fields such as the neuropsychological functions, neurophysiological test, and functional neuroimaging. Fifth, considering psychoactive medications and intellectual disability in individuals with ASD and intra-subject/inter-subject variability response to rTMS and TBS (Y. Z. Huang et al., 2017; Oberman et al., 2016), studies with a larger sample size are needed.

Conclusion

In the past 10 years, TBS has been popular and proven as a useful technique to modify cortical function, and has shown therapeutic potential in several neurological and psychiatric disorders. In comparison with other protocols of rTMS, TBS requires shorter stimulation duration and use of lower stimulus intensity. These advantages make TBS convenient and acceptable to the individuals with ASD (Ni et al., 2017; Suppa et al., 2016). Although only a limited number of study on the therapeutic effect of TBS on ASD, the evidence from preliminary results are encouraging. More studies are expected to clarify currently unknown issues and provide more solid evidences in the future.

References

Accordino, R. E., Kidd, C., Politte, L. C., Henry, C. A., & McDougle, C. J. (2016). Psychopharmacological interventions in autism spectrum disorder. *Expert Opinion on Pharmacotherapy, 17*(7), 937–952.

Aydin-Abidin, S., Trippe, J., Funke, K., Eysel, U. T., & Benali, A.

(2008). High- and low-frequency repetitive transcranial magnetic stimulation differentially activates c-Fos and zif268 protein expression in the rat brain. *Experimental Brain Research, 188*(2), 249–261.

Bakker, N., Shahab, S., Giacobbe, P., Blumberger, D. M., Daskalakis, Z. J., Kennedy, S. H., & Downar, J. (2015). rTMS of the dorsomedial prefrontal cortex for major depression: Safety, tolerability, effectiveness, and outcome predictors for 10 Hz versus intermittent theta-burst stimulation. *Brain Stimulation, 8*(2), 208–215.

Benali, A., Trippe, J., Weiler, E., Mix, A., Petrasch-Parwez, E., Girzalsky, W., . . . Funke, K. (2011). Theta-burst transcranial magnetic stimulation alters cortical inhibition. *Journal of Neuroscience, 31*(4), 1193–1203.

Brondino, N., Fusar-Poli, L., Panisi, C., Damiani, S., Barale, F., & Politi, P. (2016). Pharmacological modulation of GABA function in autism spectrum disorders: A Systematic review of human studies. *Journal of Autism and Developmental Disorders, 46*(3), 825–839.

Casanova, M. F., Baruth, J. M., El-Baz, A., Tasman, A., Sears, L., & Sokhadze, E. (2012). Repetitive transcranial magnetic stimulation (rTMS) modulates event-related potential (ERP) indices of attention in autism. *Translational Neuroscience, 3*(2), 170–180.

Chou, Y. H., Hickey, P. T., Sundman, M., Song, A. W., & Chen, N. K. (2015). Effects of repetitive transcranial magnetic stimulation on motor symptoms in Parkinson disease: A systematic review and meta-analysis. *JAMA Neurology, 72*(4), 432–440.

Dayan, E., Censor, N., Buch, E. R., Sandrini, M., & Cohen, L. G. (2013). Noninvasive brain stimulation: From physiology to network dynamics and back. *Nature Neuroscience, 16*(7), 838–844.

Di Lazzaro, V., Pilato, F., Dileone, M., Profice, P., Oliviero, A., Mazzone, P., . . . Rothwell, J. C. (2008). The physiological basis of the effects of intermittent theta burst stimulation of the human motor cortex. *Journal of Physiology, 586*(16), 3871–3879.

Di Lazzaro, V., Profice, P., Pilato, F., Dileone, M., Oliviero, A., & Ziemann, U. (2010). The effects of motor cortex rTMS on corticospinal descending activity. *Clinical Neurophysiology, 121*(4), 464–473.

Di Lazzaro, V., & Rothwell, J. C. (2014). Corticospinal activity evoked and modulated by non-invasive stimulation of the intact human motor cortex. *Journal of Physiology, 592*(19), 4115–4128.

Eberle, M. C., Wildgruber, D., Wasserka, B., Fallgatter, A. J., & Plewnia, C. (2010). Relief from chronic intractable auditory hallucinations after long-term bilateral theta burst stimulation. *American Journal of Psychiatry, 167*(11), 1410.

Ecker, C., Bookheimer, S. Y., & Murphy, D. G. (2015). Neuroimaging in autism spectrum disorder: Brain structure and function across the

lifespan. *Lancet. Neurology, 14*(11), 1121–1134.
Edwards, M. J., Huang, Y. Z., Mir, P., Rothwell, J. C., & Bhatia, K. P. (2006). Abnormalities in motor cortical plasticity differentiate manifesting and nonmanifesting DYT1 carriers. *Movement Disorders, 21*(12), 2181–2186.
Eldevik, S., Hastings, R. P., Hughes, J. C., Jahr, E., Eikeseth, S., & Cross, S. (2009). Meta-analysis of early intensive behavioral intervention for children with autism. *Journal of Clinical Child and Adolescent Psychology, 38*(3), 439–450.
Enticott, P. G., Kennedy, H. A., Zangen, A., & Fitzgerald, P. B. (2011). Deep repetitive transcranial magnetic stimulation associated with improved social functioning in a young woman with an autism spectrum disorder. *Journal of ECT, 27*(1), 41–43.
Enticott, P. G., Fitzgibbon, B. M., Kennedy, H. A., Arnold, S. L., Elliot, D., Peachey, A., . . . Fitzgerald, P. B. (2014). A double-blind, randomized trial of deep repetitive transcranial magnetic stimulation (rTMS) for autism spectrum disorder. *Brain Stimulation, 7*(2), 206–211.
Fang, J. H., Huang, Y. Z., Hwang, I. S., & Chen, J. J. (2014). Selective modulation of motor cortical plasticity during voluntary contraction of the antagonist muscle. *European Journal of Neuroscience, 39*(12), 2083–2088.
Fecteau, S., Agosta, S., Oberman, L., & Pascual-Leone, A. (2011). Brain stimulation over Broca's area differentially modulates naming skills in neurotypical adults and individuals with Asperger's syndrome. *European Journal of Neuroscience, 34*(1), 158–164.
Fernández, M., Mollinedo-Gajate, I., & Peñagarikano, O. (2017). Neural circuits for social cognition: Implications for autism. *Neuroscience, 370*, 148-162.
Hallmayer, J., Cleveland, S., Torres, A., Phillips, J., Cohen, B., Torigoe, T., . . . Risch, N. (2011). Genetic heritability and shared environmental factors among twin pairs with autism. *Archives of General Psychiatry, 68*(11), 1095–1102.
Hoogendam, J. M., Ramakers, G. M., & Di Lazzaro, V. (2010). Physiology of repetitive transcranial magnetic stimulation of the human brain. *Brain Stimulation, 3*(2), 95–118.
Hsieh, T. H., Huang, Y. Z., Rotenberg, A., Pascual-Leone, A., Chiang, Y. H., Wang, J. Y., & Chen, J. J. (2015). Functional dopaminergic neurons in substantia nigra are required for transcranial magnetic stimulation-induced motor plasticity. *Cerebral Cortex, 25*(7), 1806–1814.
Huang, Y. W., Jeng, J. S., Tsai, C. F., Chen, L. L., & Wu, R. M. (2007). Transcranial imaging of substantia nigra hyperechogenicity in a Taiwanese cohort of Parkinson's disease. *Movement Disorders, 22*(4), 550–555.
Huang, Y. Z. (2010). The modulation of cortical motor circuits and

spinal reflexes using theta burst stimulation in healthy and dystonic subjects. *Restorative Neurology and Neuroscience, 28*(4), 449–457.

Huang, Y. Z. (2016). What do we learn from the influence of motor activities on the after-effect of non-invasive brain stimulation? *Clinical Neurophysiology, 127*(2), 1011–1012.

Huang, Y. Z., Edwards, M. J., Rounis, E., Bhatia, K. P., & Rothwell, J. C. (2005). Theta burst stimulation of the human motor cortex. *Neuron, 45*(2), 201–206.

Huang, Y. Z., Chen, R. S., Rothwell, J. C., & Wen, H. Y. (2007). The after-effect of human theta burst stimulation is NMDA receptor dependent. *Clinical Neurophysiology, 118*(5), 1028–1032.

Huang, Y. Z., Rothwell, J. C., Edwards, M. J., & Chen, R. S. (2008). Effect of physiological activity on an NMDA-dependent form of cortical plasticity in human. *Cerebral Cortex, 18*(3), 563–570.

Huang, Y. Z., Rothwell, J. C., Lu, C. S., Wang, J., Weng, Y. H., Lai, S. C., . . . Chen, R. S. (2009). The effect of continuous theta burst stimulation over premotor cortex on circuits in primary motor cortex and spinal cord. *Clinical Neurophysiology, 120*(4), 796–801.

Huang, Y. Z., Rothwell, J. C., Chen, R. S., Lu, C. S., & Chuang, W. L. (2011). The theoretical model of theta burst form of repetitive transcranial magnetic stimulation. *Clinical Neurophysiology, 122*(5), 1011–1018.

Huang, Y. Z., Lu, C. S., Rothwell, J. C., Lo, C. C., Chuang, W. L., Weng, Y. H., . . . Chen, R. S. (2012). Modulation of the disturbed motor network in dystonia by multisession suppression of premotor cortex. *PLoS One, 7*(10), e47574.

Huang, Y. Z., Lu, M. K., Antal, A., Classen, J., Nitsche, M., Ziemann, U., . . . Rothwell, J. (2017). Plasticity induced by non-invasive transcranial brain stimulation: A position paper. *Clinical Neurophysiology, 128*(11), 2318–2329.

Iwabuchi, S. J., Raschke, F., Auer, D. P., Liddle, P. F., Lankappa, S. T., & Palaniyappan, L. (2017). Targeted transcranial theta-burst stimulation alters fronto-insular network and prefrontal GABA. *Neuroimage, 146*, 395–403.

Jacobs, M. F., Zapallow, C. M., Tsang, P., Lee, K. G., Asmussen, M. J., & Nelson, A. J. (2012). Current direction specificity of continuous theta-burst stimulation in modulating human motor cortex excitability when applied to somatosensory cortex. *Neuroreport, 23*(16), 927–931.

Jung, P., & Ziemann, U. (2009). Homeostatic and nonhomeostatic modulation of learning in human motor cortex. *Journal of Neurosci, 29*(17), 5597–5604.

Katayama, T., & Rothwell, J. C. (2007). Modulation of somatosensory evoked potentials using transcranial magnetic intermittent theta burst stimulation. *Clinical Neurophysiology, 118*(11), 2506–2511.

Katayama, T., Suppa, A., & Rothwell, J. C. (2010). Somatosensory evoked potentials and high frequency oscillations are differently modulated by theta burst stimulation over primary somatosensory cortex in humans. *Clinical Neurophysiology, 121*(12), 2097–2103.

Kemp, N., & Bashir, Z. I. (2001). Long-term depression: A cascade of induction and expression mechanisms. *Progress in Neurobiology, 65*(4), 339–365.

Kishore, A., Popa, T., Velayudhan, B., Joseph, T., Balachandran, A., & Meunier, S. (2012). Acute dopamine boost has a negative effect on plasticity of the primary motor cortex in advanced Parkinson's disease. *Brain, 135*(7), 2074–2088.

Klomjai, W., Katz, R., & Lackmy- Vallée, A. (2015). Basic principles of transcranial magnetic stimulation (TMS) and repetitive TMS (rTMS). *Annals of Physical and Rehabilitation Medicine, 58*(4), 208–213.

Koch, G., Mori, F., Marconi, B., Codecà, C., Pecchioli, C., Salerno, S., . . . Caltagirone, C. (2008). Changes in intracortical circuits of the human motor cortex following theta burst stimulation of the lateral cerebellum. *Clinical Neurophysiology, 119*(11), 2559–2569.

Krishnan, A., Zhang, R., Yao, V., Theesfeld, C. L., Wong, A. K., Tadych, A., . . . Troyanskaya, O. G. (2016). Genome-wide prediction and functional characterization of the genetic basis of autism spectrum disorder. *Nature Neuroscience, 19*(11), 1454–1462.

Kuo, M. F., Paulus, W., & Nitsche, M. A. (2014). Therapeutic effects of non-invasive brain stimulation with direct currents (tDCS) in neuropsychiatric diseases. *Neuroimage, 85*(3), 948–960.

Lai, M. C., Lombardo, M. V., & Baron-Cohen, S. (2014). Autism. *Lancet, 383*(9920), 896–910.

Li, C. T., Chen, M. H., Juan, C. H., Huang, H. H., Chen, L. F., Hsieh, J. C., . . . Su, T. P. (2014). Efficacy of prefrontal theta-burst stimulation in refractory depression: A randomized sham-controlled study. *Brain, 137*(7), 2088–2098.

Li, C. T., Hsieh, J. C., Huang, H. H., Chen, M. H., Juan, C. H., Tu, P. C., . . . Su, T. P. (2016). Cognition-modulated frontal activity in prediction and augmentation of antidepressant efficacy: A randomized controlled pilot study. *Cerebral Cortex, 26*(1), 202–210.

Li Voti, P., Conte, A., Rocchi, L., Bologna, M., Khan, N., Leodori, G., & Berardelli, A. (2014). Cerebellar continuous theta-burst stimulation affects motor learning of voluntary arm movements in humans. *European Journal of Neuroscience, 39*(1), 124–131.

Malenka, R. C., & Nicoll, R. A. (1999). Long-term potentiation--a decade of progress? *Science, 285*(5435), 1870–1874.

Mancini, M., Mastropasqua, C., Bonni, S., Ponzo, V., Cercignani, M., Conforto, S., . . . Bozzali, M. (2017). Theta burst stimulation of the precuneus modulates resting state connectivity in the left temporal pole. *Brain Topography, 30*(3), 312–319.

McClintock, S. M., Reti, I. M., Carpenter, L. L., McDonald, W. M., Dubin, M., Taylor, S. F., . . . Treatments. (2017). Consensus recommendations for the clinical application of repetitive transcranial magnetic stimulation (rTMS) in the treatment of depression. *Journal of Clinical Psychiatry*, 79(1), 16cs10905.

Moore, S. J., Cooper, D. C., & Spruston, N. (2009). Plasticity of burst firing induced by synergistic activation of metabotropic glutamate and acetylcholine receptors. *Neuron, 61*(2), 287–300.

Ni, H. C., Hung, J., Wu, C. T., Wu, Y. Y., Chang, C. J., Chen, R. S., & Huang, Y. Z. (2017). The impact of single session intermittent theta-burst stimulation over the dorsolateral prefrontal cortex and posterior superior temporal sulcus on adults with autism spectrum disorder. *Frontiers in Neuroscience, 11*, 255.

Oberman, L., Ifert-Miller, F., Najib, U., Bashir, S., Woollacott, I., Gonzalez-Heydrich, J., . . . Pascual-Leone, A. (2010). Transcranial magnetic stimulation provides means to assess cortical plasticity and excitability in humans with fragile x syndrome and autism spectrum disorder. *Frontiers in Synaptic Neuroscience, 2*, 26.

Oberman, L., Eldaief, M., Fecteau, S., Ifert-Miller, F., Tormos, J. M., & Pascual-Leone, A. (2012). Abnormal modulation of corticospinal excitability in adults with Asperger's syndrome. *European Journal of Neuroscience, 36*(6), 2782–2788.

Oberman, L. M., Pascual-Leone, A., & Rotenberg, A. (2014). Modulation of corticospinal excitability by transcranial magnetic stimulation in children and adolescents with autism spectrum disorder. *Frontiers in Human Neuroscience, 8*, 627.

Oberman, L. M., Enticott, P. G., Casanova, M. F., Rotenberg, A., Pascual-Leone, A., McCracken, J. T., et al. (2016). Transcranial magnetic stimulation in autism spectrum disorder: Challenges, promise, and roadmap for future research. *Autism Research, 9*(2), 184–203.

Orth, M., Schippling, S., Schneider, S. A., Bhatia, K. P., Talelli, P., Tabrizi, S. J., & Rothwell, J. C. (2010). Abnormal motor cortex plasticity in premanifest and very early manifest Huntington disease. *Journal of Neurology, Neurosurgery, and Psychiatry, 81*(3), 267–270.

Ospina, M. B., Krebs Seida, J., Clark, B., Karkhaneh, M., Hartling, L., Tjosvold, L., . . . Smith, V. (2008). Behavioural and developmental interventions for autism spectrum disorder: A clinical systematic review. *PLoS One, 3*(11), e3755.

Pedapati, E. V., Gilbert, D. L., Erickson, C. A., Horn, P. S., Shaffer, R. C., Wink, L. K., . . . Wu, S. W. (2016). Abnormal cortical plasticity in youth with autism spectrum disorder: A transcranial magnetic stimulation case-control pilot study. *Journal of Child and Adolescent Psychopharmacology, 26*(7), 625–631.

Pell, G. S., Roth, Y., & Zangen, A. (2011). Modulation of cortical excitability induced by repetitive transcranial magnetic stimulation: Influence of timing and geometrical parameters and underlying mechanisms. *Progress in Neurobiology, 93*(1), 59–98.

Poleszczyk, A. (2015). Transcranial magnetic stimulation in treatment of various psychiatric disorders - review of the most prominent studies and the latest news. *Psychiatria Polska, 49*(4), 779–789.

Rastogi, A., Cash, R., Dunlop, K., Vesia, M., Kucyi, A., Ghahremani, A., . . . Chen, R. (2017). Modulation of cognitive cerebello-cerebral functional connectivity by lateral cerebellar continuous theta burst stimulation. *Neuroimage, 158*, 48–57.

Rotenberg, A., Horvath, J.C., & Pascual-Leone, A. (2014). *Transcranial magnetic stimulation.* New York: Human Press.

Roth, Y., Amir, A., Levkovitz, Y., & Zangen, A. (2007). Three-dimensional distribution of the electric field induced in the brain by transcranial magnetic stimulation using figure-8 and deep H-coils. *Journal of Clinical Neurophysiology, 24*(1), 31–38.

Schreibman, L., Dawson, G., Stahmer, A. C., Landa, R., Rogers, S. J., McGee, G. G., . . . Halladay, A. (2015). Naturalistic developmental behavioral interventions: Empirically validated treatments for autism spectrum disorder. *Journal of Autism and Developmental Disorders, 45*(8), 2411–2428.

Sheng, M., & Kim, M. J. (2002). Postsynaptic signaling and plasticity mechanisms. *Science, 298*(5594), 776–780.

Slotema, C. W., Blom, J. D., Hoek, H. W., & Sommer, I. E. (2010). Should we expand the toolbox of psychiatric treatment methods to include repetitive transcranial magnetic stimulation (rTMS)? A meta-analysis of the efficacy of rTMS in psychiatric disorders. *Journal of Clinical Psychiatry, 71*(7), 873–884.

Sokhadze, E. M., El-Baz, A., Baruth, J., Mathai, G., Sears, L., & Casanova, M. F. (2009). Effects of low frequency repetitive transcranial magnetic stimulation (rTMS) on gamma frequency oscillations and event-related potentials during processing of illusory figures in autism. *Journal of Autism and Developmental Disorders, 39*(4), 619–634.

Sokhadze, E., Baruth, J., Tasman, A., Mansoor, M., Ramaswamy, R., Sears, L., . . . Casanova, M. F. (2010). Low-frequency repetitive transcranial magnetic stimulation (rTMS) affects event-related potential measures of novelty processing in autism. *Applied Psychophysiology and Biofeedback, 35*(2), 147–161.

Spreckley, M., & Boyd, R. (2009). Efficacy of applied behavioral intervention in preschool children with autism for improving cognitive, language, and adaptive behavior: A systematic review and meta-analysis. *Journal of Pediatrics, 154*(3), 338–344.

Stagg, C. J., Wylezinska, M., Matthews, P. M., Johansen-Berg, H., Jezzard, P., Rothwell, J. C., & Bestmann, S. (2009). Neurochemical effects of theta burst stimulation as assessed by magnetic

resonance spectroscopy. *Journal of Neurophysiology, 101*(6), 2872–2877.
Suppa, A., Belvisi, D., Bologna, M., Marsili, L., Berardelli, I., Moretti, G., . . . Berardelli, A. (2011). Abnormal cortical and brain stem plasticity in Gilles de la Tourette syndrome. *Movement Disorders, 26*(9), 1703–1710.
Suppa, A., Huang, Y. Z., Funke, K., Ridding, M. C., Cheeran, B., Di Lazzaro, V., . . . Rothwell, J. C. (2016). Ten years of theta burst stimulation in humans: Established knowledge, unknowns and prospects. *Brain Stimulation, 9*(3), 323–335.
Teo, J. T., Swayne, O. B., & Rothwell, J. C. (2007). Further evidence for NMDA-dependence of the after-effects of human theta burst stimulation. *Clinical Neurophysiology, 118*(7), 1649–1651.
Trippe, J., Mix, A., Aydin-Abidin, S., Funke, K., & Benali, A. (2009). Theta burst and conventional low-frequency rTMS differentially affect GABAergic neurotransmission in the rat cortex. *Experimental Brain Research, 199*(3–4), 411–421.
Vanya, M., Szucs, S., Vetro, A., & Bartfai, G. (2017). The potential role of oxytocin and perinatal factors in the pathogenesis of autism spectrum disorders - review of the literature. *Psychiatry Research, 247*, 288–290.
Vidal-Piñeiro, D., Martin-Trias, P., Falcón, C., Bargalló, N., Clemente, I. C., Valls-Solé, J., . . . Bartrés-Faz, D. (2015). Neurochemical modulation in posteromedial default-mode network cortex induced by transcranial magnetic stimulation. *Brain Stimulation, 8*(5), 937–944.
Vorstman, J. A. S., Parr, J. R., Moreno-De-Luca, D., Anney, R. J. L., Nurnberger, J. I., Jr., & Hallmayer, J. F. (2017). Autism genetics: Opportunities and challenges for clinical translation. *Nature Reviews. Genetics, 18*(6), 362–376.
Wang, Y., Hensley, M. K., Tasman, A., Sears, L., Casanova, M. F., & Sokhadze, E. M. (2016). Heart rate variability and skin conductance during repetitive TMS course in children with autism. *Applied Psychophysiology and Biofeedback, 41*(1), 47–60.
Wankerl, K., Weise, D., Gentner, R., Rumpf, J. J., & Classen, J. (2010). L-type voltage-gated Ca^{2+} channels: A single molecular switch for long-term potentiation/long-term depression-like plasticity and activity-dependent metaplasticity in humans. *Journal of Neuroscience, 30*(18), 6197–6204.
Wu, C. C., Tsai, C. H., Lu, M. K., Chen, C. M., Shen, W. C., & Su, K. P. (2010). Theta-burst repetitive transcranial magnetic stimulation for treatment-resistant obsessive-compulsive disorder with concomitant depression. *Journal of Clinical Psychiatry, 71*(4), 504–506.
Yang, S. N., Tang, Y. G., & Zucker, R. S. (1999). Selective induction of LTP and LTD by postsynaptic $[Ca^{2+}]_i$ elevation. *Journal of*

Neurophysiology, *81*(2), 781–787.
Ziemann, U. (2004). TMS induced plasticity in human cortex. *Reviews in Neuroscience*, *15*(4), 253–266.

6

Non-Invasive Brain Stimulation in Children With Autism Spectrum Disorder

Lázaro Gómez,[1,3] Belkis Vidal,[2,4] Lilia Morales,[3] Sheyla Berrillo,[3] Margarita Báez,[3] Carlos Maragoto,[1,4] and Héctor Vera[1,4]

A Brief History About Non-Invasive Brain Stimulation

Electric and magnetic stimulation to treat medical conditions has been used for centuries in different locales such as Asia, Egypt and Africa, including for muscular pain, gout pain, headache, prolapsed anus or even mystical release from devils. Early records mention Hippocrates (Greece, 460 BC), the Roman physician Scribonius Largus and from Greece, Dioscorides (43 A.D.) using torpedo fish for pain relieving; Galeno (131–201) and Avicenna (980–1037) also used torpedo fish and magnets to heal pain among other conditions. Later in the 16th century Paracelsus described how to use magnets to stop bleeding; and in the 17th century the first devices designed specifically for electric stimulation were designed. The 18th century was essential in the development and application of electricity and magnetic fields in medicine. Electricity was used to treat depression in England in 1814, and Mesmer apparently successfully used static magnetic fields in his efforts to treat hysteria as he developed his "animal magnetism"

---

[1]Non-Invasive Brain Stimulation Unit, International Center for Neurological Restoration, Havana, Cuba
[2]Child and Adolescent Mental Health Service, Borrás-Marfán Hospital, Havana, Cuba
[3]Clinical Neurophysiology Department, International Center for Neurological Restoration, Havana, Cuba
[4]Neuropediatric Clinic, International Center for Neurological Restoration, Havana, Cuba

theory. In 1870, Fritsch and Hitzig evoked movement in dog limbs after motor cortex electrical stimulation and in 1874, Bartholow performed the first well documented electrical stimulation of the brain in an awake human. In 1831, Michael Faraday experimentally demonstrated the principle of electromagnetic induction. Later in 1896, d'Arsonval and Thompson described the occurrence of phosphenes after cranial stimulation between coils. After the development of the electric battery by Volta (19th century), Giovanni Aldini was the first to use an electric battery to induce mood improvement in patients with depression, or "melancholia" as it was known then, which seems to be one of the first clinical uses of tDCS from a non-animal source of electricity. The experiments of Penfield and Jasper during brain surgery (1954) were essential for the recognition of motor homunculus and remain an important reference for non-invasive brain stimulation (NIBS). In 1973, deep brain stimulation (DBS) was formally born with the development of chronic thalamic stimulation for the treatment of facial pain. Much research focused on electroconvulsive therapy (ECT) and DBS during the following decades due to the objectively good clinical results observed in patients (Nitsche & Paulus, 2011; Schonfeldt-Lecuona et al., 2002; Steinberg, 2013; Wexler, 2017).

In 1957, tDCS was reintroduced as electrosleep therapy and in the early sixties as electro-anesthesia. In 1964, Lippold and Redfearn used 50–500 μA DC currents in healthy subjects and reported opposite effects with anodal and cathodal stimulation in alertness, mood and motor activity (anode facilitated). Similarly in France, Germany, Russia and Italy the same therapy with high frequency and low intensity magnetic fields saw major development in psychiatry. In 1965, Bickford and Fremming demonstrated the ability to stimulate facial nerves; and 17 years later, Polson (1982) designed a magnetic stimulator for peripheral nerves, and for the first time recorded the motor evoked potential after peripheral nerve stimulation. In addition to ECT, the first clinically and scientifically applicable method of pulsed transcranial electrical stimulation was developed in 1980 by Merton and Morton demonstrating that the use of a single high-voltage discharge over the motor cortex could produce a twitch of contralateral body muscles, and over the visual cortex producing phosphenes (Sarmiento, San-Juan, & Prasath, 2016; Steinberg, 2013; Wexler, 2017).

In 1985, in England, another important event took place when Anthony Barker made the first public presentation of motor evoked potential recording after transcranial magnetic stimulation (TMS) during a meeting of the Physiological Society in Sheffield, using a newly designed machine suitable for clinical use (Barker, Jalinous, & Freeston, 1985). Initially, pulsed transcranial magnetic stimulation (TMS) was used for research and functional diagnosis exploring corticospinal pathways. In the early nineties, Pascual-Leone et al found evidence in favor of its potential therapeutic use (Dhuna, Gates, & Pascual-Leone, 1991; Gates, Dhuna, & Pascual-Leone, 1992; Pascual-Leone et al., 1993; Pascual-Leone, Valls-Sole, Wassermann, & Hallett, 1994). The following years saw numerous articles describing an increasing amount of high quality evidence in favor of the use of TMS as therapy for depression and its approval by various regulatory institutions as the most widely applied treatment of its kind to the present (O'Reardon et al., 2007). In part the development of TMS and repetitive TMS (rTMS) was responsible for the rediscovery of tDCS and its extension with therapeutic purposes but it was not until the end of the nineties and the early 2000s when tDCS gained interest in the scientific community and there was a huge increase in the number of research papers examining potential clinical applications (Nitsche & Paulus, 2000, 2001; Priori, 2003). Presently both rTMS and tDCS are in fact the two principal methods of NIBS.

Physiology of NIBS

Thousands of years after Hippocrates and Scribonius Largus, we are just beginning to understand how tDCS and rTMS work. The brain is essentially an electric organ, and both rTMS and tDCS can add a small amount of electricity in a focal way to a specific cortical area. As a result, we can modulate cortical inhibition/excitation balance with behavioral and physiological consequences that outlast the moment of stimulation, and when a series of daily sessions is applied we can expect a lasting effect of several weeks or months. That is why NIBS may be useful as adjuvant to conventional therapy in many psychiatric and neurological diseases with well-known altered brain function. Of course, the knowledge of each disease pathophysiology is the key for designing appropriate stimulation protocols. Despite rTMS and tDCS sharing common general effects at the physiological level, their physical properties are not the same as explained in the following sections.

Repetitive Transcranial Magnetic Stimulation (rTMS)

Studies from Valero-Cabré et al. demonstrated a frequency dependent effect when using rTMS. They used autoradiograph techniques based on 14C-2DG , and demonstrated in the cat visuo-parietal cortex that low (≤ 1 Hz) and high (≥ 5 Hz) frequencies suppress neuronal firing during stimulation, with an off-line effect that deferred between both alternatives: local uptake of the radiopharmaceutical substance is increased in the stimulated area after high frequency stimulation, and decreased after low frequency stimulation, and with distant effects in other areas (Valero-Cabre, Payne, Rushmore, Lomber, & Pascual-Leone, 2005). Distant effects have been described at the cortical and subcortical level in brain structures far away from the directly stimulated site, such as caudate nucleus for example, inducing an increase of endogenous dopamine release. (Strafella, Paus, Barrett, & Dagher, 2001).

At the cellular level, high frequency rTMS (> 5 Hz) typically induces long term potentiation (LTP)-like plasticity, whereas low frequency rTMS (≤ 1 Hz) induces long term depression (LTD)-like plasticity (Korchounov & Ziemann, 2011; Rajji et al., 2011). This change in synaptic efficiency is associated with long-lasting (hours after rTMS) increases in AMPA receptor mediated synaptic transmission and increases in dendritic spine diameter in pyramidal neuron populations on CA1 (Lenz et al., 2016; Muller-Dahlhaus & Vlachos, 2013). These changes take place mainly at the proximal dendrites, and similar findings have been described in classical LTP paradigms. It is supposed that change in AMPA receptor functioning mediates low-frequency stimulation effects (Thickbroom, 2007).

Also, non-synaptic mechanisms seem to play an important role in functional synaptic changes; human studies show upregulation of serum BDNF after high frequency rTMS. Low and high-frequency stimulation enhance the expression of the c-Fos and zif268 gene in the cortex (Aydin-Abidin, Trippe, Funke, Eysel, & Benali, 2008) and rTMS influences a wide range of cell types including glial and endothelial cells. There are likely more than LTP and LTD changes in its mechanism of action in the brain. There is a probable neuroprotective mechanism associated with the induction of macroscopic changes in gray matter volume at the stimulated site (May et al. (2007). It is suggested that these macroscopic changes depend of neurogenesis and the establishment of new synapses, blood vessels and glias (Ueyama et al., 2011).

Transcranial Direct Current Stimulation (tDCS)

tDCS does not induce neuronal firing by neuronal depolarization but rather modulates spontaneous neuronal activity through changes in the resting membrane potential, thus varying its polarization. Studies in animals using direct cortical stimulation in the early sixties showed that anodal stimulation over the vertex increased spontaneous neuronal activity.

whereas cathodal stimulation reduced it. In 1998, Priori et al. published the first modern study demonstrating excitability changes in cortical excitability induced by tDCS over the motor cortex, with changes in the amplitude of motor-evoked potential induced by transcranial magnetic stimulation elicited in small hand muscles in 15 healthy subjects. It was the first paper reporting a neuromodulatory effect of tDCS over cortical function induced by a very small electrical field over the skull (Priori, Berardelli, Rona, Accornero, & Manfredi, 1998). Later, with a better methodology, Nitsche and Paulus (2000) corroborated motor cortex excitability changes induced by tDCS, and they also noted that these changes were polarity-dependent: anodal tDCS increases motor-cortex excitability, whereas cathodal tDCS decreases it. In their experiment, they showed that anodal tDCS increased MEP amplitude evoked by TMS by about 40%, whereas cathodal tDCS decreased it. (Nitsche & Paulus, 2000)

Liebetanz, Nitsche, & Paulus (2003), using the NMDA antagonist dextromethorphan, demonstrated that the induction of long-lasting after-effects was mediated by NMDA receptors resulting in the drug preventing the expected tDCS effects, whatever the polarity used. Other authors have published similar results supporting this hypothesis blocking the D2 receptor with sulpiride and thus blocking the expected effect of tDCS. Stagg et al., using magnetic resonance spectroscopy, described how GABA concentration decreased significantly after anodal stimulation, with no change in glutamate concentration; and how both glutamate and GABA concentration decreased after cathodal stimulation (with higher reduction in glutamate). Thus both factors probably mediate tDCS effects through changes in cortical neurotransmitters and modification in NMDA-receptor sensitivity for both polarities. Other neurotransmitters are also involved in tDCS effects including dopamine, acetylcholine and serotonin (Nitsche et al., 2006;

Stagg et al., 2009; Stagg et al., 2011).

There is a well-known effect on functional connectivity in both normal and clinical populations, as demonstrated in functional magnetic resonance imaging or EEG studies. Stagg et al. (2013) assessed the modulation of cerebral perfusion during and after tDCS application to the left dorsolateral prefrontal cortex, and they described that during stimulation with anodal tDCS, there was an increase in the perfusion of the primary sensory-motor cortex, cingulate cortex and left parietal cortex as compared with baseline perfusion. On the other hand, cathodal tDCS decreased perfusion in thalamus and in temporal lobe compared with baseline state.

NIB in Pediatric Populations, Safety and Adverse Effects

Ethical issues with regard to NIBS use in children have been discussed since the beginning of clinical application of rTMS and tDCS (Garvey & Gilbert, 2004; Lin & Pascual-Leone, 2002; Quintana, 2005). Besides safety issues many other concerns arise regarding children's capacity to cooperate and to make informed decisions about the treatment. Adult and child brains have obvious anatomic and functional differences when considering skull and skin thickness, and excitability levels which can all influence the amount of current induced in the brain networks and its modulatory effects (Minhas, Bikson, Woods, Rosen, & Kessler, 2012).

For these reasons, NIBS has been used in children in only a few conditions, i.e., cerebral palsy, attention deficit hyperactivity disorder, epilepsy, autism spectrum disorder and Tourette syndrome. One important conclusion from all the studies is that no serious adverse effects have been reported in any case to date and described effects in children are similar to those reported in adults: headache, neck pain, drowsiness and local discomfort. Despite the absence of evidence for significant adverse effects in children, there are markedly fewer studies in pediatric population than in adults. Fortunately, today we have more evidence about safety of NIBS procedures and it is increasingly used in pediatric populations (Allen, Kluger, & Buard, 2017; Krishnan, Santos, Peterson, & Ehinger, 2015).

Evidence for brain injury by DCS in animal models occurs at intensities much higher than the ones that are usually induced by rTMS or tDCS. After more than 30 years of use of tDCS and more than 20 years of use of TMS in human and animals, there is no evidence for irreversible injury produced by conventional stimulating protocols following the safety guidelines established by the International Federation of Clinical Neurophysiology (Rossi, Hallett, Rossini, & Pascual-Leone, 2009; Rossini et al., 2015). In the case of tDCS, the most common observed adverse effect is local pain, tingling or light itching sensation under the stimulating electrodes, slight fatigue, drowsiness and headache. Skin irritation can also occur at the stimulation site but disappears promptly after finishing the stimulation (Poreisz, Boros, Antal, & Paulus, 2007; Rodriguez, Opisso, Pascual-Leone, & Soler, 2014).

Adverse effects are more commonly associated with rTMS than with tDCS and involve mainly transient headaches and scalp discomfort likely due to activation of scalp pericranial muscles. TMS can induce seizures, but the incidence rate is extremely rare (Rosa, Odebrecht, Rigonatti, & Marcolin, 2004). rTMS is associated more often with headache than tDCS, and also with neck pain or tenderness. Other rare adverse effects not well understood could include syncope, fainting, nausea, vomiting, auditory change and hypomania. In summary, both rTMS and tDCS are safe methods and are associated with only a few adverse effects, with convulsion being the most serious effect in the case of rTMS, but it is extremely rare.

Contraindications

There are absolute and relative contraindications to rTMS and tDCS. Both are absolutely contraindicated in the presence of metallic hardware in the head and neck such as aneurysm clips, deep brain stimulators, electrodes or any other sensitive devices in the body such as cardiac pacemakers, intracardiac lines, or if patients are under the effect of medications that lower the seizure threshold. In pregnant women, there are not enough data available neither for or against its use regarding the safety of the fetus and as such, it could be an ideal option for a depressed pregnant woman (Rossi et al., 2009; Wassermann, 1998).

A special mention must be made with respect to epilepsy and any history of substance abuse. In the first case low frequency rTMS and cathodal tDCS seem to have a beneficial effect, and they could be an adjuvant therapy in those patients with drug resistant epilepsy, especially when surgery is not an option (Gomes et al., 2017; San-Juan et al., 2017). Substance abuse is another interesting topic in that seizure could be a sign of acute intoxication and part of the abstinence syndrome but both high frequency rTMS and anodic tDCS over the left and right dorsolateral prefrontal cortex have shown some level of effectiveness in controlling craving (Dunlop, Hanlon, & Downar, 2017; Enokibara, Trevizol, Shiozawa, & Cordeiro, 2016).

Rationale for the Use of NIBS in Psychiatric and Neurological Disorders

The rationale for NIBS is drawn from the fact that brain functional anomalies are expressed in some way by changes in electrical potentials and spectral frequency of electrical brain activity, and any stimulating current irrupting in a brain network (such as those induced by TMS and tDCS) can potentially have a modulatory effect when an appropriate protocol is used and thus clinical deficits related to the abnormal brain electrical activity could be potentially reversed and can approximate normal functioning levels. Brain stimulation protocols can have differing effects across subjects, and those effects might be exacerbated when considering the heterogeneity of disease models, a case in point being the neurodevelopmental disorders such as ASD (Hummel & Cohen, 2006).

A simplified point of view could be that almost any brain anomaly can change neuronal network excitability, and the selection of the stimulating protocol is intended to restore the local or distant excitability balance. When a specific anomaly is known as part of the pathophysiology of the disease, it is possible to design a stimulating protocol to modulate the function of a selected network. There is significant evidence overall favoring the use of NIBS in neurological and psychiatric diseases, but with varying levels of evidences with respect to the condition in question and caution should be taken when considering the proposal of any modality of NIBS as a therapeutic option for diseases with low levels of evidence for efficacy (Chieffo, Comi, & Leocani, 2016; Kimiskidis, 2010).

It is known that in neurodevelopmental disorders such as ASD there is adequate scientific evidence supporting the existence of an intracortical inhibitory dysfunction, especially in frontal lobes. As demonstrated by Casanova, ASD patients have an abnormal structure in cortical minicolumnar architecture that can explain an inhibitory dysfunction in filtering and processing afferent information based on a poor neuropil development (Casanova, Buxhoeveden, Switala, & Roy, 2002). Nevertheless, electrophysiological research has been somewhat controversial in that some research confirms this inhibitory dysfunction while other studies report normal behavior in the study of the short intracortical inhibitory interval (SICI) and short intracortical facilitation (ICF) in ASD patients, while yet other studies report mixed results with some ASD individuals showing impaired intracortical inhibition and others showing typical responses (Enticott et al., 2013).

That is to say, there are no conclusive results, but there is interesting evidence for the possibility of using NIBS to increase local or distant excitability or potentiate local or distant inhibition when the appropriate protocol is used. In the case of ASD, following the basic idea of the presence of an intracortical inhibitory dysfunction, low frequency rTMS or cathodic tDCS could both potentially reverse this functional state and lead to an improvement in autistic symptoms (Casanova, Sokhadze, Opris, Wang, & Li, 2015; D'Urso et al., 2014).

Evidence Favoring Therapy With NIBS in Autism Spectrum Disorders

Excluding case reports, basic research articles and other papers with scarce clinical data, there are just a few published trials using NIBS in ASD patients (Table 6.1). Casanova et al. in 2009–2012 were the first to propose the use of low frequency rTMS for ASD patients, based on the possibility that low-frequency rTMS could improve GABAergic neurotransmission. They used one weekly session over 12 weeks in a group of 25 ASD patients and described an increase in gamma activity in the EEG evoked by a visual processing paradigm, with changes in Event Related Potential (ERP), improved error monitoring, and correction function in a visual recognition task after the intervention (Baruth et al., 2010; Casanova et al., 2012; E. Sokhadze et al., 2010; E. Sokhadze et al., 2009). Overall, these results showed that rTMS may be a potential therapeutic modality for ASD. Dorsolateral prefrontal cortex (DLPFC) was the preferred target due to its projections and relationships to many other cortical and subcortical structures, as for many other disease models today still being the main target for NIBS (Antal et al., 2017; Lefaucheur et al., 2014; Lefaucheur et al., 2017)

Schneider et al in 2011 used a combination of anodic tDCS and a modified version of the Bilingual Aphasia Test (BAT) in 10 children with autism and language syntax and found an improvement in syntactic accuracy when compared with the

Table 6.1
Principal Published Trials With NIBS in Patients With ASD

Author	Sample Size	Design	Protocol Details
Sokhadze (2010)	13	Open and controlled	rTMS 0.5 Hz, 6 sessions (twice a week)
Baruth (2010)	25	Open and controlled	rTMS 1 Hz Left DLPFC 160 pulses
Schneider (2011)	10	Open and not controlled	Anodic tDCS language areas. Single session
Casanova (2012)	45	Open and controlled	rTMS 1 Hz Left DLPFC 160 pulses
Panerai (2014)	43	Crossover with sham stimulation	rTMS, 1 Hz and 8 Hz, 10 sessions 1500 pulses
D'Urso (2014)	12	Open and not controlled	tDCS: Cathode F3 10 sessions
Amatachaya (2014)	20	Randomized, double blind & crossover	Target: Left DLPFC Anodal stimulation, 5 sessions
Casanova (2014)	18	Open	R/L DLPFC. 0.5 Hz. 160 pulses, 18 sessions
Sokhadze (2014)	54	Open and controlled	rTMS 1 Hz, R/L DLPFC, 18 sessions, 180 pulses
Enticott (2014)	28	Double-blind, randomized, placebo-controlled	Target: DMPFC.Deep rTMS (H-coil) 10 sessions double-blind, randomized, placebo-controlled.5 Hz, 4500 pulses
Gómez (2017)	24	Open, controlled and partially crossover	Target: Left DLPFC 20 sessions tDCS: Cathode F3 rTMS: 1 Hz, 90% MT. 1500 pulses

Aberrant BC = Aberrant Behavior Checklist;
Autism BC = Autism Behavior Checklist;
ADI = Autism Diagnostic Interview;
AQ = Autism Spectrum Quotient;
ATEC = Autism Treatment Evaluation Checklist;
BAT = Bilingual Aphasia Test;
CARS = Childhood Autism Rating Scale;
CGAS = Children's Global Assessment Scale

Outcome Measure	Follow-up	Result
Aberrant BC, SRS, RBS	2 weeks after	Improvement in all behavioral measures
Aberrant BC, SRS, RBS	2 weeks after	Significant improvement in the responses on behavioral questionnaires (i.e., irritability, repetitive behavior)
BAT	Immediately after	Improvement in language syntax and syntactic accuracy
Aberrant BC, SRS, RBS	2 weeks after	Significant improvement in the responses on behavioral questionnaires (i.e., irritability, repetitive behavior)
PEP-R, EHC	Immediately after	Improvement in eye-hand performances with 8 Hz
Aberrant BC	2 weeks	Improvement in autistic symptoms
CARS, ATEC, CGAS	1 week	Improvement in autistic symptoms
Aberrant BC, SRS, RBS-R	2 weeks after	Improvement in autistic symptoms with changes in autonomic variables
Aberrant BC, SRS, RBS-R	2 weeks after	Improvement in autistic symptoms
RAADS, AQ, IRI	1 month	Improvement in autistic symptoms
ADI, ATEC, Autism BC	6 month	Improvement in autistic symptoms

EHC = Eye-hand coordination;
IRI = Interpersonal Reactivity Index;
PEP-R = Psychoeducational Profile-Revised;
RBS = Repetitive Behavior Scale;
RBS-R = Repetitive Behavior Scale-Revised;
RAADS = Ritvo Autism Asperger Diagnostic Scale;
SRS = Social Responsiveness Scale

performance in BAT patients before and after tDCS sessions with cathode stimulation of language areas in the contralateral homologous projections. They concluded that combining a special language therapy with tDCS could be effective for improving language based on syntax acquisition in children with autism (Schneider & Hopp, 2011). In the same year Fecteau et al. published their results from a crossover sham-control study in 10 adult ASD stimulating pars opercularis and pars triangularis using MRI for language area localization for 1 Hz rTMS; they reported improvement in picture naming as the main result (Fecteau, Agosta, Oberman, & Pascual-Leone, 2011). Using another target (pre-motor cortex), Panerai et al also suggested that high frequency stimulation could help ASD patients improve hand-eye coordination (Panerai et al., 2014). In 2014, Casanova et al. published another paper describing a neuromodulatory effect of 18 sessions of low frequency rTMS over autonomic functions in a group of ASD patients, consisting of a significant increase in cardiac interval variability and a decrease of tonic SCL accompanied by behavioral improvement with decreased irritability, hyperactivity, stereotypes and compulsive behavior (Casanova et al., 2014). They emphasized a possible role of vagal and sympathetic tone in autistic symptomatology.

D'Urso et al. seem to be the first to use cathodic tDCS over the left DLPFC in a male autistic adult with grossly disturbed behavior, severe irritability, agitation, hyperactivity, and lack of compliance who was unresponsive to different psychosocial and pharmacological interventions. After 10 daily sessions they reported a remarkable improvement in his abnormal behavior based on the Aberrant Behavior Checklist score with a 40.2% reduction in the total score compared with the initial value. The same group published another experience 1 year later with the use of the same tDCS protocol in 12 young adults with autistic disorder with improvement in 80% of the patients that completed the 10 proposed sessions, and among all the subscales principal modulatory effect was related to hyperactivity and non-compliance (D'Urso et al., 2015). Interestingly Amatachaya et al. achieved similar results using anodic tDCS stimulation instead of cathodic stimulation over the same target (left DLPFC). They studied 20 patients with autism and applied a total of five sessions during consecutive days with a randomized and double-blind crossover trial and described improvement in patients from the experimental group in all the applied clinical scales 1 week after completing the intervention (Amatachaya & Auvichayapat, 2014).

With a different approach Enticott et al. applied deep rTMS (HAUT-Coil) in a group of 28 high functioning autistic adults. The target was the dorsomedial prefrontal cortex bilaterally and a prospective, double-blind, randomized, placebo-controlled design was conducted with ten 5 Hz session treatments, completing 1500 pulses per session. Those in the active condition also showed a reduction in self-oriented anxiety during difficult and emotional social situations from pre-treatment to 1-month follow-up. Deep rTMS to the bilateral dorsomedial prefrontal cortex yielded a reduction in social relation impairment and socially-related anxiety (Enticott et al., 2014).

Recently our group published the results of an open and self-controlled trial including 24 patients with ASD of medium-low severity autistic behavior using both low frequency rTMS and cathodic tDCS over the left DLPFC with tDCS used in children younger than 11 and rTMS in the older children ages 11–13. Patients received a total of 20 session of NIBS weekly and had a complete follow-up during the first 6 months after the intervention (intended to be up to 1 year after the intervention), with evaluations of the Autism Behavior Checklist, Autism Treatment Evaluation Checklist, and the Autism Diagnostic Interview. A significant reduction in the total score on the three clinical scales was observed and maintained during the first 6 months after treatment, with a slight and non-significant tendency to increase the scores in the last evaluation. Actual improvement in the treated patients persisted in most subjects up to 1 year later (Figure 6.1, unpublished results). Twenty sessions of NIBS over the L-DLPFC improved autistic symptoms in ASD children with a lasting effect of 6 months (Gomez et al., 2017). All the available evidence indicates that NIBS, either rTMS or tDCS, may at least transiently improve autistic symptoms.

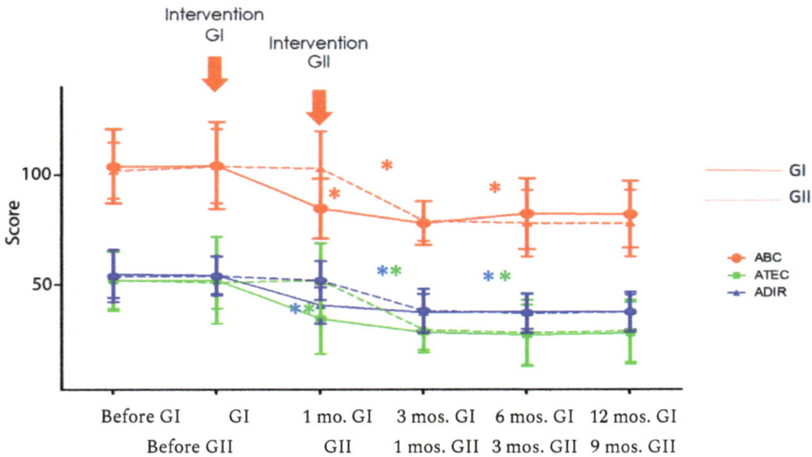

Figure 6.1. *Clinical improvement according to Autism Behavioral Checklist (ABC), Autism Treatment Evaluation Checklist (ATEC) and Autism Diagnostic Interview (ADI-R) is maintained until 1 year after completing 20 sessions of NIBS. Methodological data could be revisited in Gómez et al. until 6 month of follow-up (Gomez et al., 2017).* * $p < 0.05$

Repetitive Transcranial Magnetic Stimulation or Transcranial Direct Current Stimulation?

As a neuromodulating technique for therapeutic use, tDCS seems to be preferable to rTMS for several reasons: tDCS is less expensive than TMS, easier to use and can be delivered via a portable system. Stimulating electrodes are easily secured to the scalp, allowing patient mobility which makes its use possible without strict movement restriction during other physical activities including physical rehabilitation and occupational or speech therapy which is a great advantage when treating children or uncooperative patients. Sham stimulation is more reliable when using tDCS than rTMS because patients rarely perceive active tDCS, or at most they experience the actual stimulation in the active site though only for a few seconds, while the TMS coil emits a loud click for each stimulus delivered. Because TMS induces electric current in the scalp as well as the brain, it usually activates local sensory nerves or muscles thus causing a sensation that patients can readily perceive (Lefaucheur et al., 2017).

The techniques are also different in terms of spatial resolution of stimulation—tDCS action is less focal than TMS, so in some circumstances it can represent a further advantage over rTMS because of the large brain area that could be targeted. Therefore, no complex targeting procedure is required for tDCS, which is usually needed when using rTMS. Although tDCS has demonstrated benefits in many clinical conditions, rTMS is more widely used than tDCS in research and in clinical practice. Thus, there is more scientific evidence in favor of rTMS efficacy for therapeutic applications than for tDCS (Antal et al., 2017; Fregni et al., 2015; Lefaucheur et al., 2014; Lefaucheur et al., 2017; Perera et al., 2016; Rossi et al., 2009).

On the other hand, published results from our group support that at least in ASD patients, rTMS is associated with rather more significant change in functional connectivity than tDCS according to results from an EEG based analysis, especially in high frequency spectrum. As far as we know it is the first published study that compared clinical effects of the use of both rTMS and tDCS methods in the same population, based on objective changes in functional connectivity (Figure 6.2). Clearly more evidence is needed to establish solid conclusions, but these results are probably related to a higher value of stimulating current induced by rTMS than by tDCS, at least in our experimental setting (Gomez et al., 2017).

Principal Consensus Articles About the Use of NIBS in Autism Spectrum Disorder

The use of NIBS in ASD is growing exponentially with the development of a high number of experimental and clinical paradigms associated either with the pathophysiological research, or with attempts to treat ASD with a different strategy. Two important consensus conferences in 2014 and 2015

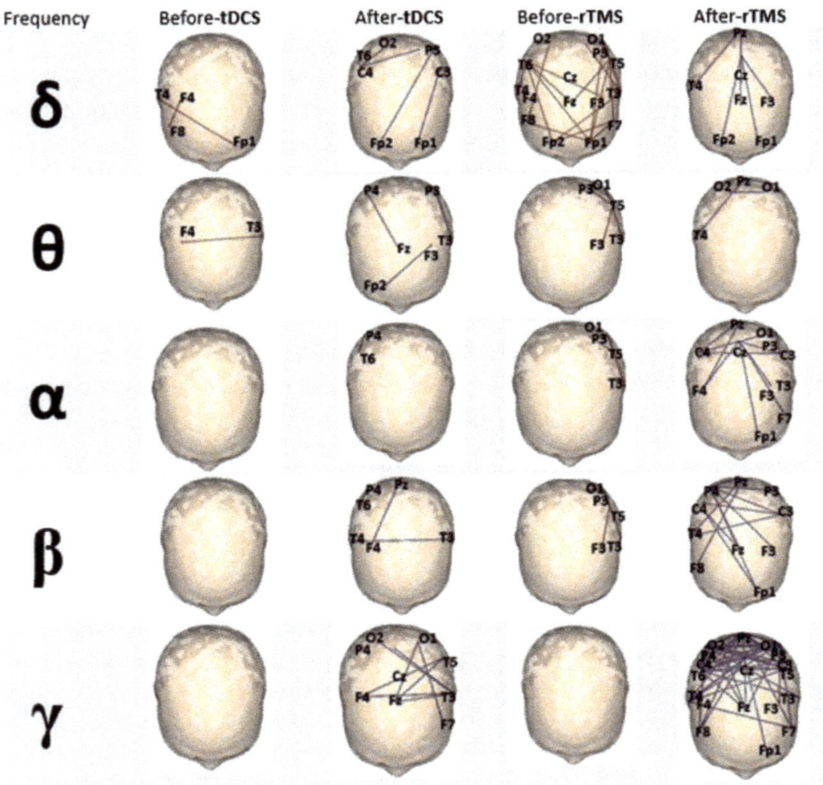

Figure 6.2. *Change in functional connectivity from an EEG based analysis in patients who received: tDCS (first two columns) or rTMS(columns 3 and 4). From Gómez et al. (2017).*

have been held to analyze the state of the art of TMS therapy in ASD (Oberman et al., 2014, 2016). Unfortunately, they only analyzed published results related to TMS, and not tDCS experiences. The expert panel confirmed that among other reasons, the need for exploring the therapeutic potential of rTMS in ASD arises from the fact that there is currently no pharmacotherapy conclusively shown to improve the core symptoms of ASD patients. One of the main conclusions is that TMS is safe in ASD when safety guidelines and recommendations are followed. There are just a few randomized double-blind trials but these studies all collectively provide preliminary support for further exploration of the potential effectiveness of rTMS for ASD. There is a wide spectrum of methodological details differentiating one study from other, including target for stimulation, stimulation frequency, number of sessions and number of pulses per sessions, all of which make for difficulty in evaluating replicability of results.

For many reasons, inclusion criteria tend to be restrictive, excluding severely symptomatic patients; but it should be understood that a moderate grade of collaboration is required for steady coil placement in the case of rTMS, or stimulating electrodes placement for tDCS. In the latter case, there are much fewer published studies, however because of its relative simplicity, tDCS could be easier to apply in ASD patients than rTMS. The absence of a biological marker or objective measures for diagnosis and management of ASD is a great obstacle even using the best inclusion criteria, and for the follow up and establishment of good outcome measures. All in all, preliminary results regarding therapeutic effectiveness in ASD patients are encouraging, indicating a positive effect in the majority of patients; but we are still far from a definition of the best approach of NIBS for ASD patients, even if there is a specific response to low or high frequency rTMS, or a polarity dependent effect in the case of tDCS. As the expert panel stated: "TMS represents an innovative research tool and a novel, possibly transformative approach to the treatment of neurodevelopmental disorders" (Oberman et al., 2016). In any case, the small study samples and the low number of randomized double-blind trials are the main limitations to obtaining solid conclusions.

Conclusions

Although the presence of scientific evidence is limited, it is thus far uniformly positive and provides further support to consider NIBS as a potential symptomatic treatment for ASD; though more basic and clinical research is needed with well-designed randomized and double-blind trials. For neuroscience, NIBS therapy for ASD is a pathway to be explored.

References

Allen, C. H., Kluger, B. M., & Buard, I. (2017). Safety of transcranial magnetic stimulation in children: A systematic review of the literature. *Pediatric Neurology, 68*, 3–17.

Amatachaya, A., & Auvichayapat, N. (2014). Effect of anodal transcranial direct current stimulation on autism: A randomized double-blind crossover trial. *Behavioural Neurology, 2014,*173073.

Antal, A., Alekseichuk, I., Bikson, M., Brockmoller, J., Brunoni, A. R., Chen, R., . . . Paulus, W. (2017). Low intensity transcranial electric stimulation: Safety, ethical, legal regulatory and application guidelines. *Clinical Neurophysiol*ogy, *128*(9), 1774–1809.

Aydin-Abidin, S., Trippe, J., Funke, K., Eysel, U. T., & Benali, A. (2008). High- and low-frequency repetitive transcranial magnetic stimulation differentially activates c-Fos and zif268 protein expression in the rat brain. *Experimental Brain Research, 188*(2), 249–261.

Barker, A. T., Jalinous, R., & Freeston, I. L. (1985). Non-invasive magnetic stimulation of human motor cortex. *Lancet, 1*(8437), 1106–1107.

Baruth, J. M., Casanova, M. F., El-Baz, A., Horrell, T., Mathai, G., Sears, L., & Sokhadze, E. (2010). Low-frequency repetitive transcranial magnetic stimulation (rTMS) modulates evoked-gamma frequency oscillations in autism spectrum disorder (ASD). *Journal of Neurotherapy, 14*(3), 179–194.

Casanova, M. F., Buxhoeveden, D. P., Switala, A. E., & Roy, E. (2002). Minicolumnar pathology in autism. *Neurology, 58*(3), 428–432.

Casanova, M. F., Baruth, J. M., El-Baz, A., Tasman, A., Sears, L., & Sokhadze, E. (2012). Repetitive transcranial magnetic stimulation (rTMS) modulates event-related potential (ERP) indices of attention in autism. *Translational Neuroscience, 3*(2), 170–180.

Casanova, M. F., Hensley, M. K., Sokhadze, E. M., El-Baz, A. S., Wang, Y., Li, X., & Sears, L. (2014). Effects of weekly low-frequency rTMS on autonomic measures in children with autism spectrum disorder. *Frontiers in Human Neuroscience, 8*, 851.

Casanova, M. F., Sokhadze, E., Opris, I., Wang, Y., & Li, X. (2015). Autism spectrum disorders: Linking neuropathological findings to treatment with transcranial magnetic stimulation. *Acta Paediatrica, 104*(4), 346-355.

Chieffo, R., Comi, G., & Leocani, L. (2016). Noninvasive neuromodulation in poststroke gait disorders: Rationale, feasibility, and state of the art. *Neurorehabilitation and Neural Repair, 30*(1), 71–82.

D'Urso, G., Ferrucci, R., Bruzzese, D., Pascotto, A., Priori, A., Altamura, C. A., . . . Bravaccio, C. (2014). Transcranial direct current stimulation for autistic disorder. *Biological Psychiatry, 76*(5), e5–6.

D'Urso, G., Bruzzese, D., Ferrucci, R., Priori, A., Pascotto, A., Galderisi, S., . . . Bravaccio, C. (2015). Transcranial direct current stimulation for hyperactivity and noncompliance in autistic disorder. *World Journal of Biological Psychiatry, 16*(5), 361–366.

Dhuna, A., Gates, J., & Pascual-Leone, A. (1991). Transcranial magnetic stimulation in patients with epilepsy. *Neurology, 41*(7), 1067–1071.

Dunlop, K., Hanlon, C. A., & Downar, J. (2017). Noninvasive brain stimulation treatments for addiction and major depression. *Annals of New York Academy of Sciences, 1394*(1), 31–54.

Enokibara, M., Trevizol, A., Shiozawa, P., & Cordeiro, Q. (2016). Establishing an effective TMS protocol for craving in substance addiction: Is it possible? *American Journal of Addictions, 25*(1), 28–30.

Enticott, P. G., Kennedy, H. A., Rinehart, N. J., Tonge, B. J., Bradshaw, J. L., & Fitzgerald, P. B. (2013). GABAergic activity in autism spectrum disorders: an investigation of cortical inhibition via transcranial magnetic stimulation. *Neuropharmacology, 68*, 202–209.

Enticott, P. G., Fitzgibbon, B. M., Kennedy, H. A., Arnold, S. L., Elliot, D., Peachey, A., . . . Fitzgerald, P. B. (2014). A double-blind, randomized trial of deep repetitive transcranial magnetic stimulation (rTMS) for autism spectrum disorder. *Brain Stimulation, 7*(2), 206–211.

Fecteau, S., Agosta, S., Oberman, L., & Pascual-Leone, A. (2011). Brain stimulation over Broca's area differentially modulates naming skills in neurotypical adults and individuals with Asperger's syndrome. *European Journal of Neuroscience, 34*(1), 158–164.

Fregni, F., Nitsche, M. A., Loo, C. K., Brunoni, A. R., Marangolo, P., Leite, J., . . . Bikson, M. (2015). Regulatory considerations for the clinical and research use of transcranial direct current stimulation (tDCS): Review and recommendations from an expert panel. *Clinical Research and Regulatory Affairs, 32*(1), 22–35.

Garvey, M. A., & Gilbert, D. L. (2004). Transcranial magnetic stimulation in children. *European Journal of Paediatric Neurology, 8*(1), 7–19.

Gates, J. R., Dhuna, A., & Pascual-Leone, A. (1992). Lack of pathologic changes in human temporal lobes after transcranial magnetic stimulation. *Epilepsia, 33*(3), 504–508.

Gomes, J. S., Dias, A. M., Scorza, F. A., Cordeiro, Q., Sato, I. A., Akiba, H., . . . Trevizol, A. P. (2017). Transcranial direct current stimulation for refractory major depressive disorder temporal lobe epilepsy: A quantitative electroencephalography study. *Epilepsy & Behavior, 72*, 205–207.

Gomez, L., Vidal, B., Maragoto, C., Morales, L. M., Berrillo, S., Vera Cuesta, H., . . . Robinson, M. (2017). Non-Invasive brain stimulation for children with autism spectrum disorders: A short-term outcome study. *Behavioral Sciences (Basel), 7*(3), E63.

Hummel, F. C., & Cohen, L. G. (2006). Non-invasive brain stimulation: A new strategy to improve neurorehabilitation after stroke? *Lancet. Neurology, 5*(8), 708–712.

Kimiskidis, V. K. (2010). Transcranial magnetic stimulation for drug-resistant epilepsies: Rationale and clinical experience. *European Neurology, 63*(4), 205–210.

Korchounov, A., & Ziemann, U. (2011). Neuromodulatory neurotransmitters influence LTP-like plasticity in human cortex: A pharmaco-TMS study. *Neuropsychopharmacology, 36*(9), 1894–1902.

Krishnan, C., Santos, L., Peterson, M. D., & Ehinger, M. (2015). Safety of noninvasive brain stimulation in children and adolescents. *Brain Stimulation, 8*(1), 76–87.

Lefaucheur, J. P., Andre-Obadia, N., Antal, A., Ayache, S. S., Baeken, C., Benninger, D. H., . . . Garcia-Larrea, L. (2014). Evidence-based guidelines on the therapeutic use of repetitive transcranial magnetic stimulation (rTMS). *Clinical Neurophysiology, 125*(11), 2150–2206.

Lefaucheur, J. P., Antal, A., Ayache, S. S., Benninger, D. H., Brunelin, J., Cogiamanian, F., . . . Paulus, W. (2017). Evidence-based guidelines on the therapeutic use of transcranial direct current stimulation (tDCS). *Clinical Neurophysiology, 128*(1), 56–92.

Lenz, M., Galanis, C., Muller-Dahlhaus, F., Opitz, A., Wierenga, C. J., Szabo, G., . . . Vlachos, A. (2016). Repetitive magnetic stimulation induces plasticity of inhibitory synapses. *Nature Communications, 7*,

10020.
Liebetanz, D., Nitsche, M. A., & Paulus, W. (2003). Pharmacology of transcranial direct current stimulation: Missing effect of riluzole. *Supplements to Clinical Neurophysiology, 56*, 282–287.
Lin, K. L., & Pascual-Leone, A. (2002). Transcranial magnetic stimulation and its applications in children. *Chang Gung Medical Journal, 25*(7), 424–436.
Minhas, P., Bikson, M., Woods, A. J., Rosen, A. R., & Kessler, S. K. (2012). Transcranial direct current stimulation in pediatric brain: A computational modeling study. *Conference Proceedings IEEE Engineering in Medicine and Biology Society, 2012*, 859–862.
Muller-Dahlhaus, F., & Vlachos, A. (2013). Unraveling the cellular and molecular mechanisms of repetitive magnetic stimulation. *Frontiers in Molecular Neuroscience, 6*, 50.
Nitsche, M. A., & Paulus, W. (2000). Excitability changes induced in the human motor cortex by weak transcranial direct current stimulation. *Journal of Physiology, 527*(3), 633–639.
Nitsche, M. A., & Paulus, W. (2001). Sustained excitability elevations induced by transcranial DC motor cortex stimulation in humans. *Neurology, 57*(10), 1899–1901.
Nitsche, M. A., Lampe, C., Antal, A., Liebetanz, D., Lang, N., Tergau, F., & Paulus, W. (2006). Dopaminergic modulation of long-lasting direct current-induced cortical excitability changes in the human motor cortex. *European Journal of Neuroscience, 23*(6), 1651–1657.
Nitsche, M. A., & Paulus, W. (2011). Transcranial direct current stimulation—update 2011. *Restorative Neurology and Neuroscience, 29*(6), 463–492.
O'Reardon, J. P., Solvason, H. B., Janicak, P. G., Sampson, S., Isenberg, K. E., Nahas, Z., . . . Sackeim, H. A. (2007). Efficacy and safety of transcranial magnetic stimulation in the acute treatment of major depression: A multisite randomized controlled trial. *Biological Psychiatry, 62*(11), 1208–1216.
Oberman, L. M., Enticott, P. G., Casanova, M. F., Rotenberg, A., Pascual-Leone, A., & McCracken, J. T. (2014). Transcranial magnetic stimulation (TMS) therapy for autism: An international consensus conference held in conjunction with the international meeting for autism research on May 13th and 14th, 2014. *Frontiers in Human Neuroscience, 8*, 1034.
Oberman, L. M., Enticott, P. G., Casanova, M. F., Rotenberg, A., Pascual-Leone, A., & McCracken, J. T. (2016). Transcranial magnetic stimulation in autism spectrum disorder: Challenges, promise, and roadmap for future research. *Autism Research, 9*(2), 184–203.
Panerai, S., Tasca, D., Lanuzza, B., Trubia, G., Ferri, R., Musso, S., . . . Elia, M. (2014). Effects of repetitive transcranial magnetic stimulation in performing eye-hand integration tasks: Four

preliminary studies with children showing low-functioning autism. *Autism, 18*(6), 638–650.
Pascual-Leone, A., Houser, C. M., Reese, K., Shotland, L. I., Grafman, J., Sato, S., . . . et al. (1993). Safety of rapid-rate transcranial magnetic stimulation in normal volunteers. *Electroencephalography and Clinical Neurophysiology, 89*(2), 120–130.
Pascual-Leone, A., Valls-Sole, J., Wassermann, E. M., & Hallett, M. (1994). Responses to rapid-rate transcranial magnetic stimulation of the human motor cortex. *Brain, 117*(4), 847–858.
Perera, T., George, M. S., Grammer, G., Janicak, P. G., Pascual-Leone, A., & Wirecki, T. S. (2016). The clinical TMS society consensus review and treatment recommendations for TMS therapy for major depressive disorder. *Brain Stimulation, 9*(3), 336–346.
Poreisz, C., Boros, K., Antal, A., & Paulus, W. (2007). Safety aspects of transcranial direct current stimulation concerning healthy subjects and patients. *Brain Research Bulletin, 72*(4–6), 208–214.
Priori, A., Berardelli, A., Rona, S., Accornero, N., & Manfredi, M. (1998). Polarization of the human motor cortex through the scalp. *Neuroreport, 9*(10), 2257–2260.
Priori, A. (2003). Brain polarization in humans: A reappraisal of an old tool for prolonged non-invasive modulation of brain excitability. *Clinical Neurophysiology, 114*(4), 589–595.
Quintana, H. (2005). Transcranial magnetic stimulation in persons younger than the age of 18. *Journal ECT, 21*(2), 88–95.
Rajji, T. K., Liu, S. K., Frantseva, M. V., Mulsant, B. H., Thoma, J., Chen, R., . . . Daskalakis, Z. J. (2011). Exploring the effect of inducing long-term potentiation in the human motor cortex on motor learning. *Brain Stimulation, 4*(3), 137–144.
Rodriguez, N., Opisso, E., Pascual-Leone, A., & Soler, M. D. (2014). Skin lesions induced by transcranial direct current stimulation (tDCS). *Brain Stimulation, 7*(5), 765–767.
Rosa, M. A., Odebrecht, M., Rigonatti, S. P., & Marcolin, M. A. (2004). [Transcranial magnetic stimulation: review of accidental seizures]. *Revista Brasileira Psiquiatria, 26*(2), 131–134.
Rossi, S., Hallett, M., Rossini, P. M., & Pascual-Leone, A. (2009). Safety, ethical considerations, and application guidelines for the use of transcranial magnetic stimulation in clinical practice and research. *Clinical Neurophysiology, 120*(12), 2008–2039.
Rossini, P. M., Burke, D., Chen, R., Cohen, L. G., Daskalakis, Z., Di Iorio, R., . . . Ziemann, U. (2015). Non-invasive electrical and magnetic stimulation of the brain, spinal cord, roots and peripheral nerves: Basic principles and procedures for routine clinical and research application. An updated report from an I.F.C.N. Committee. *Clinical Neurophysiology, 126*(6), 1071–1107.
San-Juan, D., Espinoza Lopez, D. A., Vazquez Gregorio, R., Trenado, C., Fernandez-Gonzalez Aragon, M., Morales-Quezada, L., . .

. Fregni, F. (2017). Transcranial direct current stimulation in mesial temporal lobe epilepsy and hippocampal sclerosis. *Brain Stimulation, 10*(1), 28–35.

Sarmiento, C. I., San-Juan, D., & Prasath, V. B. (2016). Letter to the editor: Brief history of transcranial direct current stimulation (tDCS): From electric fishes to microcontrollers. *Psychological Medicine, 46*(15), 3259–3261.

Schneider, H. D., & Hopp, J. P. (2011). The use of the Bilingual Aphasia Test for assessment and transcranial direct current stimulation to modulate language acquisition in minimally verbal children with autism. *Clinical Linguistics & Phonetics, 25*(6–7), 640–654.

Schönfeldt-Lecuona, C., Walter, H., Connemann, B. J., Kassubek, J., Spitzer, M., & Herwig, U. (2002). [Historical review and recent research trends of the antidepressant repetitive transcranial magnetic stimulation (rTMS)]. *Fortschritte der Neurologie-Psychiatrie, 70*(10), 520–530.

Sokhadze, E. M., El-Baz, A., Baruth, J., Mathai, G., Sears, L., & Casanova, M. F. (2009). Effects of low frequency repetitive transcranial magnetic stimulation (rTMS) on gamma frequency oscillations and event-related potentials during processing of illusory figures in autism. *Journal of Autism and Developmental Disorders, 39*(4), 619–634.

Sokhadze, E., Baruth, J., Tasman, A., Mansoor, M., Ramaswamy, R., Sears, L., . . . Casanova, M. F. (2010). Low-frequency repetitive transcranial magnetic stimulation (rTMS) affects event-related potential measures of novelty processing in autism. *Applied Psychophysiology and Biofeedback, 35*(2), 147–161.

Stagg, C. J., Best, J. G., Stephenson, M. C., O'Shea, J., Wylezinska, M., Kincses, Z. T., . . . Johansen-Berg, H. (2009). Polarity-sensitive modulation of cortical neurotransmitters by transcranial stimulation. *Journal of Neuroscience, 29*(16), 5202–5206.

Stagg, C. J., Bestmann, S., Constantinescu, A. O., Moreno, L. M., Allman, C., Mekle, R., . . . Rothwell, J. C. (2011). Relationship between physiological measures of excitability and levels of glutamate and GABA in the human motor cortex. *Journal of Physiology, 589*(23), 5845–5855.

Stagg, C. J., Lin, R. L., Mezue, M., Segerdahl, A., Kong, Y., Xie, J., & Tracey, I. (2013). Widespread modulation of cerebral perfusion induced during and after transcranial direct current stimulation applied to the left dorsolateral prefrontal cortex. *Journal of Neuroscience, 33*(28), 11425–11431.

Steinberg, H. (2013). Letter to the editor: Transcranial direct current stimulation (tDCS) has a history reaching back to the 19th century. *Psychological Medicine, 43*(3), 669–671.

Strafella, A. P., Paus, T., Barrett, J., & Dagher, A. (2001). Repetitive transcranial magnetic stimulation of the human prefrontal cortex induces dopamine release in the caudate nucleus. *Journal of Neuroscience, 21*(15), Rc157.

Thickbroom, G. W. (2007). Transcranial magnetic stimulation and synaptic plasticity: Experimental framework and human models. *Experimental Brain Research, 180*(4), 583–593.

Ueyama, E., Ukai, S., Ogawa, A., Yamamoto, M., Kawaguchi, S., Ishii, R., & Shinosaki, K. (2011). Chronic repetitive transcranial magnetic stimulation increases hippocampal neurogenesis in rats. *Psychiatry and Clinical Neurosciences, 65*(1), 77–81.

Valero-Cabré, A., Payne, B. R., Rushmore, J., Lomber, S. G., & Pascual-Leone, A. (2005). Impact of repetitive transcranial magnetic stimulation of the parietal cortex on metabolic brain activity: A 14C-2DG tracing study in the cat. *Experimental Brain Research, 163*(1), 1–12.

Wassermann, E. M. (1998). Risk and safety of repetitive transcranial magnetic stimulation: Report and suggested guidelines from the International Workshop on the Safety of Repetitive Transcranial Magnetic Stimulation, June 5–7, 1996. *Electroencephalography and Clinical Neurophysiology, 108*(1), 1–16.

Wexler, A. (2017). Recurrent themes in the history of the home use of electrical stimulation: Transcranial direct current stimulation (tDCS) and the medical battery (1870–1920). *Brain Stimulation, 10*(2), 187–195.

7

Sympathetic Resonance as a Way of Altering Brain Waves and Behavioral States

Manuel F. Casanova,[1,2] Estate Sokhadze,[1] Emily L. Casanova,[1] Thomas Roussel,[3] Saliya Kirigeeganage,[4] and John F. Naber[4]

The brain is a function-generating power supply that creates relatively low frequency, low amplitude voltages that vary over time. In a simplistic way, we can envision the brain as a "black box" that can be studied by attaching two or more electrodes to its surface. There are a limited number of direct electrical measurements that can be made in such a setup, the simplest one being an open circuit voltage reading when no current is being drawn. Theoretically, this would be the highest voltage that can be obtained from the system. The resultant voltage is a time dependent variable that, after proper manipulation (i.e., amplification and filtering), can be displayed on an oscilloscope or recording chart. The tracing thus obtained, using the brain as a load, is an electroencephalogram (EEG). The frequencies contained within the signals recorded by the EEG are typically divided into different bandwidths according to their association with different behavioral states and levels of consciousness. Low frequencies such as delta waves (1–4 Hz) are associated with deep dreamless sleep and high frequencies (30 to 100 Hz) with states of ecstasy and concentration.

The gelatinous consistency of the brain makes it susceptible to injury. The skull provides a protective covering to the

[1]University of South Carolina School of Medicine Greenville, Department of Biomedical Sciences
[2]Greenville Health System, Department of Pediatrics
[3]University of Louisville, Department of Bioengineering
[4]University of Louisville, Department of Electrical and Computer Engineering

brain that isolates and guards it from the immediate environment. The structure cushions impacts and, in doing so, has spared humans from countless episodes of traumatic brain injury throughout our evolutionary history. While the protective nature of the skull directly shields the brain from physical trauma, it does little, if anything, to block or attenuate electromagnetic fields. The composition of bone, i.e., collagenous fibers and minerals, makes for a poorly conductive material and has little effect on the electromagnetic field at low frequencies. This is in stark contrast to a grounded metal mesh (i.e., a Faraday cage), as the latter is able to attenuate the electromagnetic field at all frequencies without allowing its internal contents to be affected (e.g., the brain).

The skull is virtually transparent to ambient electromagnetic radiation thus allowing the brain to be susceptible to their effects. The Earth is surrounded by a mixture of gasses held in place by gravity. There are electromagnetic waves generated by electrical activity in the atmosphere (e.g., lightning storms, solar flares, sunspots) from the surface of the earth to the border of the ionosphere, approximately 55 kilometers in altitude. The baseline (fundamental) frequency of these types of electromagnetic radiation is about 7.8 Hz with a daily variation as high as + 0.7 Hz (Chand, Israil, & Rai, 2009). This frequency and its overtones are known by the eponym of "Schumann resonance frequencies," named after its discoverer Winfried Otto Schumann. Early studies by Herbert König (1977) showed a direct correlation between electromagnetic fields in the environment and alpha brain frequencies (8–13 Hz) in humans (for reviews see Beck, 1978 and Schlegel & Füllekrug, 2002).

In a recent article in the *Scientific American*, the question of whether electromagnetic radiation can affect brain function was answered with a definite "yes" (Raz, 2006). The effect of electromagnetic radiation on the brain is not limited to low frequencies, like the Schumann resonance frequency previously discussed, but is also affected at higher frequencies as well. Kramarenko and Tan (2003) reported the generation of low frequency voltages in contralateral frontal and temporal lobes as a result of exposure to a cell phone antenna (800 MHz to 1900 MHz). The phenomenon occurred some 20 to 40 seconds after initiating its use and recorded using a telemetric electroencephalograph (ExpertTM). The phenomenon was observed in both adults and children, except that in children the frequencies were lower and of longer duration.

Electrophysiology and the Brain

Present day attempts at modulating the activity of the brain rely on four different mechanisms:

The induction of electrical activity by the action of a varying magnetic field upon anatomical elements within the brain. This is the basic mechanism by which transcranial magnetic stimulation (TMS) works. TMS has been approved by the FDA as a therapeutic modality for treatment of drug resistant depression.

Passing an electric current directly through the brain. The applied current triggers a brief seizure in electroconvulsive therapy (ECT or shock treatment). In order to avoid some side effects of convulsions (e.g., bone fractures, dislocation of the long bones), the psychiatrist pre-treats ECT patients with anesthetics and muscle relaxants. Some patients exhibit confusion and memory loss after treatment. ECT is currently used in the treatment of major depression, mania and catatonia.

- Training the brain by watching a real-time display of its activity—a technique called neurofeedback. An individual may learn how to self-regulate his/her brain function using neurofeedback. Potential mechanisms of action for neurofeedback are changes in global neural connectivity, neuroplasticity, and/or reinforcement of the default mode network, central executive network, and salience network (Niv, 2013). Neurofeedback is frequently used in attention deficit hyperactivity disorder (ADHD). Fatigue, both physical and mental, is the most commonly reported side effect, and is often the result of overexertion during training.

- Neural or brainwave entrainment refers to procedures that cause the brain to synchronize its frequency with a periodic sensory stimulus such as sound, vibration or light. Probably the earliest use of acoustic neural entrainment was the beating of drums at a constant rate in shamanic rituals. According to Bennett and associates (2002), "Such entrainment occurs because small amounts of energy are transferred between the two systems when they are out of phase in such a way as to produce negative feedback. As they assume a more stable phase relationship, the amount of energy gradually reduces to zero, with the system of greater frequency slowing down, and the other speeding up." Other types of entrainment have used photic (i.e., light) stimulation. It is believed that strobe flashes at certain frequencies may entrain brainwaves and that individuals susceptible to these frequencies may manifest seizures. (Note: In 1997, a Japanese television station broadcasted a cartoon where light and sound caused a strobe effect. Shortly afterwards 700 children were taken to hospitals with seizures and many others complaining of headaches, dizziness and nausea)
- In addition, entrainment using electromagnetic fields has been achieved using solenoids to produce small magnetic fields in the nanoT and microT range (Persinger, Richards, & Koren,1997). This technique has been used within several experimental contexts (Bell, Marino, & Chesson, 1992; von Klitzing, 1991; note:

Solenoids are coils of wire often wrapped around a solid core material whose purpose is to generate a magnetic field that typically actuates the movement of a mechanical mechanism such as a piston).

Historical Highlights

It can be said that modulatory attempts by using the principle of induction of electricity and by passing a current directly through the brain have their origin in Hippocratic thought. Hippocrates (460–370 BC) believed that our human emotions and behaviors were the result of a balance between different body fluids or "humors." The normal or healthy condition was a result of the proper balance between the body fluids and the external environment. An excess or deficiency of these humors produced changes in temperament and/or in health. In modern times this "push-pull" type of mentality has made its way into our therapeutic armamentarium. Pathology is now ascribed to hyper- or hypoactivity of brain areas and treatment is offered in order to counteract these metabolic states. This monolithic way of thinking does not take into account how different brain areas work together in different networks (Wheeler, 2012), how areas of the brain may be affected when they serve as a hub of connectivity, or the cascading effect that they may have on other areas of the brain at subthreshold levels.

In more modern times, early 1900's, Dr. Albert Abrams popularized the idea that living beings, including humans, functioned within the bounds of frequencies detectable throughout their tissues (Evans, 2017). According to this school of thought, which he named Radionics, disease occurred when the body worked outside the normal range of frequencies. These frequencies radiated outwards from the body and were detectable with special devices that he created. Wires from his device would be attached to a drop of blood from the patient and other wires to the forehead of a normal volunteer. He would then tap the body of the volunteer looking for areas of dullness. These areas pinpointed, by proxy, the health problem of the patient providing the blood sample. Radionics claimed that matching the frequency of the patient to that of healthy controls would promote their cure.

Dr. Abrams misused the term frequency in order to make reference to a certain type of energy similar to that of dowsing (the use of divination rods) or Kirlian (aura) photography. His instruments did not provide for an operational electrical circuit, and many times did not require a power cord. Although Radionics attracted a large following it has no scientifically verifiable mechanism of action and Dr. Abrams himself received the appellation of the "Dean of 20th Century Charlatans" by the American Medical Association (Wilfried & Nowak, 2007).

Contemporaneously to Radionics, Royal Raymond Rife developed a frequency generator meant to kill disease causing organisms in cells. The machine used the principle of resonance in order to match the presumed frequency generated by pathogens to that of the generator. Over the years, claims were made that the Rife machine could cure anything from hair loss and anal itching to cancer. Patients would hold electrodes or pads from a machine tuned to a particular frequency that was compatible with the ailment. In some cases, a piezo buzzer allowed you to hear the tone generated by the machine. These pad type devices were usually powered by 12-volt batteries while others, using plasma tubes, required higher power sources. The plasma tubes, made for patient contact or not, generated high radio frequency emissions along with respective sidebands. These devices are not registered by the US Food and Drug Administration and have figured prominently in many cases of health fraud (for more information see Evans, 2017).

In recent years pulsed electromagnetic field therapy (pEMF) devices have been created to deliver various frequencies at different intensities through full body mats or localized pads (Meyers, 2014). In many cases practitioners of these techniques have adopted the idea of a "biofield" and attempt to treat the averaged frequencies of cells throughout the whole body. One recent attempt is that of NeuroField (Dogris, 2009) that does not use contact electrodes and is sometimes used in conjunction with neurofeedback. The NeuroField device is presently registered with the FDA as a 510K exempt equipment. It generates frequencies from 0.3 Hz to 300,000 Hz with an output intensity range from 1 to 50 microTesla and the ability to generate sine, triangle, and square wave forms.

Sympathetic Resonance (Passive Resonance or Coupled Oscillators)

A major problem with present day electrophysiological interventions is the fact that they operate or are administered at a different energy level from that observed in the normal brain. Hodgkin and Huxley characterized the current density through the giant axon of the squid as 1 mA/cm2. In a typical synapse, with a much smaller cross-sectional area compared to the squid axon, the response may be only a few picoAmps (10-12 Amps) (Pugh, 2000) for a fraction of a second. In contrast, ECT passes approximately 900 mA through the brain and the current is sustained for several seconds. Electrophysiological methods in this regard bombard the brain with stimuli of much higher amplitudes to what it is accustomed. The end result in using ECT or TMS for the brain is the induction of a high amplitude signal whose effects may be non-linear and non-physiological. It is for this reason that other therapeutic techniques that work within the physiological range of activity of the brain are required.

Sympathetic resonance describes the phenomenon by which a passive vibratory object responds to external vibrations to which it has a harmonic likeness. The classic example for this is when two identical tuning forks are brought in close proximity and are placed nearby on top of a wooden table. If one of them is struck making its tines vibrate, the unstruck mounted tuning fork will also vibrate. Another example is the rattling of a windowpane when a train passes nearby. These are passive phenomena that make an object react or adapt to an external exigency while working within their own resonance limits. In other words, with sympathetic resonance the object works within its biological operational parameters and does not exert itself.

A sympathetic resonator works with the brain and helps it adjust to required frequencies according to the behavioral state of the individual. In effect, this would be a non-invasive pacemaker for the brain where low frequency outputs from a radio frequency (RF) signal generator are radiated and "experienced" by the brain. The exact mechanisms by which different electrophysiological techniques work (e.g., TMS, ECT) are not well known. By way of contrast sympathetic or passive resonance starts with a mechanism of action and has then looked for appropriate medical conditions wherein applying the same would be of use.

In terms of the equipment required, an antenna serves to optimize and control the emitted radiation (e.g., the strength of the radiated field in a given direction) so as to maximize coupling of the energy from the signal generator to free space. The distance to the target is very small providing for little attenuation and no free space path loss. The scenario is different from the loss of power observed during traditional radio transmission where one millionth-millionth of the power leaving the transmitter is coupled into the receiver (Sinclair, 1997).

Radiation from an antenna can be envisioned by means of an analogy. Imagine using your hand as a paddle and waving it back and forth over a bowl of water in order to create waves. By increasing the speed of your hand, a frequency will be reached at which a large body of water will move in unison and splash over the border of the bowl. Whether splashing occurs depends on the length of the bowl and frequency of your hand movement. Similar to this analogy, radiation from an antenna (splashing of the water outside of the bowl) will depend on its length and the frequency of the voltage (length of bowl and how rapidly your hand is moving).

In sympathetic resonance, the wavelength of the electromagnetic radiation, from 2–60 Hz, assures activity in the inductive or near field. (Note: near field is named because its effects are concentrated near the source and makes reference to a distance less than one wavelength from the antenna). The inductive field is the region where energy is being shifted back and forth between the electric circuit and the field. In this space, the nature of the wave depends on source characteristics rather than on the propagation medium. Also, in near field the use of high currents/low voltages provides mainly for magnetic radiation or effects. Outside of the inductive region the field loses its connection to the source and radiates as a combination of electrical and magnetic waves. Absorption of radiation in the far field decreases as the square of the distance and absorption does not feed-back or affect the load of the transmitter.

Resonant lengths of a conductor (half a wavelength of the antenna or an odd multiple of the same) can be used to give directionality to the radiation (note: this is the Yagi type of antenna). These extra conductors or parasitic elements[1] have a maximum effect when placed side-on the incident wavefront and have a zero effect when the conductor is placed end-on. Parasitic elements longer than the resonant length will reflect

[1]Conductors that affect the directionality of a signal and are not powered are called parasitic. Those that minimize radiation in their direction are called reflectors and those that maximize the signal in their direction are called directors.

a signal away from its direction while shorter ones will lead the signal to greater concentrations in its direction.

The signal generator allows for the selection of frequency, voltage amplitude and type of wave (e.g., sinusoidal, square) while a reflectometer provides a measure of impedance matching and reflected waves. The use of multiple leads helps entrain brain areas to develop coherence in medical conditions where neural binding has been shown to be abnormal (e.g., autism, schizophrenia).

Brain waves are considered to be extremely low frequency and as such have correspondingly long wavelengths, i.e., more than 10,000 kilometers. Because of the difficulty in building antennas capable of radiating these low frequencies, the information or intelligence is delivered to the brain by using a high frequency carrier wave. Think of modulation as mailing a letter. The information is in the letter and the carrier wave is the envelope. The mailing route is the direction the radio frequencies travel after leaving the antenna. In amplitude modulation, the intelligence or information is contained within the contour of the modulated waveform. The high frequency carrier allows for radiation of the signal while its higher energy level ensures penetration of the biological system. The higher frequency also helps to focus the energy in the wave (inversely lower frequencies tend to radiate in a broader area over distance). The close apposition of the transmitting antenna to the skull minimizes noise (i.e., any unwanted interference with the signal).

High frequency waves (e.g., radio waves) are well above the response capabilities (ability to establish resonance) of the brain or the human ear. For practical purposes this carrier frequency, as well as its sidebands (for standard AM), will be invisible to the brain (note: this point may be arguable, see Fields, 2008, Kramarenko & Tan, 2003). Riding on this carrier wave is the desired low frequency that affects the brain. The amplitude of the high frequency is varied in accordance with the low or intelligent frequency and the multiple leads help establish coherence between different brain regions. The modulated signal causes the less powerful brain frequency to fall into a desired rhythm and consequent behavioral state.

High-end function generators have the inbuilt capacity to produce high frequency signals and modulated waveforms. They allow the use of different carrier waveforms at high frequencies (GHz), adjustment of the voltage level, the selection of various analogue modulation techniques, the depth of modulation, and the source for coupling (i.e., internal or external to the function generator). Most function generators have oscillators that produce a high-quality sine wave. This is of importance as imperfections to the sine wave may be misinterpreted as information. The generator may also use an amplifier to increase its power output or one may be serially added to the same.

The availability of a high-end function generator is an absolute requirement as there are multiple analog circuit designs capable of generating amplitude modulated signals. Some of the simplest ones allow miniaturization of the passive resonator. These circuits use crystals, audio transformers, transistors, or audio operational amplifiers like the LM358. Although the radiated waveforms of these simple circuits are of low power they may be of use in "take home" applications such as the treatment of insomnia or increasing the attention skills of gamers.

The preferred antenna is the magnetic or small loop type, essentially a coil, which due to its small size can be more easily apposed to the scalp of the patient. In addition, contrary to a rod antenna that generates an omnidirectional radiation pattern, a small loop antenna can be oriented to maximize the direction of radiation. The size of the small loop antenna is smaller than a wavelength of the carrier frequency. In order to increase its radiation efficiency a ferrite rod can be inserted inside the windings of the antenna. The inductive reactance of the antenna can be cancelled by a variable capacitor placed in parallel to the coil. The inductor or coil with the parallel capacitor would form a tuned or resonant/tank circuit. Also, the wire can be wound with litz (braided) wire to reduce skin effect losses.

When using passive resonance some care should be taken in the testing environment. There are many metal surfaces that could form resonant reflectors and whose overall effect will depend on the power and wavelength of the radiation. Although the low power employed in passive resonance may remove possible side effects from consideration, it is useful to remember that stray resonances may cause localized hot spots that may prove hazardous to those chronically exposed. Indeed, dielectric heating is the process by which a radio wave heats an insulator or dielectric material. The human body can act as a dielectric and receive severe burns when standing near a high-power transmitter. The resultant injury would be similar to that received if the dielectric was placed inside of a microwave oven. Since the heating effect varies with the power of the transmission, it is doubtful that passive resonance poses any serious peril in this regard. Safety indices based on specific absorption rates (SAR) have been published based on the International Commission on Non-Ionizing Radiation Protection (ICNIRP, 1998).

Electromagnetic Modelling of Induced Signals Into the Brain

Various electrophysiological techniques have been discussed to modulate the brain activity for therapeutic or other reasons. Although the desired results can be achieved, the exact mechanisms of the workings of these techniques are not well understood. Furthermore, questions have been raised about the effects of EM waves on human health as man-made EM activities keep increasing. Specifically, the high-frequency effects on the human brain due to the use of mobile phones have been studied extensively. Modelling the effects of EM waves in the human brain is one of the best methods to provide insight into understanding this behavior and their effects on the brain.

Researchers utilize different simulation and modelling techniques to study the effects of EM waves in the brain (Elloian, Noetscher, Makarov, & Pascual-Leone, 2014; Gabran, Saad, Salama, & Mansour, 2009; Schmidt & Van Rienen, 2012). One such modelling technique is to utilize data from a brain atlas such as the SRI24 multi-channel atlas (Rohlfing, Zahr, Sullivan, & Pfefferbaum, 2010). The brain atlas can produce detailed models using MRI images and tissue segmentation data. Less detailed models can be used depending on the purposes of the simulation. In such cases, simplified finite element method (FEM) models are used. However, if time domain simulations were also performed using FEM for a range of frequencies, different simulation runs would have to be run to account for the different frequency regions. It is very time consuming and tedious to perform different simulation runs for each set of frequencies. In such situations, finite difference time domain (FDTD) simulations are primarily used. A single simulation run of a FDTD simulation can cover a range of frequencies giving more flexibility to the user. Although these techniques can provide better insights to the brain and the effects of EM waves on it, the simulations can take significant time and use extensive computer resources. Therefore, other recent techniques have been proposed and explored to increase the computational efficiency of these type of simulations. One such technique is to scale the material parameters inside the head and to perform the simulations at a higher frequency (Jain, Mittra, & Wiart, 2015). These results are then extrapolated to an actual system at a lower frequency. This technique is used to model brainwaves that are modelled as EM waves operating in the frequency range of 0.1–100 Hz.

As stated before, the modelling and simulation of electrophysiological behavior in the brain can reveal information that is not well known or understood and help improve the effectiveness of such techniques. The first computational study comparing the electric fields induced by different electroconvulsive therapy (ECT) and magnetic seizure therapy (MST) techniques was Zhi-De et al. (2011). They concluded that the typical ECT pulse amplitude of 800–900mA exceeds the required threshold for seizure induction by more than six times. This study also suggests possible biophysical explanations for the reduced side effects of MST compared to ECT. In another FEM study, researchers have explored the alterations to the transcranial magnetic stimulation (TMS) induced current density distributions due to symmetric brain atrophy and widened sulci (Wagner et al., 2008). Although the presence of such structural abnormalities to the extent of the models in the simulation study is unlikely, a combination of both, to a certain degree, has always been observed. This study predicts that atrophy and/or widened sulci could create unintended perturbations in the TMS induced current densities and lead to unreliable results that could even be dangerous. Other simulation studies that use minimum simplifications to the cell properties have also been performed to better understand the mechanisms of TMS, TES (transcranial electric stimulation) and ECT (Wu, Fan, Lee, & Li, 2016). Such studies have made revelations that were not predicted by previous studies exhibiting the importance of further simulation studies.

In summary, sympathetic resonance couples the oscillatory voltage stemming from the brain and thus retains the neurophysiological properties of the system. The applied frequencies of a passive resonator reinforce or intensify intrinsic brainwave frequencies therefore propitiating targeted behavioral states. The use of sympathetic resonance would be of benefit in multiple medical conditions including autism, dyslexia, ADHD, major depression and schizophrenia. Low frequencies could be applied to help people fall and remain asleep in cases of insomnia, while portable helmets and higher frequencies could help individuals remain alert as in the case of fighter pilots (Beck, 1978), traffic controllers, and gamers. In the future, passive or sympathetic resonance could be combined with neurofeedback and/or cognitive behavioral therapy (CBT). Sympathetic resonance should have very little, if any side effects, and differ in this regard substantially from pharmacological interventions. Furthermore, sympathetic resonance as a therapeutic modality is not meant to be symptomatic but aimed at some of the core pathology of the conditions to which it is applied. Although simulation studies have not been performed until present, they may serve to pinpoint mechanisms and limitations of the technique.

References

Beck, R. C. (1978). Preliminary research report ELF magnetic fields and EEG entrainment. Retrieved from http://www.elfis.net/elfol8/e8elfeeg2.htm

Bell, G., Marino, A.A., & Chesson, A. L. (1992). Alterations in brain electrical activity caused by magnetic fields: Detecting the detection process. *Electroencephalography and Clinical Neurophysiology, 83,* 389–397.

Bennett, M., Schatz, M. F., Rockwood, H., & Wiesenfeld, K. (2002). Huygens's clocks. *Proceedings: Mathematics, Physical and Engineering Sciences, 458*(2019), 563–579.

Chand, R., Israil, M., & Rai, J. (2009). Schumann resonance frequency variations observed in magnetotelluric data recorded from Garhwal Himalayan region India. *Annales Geophysicae, 27*, 3497–3507.

Dogris, N. (2009). NeuroField. *NeuroConnections, ISNR, Winter,* 21–24.

Elloian, J. M., Noetscher, G. M., Makarov, S. N., & Pascual-Leone, A. (2014). Continuous wave simulations on the propagation of electromagnetic fields through the human head. *IEEE Transactions on Biomedical Engineering, 61*(6), 1676–1683.

Evans, J. R. (2017). Historical overview of rhythmic stimulation procedures in health and disease. In J. R. Evans & R. P. Turner

(Eds.), *Rhythmic stimulation procedures in neuromodulation* (pp. 1–31). London, UK: American Academy Press.
Fields, R.D. (2008, May 7) Mind control by cell phone, *Scientific American*.
Gabran, S. R., Saad, J. H., Salama, M. M., & Mansour, R. R. (2009). Finite difference time domain (FDTD) modeling of implanted deep brain stimulation electrodes and brain tissue. *Conference proceedings: Annual International Conference of the IEEE Engineering in Medicine and Biology Society, 2009*, 6485–6488.
International Commission on Non-Ionizing Radiation Protection. (1998). Guidelines for limiting exposure to time-varying electric, magnetic, and electromagnetic fields (up to 300 GHz). *Health Physics, 74*(4), 494–522.
Jain, S., Mittra, R., & Wiart, J. (2015). Full wave modelling of brain waves as electromagnetic waves (invited paper). *Progress in Electromagnetics Research, 151*, 95–107.
König, H. L. (1977). *Unsichtbare umwelt*. München: Eigenverlag Herbert L. König.
Kramarenko, A. V., & Tan, U. (2003). Effects of high-frequency electromagnetic fields on human EEG: A brain mapping study. *International Journal of Neuroscience, 113*(7), 1007–1019.
Meyers, B. A. (2014). *PEMF: The 5th element of health*. Bloomington, IN: Balboa Press.
Niv, S. (2013). Clinical efficacy and potential mechanism of neurofeedback. *Personality and Individual Differences, 54*(6), 676–686.
Persinger, M. A., Richards, P. M., & Koren, S. (1997). Differential entrainment of electroencephalographic activity by weak complex electromagnetic fields. *Perceptual and Motor Skills, 84*,527–536.
Pugh, O. (2000). What is the amperage of the electric current running through neurons? Retrieved from http://www.madsci.org/posts/archives/2000-04/955661195.Cb.r.html
Raz, A. (2006, April 24). Could certain frequencies of electromagnetic waves or radiation interfere with brain function? Scientific American. Retrieved from http://www.scientificamerican.com/article/could-certain-frequencies/
Rensberger, B. (1976, March 6). Jell-O test finds lifelike signal. NY Times, C6.
Rohlfing, T., Zahr, N. M., Sullivan, E. V., & Pfefferbaum, A. (2010). The SRI24 multi-channel atlas of normal adult human brain structure. *Human Brain Mapping, 31*(5), 798–819.
Schlegel, K., & Füllekrug, M. (2002). 50 years of Schumann resonance. *Physik in unserer Zeit, 33*(6), 256-261. A version translated into English can be found at http://www.hese-project.org/hese-uk/en/niemr/50_yrs_schumann.pdf
Schmidt, C., & Van Rienen, U. (2012). Modeling the field distribution

in deep brain stimulation: The influence of anisotropy of brain tissue. *IEEE Transactions on Biomedical Engineering, 59*(6), 1583–1592.

Sinclair, J. (1997). How radio signals work. New York: McGraw - Hill.

Von Klitzing, L. (1991). A new encephalomagnetic effect in human brain generated by static magnetic fields. *Brain Research, 540*(1–2), 295–296.

Wagner, T., Eden, U., Fregni, F., Valero-Cabre, A., Ramos-Estebanez, C., Pronio-Stelluto, V., ... Pascual-Leone, A. (2008). Transcranial magnetic stimulation and brain atrophy: A computer-based human brain model study. *Experimental Brain Research, 186*(4), 539–550.

Wheeler, M. (2012, February 27). Hyperactivity in brain may explain multiple symptoms of depression. UCLA Newsroom. Retrieved from http://newsroom.ucla.edu/releases/hyperactivity-in-brain-may-explain-228954

Wilfried, A., & Nowak, H. (2007). Magnetism in medicine: A handbook. New York: Wiley.

Wu, T., Fan, J., Lee, K. S., & Li X. (2016). Cortical neuron activation induced by electromagnetic stimulation: A quantitative analysis via modelling and simulation. *Journal of Computational Neuroscience, 40*(1), 51-64.

Zhi-De, D., Sarah, H. L., & Angel, V. P. (2011). Electric field strength and focality in electroconvulsive therapy and magnetic seizure therapy: A finite element simulation study. *Journal of Neural Engineering, 8*(1), 016007.

8

Research and Treatment Applications of Transcranial Direct Current Stimulation (tDCS) in Autism Spectrum Disorder

Dinisha Parmar, Freya J. Stockman, Soukayna Bekkali, Natalia Albein-Urios, Peter H. Donaldson, and Peter G. Enticott

Cognitive Neuroscience Unit, School of Psychology, Deakin University, Geelong, Victoria, Australia

What is tDCS?

Transcranial direct current stimulation (tDCS) is a non-invasive brain stimulation technique that involves the application of weak electrical currents to the brain. Typically, this involves connecting a positive electrode (anode) and a negative electrode (cathode) to a battery powered device and running the current from the anode to the cathode. When placed against the scalp, some of the current generated by these electrodes is able to pass through brain tissue and deliver subtle neural stimulation. tDCS is used with the express purpose of modulating activity in one or more regions of the brain and examining the effects (physiological, cognitive-behavioral, or clinical) of this presumed modulation.

In both basic and clinical sciences, tDCS is used widely. For instance, tDCS is used in physiological research to probe the properties of the human motor system, in cognitive neuroscience to examine brain-behavior relationships, and in psychiatry and neurology for the development of new treatment

---

Correspondence to: Professor Peter G. Enticott, School of Psychology, Deakin University, 221 Burwood Highway, Burwood, Victoria, 3125, AUSTRALIA
Email: peter.enticott@deakin.edu.au
Phone: +61 3 9244 5504

Thank you to Ms. Emily Grundy for assistance with manuscript preparation.

applications. These are all relevant to potential applications of tDCS in autism spectrum disorder (ASD). tDCS might be used to better understand the neuropathophysiology of ASD (including links to neurocognitive aspects of ASD), but also to modulate brain activity for therapeutic purposes.

There are a number of advantages to tDCS. It is relatively inexpensive, easy to use, and does not necessarily require extensive medical expertise or infrastructure (see section *Safety and Ethical Considerations*, this chapter). Before reviewing the use of tDCS in ASD, we provide a brief overview of the technique.

How does tDCS work?

While tDCS is often considered alongside other brain stimulation techniques such as transcranial magnetic stimulation (TMS), its biological mechanism of action is very different. tDCS is thought to exert an effect on neural excitability by influencing the flow of ions across the cellular membrane (Woods et al., 2016). The weakness of the current, which is necessary to avoid skin burns or lesions, prevents the direct generation of an axonal action potential (as is seen with TMS). It does, however, transiently change the resting membrane permeability of the stimulated cell, either depolarising or hyperpolarising the neuron. These changes are detectable following a sustained period of stimulation (typically 15-30 minutes), and often last beyond the period of stimulation. There may be a cumulative, longer-lasting effect of repeated sessions. Ultimately, tDCS results in neurons being either more excitable/likely to fire (i.e., during the period of depolarisation), or less excitable/likely to fire (i.e., during the period of hyperpolarisation).

The conventional wisdom is that neurons beneath the anode will depolarise, thus increasing excitability, while neurons beneath the cathode will hyperpolarise, thus decreasing excitability. This can be thought of as somewhat analogous to varying the frequency of TMS, where low-frequency stimulation (1Hz) seems to reduce cortical excitability and high-frequency stimulation (usually ≥5Hz) seems to increase cortical excitability. As with TMS, however, this understanding is derived primarily from studies of the primary motor cortex where changes in excitability can be easily probed by examining motor-evoked potentials MEPs). This involves administering single TMS pulses to the primary motor cortex and recording the response in peripheral muscle (typically hand) via electromyography (EMG). There is also no certainty that the effects will be identical when stimulating non-motor brain regions. Indeed, there is a good deal of evidence to suggest that these effects (i.e., anodal = excitatory, cathodal = inhibitory) do not apply across other brain regions, or at least that they do not apply consistently (Yavari, Jamil, Mosayebi Samani, Vidor, & Nitsche, 2018). Also similar to TMS, there is substantial inter-individual variability in the response to tDCS. For instance, some individuals will show either no effect of anodal or cathodal stimulation of M1, or the opposite effects (where cathodal stimulation actually increases excitability and vice-versa). There is a significant amount of controversy surrounding the use of tDCS, particularly in terms of the replicability of cognitive effects across studies (Horvath, Forte, & Carter, 2015).

How do we target specific brain regions with tDCS?

Conventional tDCS should not be considered a focal technique for targeting discrete brain regions. Where there is a single channel (i.e., two electrodes: one anode, one cathode) with typically sized electrodes (25-35cm^2) placed over opposite cerebral hemispheres, field modelling indicates that current will pass through a significant proportion of total brain tissue (see Figures 8.1 and 8.2). Even if current is maximal in the tissue under each electrode, the passing of current from one electrode to the next, and the "shunting" of current when penetrating the skull, ensures that brain stimulation will actually be quite diffuse. Although tDCS is often administered with the intention of modulating cortical excitability within a single region (e.g., M1, dorsolateral prefrontal cortex [DLPFC]), the placement of the other electrode, typically over another section of the head, ensures that maximal stimulation effects are unlikely to be limited to the region of interest, and that there may be opposite, unwanted effects (e.g., reduced excitability due to cathodal stimulation) at the so-called "reference" electrode site.

A recent development in tDCS technology, high-definition transcranial direct current stimulation (HD-tDCS), represents a promising alternative to conventional tDCS for enhancing stimulation focality. Rather than using a single anode and single cathode, HD-tDCS involves using an array of smaller electrodes to distribute current in a more controlled manner. A standard HD-tDCS montage is the 4 x 1 "ring" montage, which involves an anodal electrode surrounded by 4 cathodal electrodes (or vice-versa; see Figures 8.1 and 8.2). Current is then distributed from the anodal electrode across the cathodal electrodes, resulting in a reduced spread of current in the brain and more focal stimulation. Several software packages are available for modelling a montage's associated current induction in the brain, where the aim is usually to stimulate a region of interest and minimise the spread of current beyond that region. One disadvantage is that HD-tDCS often involves smaller intensities; when the stimulation intensity (measured in milliamperes, or mA) is held constant, the use of smaller electrodes will result in higher current density, which increases the risk of skin irritation or skin lesioning at the site of stimulation. Safety guidelines provide recommended maximum current densities for applying tDCS (Bikson et al., 2016).

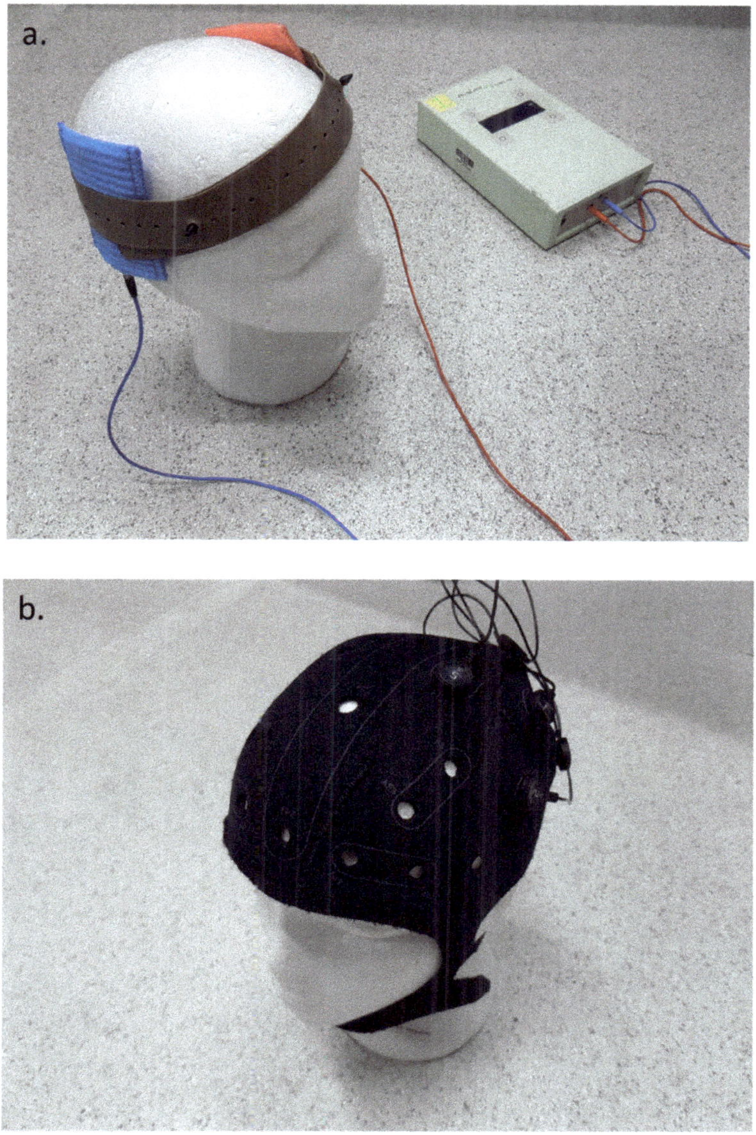

Figure 8.1. Example setup for standard tDCS (a. DC-STIMULATOR, neuroConn, Ilmenau, Germany) and HD-tDCS (b. STARSTIM, Neuroelectrics, Barcelona, Spain)

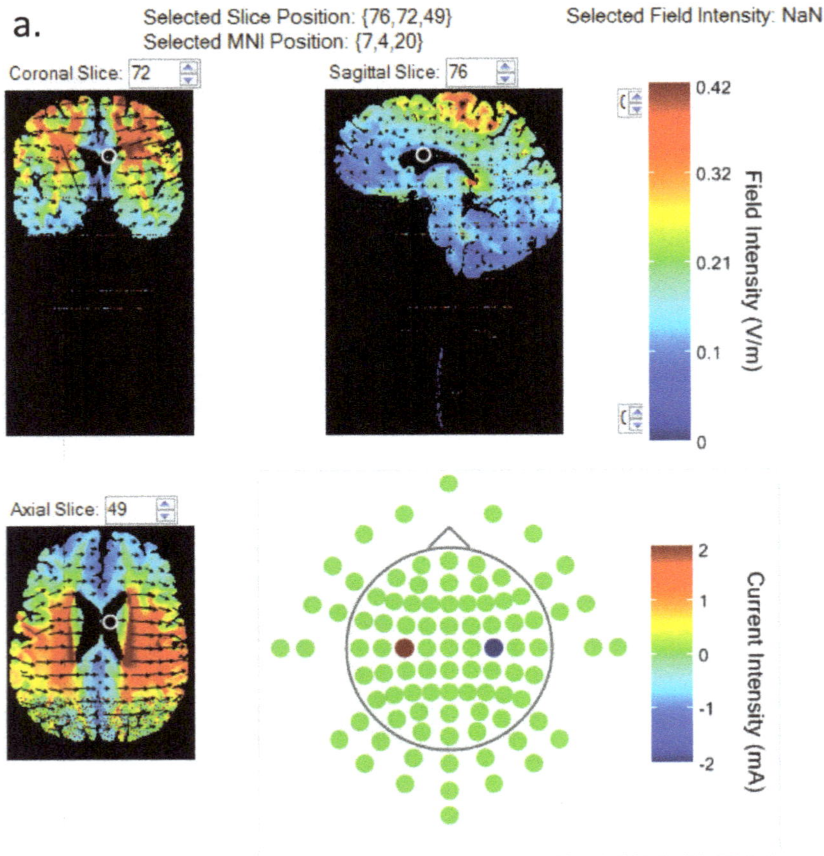

Figure 8.2. Example field induction for 2mA anodal M1 stimulation for standard tDCS (a.) and 4 x 1 HD-tDCS (b.).
Note the difference in field intensity scales.
Modelled using HD-Explore software, Soterix Medical, New York, NY

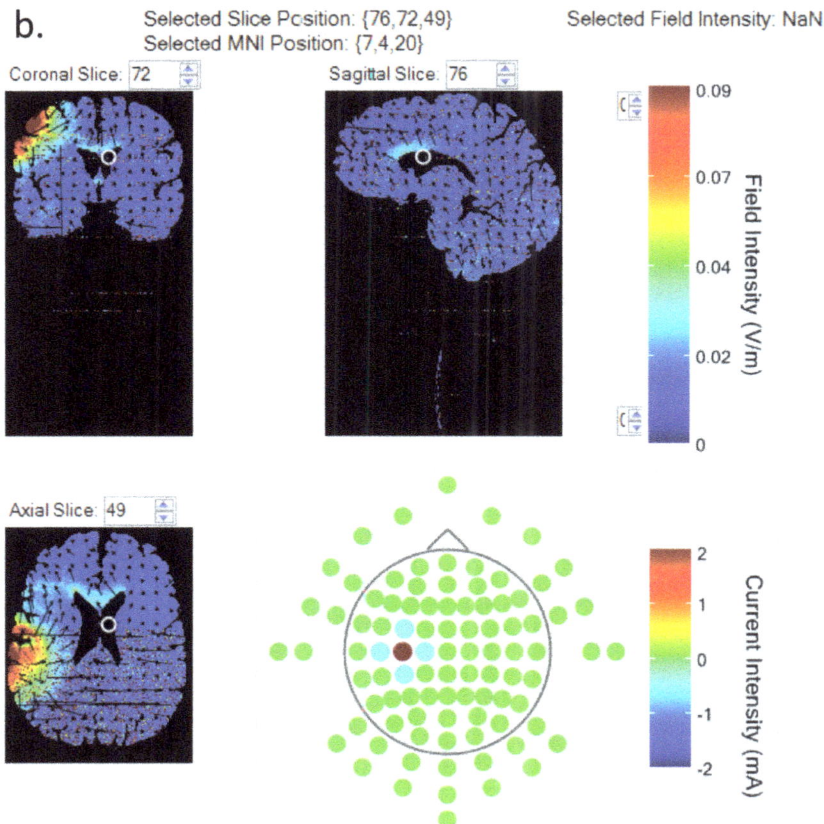
b.
Selected Slice Position: {76,72,49}
Selected MNI Position: {7,4,20}
Selected Field Intensity: NaN
Coronal Slice: 72
Sagittal Slice: 76
Axial Slice: 49
0.09
0.07
0.04
0.02
0
Field Intensity (V/m)
2
1
0
-1
-2
Current Intensity (mA)

Table 8.1
Published Reports of Therapeutic Application of tDCS, HD-tDCS, TACS, and TES in ASD (continued)

Paper	Diagnosis	Intellectual Disability	*n* (handedness)	Mean age (years)
Schneider and Hopp (2011), *Clinical Linguistics and Phonetics* (pre-post experimental design)	ASD	(n/a)	10 (right)	9.8
Amatachaya et al. (2014), *Behavioural Neurology* (RCT with sham control)	ASD	(n/a)	20 (8 left, 12 right)	6.4
D'Urso et al. (2014), *Biological Psychiatry* (case study)	ASD	(n/a)	1 (n/a)	(n/a)
Amatachaya et al. (2015), *Behavioural Neurology* (RCT with sham control)	ASD	None	20 (8 left, 12 right)	6.4
Costanzo et al. (2015), *Brain Stimulation* (case study)	ASD	Mild	1 (n/a)	(n/a)

Note. No studies used tACS, Abbreviations: ASD = Autism Spectrum Disorder; DLPFC = dorsolateral prefrontal cortex; HD-tDCS = high definition-transcranial magnetic stimulation; HFA = high functioning autism; IFC = inferior frontal cortex; IFG = inferior frontal gyrus; PPC = posterior parietal cortex; RCT = randomized control trial; TACS = transcranial alternating current stimulation; tDCS = transcranial direct current stimulation; TES = transcranial electrical stimulation; TPJ = temporoparietal junction.

Gender	Medication	Stimulation	Anode
M (8), F (2)	(n/a)	tDCS	DLPFC (F3)
M	Pyritinol, Ritalin, Risperidone	tDCS	Left DLPFC (F3)
M	(n/a)	tDCS	None
M	Pyritinol, methylphenidate, Risperidone	tDCS	Left DLPFC (F3)
F	Promazine, Quetiapine, Carbolithium	tDCS	Left DLPFC

(continued)

Table 8.1
Published Reports of Therapeutic Application of tDCS, HD-tDCS, TACS, and TES in ASD (continued)

Paper	Diagnosis	Intellectual Disability	*n* (handedness)	Mean age (years)
D'Urso et al. (2015), *The World Journal of Biological Psychiatry* (pre-post experimental design)	ASD (all), epilepsy (1), down syndrome (1)	Mild to severe	10 (n/a)	20.2
Donaldson et al. (2017), *European Journal of Neuroscience* (RCT with sham control)	Healthy	None	53 (right)	25.1
English et al. (2017), *Autism Research* (pilot study)	Healthy	(n/a)	38 (right)	21.3
Gómez et al. (2017), *Behavioural Sciences* (RCT between-groups crossover design)	ASD	Mild to moderate	24 (n/a)	12.2
Nobusako et al. (2017), *Frontiers in Behavioral Neuroscience* (within-groups design with sham control)	Healthy	None	30 (right)	21.4
Van Steenburgh et al. (2016), *Molecular Autism* (Crossover design with sham control)	HFA	None	12 (n/a)	32.1

Gender	Medication	Stimulation	Anode
M (9), F (3)	Carbamazepine, Delorazepam, Lacosamide, Levetiracetam, Levomepromazine, Lithium, Lorazepam, Lormetazepam, Melatonine, Olanzapine, Oxcarbazepine, Paliperidone, Periciazine, Risperidone, Valproate	tDCS	Contralateral arm (lateral aspect)
M (23), F (30)	(n/a)	HD-tDCS	Right TPJ (P6)
M (18), F (16)	(n/a)	tDCS	Right PPC (P4 active, Cz reference)
(n/a)	(n/a)	(i) tDCS (*n*=4), (ii) rTMS (*n*=20)	(i) Proximal right arm
M (15), F (15)	(n/a)	tDCS	(i) Right TPJ (CP6), (ii) right IFC (FC6)
M (10), F (2)	(n/a)	(i) Left anodal tDCS, (ii) right anodal tDCS, (iii) sham tDCS	(i) Left DLPFC (F3), (ii) right DLPFC (F4), (iii) F3

(continued)

Table 8.1
Published Reports of Therapeutic Application of tDCS, HD-tDCS, TACS, and TES in ASD (continued)

Paper	Cathode
Schneider and Hopp (2011)	Right supraorbital region
Amatachaya et al. (2014)	Contralateral shoulder
D'Urso et al. (2014)	Left DLPFC (F3)
Amatachaya et al. (2015)	Contralateral shoulder
Costanzo et al. (2015)	Right DLPFC
D'Urso et al. (2015)	Left DLPFC (F3)
Donaldson et al. (2017)	Right TPJ (C6, TP8, PO8, P2)
English et al. (2017)	Right PPC (Cz active, P4 reference)
Gómez et al. (2017)	(i) Left DLPFC (F3)
Nobusako et al. (2017)	(i) Vertex, (ii) vertex
Van Steenburgh et al. (2016)	(i) F4, (ii) F3, (iii) F4

Intensity	Duration	Sessions	Blinding
2.0 mA	30 min (tDCS)	1	None
1.0 mA	(i) 20 min (tDCS), (ii) 20 min (sham)	5	Double
1.5 mA	20 min	10	(n/a)
1.0 mA	(i) 20 min (tDCS), (ii) 20 min (sham)	2	Double
1.0 mA	20 min (tDCS)	28	None
1.5 mA	20 min	10	(n/a)
2.0 mA	(i) 20 min (HD-tDCS), (ii) 20 min (sham)	1	Double
2.0 mA	(i) 9.76 min (tDCS), (ii) 20 min (sham)	2	(n/a)
1.0 mA	20 min (tDCS)	20	(n/a)
1.0 mA	(i) 20 min (TPJ tDCS), (ii) 20 min (IFC tDCS), (iii) 20 min (sham)	1	(n/a)
1.5 mA	(i) 39.5 min (left anodal tDCS), (ii) 39.5 min (right anodal tDCS), (iii) 39.5 min (sham)	3	Single

(continued)

Table 8.1
Published Reports of Therapeutic Application of tDCS, HD-tDCS, TACS, and TES in ASD (continued)

Paper	Measures	Assessment Times	Side Effects
Schneider and Hopp (2011)	Vocabulary Test, Syntax (VTS), Comprehension Test	Pre-treatment, post-treatment	(n/a)
Amatachaya et al. (2014)	Childhood Autism Rating Scale (CARS), Autism Treatment Evaluation Scale (ATEC), Children's Global Assessment Scale (CGAS), Clinical Global Impression-Improvement (CGI-I)	Pre-treatment, 7-days post-treatment	Well tolerated
D'Urso et al. (2014)	Aberrant Behavior Checklist (ABC)	Pre-treatment, post-treatment	(n/a)
Amatachaya et al. (2015))	ATEC, Peak alpha frequency (PAF)	Pre-treatment, immediately after, 24-hours, 48-hours, 72-hours, 7-days post-treatment	Transient erythematous rash post-active tDCS (*n*=3)

Reported Effects
Vocabulary mean scores significantly improved post-tDCS. Syntax mean scores significantly improved post-tDCS.
Autistic symptom severity decreased significantly post-tDCS with a lasting effect of 7-days. Social, sensory-cognitive awareness and health-behavioral problems were significantly improved post-tDCS with a lasting effect of 7-days. Psychosocial functioning was significantly improved post-tDCS with a lasting effect of 7-days. Global impressions of autistic symptoms improved significantly post-tDCS. No significant changes were observed in the sham group across all outcome measures.
A reduction in irritability (30%), social withdrawal (45%), and hyperactivity, non-compliance (58%) was recorded post-tDCS.
Significant negative association between changes in PAF (F3) and changes in ATEC total scores, health-behavioral problem scores, and social scores post-tDCS. Relative to baseline, PAF significantly increased immediately post-tDCS (Fp1, F7, F3, Fz), 24-hours post-tDCS (F3), and 72-hours post-tDCS (Fp2). No significant changes in PAF relative to baseline were observed following sham tDCS. ATEC social and health and behavioral problems scores decreased significantly 7-days post-tDCS relative to baseline. Autism problems reduced significantly post-tDCS relative to baseline with a lasting effect of 7-days, as well as 48-hours post-sham tDCS. No significant changes in ATEC total score, social scores, or health and behavioral problem scores observed following sham tDCS. No significant changes in language performance or sensory and cognitive awareness in either the tDCS or sham group.

(continued)

Table 8.1
Published Reports of Therapeutic Application of tDCS, HD-tDCS, TACS, and TES in ASD (continued)

Paper	Measures	Assessment Times	Side Effects
Costanzo et al. (2015)	Kanner Scale (KCRS)	Pre-treatment, 10th session, 20th session, 28th session, 1-month post-treatment	(n/a)
D'Urso et al. (2015)	ABC	Pre-treatment, post-treatment	Mild skin irritation (stimulation site)
Donaldson et al. (2017)	Autism-Spectrum Quotient (AQ), event-related potentials (ERPs), Fear Surprise Task (FST), Reading the Mind in the Eyes task (RME)	Pre-treatment, post-treatment	(n/a)

Reported Effects
Catatonic symptoms reduced by 30% (from 70 to 28) post-tDCS. Full recovery of autistic symptoms including impulsivity, grimacing, rigidity, stereotypy, eating competency, and excitement post-28-sessions of tDCS. Mildly improved mutism, staring, negativism, and combativeness post-28-sessions of tDCS. Improved grasp reflex, motor planning and waxy flexibility. Symptom reduction was stable at 1-month follow-up evaluation. Slight worsening of posturing detected.
Eighty percent of participants showed a 26.7% average reduction in abnormal behavior relative to pre-tDCS scores. Twenty percent of participants showed no significant changes post-tDCS relative to pre-tDCS scores. On average, participants showed a 23.7% significant reduction in ABC total scores post-tDCS. Autistic symptoms reduced significantly post-tDCS including irritability, agitation, crying, social withdrawal, lethargy, hyperactivity, and non-compliance.
Following sham-tDCS, higher AQ Switching scores were associated with improved RME accuracy. Cathodal tDCS accounted for 37.8% of variance in AQ Social scores which was non-significant, and 59.2% of variance in AQ Switching scores which was significant. Anodal tDCS accounted for 27% of variance in AQ Social scores which was non-significant. Following cathodal HD-tDCS, reduced improvements in static/surprise accuracy and static/fear reaction time were associated with higher AQ Social and AQ Switching scores. Following anodal HD-tDCS, increased latencies were associated with higher AQ Social scores. Increased left-hemisphere latencies were associated with higher AQ Social scores relative to right hemisphere. Sham HD-tDCS accounted for 69.2% of variance in RME accuracy change and active tDCS explained no variance. Higher AQ Switching scores were associated with improved RME accuracy post sham HD-tDCS, but not after active HD-tDCS.

(continued)

Table 8.1
Published Reports of Therapeutic Application of tDCS, HD-tDCS, TACS, and TES in ASD (continued)

Paper	Measures	Assessment Times	Side Effects
English et al. (2017)	AQ, Greyscales Task	During treatment	(n/a)
Gómez et al. (2017)	ABC, Autism Diagnostic Interview-Revisited Edition (ADI-R), ATEC, Global Clinical Impression Scale (GCIS)	One week pre-treatment, 1-week, 1-month, 3-months, 6-months post-treatment	(n/a)
Nobusako et al. (2017)	AQ, Imitation-Inhibition Task (IIT), Visual Perspective-Taking Task (VPTT)	Post-treatment	(n/a)
Van Steenburgh et al. (2016))	Brief Test of Attention (BTA), Wechsler Memory Scale, 3rd Edition (WMS-III)	Pre-treatment, 40 min post-treatment,	Well tolerated

Reported Effects
Anodal tDCS significantly increased pseudo-neglect (leftward bias) in the high-trait group, relative to sham tDCS, but had a no effect on the low-trait group. No significant changes in pseudo-neglect were recorded in the low-trait or high-trait group post-cathodal tDCS.
Global improvement in autistic symptoms according to pre-to-post scale scores. Significant reduction in ATEC, ADI-R, ABC total scores with lasting effect of 6-months. Increased brain functional connectivity was observed, predominantly the higher frequencies (alpha, beta and gamma).
Anodal tDCS applied over the TPJ and IFC significantly decreased the cost of perspective thinking in a perspective thinking task relative to sham tDCS. Anodal tDCS applied over the TPJ and IFC significantly decreased the interference effect in an imitation-inhibition task relative to sham tDCS. Reaction time significantly increased across all groups during incongruent trails compared to congruent trials. The cost of reaction time for perspective-taking significantly decreased in the IFC group, compared to the sham group. The interference effect for reaction time significantly decreased for the TPJ and IFC group compared to sham. Accuracy rate significantly decreased following sham tDCS compared to control conditions, but did not differ between TPJ and IFC groups. No significant differences in accuracy rate and reaction time in the IFC or TPJ group under experimental and control conditions. No significant changes were observed in AQ total scores or AQ subscale scores post-tDCS.
Participants who received right and left anodal active tDCS performed significantly better in working memory, relative to sham tDCS. Left anodal tDCS and right anodal tDCS were significantly associated with longer maximum spatial spans relative to sham group. Right anodal tDCS was significantly better than sham tDCS and left anodal tDCS in attention performance. Attention performance did not differ between left anodal tDCS and sham tDCS.

Transcranial Alternating Current Stimulation (tACS)

Transcranial electrical stimulation (tES) has multiple modes, including tDCS. Although it is the most widely used form of tES it is not the only one. Transcranial alternating current stimulation (tACS) is similar to tDCS, but instead of channelling current from anode to cathode at a fixed intensity, current direction switches back and forth between electrodes. It is possible to select a relatively high frequency of stimulation and there is evidence to suggest that neural activity can be "entrained" to oscillate at the same frequency as the frequency of stimulation (typically detected via electroencephalography [EEG]). For instance, if attempting to invoke greater gamma oscillatory power, tACS might be set at 40Hz (Janik, Rezlescu, & Banissy, 2015). This is particularly useful if certain frequencies or combinations of frequencies have been shown to be abnormal in a given clinical disorder, or if there is a particular frequency that is associated with superior cognitive performance. tACS, however, does not always produce detectable entrainment and the factors underpinning successful entrainment are not well understood.

tDCS Research in ASD

It is only in recent years that researchers have begun to investigate the use of tDCS in ASD. Unlike most entries in the DSM-5, there are no well-validated biomedical treatments for the core symptoms of ASD. The recent prevalence increase in ASD highlights the need for innovative intervention development, both cognitive-behavioral and biomedical. tDCS is one such potential intervention and this promise is derived from emerging studies investigating the behavioral and neural changes in children and young adults with ASD (see Table 8.1. Published Reports of Therapeutic Application of tDCS, HD-tDCS, TACS, and TES in ASD).

One of the first tDCS studies conducted in ASD was an open-label trial conducted by Schneider and Hopp (2011).

Participants included 10 individuals with ASD (aged 6-21 years). Language ability was evaluated before and after a single 30-minute session of anodal tDCS stimulation over the left DLPFC (2 mA). The corresponding cathode (reference) electrode was placed over the right supraorbital region. This is a widely used montage for DLPFC stimulation. The authors reported a significant improvement in mean scores for vocabulary and syntax comprehension following tDCS.

Subsequent research conducted by Amatachaya et al. (2014) investigated and evaluated the efficacy of anodal tDCS in 20 male participants (aged 5-8 years) with mild and moderate ASD. In this randomized, double-blind, cross over trial, improvements in ASD symptoms were measured by the Childhood Autism Rating Scale (CARS) and Autism Treatment Evaluation Checklist (ATEC) subscales, before and seven days after participants completed five consecutive days of both active tDCS and sham (non-active or placebo) stimulation. Participants received 1 mA of anodal stimulation over the left DLPFC for 20 minutes, while the reference cathodal electrode was placed on the right shoulder. Results from this study indicated the CARS and ATEC sociability, sensory, and cognitive awareness subscales improved significantly after active tDCS stimulation compared with sham.

Further published work from this group (Amatachaya et al., 2015) used the same sample and tDCS methods to report EEG outcomes. Comparing anodal and sham conditions, tDCS was associated with an increase of peak alpha frequency (PAF; i.e., precise frequency within the alpha range at which the individual shows the greatest power), which was thought to reflect increased cortical activity in the frontal regions. These findings were also linked to symptoms: PAF was associated with improvements on the ATEC social and health/behavioral subscales, suggesting that tDCS may have the potential to improve ASD symptoms.

In another trial, D'Urso et al. (2015) enrolled 12 adult participants (18+) with ASD and an intellectual disability in a cathodal DLPFC study. Change in clinical symptoms was measured using the Aberrant Behavior Checklist (ABC) autism scale. Only 10 participants completed the trial, which involved 20 minutes of only 1.5 mA of tDCS for 10 consecutive weekdays. From the 10 participants, two showed no improvements in clinical symptoms after the trial, whereas the remaining eight participants reported statistical improvement in abnormal behaviors and an average reduction of 26.7% of the total ABC score compared to baseline, including hyperactivity and non-compliance. Interestingly, the subscales which showed significant decreases in order were, subscale 4 (hyperactivity and non-compliance); subscale 1 (irritability, agitation and crying) and subscale 2 (social withdrawal and lethargy).

In a study providing perhaps the strongest evidence for the utility of tDCS in ASD thus far, working memory impairment was investigated by Van Steenburgh, Varvaris, Schretlen, Vannorsdall, and Gordon (2016) in 12 adults with "high-functioning" ASD (i.e., no intellectual disability). Using a single-blind, randomised crossover design, each participant received 40 minutes of left anodal/right cathodal stimulation, right anodal/left cathodal stimulation, or sham stimulation over the DLPFC on three separate days. During stimulation, participants engaged in working memory tasks including backward spatial span, backward digit span, spatial n-back, and letter n-back. Active tDCS (both left and right anodal stimulation) administered during working memory tasks was found to enhance performance, suggesting tDCS could reduce deficits of ASD related broadly to cognition and executive functioning.

Finally, Gómez et al. (2017) aimed to investigate the enduring effects of non-invasive brain stimulation (NBIS) techniques in ASD by using both repetitive transcranial magnetic stimulation (rTMS) and tDCS. Follow-up assessments were conducted at one, three, and six months after treatment. Twenty-four participants underwent either twenty sessions of tDCS (children under 11 years) or rTMS (children 11-13 years). Of these, four participants received 20 sessions of 1 mA tDCS with the cathode positioned over the left DLPFC and the anode over the proximal right arm. After one-month, specific improvements were seen in the total score of the Autism Disorder Interview – Revised (ADI-R), Autism Behavioral Checklist (ABC), and the ATEC. Interestingly, at six months the effects appeared to be maintained. Despite a slight rebound in total score on the ADI-R, ABC, and the ATEC, the observed difference remained lower than pre-treatment assessments.

While abovementioned studies provide valuable insight into the potential benefits of tDCS in ASD, researchers must be circumspect when interpreting these findings in light of methodological limitations. The sample size for most studies was around 10 participants (D'Urso et al., 2015; Gómez et al., 2017; Schneider & Hopp, 2011; van Steenburgh et al., 2016) and only one study recruited 20 participants (Amatachaya et al., 2014; Amatachaya et al., 2015). This has ramifications for both statistical power and sample representativeness, with the majority of the participants being male. A small sample size is concerning given (a) symptom heterogeneity in ASD, (b) the strong possibility of underpowered results, and (c) an increased likelihood of conflicting research and clinical findings. More critically, apart from Amatachaya et al. (2014; 2015) trials, several studies were not designed using strict clinical trial designs such as randomisation (D'Urso et al., 2015; Schneider & Hopp, 2011), double blinding with appropriate sham or active control conditions (Schneider & Hopp, 2011), or unambiguous ASD measures (Schneider & Hopp, 2011). Lack of blinding or use of sham-controlled conditions in most of the preliminary studies heightens concerns around the generalisation of studies. Studies that include a single tDCS session with a small sample size should be interpreted with extreme caution. Later in the chapter we discuss recommendations for future studies involving tDCS in ASD.

Case Studies of tDCS in Autism

Several tDCS case studies of ASD have been published, typically where biomedical and/or behavioral treatments have failed and clinical presentation has deteriorated. For example, D'Urso et al. (2014) reported on the case of a 26-year-old male with ASD who had an IQ score of 30 and presented with severe irritability, agitation, hyperactivity, and lack of compliance. Following 10 consecutive weekday sessions of twenty minutes 1.5 mA cathodal tDCS over the left DLPFC (anode placed extracephalically over the contralateral deltoid) a 40.2% reduction in behavioral symptoms was measured on the Aberrant Behavior Checklist after tDCS stimulation. Reduced symptom expression was stable at the three-month follow up.

Similarly, Costanzo et al. (2015) administered 28 consecutive sessions (excluding weekends) of tDCS to a 14-year old girl diagnosed with ASD, catatonia (alterations in motor, vocal and Behavioral signs), and mild intellectual disability (IQ = 58). After applying 1 mA of cathodal tDCS over the right DLPFC and anodal over the left DLPFC, a 30% reduction in catatonic symptoms was documented at the end of treatment. This was maintained at the one-month follow up. Importantly, Costanzo et al. state that symptoms including excitement, grimacing, stereotypy, rigidity, impulsivity, and refusal to eat and to drink had fully recovered for the adolescent patient.

Both case studies conducted by D'Urso et al. (2014) and Costanzo et al. (2015) included behavioral ratings based on parent reports. Although parent outcome measures are crucial in research with ASD participants, the effects recorded might have been biased by the positive expectations from treatment. Nevertheless, while the clinical findings from case studies cannot be generalised, they do provide promising results for further hypothesis-driven tDCS research in ASD.

Autism-Related Measures to Assess tDCS in Neurotypical Individuals

Recently published studies assessing tDCS or HD-tDCS in neurotypical individuals have employed autism-related measures (Donaldson, Kirkovski, Rinehart, & Enticott, 2017; English, Kitching, Maybery, & Visser, 2017; Nobusako et al., 2017) to better understand how brain stimulation and autistic traits might interact. While these studies have provided valuable insight into potential future applications for tDCS and HD-tDCS in ASD, the results reported among these studies vary in relation to ASD outcome measures.

Nobusako et al. (2017) applied tDCS to either the right temporoparietal junction (TPJ) or right inferior frontal cortex (IFC). As lesions to these brain regions have been reported to affect the severity of ASD, 30 healthy participants were divided into three equal groups: TPJ tDCS, IFC tDCS, or sham tDCS. This study was designed to assess whether anodal tDCS over the right IFC and TPJ affects imitation-inhibition and perspective taking, and the degree to which this might modulate autism spectrum quotient (AQ) scores. The authors found a significant improvement in the two tasks assessing imitation-inhibition and visual perspective-taking after 1 mA tDCS for 20 minutes, but no reduced effect on total AQ score or its subscale scores (social skills, attention switching, attention to detail, communication and imagination). Given that the AQ is a trait-based measure that evaluates behavior across long periods of time, it is not surprising that no immediate or short-term effect on AQ was observed.

In another trial conducted by our group, Donaldson et al. (2017) applied 20 minutes of HD-tDCS over the right TPJ (anodal, cathodal, or sham; between-subjects) in 53 healthy adults.

This is the only study published within the ASD literature that has included HD-tDCS, which achieves more focal stimulation than standard tDCS. Here, the aim of the study was to examine the interaction between the effect of HD-tDCS on social cognition (and event-related potentials [ERPs] relevant to facial emotion processing) and the AQ scores on the Social Skills and Attention sub-scales. Following cathodal stimulation, there was a reduction in emotional attribution in participants with high AQ switching and social scores, while anodal stimulation appeared to increase ERP latencies for those with higher AQ scores. The authors further suggested that depending on ASD trait levels, cathodal and anodal simulation may have varying effects across these domains.

In a pilot study by English et al. (2017), tDCS was administered over the right posterior parietal cortex to neuro-typical individuals with low levels and high levels of autistic traits. During the application of 2 mA tDCS, participants completed a greyscales tasks that assesses differences in attentional bias between low and high autism-like groups. Anodal tDCS increased leftward bias (pseudo-neglect) for high-trait autism but had no effect for low-trait individuals. There were no effects reported from cathodal tDCS.

Collectively, these studies yield interesting findings, but it is important to consider that they involve non-clinical samples, and generalisation to ASD populations in unclear. Active stimulation conditions in non-clinical participants may yield very different or mixed results compared with what would be seen in ASD. Despite this, these preliminary findings with neuro-typical individuals have the potential to enhance our understanding of the way in which brain stimulation interacts with autism traits and may inform future clinical studies.

Safety and Ethical Considerations

Of all non-invasive brain stimulation techniques currently in use, tDCS has perhaps the best safety profile. Unlike TMS, which has a small potential for seizure induction, there are no serious adverse neurological consequences that have been reported in relation to tDCS. Nevertheless, there are some possible side-effects. For instance, during stimulation, tDCS can produce uncomfortable burning, tingling, or itching sensations on the scalp (although these typically dissipate within minutes) (Bikson et al., 2016).

Despite this excellent safety profile, almost all tDCS work has been conducted on adults. Thus, relatively little is known regarding the impact of tDCS on the developing brain. Where tDCS is used in children, a conservative approach is strongly recommended. In a research context, this could involve beginning with short stimulation durations and low stimulation intensities, and only introducing gradual increases in duration and intensity if there is no evidence for serious side-effects (i.e., beyond those minor events typically seen with tDCS) or adverse events. Participants should be closely monitored both during and after stimulation, and neuropsychological assessment is also warranted to ensure that there is no discernible negative impact on cognitive function. As with all medical devices, clinical use should only be considered where there is ample empirical evidence for both safety and efficacy.

With respect to clinical trials, the use of standardised, comprehensive measures for assessing tolerability, side-effects, and adverse events should be considered mandatory. Unfortunately, many brain stimulation clinical trials involving TMS and tDCS do not collect such data, or at least do not report this in a systematic or comprehensive manner. There are exceptions though: for instance, Andrade et al. (2014) conducted a feasibility study of tDCS in 5-12-year-old children with ASD, stimulating Broca's area at 2 mA each weekday for two weeks. This is generally the highest stimulating intensity that would be delivered, so should be considered a robust initial assessment of feasibility and tolerability. While there were some adverse effects reported (tingling, itching, irritability, mood effects), it was concluded that tDCS in children with ASD was feasible and tolerable (with more data required around safety).

Future Directions for tDCS, HD-tDCS in ASD

The above-reviewed work is promising, but there are a number of recommendations that can be made for future directions in tDCS research for ASD applications. First and foremost, we require clinical trials that are much larger, double-blind, and sham-controlled. Outcome measures should be multimodal and comprehensive, including clinical, neuropsychological, neurophysiological, and tolerability assessment. There should be long periods of follow-up (e.g., 6-12 months) to determine the lasting effects of any changes. Work of this nature is both intensive and expensive; as with TMS for ASD, it is likely to be best achieved by collaborative, multisite trials (Oberman et al., 2016).

There are a number of additional, unanswered questions that will require extensive research. This includes determining the best schedule for stimulation delivery. For instance, initial evidence suggests that multiple, spaced sessions may increase the duration of behavioral effects to several weeks (Boggio et al., 2007; Boggio, Zaghi, Lopes, & Fregni, 2008; Reis et al., 2009). If tDCS is to prove safe and effective in ASD, it is entirely unclear as to which site or sites should be targeted and this must be clearly matched to the intended clinical effect. For instance, if targeting social relating, there are very well-defined cortical sites that contribute to the "social brain" and have shown abnormal activation in ASD (Kirkovski, Enticott, Hughes, Rossell, & Fitzgerald, 2016). The focality of stimulation is also likely to be very important, particularly when attempting to target very specific cortical regions as well as avoid unwanted effects at adjacent sites. HD-tDCS approaches seem to hold the most promise here(Edwards et al., 2013; Hogeveen et al., 2016; Villamar et al., 2013), and there are now a number of devices on the market that will allow this mode of stimulation. Finally, while most work has been done with tDCS, other TES approaches that attempt to entrain neural oscillations, such as tACS or transcranial pulsed current stimulation (tPCS), may be more amendable to remedying the synaptic and network-based deficits in ASD. These alternative forms of stimulation should be considered for clinical trial work.

Conclusion

tDCS is one of several non-invasive brain stimulation techniques that is being trialled in ASD and as with other techniques (e.g., TMS), it remains at a very preliminary stage. The small number of studies conducted to date are supportive of the potential efficacy and safety of tDCS in ASD, but this work has significant methodological limitations and we are a long way from clinical implementation of tDCS in ASD. There is, however, ample justification for continued research in this area. While this clinical trial work is resource-intensive and expensive to conduct, studies should strive to employ large samples, gold-standard assessment, and best-practice clinical trial methods for determining the short-, medium-, and long-term safety, efficacy, and neurophysiology of tDCS in ASD.

References

Amatachaya, A., Auvichayapat, N., Patjanasoontorn, N., Suphakunpinyo, C., Ngernyam, N., Aree-uea, B., . . . Auvichayapat, P. (2014). Effect of anodal transcranial direct current stimulation on autism: A randomized double-blind crossover trial. *Behavioral Neurology, 2014*, 173073.

Amatachaya, A., Jensen, M. P., Patjanasoontorn, N., Auvichayapat, N., Suphakunpinyo, C., Janjarasjitt, S., . . . Auvichayapat, P. (2015). The short-term effects of transcranial direct current stimulation on electroencephalography in children with autism: A randomized crossover controlled trial. *Behavioral Neurology, 2015, 928631*.

Andrade, A. C., Magnavita, G. M., Allegro, J. V. B. N., Neto, C. E. B. P., Lucena, R. d. C. S., & Fregni, F. (2014). Feasibility of transcranial direct current stimulation use in children aged 5 to 12 years. *Journal of Child Neurology, 29*(10), 1360–1365.

Bikson, M., Grossman, P., Thomas, C., Zannou, A. L., Jiang, J., Adnan,

T., . . . Woods, A. J. (2016). Safety of transcranial direct current stimulation: Evidence based update 2016. *Brain Stimulation, 9*(5), 641–661.

Boggio, P. S., Nunes, A., Rigonatti, S. P., Nitsche, M. A., Pascual-Leone, A., & Fregni, F. (2007). Repeated sessions of noninvasive brain DC stimulation is associated with motor function improvement in stroke patients. *Restorative Neurology and Neuroscience, 25*(2), 123–129.

Boggio, P. S., Zaghi, S., Lopes, M., & Fregni, F. (2008). Modulatory effects of anodal transcranial direct current stimulation on perception and pain thresholds in healthy volunteers. *European Journal of Neurology, 15*(10), 1124–1130.

Costanzo, F., Menghini, D., Casula, L., Amendola, A., Mazzone, L., Valeri, G., & Vicari, S. (2015). Transcranial direct current stimulation treatment in an adolescent with autism and drug-resistant catatonia. *Brain Stimulation: Basic, Translational, and Clinical Research in Neuromodulation, 8*(6), 1233–1235.

D'Urso, G., Ferrucci, R., Bruzzese, D., Pascotto, A., Priori, A., Altamura, C. A., . . . Bravaccio, C. (2014). Transcranial direct current stimulation for autistic disorder. *Biological Psychiatry, 76*(5), e5–e6.

D'Urso, G., Bruzzese, D., Ferrucci, R., Priori, A., Pascotto, A., Galderisi, S., . . . Bravaccio, C. (2015). Transcranial direct current stimulation for hyperactivity and noncompliance in autistic disorder. *The World Journal of Biological Psychiatry, 16*(5), 361–366.

Donaldson, P. H., Kirkovski, M., Rinehart, N. J., & Enticott, P. G. (2017). Autism-relevant traits interact with temporoparietal junction stimulation effects on social cognition: A high-definition transcranial direct current stimulation and electroencephalography study. *European Journal of Neuroscience, 47*(6), 669–681.

Edwards, D., Cortes, M., Datta, A., Minhas, P., Wassermann, E. M., & Bikson, M. (2013). Physiological and modeling evidence for focal transcranial electrical brain stimulation in humans: A basis for high-definition tDCS. *Neuroimage, 74*, 266–275.

English, M. C., Kitching, E. S., Maybery, M. T., & Visser, T. A. (2018). Modulating attentional biases of adults with autistic traits using transcranial direct current stimulation: A pilot study. *Autism Research, 11*(2), 385–390.

Gómez, L., Vidal, B., Maragoto, C., Morales, L. M., Berrillo, S., Vera Cuesta, H., . . . Cabrera, Y. (2017). Non-invasive brain stimulation for children with autism spectrum disorders: A short-term outcome study. *Behavioral Sciences, 7*(3), 63.

Hogeveen, J., Grafman, J., Aboseria, M., David, A., Bikson, M., & Hauner, K. (2016). Effects of high-definition and conventional tDCS on response inhibition. *Brain Stimulation: Basic, Translational, and Clinical Research in Neuromodulation, 9*(5), 720–729.

Horvath, J. C., Forte, J. D., & Carter, O. (2015). Evidence that transcranial direct current stimulation (tDCS) generates little-to-no reliable neurophysiologic effect beyond MEP amplitude modulation in healthy human subjects: A systematic review. *Neuropsychologia, 66*, 213–236.

Janik, A. B., Rezlescu, C., & Banissy, M. J. (2015). Enhancing anger perception with transcranial alternating current stimulation induced gamma oscillations. *Brain Stimulation, 8*(6), 1138–1143.

Kirkovski, M., Enticott, P. G., Hughes, M. E., Rossell, S. L., & Fitzgerald, P. B. (2016). Atypical neural activity in males but not females with autism spectrum disorder. *Journal of Autism and Developmental Disorders, 46*(3), 954–963.

Nobusako, S., Nishi, Y., Shuto, T., Asano, D., Osumi, M., & Morioka, S. (2017). Transcranial direct current stimulation of the temporoparietal junction and inferior frontal cortex improves imitation-inhibition and perspective-taking with no effect on the autism-spectrum quotient score. *Frontiers in behavioral neuroscience, 11*, 84.

Oberman, L. M., Enticott, P. G., Casanova, M. F., Rotenberg, A., Pascual-Leone, A., McCracken, J. T., & TMS in ASD Consensus Group. (2016). Transcranial magnetic stimulation in autism spectrum disorder: challenges, promise, and roadmap for future research. *Autism Research, 9*(2), 184-203.

Reis, J., Schambra, H. M., Cohen, L. G., Buch, E. R., Fritsch, B., Zarahn, E., . . . Krakauer, J. W. (2009). Noninvasive cortical stimulation enhances motor skill acquisition over multiple days through an effect on consolidation. *Proceedings of the National Academy of Sciences, 106*(5), 1590–1595.

Schneider, H. D., & Hopp, J. P. (2011). The use of the Bilingual Aphasia Test for assessment and transcranial direct current stimulation to modulate language acquisition in minimally verbal children with autism. *Clinical Linguistics & Phonetics, 25*(6–7), 640–654.

van Steenburgh, J., Varvaris, M., Schretlen, D., Vannorsdall, T., & Gordon, B. (2016). Bifrontal transcranial direct current stimulation enhances working memory in adults with high-functioning autism. *Neurology, 86*(Suppl.16), S9. 001.

Villamar, M. F., Volz, M. S., Bikson, M., Datta, A., DaSilva, A. F., & Fregni, F. (2013). Technique and considerations in the use of 4x1 ring high-definition transcranial direct current stimulation (HD-tDCS). *Journal of Visualized Experiments*, (77), e50309.

Woods, A. J., Antal, A., Bikson, M., Boggio, P. S., Brunoni, A. R., Celnik, P., . . . Nitsche, M. A. (2016). A technical guide to tDCS, and related non-invasive brain stimulation tools. *Clinical Neurophysiology, 127*(2), 1031–1048.

Yavari, F., Jamil, A., Mosayebi Samani, M., Vidor, L. P., & Nitsche, M. A. (2018). Basic and functional effects of transcranial electrical stimulation (tES)—An introduction. *Neuroscience and Biobehavioral Reviews, 85*, 81–92.

9

Autonomic Nervous System Dysfunctions in Children With Autism Spectrum Disorder

Estate M. Sokhadze,[1] Manuel F. Casanova,[1] Emily L. Casanova,[1] Jessica Klusek,[2] and Jane Roberts[2]

Many children with autism spectrum disorder (ASD) exhibit symptoms associated with autonomic dysfunction. The autonomic nervous system (ANS) is directly involved in manifestations of affect, emotional expression, facial gestures, social-communication, and other social engagement behaviors. The ANS is responsible for multiple physiological functions, and dysfunction of this system is often hypothesized as contributing to abnormalities of cognitive, emotional, and behavioral responses in children with ASD (Benevides & Lane, 2015; Klusek, Roberts, & Losh, 2015). Investigation of atypicality of basal ANS activity and autonomic reactivity may provide insight into behavioral dysregulation and clinical symptoms in children with ASD. The purpose of this review chapter is to describe commonly reported cardiac autonomic balance indices and electrodermal measures as well as to discuss theoretical models and concepts linking ANS parameters with functional measures of central nervous system (CNS) activity. There is a need to justify usefulness of autonomic measures in ASD research and treatment and to provide researchers in this area with a basic foundation for the use of ANS activity recording and analysis methods. This may have important implications for both research and clinical applications.

[1]University of South Carolina School of Medicine-Greenville, Greenville, SC
[2]University of South Carolina, Columbia, SC

The electrophysiological correlates of autonomic dysfunctions in ASD at resting baseline and during exposure to emotional stimuli were not sufficiently well explored in the past. However, autonomic regulation deficits in ASD recently started attracting substantial interest from the scientific and clinical community resulting in numerous research studies and reviews on this topic (Casanova et al., 2014; Chang et al., 2012; Cohen, Masyn, Mastergeorge, & Hessl, 2015; Klusek, Martin, & Losh, 2013; Klusek et al., 2015; Kushki et al., 2013; Kylliäinen et al., 2012; Lydon et al., 2014; Ming, Patel, Kang, Chokroverty, & Julu, 2016; Panju, Brian, Dupuis, Anagnostou, & Kushki, 2015; Patriquin, Scarpa, Friedman, & Porges, 2013a; Smeekens, Dibben, & Verhoeven, 2015; Schaaf, Benevides, Leiby, & Sendecki, 2015; G. Sokhadze et al., 2017; Wang et al., 2016).

Cardiac and electrodermal measures

Heart rate. The present methodologic review will focus on cardiac and electrodermal activity indices as those are the most often used autonomic activity measures in ASD research and treatment. Heart rate (HR) is known as a traditional measure in developmental psychophysiology. The parameters of HR include directional changes (HR deceleration and acceleration) and magnitude of HR changes in response to particular eliciting stimulus that might be in various modalities such as auditory, visual, tactile, etc. (Fox & Calkins, 1993). The evoked heart rate responses are controlled by the sympathetic and parasympathetic nervous systems. Heart rate acceleration is assumed to be a manifestation of excitatory sympathetic influences, and heart rate deceleration to be a manifestation of the inhibitory parasympathetic influences via the vagus nerve (n. vagus). However, in virtually every situation in developmental psychophysiological research, the phasic HR changes are primarily mediated by the nervus vagus (Porges & Fox, 1986). Thus, although the mean HR is determined by the additive input of the tonic sympathetic and parasympathetic systems, the evoked heart rate response in infants and young children is determined by the changing vagal tone (Porges, 1995; Porges & Fox, 1986; Porges, Doussard-Roosevelt, Portales, & Greenspan, 1996). Changes in HR can be a rich source of information concerning attention and cognitive processing, and their developmental changes. Also, the magnitude and the direction of the heart rate response have been used as indicators of the central information processing in children (Graham et al., 1970; Jennings, van der Molen, Pelham, Brock, & Hoza, 1997; Suess, Porges, & Plude, 1994; Weber, Van der Molen, & Molenaar, 1994). Abnormalities in direction (e.g., acceleration vs. deceleration) and intensity (i.e., magnitude) of cardiac chronotropic response in a form of heart rate changes can provide an important input to our understanding of autonomic dysfunctions and their role in atypical behavioral responses observed in children with autism.

Heart rate variability. Because beat-to-beat HR changes are influenced by both parasympathetic and sympathetic factors, additional heart rate variability (HRV) analysis in high frequency (HF) range (0.14-0.40 Hz) needs to illuminate the specific role of parasympathetic factors (Berntson et al., 1997). The HF component of HRV is often referred to as respiratory sinus arrhythmia (RSA), the physiological phenomenon extracted by spectral analysis (Berntson et al., 1997) or other quantitative methods including the "moving polynomial filtering" (Porges et al., 1996), time domain methods (e.g., standard deviation of HR, etc.), and the "peak-to-valley" technique (Grossman & Wientjes, 1986; Grossman, van Beek, & Wientjes,

1990). The power of the HF component and magnitude of RSA are assumed to be reliable non-invasive indices of parasympathetic influences on the heart.

Vagal tone reflects the level of parasympathetic inhibition on the heart and is thought to be a valuable biomarker of psychophysiological reactivity, chronotropic regulatory control, and autonomic flexibility (Sohn, E. Sokhadze, & Watanuki, 2001). Porges (1991) considered vagal tone as the most important autonomic mediator of affect in children. He further developed this position through development of the "polyvagal" theory, emphasizing that RSA and tonic vagal control of the heart could be two distinct vagally-mediated influences controlled by different centers in the brainstem (Porges, 1995, 2003). The hypothesis of higher vagal tone associated with better social functioning and greater inhibitory control has been supported by empirical findings. For instance, studies with infants found vagal tone to be positively correlated with emotional reactivity to positive, novel and negative situations (Calkins, 1997). Infants with high vagal tone were more sociable and adjusted better to new social environments (Fox, 1989; Fox & Field, 1989). Preschool children with an inhibited temperament, a potential precursor of anxiety in school-aged children, exhibited reduced HRV (Kagan, Reznick, & Snidman, 1987) suggesting that reduced parasympathetic activity might contribute to the association between elevated HR and anxiety in school-age children. Reports from various researches suggest that lower RSA in childhood can be considered a predictor of affective disorders (Rechlin, Weis, Spitzer, & Kaschka, 1994). Porges et al. (1996) found that infants who exhibited deficient RSA modulation manifested more behavioral problems as preschoolers, supporting the role of the parasympathetic system in behavioral and affective disorders. The ability to suppress vagal tone was related to fewer behavioral problems in preschool, greater sustained attention, and better behavior regulation (Calkins, 1997; Porges et al., 1996; Suess et al., 1994). This implies that individual differences in parasympathetic control may be important for assessing heart rate responses to emotion-eliciting stimulation in autism research.

The cardiovascular system exhibits massive age-related changes that reflect maturation of both end-organ and neural components. The neural influence of the sympathetic and vagus inputs change with age as sympathetic influences increase, and vagal influences decrease (Porges & Fox, 1986). The mechanisms underlying the decreased vagal efferent influence on the heart may be due to a reduced number of baroreceptors, to decreased compliance of the arterial wall in the pressoreceptor area or the greater elasticity of arterial walls in children (Porges & Fox, 1986).

The spectral analysis of HRV provides quantification of heart rate oscillations and allows researchers to evaluate not only the high frequency (0.015-0.4 Hz) component, primarily influenced by vagal activity, but also slower low frequency (LF, 0.04-0.15 Hz) component reflecting both sympathetic and parasympathetic activity mediated through baroreflex (Task Force, 1996). It is important to note that spectral activity in the high frequency band (HF of HRV 0.015-0.4 Hz) is accepted as an index of cardiac vagal control (Task Force, 1996). In children, especially in infants, the range of the HF window is sometimes adjusted to higher values because of the higher respiration rate in younger children. The majority of HRV studies considers LF/HF ratio of HRV as a reliable index of cardiac autonomic balance (Berntson et al., 1997; Task Force, 1996).

Among the most popular time domain measures of HRV are those derived from R-R interval (NN) differences including

RMSSD, the square root of the mean squared differences of successive NN intervals, *NN50*, the number of interval differences of successive NN intervals greater than 50 ms, and *pNN50* the proportion derived by dividing NN50 by the total number of NN intervals. However, the NN50 can have reduced accuracy in children does not do a good job of reflecting HRV and is therefore not used on a regular basis.

Electrodermal activity. Electrodermal activity (EDA) refers to changes in the electrical activity of the skin. Electrodermal responses are considered as informative measures of autonomic reactivity as they reflect activity of the eccrine sweat glands known to be innervated solely by the sympathetic branch of the ANS (Boucsein, 1992, 2012; Fowles, Kochanska, & Murray, 2000). Electrodermal activity (EDA) is therefore an important and widely used measure in emotion research based on psychophysiological approaches. Most popular phasic and tonic EDA measures such as the skin conductance response (SCR) magnitude; non-specific skin conductance response (NS.SCR) frequency and skin conductance level (SCL) contain considerable information that may explain the components of variance in distinct emotional states as it was outlined by Boucsein (2012). Since the magnitude of EDA corresponds to the strength of an elicited emotion it can be used as an indicator of the quantitative aspects of emotional arousal (Boucsein, 1999). On the other hand, intensity of emotional response is most appropriately represented by such tonic measure as the NS.SCR frequency (Boucsein, 1992, 2012). There is a certain covariation between electrodermal variables and emotional dimension such as arousal and valence. Studies of Lang (Lang, 1994, 1995; Lang, Bradley, & Cuthbert, 1997) indicate that electrodermal responses are more sensitive to the arousal dimension of emotion, and less informative as correlates along the valence (pleasantness) dimension in the two-dimensional affective space. At the same time, it should be noted that electrodermal responses by themselves are not capable of distinguishing one emotion from another, and they have to be combined with other ANS parameters (Collet, Vernet-Maury, Delhomme, & Dittmar, 1997).

The autonomic response to stressors that evoke "the fight or flight" type response, generally involves the activation of the sympathetic and inhibition of the parasympathetic branches of the ANS. This stress response results in several psychophysiological reactions including changes in cardiac and electrodermal activity. The sympathetic and parasympathetic branches of the ANS are known to exert excitatory and inhibitory effects on cardiac activity, respectively (Berntson, Cacioppo, & Quigley, 1993). The sympathetic system activation during exposure to stressors increases heart rate and cardiac contractibility and increases perspiration of the skin. Eccrine sweat glands have predominantly sympathetic cholinergic innervations and are activated during sympathetic response to stress. In contrast to thermoregulatory sweating which occurs over the entire body, this type of sweating' occurs in the palms of the hands, as well as the soles of the feet. Since the perspiration affects the conductance of the skin, sympathetically-induced changes serve to adjust the EDA.

Cardiovascular and electrodermal activity in children with ASD

Before moving to a more detailed description of specific indices and measures of autonomic activity and their abnormalities in children with ASD, it would be useful to provide a brief overview of several notable differences of ANS activity found in individuals with ASD. Among the most well-established finding in ASD, besides high basal autonomic arousal, is a blunted cardiac response to visual and auditory social stimuli (Hirstein, Iversen, & Ramachandran, 2001; Palkovitz & Wiesenfeld, 1980), a response important for understanding social situations. In general, developmental deficits in autonomic regulation of cardiac activity may result in diminished ability to engage in social communication in children with autism (Porges, 2001, 2003). Evidence of more recent studies supports autonomic activity dysregulation in a majority of individuals with ASD and is manifested as sympathetic hyperarousal and dampened parasympathetic vagal tone (Klusek et al., 2015). Furthermore, there is growing data to support a link between aberrant autonomic control of cardiac activity and core deficits associated with ASD, such as social-communication deficits (Klusek et al., 2013; Watson et al., 2010, 2012). The recent study of Patriquin et al. (2013a) examined the relationship between autonomic activity and language delays in children with ASD. Resting respiratory sinus arrhythmia (RSA) and heart rate (HR) were assessed in 23 children (age 4-7-years) with ASD. The relationship between heart rate, RSA, and behavioral symptoms of ASD was examined and results showed that children with ASD had lower basal RSA accompanied by more caregiver-reported language and cognitive delays (Patriquin, Lorenzi, & Scarpa, 2013b).

In a series of studies on this topic, Ming et al. (2005, 2011, 2016) reported evidence supportive of reduced baseline parasympathetic activity in autistic children in association with increased sympathetic tone. Cardiac parasympathetic hypofunction has often been reported in ASD as Ming et al. (2005) noted. Various respiratory dysrhythmias were detected in children with ASD, who also exhibited greater variability in respiratory rhythm and amplitudes as compared to typically developing children (Ming et al., 2016). The authors suggested that the respiratory dysrhythmia in children with ASD could be associated with lower cardiac parasympathetic activity and that respiratory and cardiac vagal hypofunction in ASD may reflect a brainstem dysfunction. Excessive sympathetic arousal along with the low parasympathetic activity could explain, in part, the chronic sensory hyperarousal state in many children with ASD. Reduced cardiac vagal tone, decreased baroreflex sensitivity, and labile respiratory rhythm in ASD were also reported by Julu et al. (2001).

Skin conductance response (SCR) studies in ASD have shown a lack of the normal habituation in the SCR to the same stimulus over time (Barry & James, 1988; van Engeland, 1984). Children with ASD had blunted cardiac and SCR responses to visual or auditory social stimuli (Hirstein et al., 2001; Palkovitz & Wiesenfeld, 1980). Higher basal tonic electrodermal activities as well as larger SCRs to sounds were also observed in earlier studies in autistic children compared to controls (Barry & James, 1988).

As it was noted above, HRV measures represent reliable assessment of cardiac autonomic responses (Berntson et al., 1997; Porges, 1995, 2003). It should be noted that reduced HRV indicative of limited psychophysiological flexibility is not a specific marker for ASD as it has been found in various psychopathologies and borderline subclinical conditions (Cohen et al., 2000; Movius & Allen, 2005; Thayer & Friedman, 2002; Thayer & Lane, 2009). Nevertheless, lower phasic and tonic HRV observed in ASD deserves further considerations. The inability to regulate autonomic activity and, more importantly, HRV during social interactions is believed to contribute to social and affective impairments present in children with ASD, in a similar manner as it was shown in differences between children and adults (Shahrestani, Stewart, Quintana, Hickie, &

Guastella, 2014). In a meta-analysis study the authors reviewed research on HRV during both socially engaging and socially disengaging tasks between children and adults to assess this difference and provided support for the role of autonomic cardiac control in the effective regulation of social engagement and social communication. Several studies indicated that autonomic activity dysfunctions may be directly related to social functioning abnormalities in individuals with ASD (Smeekens et al., 2015). The study explored the relationship of autonomic activity with social functioning in young adult males with ASD compared to young adult males without ASD. Autonomic activity (i.e., heart rate, HRV) was measured during rest and social interaction. The ASD group showed a blunted increase in heart rate from resting baseline to social interaction as compared to those without ASD. This study emphasizes once again that cardiac reactivity difference between children with ASD and typically developing children usually is more pronounced during sensory stimulation of various modalities. Schaaf et al. (2015) measured autonomic activity during sensory stimulation in 59 children with ASD (ages 6-9) in comparison to 30 typically developing controls. Multivariate comparisons revealed significant differences between groups in parasympathetic measures, and sympathetic activity, as measured by pre-ejection period, was statistically higher in ASD group. The findings suggest that children with ASD demonstrated a different pattern of autonomic activity responses during sensory stimulation. Chang et al. (2012) investigated autonomic and behavioral responses to intense auditory stimulation in 25 children with ASD and found that auditory behavioral difficulties were associated with higher sympathetic activation at rest and stronger sympathetic reactivity to sound. Stereotyped and repetitive motor behaviors, one of the core features of ASD, have been proposed as a response to reduce hyper-responsive sympathetic activity (Toichi & Kamio, 2003). Similar ideas were proposed also by other authors (Condy, Scarpa, & Friedman, 2017; Hirstein et al., 2001).

Dysfunctions of the parasympathetic system negatively affect social behavior in children with ASD by impacting their heart rate modulation. The inhibitory parasympathetic, nervus vagus, acts as a brake and slows heart rate (Porges, 2001, 2003; Porges et al., 1996). Functionally, the vagal "brake," which modulates HR, enables rapid engagement and disengagement with objects and people, a skill important for promoting social behaviors (Porges, 1995, 2003). Spectral analysis of HRV represents a measure commonly used in psychopathology research (Cohen, 2000; Thayer & Friedman, 2002) for assessment of cardiac autonomic control (Berntson et al., 1997). Reduced HRV and in particular attenuated power of high frequency (HF) component of the HRV (index of parasympathetic control) is an indicator of abnormal psychophysiological reactivity (Berntson et al., 1997; Cohen et al., 2000; Friedman & Thayer, 1998; Movius & Allen, 2005; Thayer & Lane, 2000). Deficits in the modulation of the HRV in HF range (i.e., respiratory arrhythmia) in different social tasks have been found in ASD. Typical children suppressed the HF in HRV more than children with ASD (Althaus, L. Mulder, G. Mulder, Aarnoudse & Minderaa, 1999; Hutt, Forrest, & Richer, 1975). Children with ASD, on the other hand, demonstrated dampened HR reactivity; they showed unusually small deceleratory HR responses and generally low cardiac reactions to auditory stimulation including socially relevant speech, phrases and tones (Chang et al., 2012; Corona, Dissanayake, Arbelle, Wellington, & Sigman, 1998; Palkovitz & Wiesenfeld, 1980; Zahn, Rumsey, & Van Kammen, 1987). Differences between ASD and typical children are even better manifested during challenging, anxiety provoking tasks such as for instance Stroop test. Kushki et al. (2013, 2014) measured heart rate, electrodermal activity, and skin temperature during a baseline and anxiety condition (Stroop task) in a sample of typically developing children (*n*=17) and children with ASD (*n*=12). The ASD group showed elevated heart rate during both baseline and anxiety conditions. Elevated and blunted phasic electrodermal activity was found in the ASD group both during baseline and anxiety conditions. The authors proposed that children with ASD may have atypical autonomic response to anxiety that is most consistent with sympathetic over-arousal and parasympathetic under-arousal.

Autonomic arousal in ASD

Autonomic over-arousal has several possible origins, as it may be related to sympathetic hyper-arousal, parasympathetic under-activation, or atypical interaction of these two branches of the ANS. Therefore, there is a need to have several measures of autonomic balance that reflect activity of these branches of the autonomic system. The majority of research studies have focused on either combined ANS function (e.g., heart rate and EDA measures) or parasympathetic activity (e.g., HRV measures). The latter has been of special interest due to its potential role in regulating emotional and behavioral functions (Porges, 2003). Decreased parasympathetic tone, measured by respiratory sinus arrhythmia (or HF of HRV), has also been associated with social and emotional difficulties in ASD. Given that the ANS output depends on the complex interaction of both branches of the ANS, it is important to better understand sympathetic function in ASD population. However, research on sympathetic function in ASD has been very limited. In this regard it is an important methodological advantage to add non-invasive electrophysiological indices reflective sympathetic activity, e.g., those related to electrodermal activity.

There are numerous reports that individuals with ASD present with altered psychophysiological reactivity patterns. Physiological responses (e.g., electrodermal and cardiac responses) to pictorial affective stimuli and to emotional facial expressions provided for excessive sympathetic arousal and low parasympathetic responses as derived from the autonomic balance indices based on HRV and skin conductance measures (Cohen, Masyn, Mastergeorge, & Hessl, 2015). Autonomic arousal specifics and autonomic cardiac responses regulation profiles could be useful for distinguishing groups of ASD from other neurodevelopmental disorders and may explain underlying neurobiological mechanisms resulting in well-known emotional responsivity deficits typical of ASD. Abnormal behavioral and emotional responses to a variety of affective stimuli in individuals with ASD led Lyndon et al. (2014) to conduct systematic review of the literature to explore whether such altered physiological reactivity is typical of this population. Despite the mixed results of the review, the authors concluded that individual differences in psychophysiological responses are clearly present in ASD, suggesting that additional research is needed to determine the variables relating to these differences among those with ASD and to examine the possible existence of a specific phenotype of physiological responsiveness in this population. Abnormal autonomic activity can be associated with brain activities not only during exposure to stimulation but also during resting state in ASD. As it was reported by Eilam-Stock et al. (2014) resting state electrodermal activity is correlated with different patterns of brain activity in subjects with ASD than in typical controls. These results can be considered in light of theories of atypical physiological arousal patterns in ASD (Kleberg, 2015).

Venables and Mitchell (1996) emphasized the need to take into account age and sex in studies using measures of electrodermal activity as arousal biomarkers in children. Other confounding factors include medication status. Eventually the same factors should be accounted for during analysis of cardiovascular measures of arousal in children with ASD. Among the physiological mechanisms responsible for age effects on the electrodermal reactivity are developmental processes that influence the number of sweat glands and the sympathetically mediated reactivity of the sweat glands (Porges & Fox, 1986). These developmental influences are manifested in psychophysiological research both in differences in the basal state (i.e., resting skin conductance level [SCL] and number of non-specific skin conductance responses frequency [NS.SCR]) and in the magnitude of stimulus-elicited skin conductance responses (e.g., SCR amplitude and latency measures).

Investigators have also observed higher electrodermal reactivity to emotional stimuli in younger children. Preschool children showed marginally higher NS.SCR frequency increase from baseline to happiness and had higher magnitude of SCRs under anger, boredom and annoyance situations than school children. In addition, studies have also found gender differences: boys showed higher SCR magnitude than girls in happiness within the preschool group (Sohn et al., 2001). Electrodermal responses turned out to be effective for differentiating elicited discrete emotional states. In a total sample of 138, of 7- to 9-year-olds, SCR magnitude and NS.SCR frequency were significantly higher in anger than in happiness and sadness. Furthermore, typical phasic EDA measure, such as specific SCR amplitude also clearly differentiated happiness from annoyance both in preschool and school children (Sohn et al., 2001).

Classical skin conductance response (SCR) studies in ASD have shown a lack of the normal habituation in the SCR to the same stimulus over time (James & Barry, 1984; van Engeland, 1984; van Engeland, Roelofs, Verbaten, & Slangen, 1991). Children with ASD had blunted SCR responses to visual or auditory social stimuli (Hirstein et al., 2001; Palkovitz & Wiesenfeld, 1980). Higher basal tonic electrodermal activity as well as larger SCRs to sounds were observed in autistic children compared to neurotypical controls (Barry & James, 1988). In general, the majority of studies focusing on the relationship between ASD and abnormalities of autonomic activity have also found manifestations of increased sympathetic activity reflected in various EDA measures. In addition, it has been found that children with ASD display greater fluctuations in SCL compared to controls (Angus, 1970). Also, the pilot studies from out lab support that there are excessive but less differentiated SCR to affective stimuli (sounds, visual and audio-visual stimuli) (Dombroski et al., 2014; E. Sokhadze et al., 2012;). SCL is controlled solely by sympathetic inputs (Boucsein, 2012); therefore, the above findings are indications of high sympathetic tone and low selectivity of ANS responses in ASD.

Associations between variability in sympathetic nervous system arousal and individual differences in symptom severity were examined for children with ASD in a study by Fenning et al. (2017). Thirty-four families participated in a laboratory visit that included continuous measurement of EDA during a battery of tests. Greater variability in EDA was associated with higher levels of ASD symptoms, with findings generally consistent across tasks. This led the authors to conclude that sympathetic arousal tendencies may represent an important individual difference factor for the ASD population (Fenning et al., 2017). As a result, possible implications of autonomic dysfunctions associated with abnormal arousal control in ASD provide a plausible explanation of several social, emotional and communication deficits observed in the disorder. It might be hypothesized that cardiac under-reactivity during socially engaging situations results in lower behavioral flexibility and reduced attentional capacity to attend to relevant stimuli critical for social communication development. Althaus et al. (1999) showed that children with serious problems in communication and interaction with others are features associated with significantly less cardiac responsiveness to the demands of attention task and show greater limitation in behavioral control of attention than do healthy children. There are also other studies suggesting that lower executive control of behavior is associated with decreased vagal modulation of cardiac responses and generally attenuated ANS responsiveness to task-related information processing in individuals with ASD (Mezzacappa, Kindlon, Saul, & Earls, 1998; Zahn et al., 1987). Most of these studies have found that children with ASD are less capable of flexible allocation of energy to cope with task requirements. Thus, a deficient vagal response in individuals with ASD probably reflects a reduced ability to mobilize processing resources appropriately and may result in a flattened affect and a general detachment from environment (Porges et al., 1996; Zahn et al., 1987). Beside decreased vagal tone and reduced ability to mobilize processing resources, Althaus et al. (2004) suggested that resulting decreased peripheral feedback (e.g., via vagal afferents) may fail to form coherent somatic representations (so called "somatic markers", Damasio, 1994, 1996) required for development of mental representations of somatic states. Therefore, reduced autonomic feedback may represent yet another functional aspect of unbalanced autonomic responsiveness in ASD which may negatively affect normal development of social communication skills.

Autonomic dysregulation and anxiety in ASD and theoretical models of autonomic control

Anxiety. Sympathetic over-activation is often associated with anxiety disorders. Children and adolescents with ASD are known to present anxiety symptoms and this is a very common problem in the clinical settings. A majority of children with ASD meet criteria for at least one anxiety disorder (de Bruin, Ferdinand, Meester, de Nijs, & Verheij, 2007; McPheeters, Davis, Navarre, & Scott, 2011). Symptoms of anxiety may be related to a reduced functional connectivity between the frontal cortex and limbic system, as a weakened normative frontal inhibition of limbic system is compromised in ASD. Development of new neuromodulation and neurotherapy methods aimed at reducing autonomic arousal in children with ASD is thus an important clinical research objective (for effects on arousal of neuromodulation based on rTMS in ASD see Casanova et al., 2014; G. Sokhadze et al., 2017; Wang et al., 2016; for HRV biofeedback effects on arousal in ASD see Friedrich et al., 2014; Thompson & Thompson, 2014). Excess of sympathetic arousal on a background of attenuated parasympathetic tonus in ASD may provide a plausible explanation of several social, emotional and communication deficits observed. It might be hypothesized that cardiac under-reactivity during socially engaging situations results in lower behavioral flexibility and reduced attentional capacity to attend to relevant stimuli critical for social communication development. Althaus et al. (1999) showed that, in children with ASD, serious problems in communication and interaction with others are features with significantly less cardiac responsiveness to the demands of attention task and show greater limitation in behavioral control of attention than do healthy children.

Interaction between central and autonomic nervous system.

Thayer and Lane (2009) reviewed neuroanatomical and neuroimaging studies that implicate inhibitory GABAergic pathways from the prefrontal lobe to the limbic system, including amygdala, along with inhibitory pathways between the amygdala and the sympathetic and parasympathetic neurons in medulla neurons known to be involved in modulation of HRV. This group of authors described earlier (Lane, 2008; Lane, McRae, Reiman, Ahern, & Thayer, 2007; Thayer & Lane, 2000; 2005) a neurovisceral integration model that is directly involved in regulation of emotion and proposed a role for dysregulation that may result in various psychopathologies, including anxiety disorder (Friedman, 2007) and potentially anxiety symptom so typical in children with ASD.

Heart rate variability is controlled by the joint activity of the sympathetic nerves and vagus nerves at the sinoatrial node. Both branches of the autonomic nervous system are tonically active with sympathetic activity associated with heart rate acceleration and parasympathetic activity associated with heart rate deceleration (reviewed in Levy, 1990). Importantly, heart rate is under tonic parasympathetic inhibitory control (Uijtdehaage & Thayer, 2000). Benarroch (1997) used the term "the central autonomic network (CAN)" and proposed connections of the CAN with the sinoatrial node of the heart via the stellate ganglia and the vagus nerve. As it was outlined by Thayer (2015) control and regulation of the output of the CAN is under tonic inhibition c/o GABAergic neurons in the nucleus of the solitary tract (NTS). Thus, the prefrontal cortex in healthy subjects exerts tonic inhibition of limbic activity via pathways to intercalated GABAergic neurons in the amygdala (Shekhar, Sajdyk, Gehlert, & Rainnie, 2003; Thayer & Lane, 2009). Disinhibition of the amygdala of frontal inhibition is weak leading to increased HR and decreased HRV. Potential mechanisms according to Thayer and Lane (2009) might be a disinhibition of tonically active sympatho-excitatory neurons in the rostral ventrolateral medulla (RVLM), or inhibition of neurons in the nucleus tractus solitarii (NTS) resulting in inhibition of tonically active nucleus ambiguus (NA) and dorsal vagal motor nucleus (DVN) neurons leading to a net decrease of parasympathetic activity. Thus, decreased tonic inhibitory output of the prefrontal cortex can lead to disinhibition of the tonically inhibited structures of central autonomic control (i.e., CAN) and result in a simultaneous disinhibition of sympatho-excitatory neurons and an inhibition of parasympatho-excitatory neurons accompanied by an increase in HR and a concomitant decrease of vagally mediated HRV.

Sympathetic branch activity circuits are under tonic inhibitory control by the prefrontal cortex (Amat et al., 2005; Thayer, 2015), via GABAergic mediated projections from the prefrontal cortex (Davidson, 1990; Thayer, 2006). Activation of inhibitory interneurons of the frontal cortex using rTMS is therefore a potential mechanism of how neuromodulation may restore normative prefrontal inhibitory tone resulting in normalization of the cardiac autonomic balance in ASD. Prolonged prefrontal cortical inactivity can lead to hypervigilance, defensiveness, and social isolation (Thayer & Lane, 2009). The CAN model predicts reduced HRV and hypofunctional vagal activity in anxiety, as it might be associated with abnormal ANS cardiac control (Friedman, 2007). This approach challenges the sympathetic over-arousal model of anxiety that overlooks the role of a hypo-functional parasympathetic system. From this perspective, disorders presenting with anxiety and dysregulated autonomic control can involve varying degrees of sympathetic over-activation and parasympathetic under-activation. The main point is to account for both autonomic branches' activation status in research aimed at understanding the nature of autonomic dysfunction.

Brain functions involved in the generation and representation of arousal state have been linked to social cognition in typical development (Critchley, 2005), suggesting that they may be important to disorders of social interaction such as ASD. According to Critchley (2005), emotional and cognitive processes evoke patterned changes in profiles of physiological measures that may signal a particular emotional state. The modulation of the visceral state is mediated by the sympathetic and parasympathetic divisions of the ANS. Moreover, neural afferents support and convey representations of the internal state of the body to the brain to further influence emotion and cognition. Feedback from the viscera is mapped in the brain to influence efferent neural signals, and at the cortical level reinforce affective responses and emotional states. The discrete cortical substrates for these representations include the anterior regions of the insula and orbitofrontal cortex, areas that have direct connections with the dorsolateral prefrontal cortex (DLPFC). The misperception of heightened arousal level (either over- or underestimation of actual autonomic arousal level status) may readily evoke significant changes in emotional behavior. Cognitive processes such as decision-making are guided by central feedback of bodily arousal responses (Damasio, 1996). The influence of transient arousal responses on aspects of affect and cognition is embodied within Damasio's "Somatic Marker Hypothesis" which proposes that emotional feelings originate in mental representations within the somatosensory cortices (Damasio, 1996). Empirical studies have implicated the insular cortex as the substrate for emotional states, supported by activity within the amygdala, ACC and orbital prefrontal regions, structures which communicate directly with the DLPFC. The anterior insula and ventromedial prefrontal cortex contribute to the integration of visceral afferent information. These observations also map into the insula theory of anxiety of Paulus and Stein (2006), who propose that feelings of anxiety emerge through mismatched representation of anticipated and perceived bodily states within the insular cortex. The role of the heightened sympathetic arousal and reduced vagal afferent activity biasing normal autonomic/visceral state representations therefore may negatively affect emotional reactivity in individuals with ASD.

Effects of autonomic disturbances on behavioral symptoms and comorbidities in ASD

ASDs are also associated with various co-morbidities, including psychiatric disorders. Kleberg (2015) emphasized that atypical autonomic arousal has been used to explain some of the core symptoms of ASD, in particular stereotyped repetitive behaviors. In effect, it has been hypothesized that either elevated or attenuated tonic arousal was a causal factor behind some of the core ASD symptoms, such as repetitive behaviors (Hirstein et al., 2001; Toichi & Kamio, 2003; Toichi et al., 1999) and avoidance of social interaction (Rogers & Ozonoff, 2005; Watson et al., 2010, 2012). According to other current theories, atypical regulation of arousal could cause impairment in attention functions, yet another feature associated with ASD, often resulting in comorbid attention deficit and hyperactivity disorder (ADHD) (Orekhova & Stroganova, 2014).

In a study by Hirstein et al. (2001) children with ASD mainly had higher than normal baseline SCL and high-amplitude SCRs. In the majority of the children, however, SCL and SCR magnitude dropped below the values observed in normal control groups as soon as they became involved in self-stimulatory activities (such as putting their hands in a bowl of dry beans). Stereotyped and repetitive motor behaviors, one of the core features of ASD, has been proposed to be a coping response to reduce hyper-responsive sympathetic activity (Hirstein et al., 2001; Toichi & Kamio, 2003; Toichi et al., 1999). Arousal dysregulation in ASD may manifest in two distinct modes of functioning. The first mode is characterized by elevated tonic arousal, anxiety, and difficulties in focusing attention. The second mode is reflected in reduced tonic arousal, self-stimulatory activities, and decreased awareness of the surroundings. In a social context study, Hirstein et al. (2001) reported that about two-thirds of their participants with ASD had heightened skin conductance during interaction with adults while the other third were hyporesponsive, suggesting that developmental heterogeneity in ASD may play a role in the inconsistent findings observed in EDA studies. Bal et al. (2010) suggested that children with ASD rely mostly on down-regulation of sympathetic arousal mostly because they fail to engage the parasympathetic system for self-regulation.

Our group's results (Casanova et al., 2014; G. Sokhadze et al., 2017; Wang et al., 2016) showed a positive correlation of LF of HRV with *Stereotypy* ratings on ABC and a positive correlation of LF/HF index with total *Repetitive and Stereotyped Behavior* scores on Repetitive Behavior Scale (RBS-R, Bodfish, Symons, & Lewis, 1999At the same time we found negative correlations of *Stereotyped Behavior* scores on both Aberrant Behavior Scale (ABC, Aman & Singh, 1994) and RBS-R with such HRV measures as SDNN, RMSSD, and standard deviation of HR. These finding are supportive of the hypothesis proposing that stereotyped repetitive behaviors can be considered as a coping mechanism for reducing sympathetic over-activation and alleviating anxiety in children with ASD. The above evidence supports the feasibility of using the ANS activity and responses measures as useful physiological markers of atypical behaviors in ASD.

Implication for emotion research in ASD and future research and treatment recommendations

Consistent with the ANS hyper-arousal hypothesis, many studies reported higher basal levels of heart rate and reduced variance in responsivity to different social and non-social stressors and other affective stimuli (e.g., facial emotional expressions) in children and youth with ASD as compared to typically developing individuals. Only few studies evaluated patterns of autonomic responses to emotional stimuli in healthy young subjects (Amrhein, Mühlberger, Pauli, & Wiedemann, 2004; Cuthbert, Schupp, Bradley, Birbaumer, & Lang, 2000; Palomba, Angrilli, & Mini,1997) and specifically developmental trajectories of emotional reactivity in typically developing children (Sohn et al., 2001). This area deserves more attention and rigorous research.

According to modern concepts of affect psychophysiology autonomic arousal is not considered merely as a function of emotion as such, but rather as a pattern of physiological responses supporting anticipated or realized action requirements of the emotional challenge (Cacioppo, Klein, Berntson, & Hatfield,1993; Levenson, 1994) thus posing emotional responses as behavioral dispositions reflecting central activation and preparation for action (Lang, 1995). They are mediated by the ANS and, therefore, can be detected by autonomic manifestations. Categorization of emotions by their behavioral dispositions tendencies and mapping them in two-dimensional affective space by their valence (pleasant *vs.* unpleasant) and arousal (relaxed *vs.* aroused) dimensions (Lang, 1994, 1995;

Witvliet & Vrana, 1995) might be effective approaches to the understanding of a role of the ANS engagement in emotion.

Though the study of autonomic manifestations of affect in adults has a long history (Cacioppo et al., 1993; Collet et al., 1997; Ekman, Levenson, & Friesen, 1983; Lang, 1995; Levenson, 1992, 1994; Sohn et al., 1998; Stemmler, 1989; Stern & Sisson, 1990), relatively little has been done in the area of children's emotion. Experimental studies with children have indicated that increases in electrodermal activity, heart rate changes associated with respiratory arrhythmia shifts and vasoconstriction are some of most commonly described autonomic concomitants of emotional arousal (Culbert & Bonfilio, 1998; Porges, 1991; Quas, Hong, Alkon, & Boyce, 2000; Scarpa, Raine, Venables, & Mednick, 1997). Our own study on preschool and elementary school children also supported the idea that the patterns of electrodermal, cardiorespiratory and thermo-vascular responses are sensitive autonomic correlates of emotions (Sohn et al., 2001).

Emotional response elicited by external affective stimuli or emotional situation have several stages, where the peak of responses of particular physiological systems may have distinct onset latencies. Maximum of response magnitude and its time course are also modulated by the strength of the elicited emotion and intensity of overt expression. Therefore, information describing specifics of emotional responsiveness should be collected both from evoked phasic responses to stimulus within several seconds latencies and tonic changes assessed on minute-long epoch basis. The important finding is that measurements should not be limited to phasic reactivity scores (i.e., short-term changes of parameters from relevant resting baselines). The phasic reactivity parameters should be additive to tonic ones, therefore emphasizing the necessity of using combined reactivity measures to avoid complications due to instability of inter-session baselines and high rate of spontaneous autonomic reactivity in children (Janes, Hesselbrock, & Stern, 1984; Porges & Fox, 1986).

In recent years, the scope of research using autonomic measures in children with ASD has widened and studies are no longer limited to the comparison of basal ANS activity differences from typically developing children, but also address ASD specifics of autonomic responsiveness to emotional and non-emotional stimulation, and to social communication context manipulations. However, some of the conceptual and methodological problems related to physiological specificity of emotions were inherited in the area of developmental psychophysiology of affect in general, and they should also be taken into account in ASD emotion reactivity research. Among the most sensitive issues to be considered are the following: the need to investigate the time courses of particular autonomic responses to affective stimulus or situation, the need to shy away from studies using a single autonomic measure (e.g., only HR or only HF of HRV or only SCL) and emphasize the analysis of patterns of several variables, the need to account for context-deviation of emotional responses (Stemmler, 1989) and the need to take into account other important factors such as the role of individual differences, physiological phenotypes, social experience, age and sex.

Substantial progress in ASD research can be been achieved using knowledge about the relevance of changes in particular electrodermal and cardiovascular responses to specific psychological processes (attention, orienting, defense, approach vs. avoidance, etc.) and deciphering of the pathways mediating these reactivity measures by the ANS. As an example of successful application of combined cardiac and electrodermal measures sensitive to activation of the specific branch of the ANS could be considered HRV parameters (RSA, HF component of HRV, etc.) as indices of tonic and dynamic parasympathetic influences on heart rate to access cardiac autonomic control status, which could be enriched by concurrent monitoring of such reliable sympathetic index as EDA.

The HRV measures were very effectively employed to understand the importance of vagal inputs and vagal efferents in affective responses in children with ASD (Porges, 1991, 1995). Furthermore, the alterations in HRV, besides those useful for understand etiology of ASD, can be linked with the risk of development of various affective and anxiety disorders (Rechlin et al., 1994) and also used as the predictors of individual differences in adjustments of children to new social environments (Fox & Field, 1989; Sohn et al., 2001).

The latest achievements in understanding the sensitivity of specific EDA measures as indicators of the intensity and strength of emotional processes reviewed by Boucsein (1999, 2012) can be adapted to developmental studies of arousal regulation deficits in ASD. This step might be done relatively easy given the fact that there is available extensive material regarding normative values of such electrodermal measures as basal SCL, reactivity to orienting and defensive stimuli (Venables & Mitchell, 1996), and role of such factors as age and sex on phasic and tonic electrodermal responses. Thus, pattern of electrodermal and cardiovascular measures can be successfully applied to understand the ANS mechanisms underlying the development of behavioral problems in children with ASD (Cole, Zahn-Waxler, Fox, Usher, & Welsh, 1996; Rechlin et al., 1994; Zahn & Kruesi, 1993).

Among such directions of research are studies aimed at analyzing putative correlations of ANS measures and behavioral symptom ratings. This approach was used, for instance, in a series of studies where effects of neuromodulation using repetitive transcranial magnetic stimulation (rTMS) on autonomic activity (HRV measures, SCL) were correlated to repetitive behavior ratings (Casanova et al., 2014; G. Sokhadze et al., 2017; Wang et al., 2016). Our results showed a positive correlation of LF of HRV with *Stereotypy* ratings on ABC and a positive correlation of LF/HF index with total *Repetitive and Stereotyped Behavior* scores on RBS-R. At the same time we found negative correlations of *Stereotyped Behavior* scores on both ABC and RBS-R with such HRV measures as SDNN, RMSSD, and standard deviation of HR. These findings support the hypotheses that stereotyped repetitive behaviors can be considered as a coping mechanism for reducing sympathetic over-activation and alleviating anxiety in children with ASD. Stereotyped and repetitive motor behaviors, one of the core features of ASD, has been proposed to be a coping response to reduce hyperresponsive sympathetic activity (Hirstein et al., 2001; Toichi & Kamio, 2003; Toichi et al., 1999). Arousal dysregulation in ASD may manifest in two distinct modes of functioning. The first mode is characterized by elevated tonic arousal, anxiety, and difficulties in focusing attention. The second mode is reflected in reduced tonic arousal, self-stimulatory activities, and decreased awareness of the surroundings. The first mode of response occurs more often in children with an ASD diagnosis.

Another important implication, directly related to findings of sympathetic over-activation and parasympathetic under-activation in ASD, is the possible implementation of biobehavioral interventions aimed at restoring autonomic balance. One of the most promising approach along this line is that of HRV biofeedback training in ASD (e.g., biofeedback training aimed at upregulation of HF of HRV, or other measures of RSA as it was strongly recommended by Thompson & Thompson, 2014) which might be further enriched by simultaneous biofeedback targeting downregulation of electrodermal activity.

References

Althaus, M., Mulder, L. J., Mulder, G., Aarnoudse, C., & Minderaa, R. (1999). Cardiac adaptivity to attention-demanding tasks in children with a pervasive developmental disorder not otherwise specified (PDD-NOS). *Biological Psychiatry*, *46*(6), 799-809.

Althaus, M., Van Roon, A. M., Mulder, L. J., Mulder, G., Aarnoudse, C., & Minderaa, R. (2004). Autonomic response patterns observed during the performance of an attention-demanding task in two groups of children with autistic-type difficulties in social adjustment. *Psychophysiology, 41*(6), 893-904.

Angus, Z. (1970). Autonomic and cognitive functions in childhood psychosis. *Bulletin of British Psychological Society, 23*, 228-229.

Aman, M. G., & Singh, N. N. (1994). *Aberrant behavior checklist - community. Supplementary manual.* East Aurora, NY: Slosson Educational Publications.

Amat, J., Baratta, M. V., Paul, E., Bland, S. T., Watkins, L., & Maier, L. F. (2005). Medial prefrontal cortex determines how stressor controllability affects behavior and dorsal raphe nucleus. *Nature Neuroscience, 8*(3), 365-371.

Amrhein, C., Mühlberger, A., Pauli, P., & Wiedemann, G. (2004). Modulation of event-related brain potentials during affective picture processing: A complement to startle reflex and skin conductance response? *International Journal of Psychophysiology, 54*(3), 231-240.

Bal, E., Harden, E., Lamb, D., Van Hecke, A. V., Denver, J. W., & Porges, S. W. (2010). Emotion recognition in children with autism spectrum disorders: Relations to eye gaze and autonomic state. *Journal of Autism and Developmental Disorders, 40*(3), 358-370.

Barry, R. J., & James, A. L. (1988). Coding of stimulus parameters in autistic, retarded, and normal children: Evidence for a two-factor theory of autism. *International Journal of Psychophysiology, 6*(2), 139-149.

Benevides, T. W., & Lane, S. J. (2015). A review of cardiac autonomic measures: Considerations for examination of physiological response in children with autism spectrum disorder. *Journal of Autism and Developmental Disorders*, *45*(2), 560-575.

Benarroch, E. E. (1997). The central autonomic network. In P. A. Low (Ed.), *Clinical autonomic disorders* (2nd ed.) (pp. 17-23). Philadelphia: Lippincott-Raven.

Berntson, G. G., Cacioppo, J. T., & Quigley, K. S. (1993). Respiratory sinus arrhythmia: Autonomic origins, physiological mechanisms, and psychophysiological implications. *Psychophysiology, 30*(2), 183-196.

Bernston, G. G., Bigger, J. T., Eckberg, D., Grossman, P., Kaufmann, P. G., Malik, M., ... Van der Molen, M. W. (1997). Heart rate variability: Origins, methods and interpretive caveats. *Psychophysiology, 34*(6), 623-648.

Bodfish, J. W., Symons, F. J., & Lewis, J. (1999). *Repetitive behavior scale.* Western Carolina Center Research Reports.

Boucsein, W. (1992.) *Electrodermal activity*. New York: Plenum.

Boucsein, W. (1999). Electrodermal activity as an indicator of emotional processes. *Korean Journal of Science of Emotion and Sensibility, 2*, 1-25.

Boucsein, W. (2012). *Electrodermal activity* (2nd ed.). New York: Springer.

Cacioppo, J. T., Klein, D. J., Berntson, G., & Hatfield, E. (1993). The psychophysiology of emotion. In M. Lewis & G. Haviland (Eds.), *Handbook of emotions* (pp.119-142). New York: Guilford.

Calkins, S. D. (1997). Cardiac vagal tone indices of temperamental reactivity and behavioral regulation in young children. *Developmental Psychobiology, 31*(2), 125-135.

Casanova, M. F., Hensley, M. K., Sokhadze, E. M., El-Baz, A. S., Wang, Y, Li, X., & Sears, L. (2014). Effects of weekly low-frequency rTMS on autonomic measures in children with autism spectrum disorder. *Frontiers in Human Neuroscience, 8*, 851.

Chang, M.C., Parham, L. D., Blanche, E.I., Schell, A., Chou, C. P., Dawson, M., & Clark, F. (2012). Autonomic and behavioral responses of children with autism to auditory stimuli. *American Journal of Occupational Therapy, 66*(5), 567-576.

Cohen, N., Benjamin, J., Geva, A. B., Matar, M. A., Kaplan, Z., & Kotler, M. (2000). Autonomic dysregulation in panic disorder and in post-traumatic stress disorder: Application of power spectrum analysis of heart rate variability at rest and in response to recollection of trauma or panic attack. *Psychiatry Research, 96*(1), 1-13.

Cohen, S., Masyn, K., Mastergeorge, A., & Hessl, D. (2015). Psychophysiological responses to emotional stimuli in children and adolescents with autism and fragile X syndrome. *Journal of Clinical Child and Adolescent Psychology, 44*(2), 250-263

Cole, P. H., Zahn-Waxler, C., Fox, N. A., Usher, B. A., & Welsh, J. D. (1996). Individual differences in emotion regulation and behavior problems in preschool children. *Journal of Abnormal Psychology, 105*(4), *518-529.*

Collet, C., Vernet-Maury, E., Delhomme, G., & Dittmar, A. (1997). Autonomic nervous system patterns specificity to basic emotions. *International Journal of Psychophysiology, 62*(1-2), 45-57.

Condy, E., Scarpa, A., & Friedman, B. H. (2017). Respiratory sinus arrhythmia predicts restricted repetitive behavior severity. *Journal of Autism and Developmental Disorders, 47*(9), 2795-2804.

Corona, R., Dissanayake, C., Arbelle, S., Wellington, P., & Sigman, M. (1998). Is affect aversive to young children with autism? Behavioral and cardiac responses to experimenter distress. *Child Development, 69*(6), 1494-1502.

Critchley, H. D. (2005). Neural mechanisms of autonomic, affective, and cognitive integration. *Journal of Comparative Neurology, 493*(1), 154-166.

Culbert, T., & Bonfilio, S. (1998). Integrating biofeedback and cognitive-behavioral therapy for children with anger management problems. *Biofeedback, 26,* 27-35.

Cuthbert, B. N., Schupp, H. T., Bradley, M. M., Birbaumer, N., & Lang, P. J. (2000). Brain potentials in affective picture processing: Covariation with autonomic arousal and affective report. (2000). *Biological Psychology, 52*(2), 95-111.

Damasio, A. R. (1994). *Descartes' error: Emotion, reason and the human brain.* New York: Grosset Putman.

Damasio, A. R. (1996). The somatic marker hypothesis and the possible functions of the prefrontal cortex. *Philosophical Transactions of the Royal Society of London, Biological Sciences, 351*(1346), 1413-1420.

Davidson, R. J., Ekman, P., Saron, C. D., Senulis, J. A., & Friesen, W. V. (1990). Approach-withdrawal and cerebral asymmetry: Emotional expression and brain physiology. *Journal of Personality and Social Psychology, 58*(2), 330-341.

De Bruin, E. L., Ferdinand, R. F., Meester, S., de Nijs, P. F., & Verheij, F. (2007). High rates of psychiatric co-morbidity in PDD-NOS. *Journal of Autism and Developmental Disorders, 37*(5), 877-886.

Dombroski, B., Kaplan, M., Kotsamanidis-Burg, B., Edelson, S. M., Hensley, M. K., Sokhadze, E.M., & Casanova, M. F. (2014). Effects of ambient prism lenses and visual-motor training on heart rate variability and behavioral outcomes in autism. In K. Siri & T. Lyons (Eds.), *Cutting-edge therapies for autism* (4th ed.) (pp.138-150). New York, NY: Skyhorse Publishing.

Eilam-Stock, T., Xu, P., Cao, M., Gu, X., van Dam, N., ... Fan, J. (2014). Abnormal autonomic and associated brain activities during rest in autism spectrum disorder. *Brain, 137*(1), 153-171.

Ekman, P., Levenson, R. W., & Friesen, W. V. (1983). Autonomic nervous system activity distinguishes among emotions. *Science, 221*(4616), 1208-1210.

Fenning, R. M., Baker, J. K., Baucom, B. R., Erath, S. A., Howland, M. A., & Moffitt, J. (2017). Electrodermal variability and symptom severity in children with autism spectrum disorder. *Journal of Autism and Developmental Disorders, 47*(4), 1062-1072.

Friedrich, E. V., Suttie, N., Sivanathan, A., Lim, T., Louchart, S., &

Pineda, J. A. (2014). Brain-computer interface game applications for combined neurofeedback and biofeedback treatment for children on the autism spectrum. *Frontiers in Neuroengineering, 7*, 21.
Fowles, D. C., Kochanska, G., & Murray, K. (2000). Electrodermal activity and temperament in preschool children. *Psychophysiology, 37*(6), 777-787.
Fox, N. A. (1989). Psychophysiological correlates of emotion reactivity during the first year of life. *Developmental Psychology, 25*, 364-372.
Fox, N. A., & Field, T. M. (1989). Individual differences in young children's adjustment to preschool. *Journal of Applied Developmental Psychology, 10*, 527-540.
Fox, N., & Calkins, S. (1993). Multiple-measure approaches to the study of infant emotion. In M. Lewis & J. Haviland (Eds.), *Handbook of emotions* (pp. 167 -184). New York: Guilford.
Friedman, B. H. (2007). An autonomic flexibility–neurovisceral integration model of anxiety and cardiac vagal tone. *Biological Psychology, 74*(2), 185-199.
Friedman, B. H., & Thayer, J. F. (1998). Anxiety and autonomic flexibility: A cardiovascular approach. *Biological Psychology, 49*(3), 303-323.
Graham, F. K., Berg, K. M., Berg, W. K., Jackson, J. C., Hatton, H. M., & Kantrowitz, S. R. (1970). Cardiac orienting response as a function of age. *Psychonomic Science, 19*, 363-365.
Grossman, P., & Wientjes, C. (1986). Respiratory sinus arrhythmia and parasympathetic cardiac control: some basic issues concerning quantification, applications and implications. In P. Grossman, K. H. L. Janssen, & D. Vaitl (Eds.), *Cardiorespiratory and cardiosomatic psychophysiology* (pp. 117-138). New York: Plenum Press.
Grossman, P., van Beek, J., & Wientjes, C. (1990). A comparison of three quantification methods for estimation of respiratory sinus arrhythmia. *Psychophysiology, 27*, 702-714.
Hirstein, W., Iversen, P., & Ramachandran, V. S. (2001). Autonomic responses of autistic children to people and objects. *Proceedings Royal Society London B Biological Sciences, **268***(1479), 1883-1888.
Hutt, C., Forrest, S. J., & Richer, J. (1975). Cardiac arrhythmia and behavior in autistic children. *Acta Psychiatrica Scandinavica, 51*(5), 361-372.
James, A. L., & Barry, R. J. (1984). Cardiovascular and electrodermal responses to simple stimuli in autistic, retarded and normal children. *International Journal Psychophysiology, 1*(2), 179-193.
Janes, C. L., Hesselbrock, V., & Stern, J. A. (1984). Parental psychopathology, age, and race as related to electrodermal activity of children. *Psychophysiology, 15*(1), 24-34.
Jennings, J. R., van der Molen, M. W., Pelham, W., Brock, K., & Hoza, B. (1997). Inhibition in boys with attention deficit disorder as

indexed by heart rate changes. *Developmental Psychology, 33*(2), 308-318.

Julu, P. O., Kerr, A. M., Apartopoulos, F., Al-Rawas, S., Engerström, I. W., Engerström, L., ... Hansen, S. (2001). Characterization of breathing and associated central autonomic dysfunction in the Rett disorder. *Archives of Disease in Childhood, 85*(1), 29-37.

Kagan, J., Reznick, J. S., & Snidman, N. (1987). The physiology and psychology of behavioral inhibition in children. *Child Development, 58*(6), 1459-1473.

Kleberg, J. L. (2015). Resting arousal state and functional connectivity in autism spectrum disorder. *Journal of Neurophysiology, 113*(9), 3035-3037.

Klusek, J., Martin, G. E., & Losh, M. (2013). Physiological arousal in autism and fragile X syndrome: Group comparisons and links with pragmatic language. *American Journal on Intellectual and Developmental Disabilities, 118*(6), 475-495.

Klusek, J., Roberts, J. E., & Losh, M. (2015). Cardiac autonomic regulation in autism and fragile X syndrome: A review. *Psychology Bulletin, 141*(1), 141-175.

Kushki, A., Drumm, E., Mobarak, M. P., Tanel, N., Dupuis, A., Chau, T., & Anagnostou, E. (2013). Investigating the autonomic nervous system response to anxiety in children with autism spectrum disorders. *PLoS One*, *8*(4), e59730.

Kushki, A., Brian, J., Dupuis, A., & Anagnostou, E. (2014). Functional autonomic nervous system profile in children with autism spectrum disorder. *Molecular Autism, 5*, 39.

Kylliäinen, A., Wallace, S., Coutanche, M. N., Leppänen, J. M., Cusack, J., Bailey, A. J., & Hietanen, J. K. (2012). Affective-motivational brain responses to direct gaze in children with autism spectrum disorder. *Journal of Child Psychology and Psychiatry, and Allied Disciplines, 53*(7), 790-797.

Lane, R. D. (2008). Neural substrates of implicit and explicit emotional processes: A unifying framework for psychosomatic medicine. *Psychosomatic Medicine, 70*(2), 214-231.

Lane, R. D., McRae, K., Reiman, E. M., Ahern, G. L., & Thayer, J. F. (2007). Neural correlates of vagal tone during emotion. *Psychosomatic Medicine, 69*, A-8.

Lang, P. J. (1994). The motivational organization of emotions: affect-reflex connections In S. van Goozen, N. E. Van de Poll, & J. A. Sergeant (Eds.), *Emotions: Essays on emotion theory* (pp. 61-93). Hillsdale, NJ: Erlbaum.

Lang, P. J. (1995). The emotion probe. Studies of motivation and attention. *American Psychologist, 50*(5), 372-385.

Lang, P. J., Bradley, M. M., & Cuthbert, B. N. (1997). Motivated attention: Affect, activation, and action. In P. J. Lang, R. F. Simons & M. T. Balaban (Eds.), *Attention and orienting* (pp. 97-135).

Hillsdale, NJ: Erlbaum.

Levenson, R. W. (1992). Autonomic nervous system patterning in emotion. *Psychological Science, 3,* 23-27.

Levenson, R. W. (1994). The search for autonomic specificity. In P. Ekman & R. J. Davidson (Eds.), *The nature of emotion* (pp. 252-257). New York: Oxford University Press.

Levy, M. N. (1990). Autonomic interactions in cardiac control. *Annals of the New York Academy of Sciences, 601*, 209-221

Lydon, S., Healy, O., Reed, P., Mulhern, T., Hughes, B., & Goodwin, M. S. (2015). A systematic review of physiological reactivity to stimuli in autism. *Developmental Neurorehabilitation, 24*, 1-21.

McPheeters, M. L., Davis, A., Navarre, J. R., & Scott, T. A. (2011). Family report of ASD concomitant with depression or anxiety among US children. *Journal of Autism and Developmental Disorders, 41*(5), 646-653.

Mezzacappa, E., Kindlon, D., Saul, J. P., & Earls, F. (1998). Executive and motivational control of performance task behavior, and autonomic heart-rate regulation in children: Physiological validation of two-factor solution inhibitory control. *Journal of Child Psychology and Psychiatry and Allied Disciplines, 39*(4), 525-531.

Ming, X., Julu, P. O., Brimacombe, M., Connor, S., & Daniels, M. L. (2005). Reduced cardiac parasympathetic activity in children with autism. *Brain & Development, 27(7)*, 509-516.

Ming, X., Bain, J. M., Smith, D., Brimacombe, M., Gold von-Simson, G., & Axelrod, F. B. (2011). Assessing autonomic dysfunction symptoms in children: A pilot study. *Journal of Child Neurology, 26*(4), 420-427

Ming, X., Patel, R., Kang, V., Chokroverty, S., & Julu, P.O. (2016). Respiratory an autonomic dysfunction in children with autism spectrum disorders. *Brain & Development, 38*(2), 225-232.

Movius, H. L., & Allen, J. J. (2005). Cardiac vagal tone, defensiveness, and motivational style. *Biological Psychology, 68*(2), 147-162.

Orekhova, E. V., & Stroganova, T. A. (2014). Arousal and attention re-orienting in autism spectrum disorders: Evidence from auditory event-related potentials. *Frontiers in Human Neuroscience, 8*, 34.

Palkovitz, R. J., & Wiesenfeld, A. R. (1980). Differential autonomic responses of autistic and normal children. *Journal of Autism and Developmental Disorders, 10*(3), 347-360.

Palomba, D., Angrilli, A., & Mini, A. (1997). Visual evoked potentials, heart rate responses and memory to emotional pictorial stimuli. *International Journal of Psychophysiology, 27*(1), 55-67.

Panju, S., Brian, J., Dupuis, A., Anagnostou, E., & Kushki, A. (2015). Atypical sympathetic arousal in children with autism spectrum disorder and its association with anxiety symptomatology. *Molecular Autism, 6*, 64

Patriquin, M. A., Scarpa, A., Friedman, B. H., & Porges, S. W. (2013a).

Respiratory sinus arrhythmia: A marker for positive social functioning and receptive language skills in children with autism spectrum disorders. *Developmental Psychobiology, 55*(2), 101-112.

Patriquin, M. A., Lorenzi, J., & Scarpa, A. (2013b). Relationship between respiratory sinus arrhythmia, heart period, and caregiver-reported language and cognitive delays in children with autism spectrum disorders. *Applied Psychophysiology Biofeedback, 38*(3), 203-207.

Paulus, M. P., & Stein, M. B. (2006). An insular view of anxiety. *Biological Psychiatry, 60*(4), 383-387.

Porges, S. W. (1991). Vagal tone: An autonomic mediator of affect. In J. Garber & K. A. Dodge (Eds.), *The development of emotion regulation and dysregulation* (pp. 111-128). Cambridge, UK: Cambridge University.

Porges, S. W. (1995). Orienting in defensive world: Mammalian modifications of our evolutionary heritage. A polyvagal theory. *Psychophysiology, 32*(4), 301-318.

Porges, S. W. (2001). The polyvagal theory: Phylogenetic substrates of a social nervous system. *International Journal of Psychophysiology, 42*(2), 123-146.

Porges, S. W. (2003). The polyvagal theory. *Physiology & Behavior, 79*(3), 503-513.

Porges, S. W., & Fox, N. A. (1986). Developmental psychophysiology. In M. G. H. Coles, E. Donchin, & S. W. Porges (Eds.), *Psychophysiology: Systems, processes and applications* (pp. 611-625). New York: Guilford.

Porges, S. W., Doussard-Roosevelt, J. A., Portales, L., & Greenspan, S. I. (1996). Infant regulation of the vagal "brake" predicts child behavioral problems: A psychobiological model of social behavior. *Developmental Psychobiology, 29*(8), 697-712.

Quas, J. A., Hong, M., Alkon, A., & Boyce, W. T. (2000). Dissociation between psychobiologic reactivity and emotional expression in children. *Developmental Psychobiology, 37*(3), 153-176.

Rechlin, T., Weis, M., Spitzer, A., & Kaschka, W. P. (1994). Are affective disorders associated with alterations of heart rate variability? *Journal of Affective Disorders, 32*(4), 271-275.

Rogers, S. J., & Ozonoff, S. (2005). Annotation: What do we know about sensory dysfunction in autism? A critical review of the empirical evidence. *Journal of Child Psychology and Psychiatry, and Allied Disciplines, 46*(12), 1255-1268.

Scarpa, A., Raine, A., Venables, P. H., & Mednick, S. A. (1997). Heart rate and skin conductance in behaviorally inhibited Mauritian children. *Journal of Abnormal Psychology, 106*(2), 182-190.

Schaaf, R. C., Benevides, T. W., Leiby, B. E., & Sendecki, J. A. (2015). Autonomic dysregulation during sensory stimulation in children with autism. *Journal of Autism and Developmental Disorders, 45*(2),

461-472.

Shahrestani, S., Stewart, E. M., Quintana, D. S., Hickie, I. B., & Guastella, A. J. (2014). Heart rate variability during social interactions in children with and without psychopathology: A meta-analysis. *Journal of Child Psychology and Psychiatry, and Allied Disciplines, 55*(9), 981-989.

Shekhar, A., Sajdyk, T. J., Gehlert, D. R., & Rainnie, D. G. (2003). The amygdala, panic disorder, and cardiovascular responses. *Annals of the New York Academy of Sciences, 985*, 308-325.

Smeekens, I., Dibben, R., & Verhoeven, E. W. (2015). Exploring the relationship of autonomic and endocrine activity with social functioning in adults with autism spectrum disorders. *Journal of Autism Developmental Disorders, 45*(2), 495-505.

Sohn, J.-H., Sokhadze, E., Yi, I., Lee, K.-H., & Choi, S. (1998). Patterns of autonomic responses to affective visual stimulation: Skin conductance responses, heart rate and respiration rate vary across discrete elicited emotions. *Korean Journal of Science of Emotion and Sensibility,1*, 79-91.

Sohn, J.- H., Sokhadze, E., & Watanuki, S. (2001). Electrodermal and cardiovascular manifestations of emotions in children. *Journal of Physiological Anthropology and Applied Human Science, 20*(2), 55-64.

Sokhadze, E. M., Baruth, J. M., Sears, L., Sokhadze, G. E., El-Baz, A. S., & Casanova, M. F. (2012). Prefrontal neuromodulation using rTMS improves error monitoring and correction functions in autism. *Applied Psychophysiology and Biofeedback, 37*(2), 91-102.

Sokhadze, G. E., Casanova, M. F., Kelly, D. P., Casanova, E. L., Russell, B., & Sokhadze, E. M. (2017). Neuromodulation based on rTMS affects behavioral measures and autonomic nervous system activity in children with autism. *NeuroRegulation, 4*(2), 65-78.

Stemmler, G. (1989). The autonomic differentiation of emotions revisited: Convergent and discriminant validation. *Psychophysiology, 26*(6), 617-632.

Stern, R. M., & Sisson, C. E. (1990). Response patterning. In J. Cacioppo & L. Tassinary (Eds.), *Principles of psychophysiology: Physical, socical and inferential elements* (pp. 193-215). Cambridge, UK: Cambridge University Press.

Suess, P. E., Porges, S. W., & Plude, D. J. (1994). Cardiac vagal tone and sustained attention in school-age children. *Psychophysiology, 31*(1), 12-17.

Task Force ESCNASPE (1996). Heart rate variability: Standards of measurement, physiological interpretation, and clinical use. *Circulation, 93*, 1043-1065.

Thayer, J. F. (2006). On the importance of inhibition: Central and peripheral manifestations of nonlinear inhibitory processes in neural systems. *Dose Response, 4*(1), 2-21.

Thayer, J. F. (2015, March 14). A neurovisceral integration perspective.

In The 46th annual meeting of the Association for Applied Psychophysiology and Biofeedback, Austin, TX.

Thayer, J. F., & Lane, R. D. (2000). A model of neurovisceral integration in emotion regulation and dysregulation. *Journal of Affective Disorders, 61*(3), 201-216.

Thayer, J. F., & Friedman, B. H. (2002). Stop that: Inhibition, sensitization, and their neurovisceral concomitants. *Scandinavian Journal of Psychology*, *43*(2), 123-130.

Thayer, J. F., & Lane, R. D. (2005). The importance of inhibition in dynamical systems models of emotion and neurobiology. *Brain and Behavioral Sciences, 28*(2), 218-219.

Thayer, J. F., & Lane, R. D. (2009). Claude Bernard and the heart–brain connection: Further elaboration of a model of neurovisceral integration. *Neuroscience and Biobehavioral Reviews, 33*(2), 81-88.

Thompson, M., & Thompson. (2014). *The neurofeedback book: An introduction to basic concepts in applied psychophysiology* (2nd ed.). Wheat Ridge, CO: AAPB Publication.

Toichi, M., & Kamio, Y. (2003). Paradoxical autonomic response to mental task in autism. *Journal of Autism and Developmental Disorders, 33*(4), 417-426.

Toichi, M., Kubota, Y., Murai, T., Kamio, Y., Sakihama, M., Toriuchi, T., ... & Miyoshi, K. (1999). The influence of psychotic states on the autonomic nervous system in schizophrenia. *International Journal of Psychophysiology, 31*(2), 147-154.

Uijtdehaage, S. H., & Thayer, J. F. (2000). Accentuated antagonism in the control of human heart rate. *Clinical Autonomic Research, 10*(3), 107-110.

van Engeland, H. (1984). The electrodermal orienting response to auditive stimuli in autistic children, normal children, mentally retarded children, and child psychiatric patients. *Journal of Autism and Developmental Disorders, 14*(3), 261-279.

van Engeland, H., Roelofs, J. W., Verbaten, M. N., & Slangen, J. L. (1991). Abnormal electrodermal reactivity to novel visual stimuli in autistic children. *Psychiatry Research, 38*(1), 27-38.

Venables, P. H., & Mitchell, D. A. (1996). The effects of age, sex and time of testing on skin conductance activity. *Biological Psychology, 43*(2), 87-101.

Wang, Y., Hensley, M. K., Tasman, A., Sears, L., Casanova, M. F., & Sokhadze, E. M. (2016). Heart rate variability and skin conductance during repetitive TMS course in children with autism. *Applied Psychophysiology and Biofeedback, 41*(1), 47-60.

Watson, L. R., Baranek, G. T., Roberts, J. E., David, F. J., & Perryman, T. Y. (2010). Behavioral and physiological responses to child-directed speech as predictors of communication outcomes in children with autism spectrum disorders. *Journal of Speech, Language, and Hearing Research, 53*(4), 1052-1064.

Watson, L. R., Roberts, J. E., Baranek, G. T., Mandulak, K. C., & Dalton, J. C. (2012). Behavioral and physiological responses to child-directed speech of children with autism spectrum disorders or typical development. *Journal of Autism and Developmental Disorders, 42*(8), 1616-1629.

Weber, E. J., Van der Molen, M. W., & Molenaar, P. C. (1994). Heart rate and sustained attention during childhood: Age-changes in anticipatory heart rate, primary bradycardia, and respiratory sinus arrhythmia. *Psychophysiology, 31*(2), 164-174.

Witvliet, C. V., & Vrana, C. R. (1995). Psychophysiological responses as indices of affective dimensions. *Psychophysiology, 32*(5), 436-443.

Zahn, T. P., Rumsey, J. M., & Van Kammen, D. P. (1987). Autonomic nervous system activity in autistic, schizophrenic, and normal men: Effects of stimulus significance. *Journal of Abnormal Psychology, 96*(2), 135-144.

Zahn, T. P., & Kruesi, M. J. (1993). Autonomic activity in boys with disruptive behavior disorders. *Psychophysiology, 30*(6), 605-614.

10

Neurofeedback Treatment for Autism Spectrum Disorder

Justin A. Barterian,[1,2] L. Eugene Arnold,[1,2] and Roger deBeus[3]

Neurofeedback is a specific form of biofeedback that involves the intentional manipulation of electroencephalogram (EEG) activity via operant conditioning (Sherlin et al., 2011). EEG frequencies (i.e., alpha, beta, delta, theta, and gamma) have been correlated with various neurological functions. For example, low frequency sub-band of beta waves (~13–21 Hz) are associated with states of purposeful outwardly focused attention, gamma waves (~30 Hz and above) are associated with problem solving/higher order thinking, and alpha waves (~8–12 Hz) are linked to relaxation (Hammond, 2011). Neurofeedback treatment for mental health/behavioral problems can be traced back to the 1960s when alpha waves were first targeted for relaxation training (Kamiya, 2011). Since then, researchers and practitioners have examined the use of neurofeedback for a variety of disorders, including ADHD (e.g., Arns, Heinrich, & Strehl, 2014; Gevensleben et al., 2009; Kerson et al., 2013; Sherlin, Arns, Lubar, & Sokhadze, 2010), learning disorders (e.g., Fernandez et al., 2003), substance abuse (reviewed in Sokhadze, Cannon, & Trudeau, 2008), and PTSD (e.g., van der Kolk et al., 2016) to name a few. Despite the accumulating research literature, there is still a substantial amount to learn about the possible utility and impact of this treatment on a variety of disorders, including autism spectrum disorder (ASD), with a need for scientifically rigorous randomized control

[1]Ohio State University – Wexner Medical Center
[2]Department of Psychiatry and Behavioral Health, Columbus, OH
[3]Advanced Psychological Services, Asheville, NC

trials that compare active neurofeedback to an indistinguishable placebo treatment. Additionally, several directions of future research are necessary to further refine neurofeedback treatment and examine constructs such as acceptability, feasibility, and cost-effectiveness.

ASD is a neurodevelopmental disorder characterized by deficits in social communication and interaction as well as restricted and repetitive behavior, interests, or activities. ASD leads to several functional difficulties for children and adults with the disorder. Individuals with ASD struggle with social relationships, which may result in fewer opportunities for learning experiences. Tasks of daily living, such as going to the doctor or dentist, may be difficult due to deficits in social communication and sensory concerns (APA, 2013). Neurofeedback has the potential to add to the current repertoire of psychosocial (e.g., applied behavioral analysis) and psychopharmacological (e.g., stimulant, atypical antipsychotic) treatments that are currently available for managing the symptoms of ASD. Additionally, given neurofeedback addresses neurological functioning, it may also have the potential to address the core symptoms of the disorder, such as communication deficits and repetitive behaviors.

Several studies have examined the neurological abnormalities associated with ASD. Difficulties with social cognition have been linked to abnormalities in the functioning of the amygdala, the superior temporal sulcus region, and the fusiform gyrus (Pelphrey, Adolphs, & Morris, 2004; Schultz, 2005). For example, Wang, A. (2004) found that children with autism did not demonstrate changes in amygdala activity when asked to switch between labeling faces and matching faces, while changes in amygdala functioning was noted in control groups. Imaging studies demonstrate that individuals with ASD demonstrate abnormal functioning in areas associated with executive functioning. For example, during a response inhibition task, participants with autism displayed decreased activation in the anterior cingulate cortex and increased activation in premotor areas (Kana, Keller, Minshew, & Just, 2007).

Abnormalities in brain function associated with ASD can be observed through EEG recordings. Coben, Chabot, and Hirshberg (2013) found that individuals with autism demonstrate several differences in EEG function compared to normal peers, including: 1) differences in absolute and relative power for delta, theta, alpha, and beta frequency bands; 2) differences in power between the two hemispheres; and 3) increased frontal coherence and decreased anterior and posterior/temporal coherence between hemispheres. Additional hypotheses include abnormal functioning in mirror neurons, which have been associated with imitation, theory of mind, language, and empathy (Oberman et al., 2005; Pineda et al., 2014ab) and atypical gamma oscillation (Casanova et al., 2013; Rojas & Wilson, 2014; Sokhadze et al., 2014, 2016).

A review of the literature shows differences in quantitative EEG (QEEG) activity between children with ASD and typically developing (TD) controls. Several studies reported found increased activity in the delta frequency range described as "slowing" (Cantor, Thatcher, & Hrybyk, & Kaye , 1986; Murias, Webb, Greenson, & Dawson, 2007; Stroganova et al., 2015) and theta increases (Coben, Clarke, Hudspeth, & Barry, 2008; Coben et al., 2013). Findings regarding alpha, beta and gamma frequency range were quite consistent. A majority of them reported reduced alpha power (Cantor et al., 1986) and increased beta (Coben et al., 2008). A review of atypical gamma activity in ASD can be found in Casanova et al. (2013), Orekhova et al. (2007) and Rojas and Wilson (2014). Studies that investigated cortical connectivity in ASD samples using QEEG coherence measures reported reduced connectivity, especially over longer distances (Cantor et al., 1986; Coben et al., 2008; Coben Sherlin, Hudspeth, McKeon, & Ricca, 2014).

Neurofeedback Training in ASD

Several potential approaches for neurofeedback treatment have been examined in the literature with varying evidence, including 1) sensorimotor rhythm (SMR) and theta to beta ratio (TBR) training (Kouijzer, de Moor, Gerrits, Congedo, van Schie,, 2009a; Kouijzer, de Moor, Gerrits, Buitelaar, & van Schie, 2009b; Kouijzer, van Schie, Gerrits, Buitelaar, & de Moor, 2013; Sichel, Fehmi, & Goldstein, 1995), 2) QEEG guided neurofeedback (Coben, 2013; Coben & Padolsky, 2007; Coben et al., 2014; Linden & Gunkelman, 2013), 3) mirror neuron (mu) activity (Datko, Pineda, & Müller, 2018; Friedrich et al., 2014, 2015; Pineda et al., 2008, 2014b), 4) connectivity-guided coherence neurofeedback (Coben & Padolsky, 2007; Coben et al., 2014), and 5) upregulation of gamma activity along with inhibition of high amplitude and low frequency rhythms (Wang, Y. et al., 2016) and the combination of transcranial magnetic stimulation (TMS) and neurofeedback to address gamma oscillations (Sokhadze et al., 2014).

Theta to Beta Ratio (TBR) and Sensorimotor Rhythm (SMR Training

Several cases studies have examined the use of TBR or SMR training for the treatment of ASD (reviewed in Arns et al., 2014; Arns, Heinrich, Ros, Rothenberger, & Strehl, 2015). Theta-to-beta ratio (TBR) training, which has been an intense area of focus for ADHD treatment research, consists of upregulation of low beta waves (13–21 Hz, sometimes 13–18 Hz instead) while simultaneously downregulating theta waves, with the intention of improving attention and executive functioning (Arns, de Ridder, Strehl, Breteler, & Coenen, 2009; Arns, Conners, & Kraemer, 2013; Lubar, 2003). SMR training is similar to TBR training; however, it occurs over the sensorimotor strip and focuses on approximately 12–15 Hz activity. Upregulation of SMR has been associated with an outward calm focus (Collura & Siever, 2009). The first case report to examine these training methods detailed the utility of down-training theta (4–8 Hz) and up-training sensorimotor rhythm activity (SMR; 12–15 Hz) via a monopolar placement on the sensory-motor strip in an 8-year-old boy. The patient with ASD received 31 neurofeedback treatments. Improvements in theta wave to SMR ratios at multiple sites were noted. Additionally, improvements across several domains, such as noticing emotions in others, seeking comfort, imitating others, sleep, headaches, self-stimulatory behavior, speech, general anxiety, and social anxiety (Sichel et al, 1995), were observed. Similarly, Scolnick (2005) completed a series of case studies. Training consisted of 30-minute sessions twice per week at school. Protocols varied slightly based on the child's individual needs, but mostly focused on increasing 12–15 Hz activity while inhibiting 4–10 Hz activity and 22–30 Hz (i.e., EMG). Both unipolar and bipolar placements were utilized, which varied by participant. Initially, 30 sessions were planned; however, the protocol was changed to 24 treatments due to difficulty completing all 30 given absences, school trips, and suspensions. Five of the 10 children enrolled did not complete all 24 sessions, due to issues such as participants withdrawing assent or transferring to another school. Parents for the five remaining cases reported changes across several domains, including: anxiety, self-esteem, flexibility, frustration tolerance, empathy, social interaction, anger, temper tantrums, and mood. No negative side effects were noted. Ten case studies of neurofeedback application in treatment of young children (4–7 years) with ASD were reported by Zivoder et al. (2015). Participants were seven males and three females diagnosed with ASD, who were high functioning. Target symptoms varied across participant, but included difficulties with attention, speech, and social relationships. Based on parent and teacher ratings, all children demonstrated improvements in target symptoms and electrophysiological measures; however, quantitative data regarding overall improvement for participants was not provided.

Jarusiewicz (2002) completed a randomized quasi-controlled trial with 40 participants. Twenty participants were randomized to active neurofeedback treatment while 20 participants were randomized to a wait-list control. Only 12 of the 20 participants randomized to active treatment completed a sufficient number of sessions to be included in the final analyses. Participants in the active group received 20 to 69 treatments, with an average of 36 sessions per participant. Training occurred at C4. A majority of children (57%) were rewarded for increasing 10–13 Hz activity while inhibiting 2–7 Hz and 22–30 Hz activity. Other protocols were used based on reported symptoms. For example, children with socialization and communication deficits received a bipolar F3-F4 electrode placement with up training from 7–10 Hz to 14.5–17.5 Hz and 2–7 Hz and 22–30 Hz inhibits. For children who exhibited emotional instability, a bipolar T3-T4 placement was used rewarding at 9–12 Hz activity and inhibiting 2–7 Hz and 22–30 Hz activity. Participants who received the active treatment exhibited significant improvements in sociability, speech/language/communication, health, and sensory/cognitive awareness. This study cannot be considered a true randomized clinical trial (RCT), since a waitlist was used as a control group, and protocol of neurofeedback in active treatment group was not uniform but used variable EEG training targets.

Kouijzer et al. (2009a) completed an open-label non-randomized pre-test-post-test control group design study that examined the TBR neurofeedback training in children with ASD to improve executive functioning deficits. Participants were required to have an IQ > 70 and a diagnosis of ASD per a health psychologist or psychiatrist. A majority of the participants were male (n = 12). Of the 14 participants, seven were randomized to active neurofeedback while the remaining seven were placed in a wait-list control group and were matched based on age, diagnosis, sex, and intelligence variables. Participants in the experimental group received two sessions of neurofeedback per week for a total of 40 sessions rewarding low beta band activity (12–15 Hz) while inhibiting theta activity (4–7 Hz) at C4. Each session consisted of seven 3-minutes segments of neurofeedback treatment separated by a 1-minute rest period between each segment. Five participants who received neurofeedback treatment demonstrated a reduction in theta activity post-treatment at cortical sites C3 and C4. Five participants showed increased beta activity at C4, while six showed improvement at C3. Delta activity (1.5–3.5 Hz) also increased in five participants. Children who receive the neurofeedback treatment demonstrated improved executive functioning in the domains of auditory selective attention, impulsivity, cognitive flexibility, goal setting, and speed and efficiency on executive functioning tasks. On questionnaires, rating scales, children in the intervention group were rated as significantly improved in several areas, including: non-verbal communication, general communication, social communication, and behavior. Parents reported that they were satisfied with the intervention and would recommend neurofeedback to other families who have children with ASD. One year after treatment ended, improvements in executive functioning noted immediately after treatment were maintained or increased (Kouijzer et al., 2009b).

EEG-Guided Neurofeedback

EEG-guided neurofeedback is the practice of using a baseline assessment of EEG functioning and comparing the outcome to established norms in order to identify appropriate treatment protocols. Thompson, Thompson, and Reid (2010a) suggested a rationale for application of neurofeedback in ASD and examined the outcomes of 150 individuals diagnosed with

Asperger's Syndrome (AS) and nine individuals diagnosed with autism across 15 years in a clinical setting (Thompson, Thompson, & Reid, 2010b). A majority of participants were children (n = 117), followed by adolescents (n = 30), and adults (n = 12). Participants were mostly males (n = 139). Several protocols were used, and treatment was driven by assessment and EEG findings. A majority of protocols focused on increasing sensorimotor rhythm (SMR) at FCz for adults and Cz for children while simultaneously decreasing amplitude and variability in slow wave activity. Some variability in training site occurred within and between patients. For example, training sites varied by session and for participant between C2, C3, and C4 in addition to FCz and Cz. Slow wave activity targeted for treatment varied from 3–7 Hz or 4–8 Hz and 8–10 Hz in individuals with very high alpha waves. Additionally, treatment focused on the reduction of spindling beta when it was present. Sometimes a bipolar placement (FCz-CPz) was used in children with hyperactivity to minimize the impact muscle artifact. Training at C3 was used for children who needed additional support with functions located in the left hemisphere, such as language. Finally, if children displayed symptoms of a reading disorder, training was designed to stimulate Wernicke's area. Continuous performance tests completed at pre- and post-testing indicated improvements in executive functioning (e.g., attention, impulsivity). Psychological testing demonstrated improvements in academic skills (i.e., reading, spelling, arithmetic), and cognitive abilities (i.e., full scale intelligence quotient, verbal comprehension, and perceptual reasoning/performance). Moreover, participants demonstrated a significant reduction in theta to beta ratio from pre- to post-test. Finally, improvements significant improvements in ADHD symptoms as measured by the Conners Global Index. More outcomes of NFB application in ASD treatment by this group can be found in Thompson and Thompson (2015).

Kouijzer et al. (Kouijzer, van Schie, de Moor, Gerrits, & Buitelaar, 2010) examined the use of QEEG guided neurofeedback that targeted excessive theta activity in 20 children between the ages of 8 and 12. Participants were mostly males (n = 17), received an IQ score over 80, and diagnosed with ASD by a health care psychologist. Training site and frequency bands trained were determined based on each child's individual EEG in conjunction with the Neuroguide database. Each participant received 40 neurofeedback treatments consisting of seven 3-minute training segments with a 1-minute break in between segments. Outcomes were evaluated against a non-treatment control group. Results indicated that participants who received neurofeedback treatment demonstrated improvements in parent- and teacher-rated social behavior and set-shifting. QEEG data indicated that participants receiving neurofeedback treatment successfully inhibited theta activity during treatment and overall changes after treatment concluded. Several treatment effects were maintained 6 months after treatment.

While Kouijzer and colleagues (2010) demonstrated an effect for neurofeedback in 20 participants, there were several limitations. The biggest limitation was the active neurofeedback treatment being compared to a no-treatment control, which may have resulted in a placebo effect for the participants receiving the active treatment. In order to address this, the same research team (Kouijzer et al., 2013) completed a randomized control trial for children (N = 38) 12 to 18 years old diagnosed with autism, Asperger disorder, or PDD-NOS. Diagnoses were given by psychiatrists or health care psychologists, according to the criteria in the DSM-IV-TR. Children with psychiatric comorbidities, such as ADHD or epilepsy were excluded. In contrast to the previous study, participants were randomized to the EEG-biofeedback, skin conductance (SC)-biofeedback, and a wait list control group.

EEG-biofeedback consisted of 40 training sessions at Cz (n = 8) or FCz (n = 5). Sensor placements and targeted frequencies were selected based on the 19-channel EEG recording using Neuroguide norms. SC-biofeedback consisted of 40 sessions of skin conductance training via an electrode attached to the participants' fingers. Participants in the EEG and SC groups did not know if they were receiving feedback based on their EEG or based on skin conductance. Finally, the wait list control group did not receive any active treatment. Each EEG or SC feedback session consisted of seven 3-minute intervals with a 1-minute break between intervals. When participants were achieving the desired physiological state, they would see a video clip or sound that the participant selected as interesting. Thresholds were set to allow participants to be receiving a reward 50% to 80% of the time. Participants who were able to successfully train their EEG (n = 5) or SC (n = 8) in the desired direction were considered "regulators." EEG-biofeedback regulators demonstrated significant improvements in the domain of cognitive flexibility, which was maintained at 6-month follow up. These changes were not found in the SC-biofeedback group. No changes were noted in the domain of ASD symptoms and 19-channel EEG recordings. This study resulted in interesting commentaries focused on validity of selected control group (Coben & Ricca, 2015; van Schie, Gerrits, Buitelaar, & Kouijzer, 2015). Coben & Ricca (2015) proposed several theories for the lack of significant findings. They posit that training at Cz or FCz may have not been optimal given findings from previous neuroimaging studies that indicate autism is a bilateral brain disorder, with abnormal communication across brain regions (e.g., Catani et al., 2008). Further, they suggest that the differences seen between the EEG-biofeedback group and the SC-biofeedback group would have been greater if coherence or connectivity neurofeedback training was implemented using a bipolar placement. The authors (van Schie et al., 2015) responded highlighting the importance of their finding that cognitive flexibility did in fact improve more in the EEG-biofeedback group. Additionally, they asserted that monopolar placements, such as the one used in their study, have the capability to impact brain connectivity, citing evidence from previous work that training at C3 impacts EEG measurements at C4 (e.g., Kouijzer et al., 2009ab). Finally, van Schie and colleagues (van Schie et al., 2015) assert that the concern regarding the placement of the electrode at Cz or FCz is unfounded, given there is not a direct one to one relationship between where an electrode is placed and the areas of the brain that are affected, meaning that training at FCz and Cz not only impacts those direct areas (i.e., frontal cortex), but other areas of the brain that may be directly linked to ASD.

Mirror Neuron (Mu) Activity Neurofeedback

Mirror neuron activity (mu) abnormalities are thought to potentially play a role in the manifestation of autism symptoms. Mirror neurons activate in response to observing an action, similarly to how they would respond if the person observing the action was completing the action themselves. This behavior is thought to play a role in motor comprehension. It is possible that mirror neurons may also be involved with other deficits associated with ASD, such as imitation deficit, social competence, theory of mind, and empathy (Oberman et al., 2005; Pineda et al., 2014a). Oberman and colleagues (2005) sought to measure mu activity via EEG in 11 individuals with autism and 13 matched control. Participants engaged in several tasks including: 1) moving their own hand, 2) watching a video of a moving hand, 3) watching a video of two bouncing balls, and 4) watching visual white noise (i.e., television static). EEG data was gathered from 13 cortical locations; however, mu rhythm is defined as oscillations in the sensorimotor cortex. Therefore, only data from C3, Cz and C4 were reported. Individuals with autism demonstrated a lack of suppression during the hand movement task potentially indicating dysfunction in the mirror neuron system. Given the difference in mirror neuron activity for individuals with and without ASD, these neurons appear to be a potential target for neurofeedback training.

Pineda and colleagues (2008) conducted two studies examining the utility of mu activity training in children with ASD. In the first study, participants (n = 8) were males ranging in age from 7 to 17, who were previously diagnosed with autism by a mental health care provider. Participants were randomly assigned to placebo (n = 4) or experimental (n = 5) conditions and were unaware of assignment. Participants randomized to the experimental treatment received 30 neurofeedback sessions consisting of 30 minutes of training three times per week targeting mu-activity at C4 and EMG activity from the trapezius muscles. Those randomized to the placebo condition received the same frequency and duration of training. These participants also trained EMG activity, but they viewed a fake mu signal. Results indicated that those receiving active neurofeedback treatment significantly manipulated the ratio of mu band to broadband spectrum in training sessions. In contrast, the placebo group did not demonstrate any changes in mu activity. EEG recordings revealed that the experimental group demonstrated a decrease in resting mu amplitude. Finally, participants in the experimental group displayed improvements in in the domain of sustained attention and sensory/cognitive awareness. The second study built upon the first by including participants who had a confirmed diagnosis of autism, using the Autism Diagnostic Observation Scale (ADOS). Furthermore, the treatment was further refined by focusing on the high mu band (10–13hz), which was identified as more responsive to training in the first study. Additionally, thresholds were set based on the initial baseline session and were only changed when the participant demonstrated adequate learning. Results were similar to the first study, but improvements were more robust. More recently, Pineda, Carrasco, Datko, Pillen and Schalles (2014b) recruited 13 participants with ASD (n = 10 males; ages 7–17 years) and 11 typically developing (TD) control subjects (n = 7 males; ages 8–17 years). All participants received approximately 30 hours of neurofeedback treatment, which consisted of enhancing mu activity (8–12 Hz) at C4 while simultaneously inhibiting theta (4–8 Hz) and beta (13–30 Hz). Results indicated that participants with ASD demonstrated more improvements in mu activity than the TD group, while the TD group demonstrated greater reductions in theta activity. Participants with ASD demonstrated improvements on parent rated behaviors including, social responsiveness and overall ASD symptoms; however, no changes were noted in functional behavior.

Recently, Datko and colleagues (2018) conducted an open-label randomized control trial examining the utility of approximately 20–30 hours of sensorimotor mu-rhythm based neurofeedback on ASD symptoms. Individuals diagnosed with ASD who met study criteria (e.g., high functioning, IQ > 80) were assigned to the neurofeedback group (n = 17). Typically developing children (n = 11) were assigned to a control group. Participants in the neurofeedback group ranged in age from 9 to 18 years old, while participants in the control group ranged from 8 to 16 years. Neurofeedback treatment consisted of training at C4 rewarding mu-activity in the 8–13 Hz range and inhibiting theta (4–8Hz) and beta (13–10 Hz). Participants received neurofeedback treatment twice per week, with each session lasting approximately 45 minutes for 20 weeks. Results of fMRI image analysis after the study was completed found a significant and positive correlation between activation in the right inferior parietal lobule and the ratio of mu/baseline power. Moreover, after neurofeedback treatment, differences in brain activation observed via fMRI during an imitation task between ASD children and typically developing children were no longer significant. Additionally, participants who received neurofeedback demonstrated significant improvements in social responsiveness.

Friedrich and colleagues (2014) provide a rationale for the combination of biofeedback with mu neurofeedback via brain computer interface (BCI) tasks that allow the participant to be virtually immersed in a specific situation (e.g., social interaction). The rationale for this approach, which is called the polyvagal theory, centers on the notion that it is not just cortical deficiencies that play a role in social difficulties experienced by individuals with ASD; rather, the abnormal peripheral physiological reactions of the autonomous nervous system to social stimuli also plays a part in the atypical response to social stimuli. Therefore, improving physiological responses to social stimuli via biofeedback may result in improvements in the domains of social engagement and emotional responsiveness. One example of a BCI task is the Social Mirroring Game. During this game, children have an avatar that interacts with a computer-generated character via the game. The participant is rewarded for imitating the facial expressions of the computer-generated character, which is accomplished by modifying brain activity, such as mu power, and peripherical physiological activation.

Friedrich and colleagues (2015) examined this approach in thirteen participants diagnosed with ASD. Participants were between the ages of 6 and 17 years old. All participants were diagnosed with ASD by a clinician. Participants were pseudo-randomly assigned to a training group. Individuals in both groups participated in 16 neurofeedback treatments two to three times per week. Training occurred at C4. Both groups of participants played the Social Mirroring Computer game;

however, participants assigned to Group 1 were rewarded for enhancing mu power during both non-social gaming episodes and social interaction sequences of the game, while children in Group 2 were rewarded for increasing mu power during non-social gaming episodes and decreasing mu activity during social interaction sequences. Children in both groups were rewarded for inhibiting theta (3–8 Hz) and high beta (18–30 Hz). To increase mu power, children were told to relax, while to decrease mu power, children were asked to envision themselves in a social interaction. Participants in both groups were able to increase and decrease EEG activity based on their assigned group. Overall, participants demonstrated improved ability to identify emotions and spontaneously imitate behavior to emotional stimuli. Parent-rated symptom scales indicated improvements in ASD symptoms, social responsiveness, and behavioral adaptation.

Connectivity-Guided Neurofeedback Aimed at Coherence Training in ASD

Coben and associates are strong proponents of advantages of EEG coherence training in autism. Coben, Clarke, Hudspeth, and Barry (2008) examined the EEG characteristics of 20 children diagnosed with ASD compared to 20 subjects who were typically developing. EEG was assessed across 19 cortical sites while participants were resting with their eyes closed. Results indicated that participants with ASD had higher levels of theta activity in the right posterior region, a reduction of beta in the right hemisphere, an increase of beta at the midline, and lower levels of absolute delta. Additionally, the authors identified abnormal connectivity/coherence across areas of the brain. Overall, children with autism demonstrated underactivity across brain regions compared to the typically developing participants. Within the same hemisphere, children with ASD demonstrated lower coherence in delta and theta both and medium distances between electrodes. Delta and theta coherence was also lower interhemispherically in the frontal region of the brain. Additionally, hypercoherence was observed in delta, theta, and alpha frequencies in the temporal areas. Finally, lower coherence was found for delta, theta, and beta waves in posterior areas. Coben, Chabot, and Hirshberg (2013) expanded upon their prior work by examining the EEG characteristics of 91 children diagnosed with ASD and 91 typically developing children. In the largest study to complete this task, the authors confirmed the previous findings, including excess relative and absolute theta power in the frontal, central, and temporal regions and higher levels of beta in frontal and central regions. Moreover, the results of this study identified excessive alpha in all regions except posterior cortical regions. Finally, results indicate power asymmetry across hemispheres. Participants with ASD had more delta and theta and less alpha in their right hemisphere and more beta power in their left hemisphere compared to their left hemisphere, which was not found in typically developing children. Finally, an overall pattern of high levels of coherence in frontal areas and decreased coherence in posterior/temporal areas was identified. Coben and colleagues assert that these findings suggest that ASD is a disorder of neural connectivity and interventions that target coherence/connectivity are likely to be effective.

Coben and Padolsky (2007) were the first to examine the efficacy of coherence training in children diagnosed with ASD. Thirty-seven participants were placed in the treatment group while 12 children who had similar characteristics to the experimental group served as the wait list control. Neurofeedback protocols based on each child's initial EEG assessment and were targeted at areas of maximal hyperconnectivity. Parent completed rating scales indicated that improvement in ASD symptoms for 89% of participants who received neurofeedback. Parents reported significant improvements on measures of overall ASD symptoms and executive functioning.

Neuropsychological measures identified significant improvements in the domains of attention, visual perceptual functioning, executive function, and language skills. Coben and Myers (2010) examined the relative effectiveness of coherence/connectivity-based neurofeedback compared to symptom-based neurofeedback by comparing the results of the Coben and Padolsky (2007) study, which utilized coherence training, to the results of a study completed by Jarusiewicz (2002), which administered neurofeedback based on symptoms. Overall, the Coben and Padolsky study was more effective in treating symptoms of autism compared to the Jarusiewicz study, with significant differences in sensory and cognitive awareness, health, and overall behavior. Moreover, these results were achieved with fewer sessions.

Coben, Sherlin, Hudspeth, McKeon and Ricca (2014) expanded upon these previous studies by examining changes in brain functioning after coherence training. Thirty-seven children with ASD were selected to receive connectivity-guided neurofeedback treatment, while 12 children were selected as wait list controls. Prior to treatment, the groups did not differ significantly on any identifiable demographic or symptom variable. After treatment, significant improvements were noted in connectivity across many areas of the brain. Specifically, results indicated a reduction in hyperconnectivity in the frontotemporal region. The major finding of their study was that connectivity-guided neurofeedback is a treatment capable of causing therapeutic neurophysiological changes in the brains of children with ASD. These findings were further substantiated by the eLORETA analysis, which showed prominent source localized changes in power in crucial regions of the brain for such children. These changes were evident across frontal, temporal, and limbic regions. The results of this study expanded upon the findings found by authors previously (Coben & Padolsky, 2007). The series of studies conducted by Coben et al. (Coben, Linden, & Myers, 2010; Coben et al., 2013, 2014) provides preliminary evidence that connectivity-guided neurofeedback is capable of producing neurophysiological changes while concurrently reducing autistic symptoms. Specifically, the findings provide support for hypothesis that links reductions in hypercoherence and source-localized power with reductions in autistic symptoms.

Gamma Neurofeedback

One more approach to neurofeedback training technique was based on observed abnormality of gamma activity in individuals with autism. Strong evidence both from animal and human experiments indicated that high frequency gamma band oscillations, especially those around 40 Hz frequencies, are most directly associated with entrainment of local networks. Some experimental studies have found that 40 Hz centered gamma activity are correlated with human perceptual binding (Herrmann & Mecklinger, 2000). This is especially true for the 35–45 Hz range gamma sub-band in EEG which was thought to be closely associated with the mechanisms of the information processing such as sensory, working memory, attention and other cognitive processes (Grice et al., 2001; Tallon-Baudry & Bertrand, 1999; Tallon-Baudry, Bertrand, Delpuech, & Pernier, 1996). Based on the above, abnormalities in the 35–45 Hz gamma oscillatory activity probably can be considered as one of the underlying causes of the cognitive deficits observed in autism. It provides a strong rationale to train 40 Hz-centered EEG frequency in NFB mode. Furthermore, EEG activity level in 40 Hz (35–45 Hz range) may serve as prospective biomarker in ASD treatment and potentially used as predictor of neurofeedback training success in ASD. Application of 40 Hz gamma neurofeedback for attention and cognition improvement in typical subjects started in late 70s but did not receive sufficient recognition (e.g., Bird,

Newton, Sheer, & Ford, 1978ab; Ford, Bird, Newton, & Sheer, 1980). This particular protocol of NFB definitely deserves more in-depth research. An exploratory study by Wang et al. (2016) using 40 Hz gamma power upregulation found that theta/beta ratios (both theta/low beta and theta/high beta) showed a significant linear decrease over 18 sessions of neurofeedback. The ratios also decreased statistically from the first to the last NFB training sessions. Another exploratory trial used 40 Hz-centered gamma upregulation following repetitive transcranial magnetic stimulation (rTMS) treatment in children with ASD (Sokhadze et al., 2014). Both of these studies reported improvements in parental ratings of aberrant behavior and repetitive and stereotype behavior ratings. The study where NFB was combined with rTMS found improved accuracy of performance on a visual oddball task and enhanced functional measures of executive functions as compared to the waitlist group outcomes (Sokhadze et al., 2014).

Clinical Efficacy

Several reviews on neurofeedback for ASD have been published including Holtmann et al. (2011) and more extensive reviews completed by Coben (2013), Coben and colleagues (2010), and Linden and Gunkelman (2013). Overall, the reviews identify that positive improvements occurred in children who received various treatments for ASD. Holtmann and colleagues (2011) raise concerns that the available studies primarily document changes in comorbid ADHD symptoms rather than symptoms of ASD. In contrast, Coben and colleagues (2013) were more positive about the results of previous research, concluding that neurofeedback treatments for ASD are possibly efficacious. All of the reviews highlighted the need for further more rigorous research.

Hurt, Arnold and Lofthouse. (2014) reviewed four small RCTs. Results of the review were interpreted to make recommendations on the use of neurofeedback for the treatment of ASD in clinical settings. In the two out of four RCTs reviewed (i.e., Kouijzer et al., 2010, 2013), means and standard deviations were reported allowing for the calculation of post-treatment effect size (ES). Combination of these two studies, resulted in a large effect size (d = 1.11) across outcome measures. However, a majority of the effect size data were drawn from one study. Hurt and colleagues (2014) note that many of the studies of neurofeedback for ASD employed some form of randomization, included children who were formally assessed for ASD, and documented changes in EEG after treatment. Despite this, the authors identified several areas for improvements, including the use of a double-blind sham-controlled RCT, follow up assessments to monitor latent treatment effects/non-effects, assessment of adverse events, and the monitoring of concurrent treatments. Using the United States Preventative Services Task Force (USPSTF) criteria for the Level of Certainty of Research Evidence and Recommendation Grade (2007), Hurt and colleagues (2014) rated neurofeedback for autism as "fair." A rating of fair is provided for treatments that have sufficient evidence to determine effects on outcomes, but the strength of the evidence is limited by the number, quality, or consistency of the individual studies, generalizability to routine practice, or indirect nature of the evidence on health outcomes. According to the most current grades provided by the USPSTF, the results of previous research suggest that neurofeedback for ASD would receive a "B" classification, as there is high certainty that the net benefit is moderate or there is moderate certainty that the net benefit is moderate to substantial. At this time, there is not a high level of certainty that neurofeedback is beneficial for the treatment of ASD due to the small number and methodological limitations of these studies; however, with improved methodology and more research, this classification could change (Hurt et al., 2014).

Conclusions and Future Directions

Neurofeedback for ASD is a promising treatment. Despite this, the currently available studies have weaknesses, such as small sample sizes and the lack of an indistinguishable placebo condition, that need to be addressed. Future research should address these weaknesses to further refine and establish the efficacy, effectiveness, and acceptability of this treatment for individuals with ASD. First, randomized placebo-controlled studies are necessary for each protocol (e.g., TBR, QEEG guided neurofeedback, coherence training) to verify efficacy and identify adverse events. Follow up assessments are necessary to examine the persistence of treatment effects over time. Second, a combination of available protocols (e.g., theta-to-beta, SMR, mu and gamma oscillation) should be examined to identify if such protocols are stronger in combination than alone. Third, once efficacy of a protocols is established, comparative intervention studies should be developed to identify the most efficacious treatment approaches. Finally, treatment acceptability and feasibility studies are needed. Some studies reviewed in this chapter noted a significant drop out rate (e.g., Scolnick, 2005), while others demonstrate a majority of participants completing treatment. Identifying factors that allow participants to persist with treatment is essential.

References

American Psychiatric Association. (2013). *Diagnostic and statistical manual of mental disorders (DSM-5®)*. American Psychiatric Publishing.

Arns, M., de Ridder, S., Strehl, U., Breteler, M., & Coenen, A. (2009). Efficacy of neurofeedback treatment in ADHD: The effects on inattention, impulsivity and hyperactivity: A meta-analysis. *Clinical EEG and Neuroscience, 40*(3), 180–189.

Arns, M., Conners, C. K., & Kraemer, H. C. (2013). A decade of EEG theta/beta ratio research in ADHD: A meta-analysis. *Journal of Attention Disorders, 17*(5), 374–383.

Arns, M., Heinrich, H., & Strehl, U. (2014). Evaluation of neurofeedback in ADHD: The long and winding road. *Biological Psychology, 95*, 108–115.

Arns, M., Heinrich, H., Ros, T., Rothenberger, A., & Strehl, U. (2015). Editorial: Neurofeedback in ADHD. *Frontiers in Human Neuroscience, 9*, 602.
Bird, B. L., Newton, F. A., Sheer, D. E., & Ford, M. (1978a). Biofeedback training of 40-Hz EEG in humans. *Biofeedback and Self-Regulation, 3*(1), 1–11.
Bird, B. L., Newton, F. A., Sheer, D. E., & Ford, M. (1978b). Behavioral and electroencephalographic correlates of 40 Hz EEG biofeedback training in humans. *Biofeedback and Self-Regulation, 3*(1), 13–28.
Cantor, D. S., Thatcher, R. W., Hrybyk, M., & Kaye, H. (1986). Computerized EEG analysis of autistic children. *Journal of Autism and Developmental Disorders, 16*(2), 169–187.
Casanova, M. F., Baruth, J. A., El-Baz, S., Sokhadze, G. E., Hensley, M., & Sokhadze, E. M. (2013). Evoked and induced gamma-frequency oscillation in autism. In M. F. Casanova, A. S. El-Baz, & J. S. Suri (Eds.), *Imaging the brain in autism* (pp. 87–106). New York, NY: Springer.
Catani, M., Jones, D. K., Daly, E., Embiricos, N., Deeley, Q., Pugliese, L., ... Murphy, D. G. (2008). Altered cerebellar feedback projections in Asperger syndrome. *Neuroimage, 41*(4), 1184–1191.
Coben, R. (2013). Neurofeedback for autistic disorders: Emerging empirical evidence. In M. F. Casanova, A. S. El-Baz, & J. S. Suri (Eds.), *Imaging the brain in autism* (pp. 107–133). New York, NY: Springer.
Coben, R., & Padolsky, I. (2007). Assessment-guided neurofeedback for autistic spectrum disorder. *Journal of Neurotherapy, 11*(1), 5–23.
Coben, R., & Myers, T. E. (2010). The relative efficacy of connectivity guided and symptom based EEG biofeedback for autistic disorders. *Applied Psychophysiology and Biofeedback, 35*(1), 13–23.
Coben, R., & Ricca, R. (2015). EEG biofeedback for autism spectrum disorder: A commentary on Kouijzer et al. (2013). *Applied Psychophysiology and Biofeedback, 40*(1), 53–56.
Coben, R., Clarke, A. R., Hudspeth, W., & Barry, R. J. (2008). EEG power and coherence in autism spectrum disorder. *Clinical Neurophysiology, 119*(5), 1002–1009.
Coben, R., Linden, M., & Myers, T. E. (2010). Neurofeedback for autistic spectrum disorder: a review of the literature. *Applied Psychophysiology and Biofeedback, 35*(1), 83–105.
Coben, R., Chabot, R. J., & Hirshberg, L. (2013). EEG analyses in the assessment of autistic disorders. In *Imaging the Brain in Autism* (pp. 349-370). New York, NY: Springer.
Coben, R., Sherlin, L., Hudspeth, W. J., McKeon, K., & Ricca, R. (2014). Connectivity-guided EEG biofeedback for autism spectrum disorder: Evidence of neurophysiological changes. *NeuroRegulation, 1*(2), 109–130.
Collura, T. F., & Siever, D. (2009). Auditory-visual entrainment

in relation to mental health and EEG. In T. H. Budzynski, H. Kogan Budzynski, J. R. Evans, A. Abarbanel (Eds.), *Introduction to Quantitative EEG and neurofeedback: Advance theory and applications* (pp. 195–225). Academic Press.

Datko, M., Pineda, J. A., & Müller, R. A. (2018). Positive effects of neurofeedback on autism symptoms correlate with brain activation during imitation and observation. *European Journal of Neuroscience*, *47*(6), 579–591.

Fernandez, T., Herrera, W., Harmony, T., Diaz-Comas, L., Santiago, E., Sanchez, L., ... Barraza, C. (2003). EEG and behavioral changes following neurofeedback treatment in learning disabled children. *Clinical Electroencephalography*, *34*(3), 145–152.

Ford, M., Bird, B. L., Newton, F. A., Sheer, D. E. (1980). Maintenance and generalization of 40-Hz EEG biofeedback effects. *Biofeedback and Self-Regulation*, *5*, 193–205.

Friedrich, E. V., Suttie, N., Sivanathan, A., Lim, T., Louchart, S., & Pineda, J. A. (2014). Brain-computer interface game applications for combined neurofeedback and biofeedback treatment for children on the autism spectrum. *Frontiers in Neuroengineering*, *7*, 21.

Friedrich, E. V., Sivanathan, A., Lim, T., Suttie, N., Louchart, S., Pillen, S., & Pineda, J. A. (2015). An effective neurofeedback intervention to improve social interactions in children with autism spectrum disorder. *Journal of Autism and Developmental Disorders*, *45*(12), 4084–4100.

Gevensleben, H., Holl, B., Albrecht, B., Vogel, C., Schlamp, D., Kratz, O., ... Heinrich H. (2009). Is neurofeedback an efficacious treatment for ADHD? A randomised controlled clinical trial. *Journal of Child Psychology and Psychiatry*, *50*(7), 780–789.

Grice, S. J., Spratling, M. W., Karmiloff-Smith, A., Halit, H., Csibra, G., de Haan, M., & Johnson, M. H. (2001). Disordered visual processing and oscillatory brain activity in autism and Williams syndrome. *NeuroReport*, *12*(12), 2697–2700.

Hammond, D. C. (2011). What is neurofeedback: An update. *Journal of Neurotherapy*, *15*(4), 305–336.

Herrmann, C. S., & Mecklinger, A. (2000). Magnetoencephalographic responses to illusory figures: Early evoked gamma is affected by processing of stimulus features. *International Journal of Psychophysiology*, *38*(3), 265–281.

Holtmann, M., Steiner, S., Hohmann, S., Poustka, L., Banaschewski, T., & Bölte, S. (2011). Neurofeedback in autism spectrum disorders. *Developmental Medicine & Child Neurology*, *53*(11), 986–993.

Hurt, E., Arnold, L. E., & Lofthouse, N. (2014). Quantitative EEG neurofeedback for the treatment of pediatric attention deficit/hyperactivity disorder, autism spectrum disorders, learning disorders, and epilepsy. *Child and Adolescent Psychiatric Clinics of North America, 23*(3), 465–486.

Jarusiewicz, B. (2002). Efficacy of neurofeedback for children in the autistic spectrum. A pilot study. *Journal of Neurotherapy, 6*(4), 39–49.

Kana, R. K., Keller, T. A., Minshew, N. J., & Just, M. A. (2007). Inhibitory control in high-functioning autism: Decreased activation and underconnectivity in inhibition networks. *Biological Psychiatry, 62*(3), 198–206.

Kamiya, J. (2011). The first communications about operant conditioning of the EEG. *Journal of Neurotherapy*, 15(1), 65–73.

Kerson, C., & Collaborative Neurofeedback Group. (2013). A proposed multisite double-blind randomized clinical trial of neurofeedback for ADHD: Need, rationale, and strategy. *Journal of Attention Disorders, 17*(5), 420–436.

Kouijzer, M. E., van Schie, H. T., Gerrits, B. J., Buitelaar, J. K., & de Moor, J. M. (2013). Is EEG-biofeedback an effective treatment in autism spectrum disorders? A randomized controlled trial. *Applied Psychophysiology and Biofeedback, 38*(1), 17–28.

Kouijzer, M. E. J., de Moor, J. M. H., Gerrits, B. J. L., Congedo, M., & van Schie, H. T. (2009a). Neurofeedback improves executive functioning in children with autism spectrum disorders. *Research in Autism Spectrum Disorders, 3*, 145–162.

Kouijzer, M. E. J., de Moor, J. M. H., Gerrits, B. J. L., Buitelaar, J. K., & van Schie, H. T. (2009b). Long-term effects of neurofeedback treatment in autism. *Research in Autism Spectrum Disorders, 3*, 496–501.

Kouijzer, M. E. J., van Schie, H. T., De Moor, J. M. H., Gerrits, B. J. L., & Buitelaar, J. K. (2010). Neurofeedback treatment in autism. Preliminary findings in behavioral, cognitive, and neurophysiological functioning. *Research in Autism Spectrum Disorders, 4*, 386–389.

Linden, M., & Gunkelman, J. (2013). QEEG-guided neurofeedback for autism: Clinical observations and outcomes. In M. F. Casanova, A. S. El-Baz, & J. S. Suri (Eds.), *Imaging the brain in autism* (pp. 45–60). New York, NY: Springer.

Lubar, J. F. (2003). Neurofeedback for the management of attention deficit disorders. In M. S. Schwartz & F. Andrasik (Eds.), *The biofeedback: A practitioner's guide* (3rd ed.) (pp. 409–437). New York: Guilford Press.

Murias, M., Webb, S. J., Greenson, J., & Dawson, G. (2007). Resting state cortical connectivity reflected in EEG coherence in individuals with autism. *Biological Psychiatry, 62*(3), 270–273.

Oberman, L. M., Hubbard, E. M., McCleery, J. P., Altschuler, E. L., Ramachandran, V. S., & Pineda, J. A. (2005). EEG evidence for mirror neuron dysfunction in autism spectrum disorders. *Cognitive Brain Research, 24*(2), 190–198.

Orekhova, E. V., Stroganova, T. A., Nygren, G., Tsetlin, M., Posikera, I., Gillberg, C., & Elam, M. (2007). Excess of high frequency electroencephalogram oscillations in boys with autism. *Biological Psychiatry, 62*(9), 1022–1029.

Pelphrey, K., Adolphs, R., & Morris, J. P. (2004). Neuroanatomical substrates of social cognition dysfunction in autism. *Developmental Disabilities Research Reviews, 10*(4), 259–271.

Pineda, J. A., Brang, D., Hecht, E., Edwards, L., Carey, S., Bacon, M., ... Rork, A. (2008). Positive behavioral and electrophysiological changes following neurofeedback training in children with autism. *Research in Autism Spectrum Disorders, 2*(3), 557–581.

Pineda, J. A., Friedrich, E. V. C., & LaMarca, K. (2014a). Neurorehabilitation of social dysfunctions: A model-based neurofeedback approach for low and high-functioning autism. *Frontiers in Neuroengineering, 7*(7), 29.

Pineda, J. A., Carrasco, K., Datko, M., Pillen, S., & Schalles, M. (2014b). Neurofeedback training produces normalization in behavioural and electrophysiological measures of high-functioning autism. *Philosophical Transactions of the Royal Society of London. Series B, Biological Sciences, 369*(1644), 20130183.

Rojas, D. C., & Wilson, L. B. (2014). Gamma-band abnormalities as markers of autism spectrum disorders. *Biomarkers in Medicine, 8*(3), 353–368.

Scolnick, B. (2005). Effects of electroencephalogram biofeedback with Asperger's syndrome. *International Journal of Rehabilitation Research, 28*(2), 159–163.

Schultz, R. T. (2005). Developmental deficits in social perception in autism: The role of the amygdala and fusiform face area. *International Journal of Developmental Neuroscience, 23*(2–3), 125–141.

Sherlin, L., Arns, M., Lubar, J., & Sokhadze, E. (2010). A position paper on neurofeedback for the treatment of ADHD. *Journal of Neurotherapy, 14*(2), 66–78.

Sherlin, L., Arns, M., Lubar, J., Heinrich, H., Kerson, C., Strehl, U., & Sterman, M. B. (2011). Neurofeedback and basic learning theory: Implications for research and practice. *Journal of Neurotherapy, 15*(4), 292–304.

Sichel, A. G., Fehmi, L. G., & Goldstein, D. M. (1995). Positive outcome with neurofeedback treatment in a case of mild autism. *Journal of Neurotherapy, 1*(1), 60–64.

Sokhadze, E. M., El-Baz, A. S., Tasman, A., Sears, L. L., Wang, Y., Lamina, E. V., & Casanova, M. F. (2014). Neuromodulation integrating rTMS and neurofeedback for the treatment of autism spectrum disorder: An exploratory study. *Applied Psychophysiology and Biofeedback, 39*(3–4), 237–257.

Sokhadze, E. M., Casanova, M. F., El-Baez, A. S., Farag, H. E., Li, X., & Wang, Y. (2016). TMS-based neuromodulation of evoked and induced gamma oscillations and event-related potentials in children with autism. *NeuroRegulation, 3*(3), 101–126.

Sokhadze, T. M., Cannon, R., & Trudeau, D. L. (2008). EEG biofeedback as a treatment for substance use disorders: Review, rating of efficacy and recommendations for future research. *Applied Psychophysiology and Biofeedback*, *33*(1), 1–28.

Stroganova, T. A., Butorina, A. V., Sysoeva, O. V., Prokofyev, A.O., Nikolaeva, A. Y., Tsetlin, M. M., Orekhova, E. V. (2015). Altered modulation of gamma oscillation frequency by speed of visual motion in children with autism spectrum disorders. *Journal of Neurodevelopmental Disorders, 7*(1), 21.

Tallon-Baudry, C., Bertrand, O., Delpuech, C., & Pernier, J. (1996). Stimulus specificity of phase-locked and non-phase-locked 40 Hz visual responses in human. *Journal of Neuroscience, 16*(13), 4240–4249.

Tallon-Baudry, C., & Bertrand, O. (1999). Oscillatory gamma activity in humans and its role in object representation. *Trends in Cognitive Sciences, 3*(4), 151–162.

Thompson, M., & Thompson, L. (2015). *The neurofeedback book* (2nd edition). Wheat Ridge, CO: The Association for Applied Psychophysiology and Biofeedback.

Thompson, L., Thompson, M., & Reid, A. (2010a). Functional neuroanatomy and the rationale for using EEG biofeedback for clients with Asperger's syndrome. *Applied Psychophysiology and Biofeedback, 35*(1), 39–61.

Thompson, L., Thompson, M., & Reid, A. (2010b). Neurofeedback outcomes in clients with Asperger's syndrome. *Applied Psychophysiology and Biofeedback*, *35*(1), 63–81.

US Preventive Services Task Force. Level of certainty of research evidence and recommendation. (2007). Available at: http://www.uspreventiveservicestaskforce.org/uspstf/grades.htm. Accessed February 2017.

van der Kolk, B. A., Hodgdon, H., Gapen, M., Musicaro, R., Suvak, M. K., Hamlin, E., & Spinazzola, J. (2016). A randomized controlled study of neurofeedback for chronic PTSD. *PLoS One*, *11*(12), e0166752.

van Schie, H. T., Gerrits, B. J. L., Buitelaar, J. K., & Kouijzer, M. E. J. (2015). EEG biofeedback for autism spectrum disorders: A reply to a commentary by Coben and Ricca. *Applied Psychophysiology and Biofeedback, 40*(1), 57–60.

Wang, A. T., Dapretto, M., Hariri, A. R., Sigman, M., & Bookheimer, S. Y. (2004). Neural correlates of facial affect processing in children and adolescents with autism spectrum disorder. *Journal of the American Academy of Child & Adolescent Psychiatry*, *43*(4), 481–490.

Wang, Y., Sokhadze, E. M., El-Baz, A. S., Li, X., Sears, L., Casanova, M. F., & Tasman, A. (2016). Relative power of specific EEG bands and their ratios during neurofeedback training in children with autism spectrum disorder. *Frontiers in Human Neuroscience, 9*, 723.

Zivoder, I., Martic-Biocina, S., Kosic, A. V., & Bosak, J. (2015). Neurofeedback application in the treatment of autistic spectrum disorders (ASD). *Psychiatria Danubina, 27*(1), S391–S394.

11

Three Cases of Autistic Disorder Assessed with Quantitative EEG and Treated With Neurofeedback

John K. Nash

Behavioral Medicine Associates, Inc.
Edina, Minnesota

St. Mary's University of Minnesota
Minneapolis, Minnesota

Autistic disorder (ICD-10 F84.0) presents in a variety of ways at different levels of severity. Deficits in social communication, self-stimulation, very limited interests and emotional outbursts when bothered by noise, changes in routine or other seemingly mild stressors are common in this disorder (Seltzer et al., 2003). Other chapters in this book discuss the typical symptoms of autistic disorder in detail and also describe electroencephalographic concomitants that have been found in group studies. This chapter presents background clinical information, quantitative electroencephalographic (qEEG) data and treatment outcomes for three patients who have been treated for several years at our clinic. There is a lot of variability in the EEGs between our patients with autistic disorder, and across time the abnormalities change within patients and are somewhat of a "moving target" as was noted by Wang et al. (2013). In that review of studies on resting state EEG in autistic disorder, the authors noted a lot of variability amongst the findings they reviewed, but commonly there was excessive power in low-frequency and high-frequency bands, abnormal functional connectivity, and enhanced power in the left hemisphere of the brain. Our experience has been that correcting the largest abnormalities often reveals new abnormalities, which we then target with further neurofeedback training. We use two channel training of power (amplitude) and/or coherence, driving BioExplorer designs that I construct with either the Brainquiry PET-2 or the Pocket-Neurobics U-Wiz hardware. We use both visual (bar and trend graph) displays and auditory feedback and typically train in 10-minute blocks for a total of 30 minutes per session, varying the electrode placements between blocks.

One patient (Case 1) has had extensive home neurofeedback four or five times a week for about 3 years. The two others have been treated in the clinic; Case 2 has had 120 sessions and Case 3 had an initial 60 sessions as a child, returned for 50 more sessions as a teen and has returned for further treatment as a young adult. Common to all these patients upon intake was a lack of normal social connection with others, stereotyped and repetitive behaviors, cognitive and emotional inflexibility and often strong emotional reactivity to unexpected events or changes in schedules.

Although we routinely record eyes closed, eyes open and during reading, listening, writing and drawing, only eyes open data is presented in this report because of space considerations. It is worth noting that there are often significant differences in power and coherence abnormalities across task conditions that are clinically relevant.

Case 1

Case 1 was first evaluated in January 2012 at the age of 12, with his mother present. Autistic disorder was diagnosed at the age of 26 months. At intake he met criteria for autism spectrum disorder (ASD), with mild intellectual impairment, Level 3, needing significant support. Mother is a certified behavior analyst and Case 1 had had lengthy and intensive treatment in the home with applied behavior analysis, beginning soon after diagnosis. His brother also has severe autistic disorder and their autism was severe enough to qualify both for placement in a residential facility, but mother had an agreement with the county for funding to keep him and his brother in the home with the help of professional staff. Case 1 had constipation and a mitochondrial dysfunction for which he continues to have weekly methyl B-12 injections, hyperbaric oxygen therapy (HBOT), a full spectrum of supplements and has had chelation therapy to extract heavy metals. Initial qEEG evaluation revealed extreme absolute power in delta, theta and beta/high beta (15–30 Hz), with frequent "beta" spindles. Case 1 frequently failed to answer direct questions and had minimal eye contact. Behaviorally, he was usually cooperative, but would become very agitated when his brother would act out loudly, or when unexpected schedule changes occurred. He frequently gestured in the air with both hands as if manipulating an invisible object and smiled or laughed doing so (self-stimulation). When he responded to questions his answers were short, overly loud and "telegraphic" (monotone). He was obsessively engaged in looking at weather reports on his iPad.

Figure 11.1 is an 8-second sample of Case 1's eyes open EEG from 02/18/2012, recorded with a Deymed 32 EEG amplifier, examined with the Neuroguide EEG editor and database in linked ear reference, 50 μV display and bandpass of 1–100 Hz (to make the distinction between spindling beta and EMG more visually apparent:

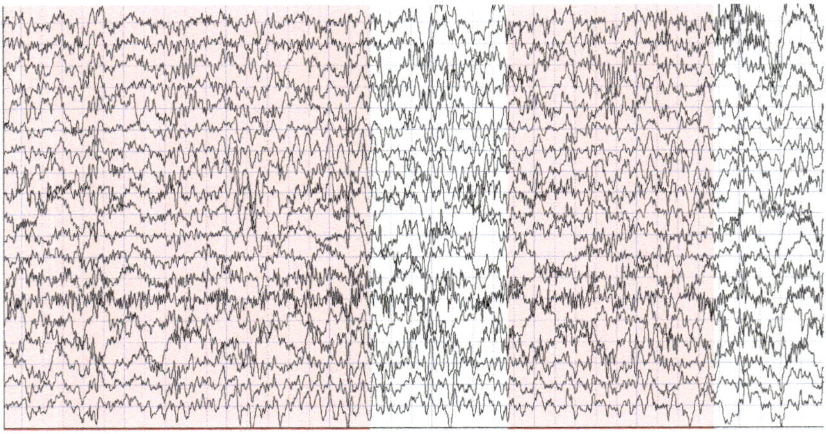

Figure 11.1. Eight-second EEG sample, 100 Hz, linked ears, 50 µV display amplitude from Case 1's EEG, 02/18/2012.

The record has some EMG on the temporal and prefrontal leads (the high frequency "buzzy" look on several channels). Spindling beta is present on the frontal/central leads. The Neuroguide summary maps show excess delta, theta, beta and high beta power, with some of the temporal high beta being EMG artifact (Figure 11.2). There was extensive, global delta hypocoherence; right hemisphere theta hypocoherence; frontal central and right frontal beta hypocoherence; and central and parietal/right temporal high beta hypocoherence. All the hypocoherence was between nearby electrodes. There was also long distance hypercoherence in theta on the left hemisphere, and more global hypercoherence in beta and high beta frequencies. There were strong phase abnormalities, mostly very short phase lags.

The neurofeedback treatment that ensued over the next 5 years was very intensive, typically 5 days a week. Mother obtained grants to acquire her own 19-channel recording and analysis hardware and software, as well as a two-channel

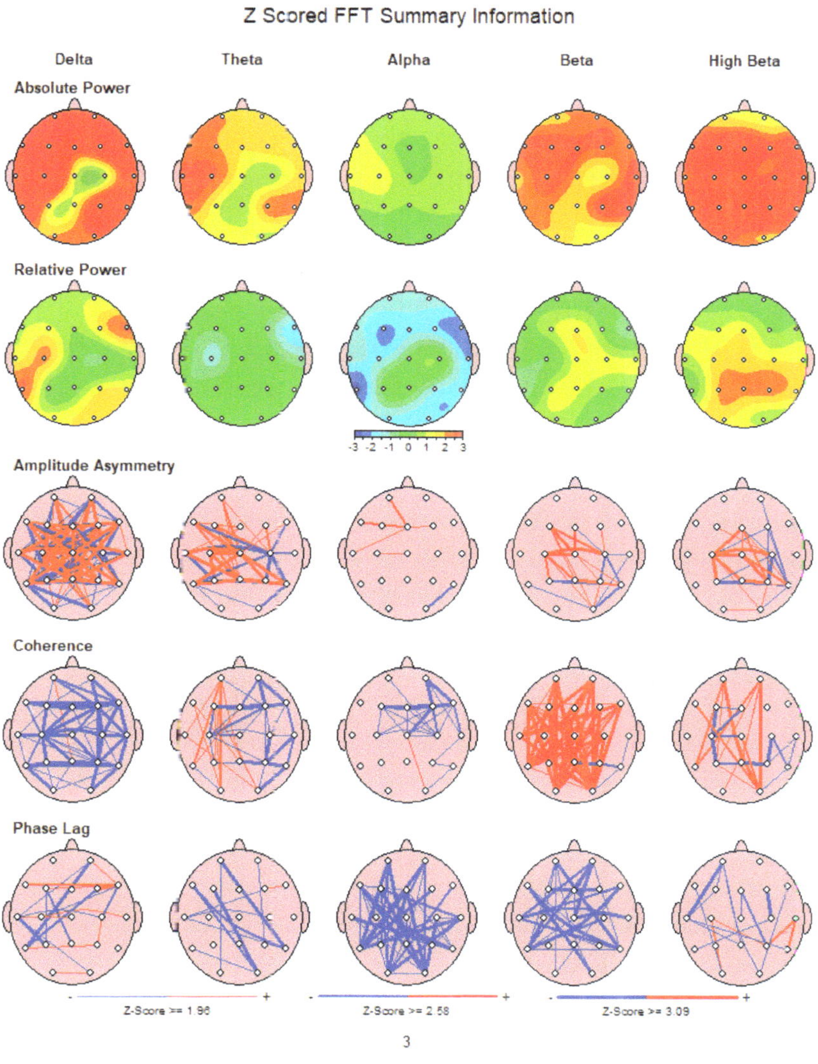

Figure 11.2. Summary z-score topographic maps from Case 1's EEG on 02/18/2012.

neurofeedback device. For the first year two channel training was used, aiming at reducing delta/theta and beta/high beta power. This resulted in patient (Case 1) becoming more verbal, calmer and showing increased self- and other-awareness. His level of awareness was indicated anecdotally by his observation that "my brother is more autistic than me" after about 18 months of treatment. At that point frontal and central spindling beta was mostly gone. There was less self-stimulation and more verbal interaction.

Now after 5 years of frequent neurofeedback Case 1 continues to show significant autistic symptoms, but has virtually no self-stimulation, answers questions readily, and is showing more appropriate non-verbal responses to human interaction. He is tracking time better and is able to remind teachers of changes in his scheduled pick-up times from school. He has become a fairly accomplished pianist, now just past his 18th birthday. He performs at hospitals and nursing homes and is quite fluent on the piano. He has six paying nursing home clients who have engaged him on an ongoing basis, weekly or biweekly to play at lunchtime for the residents. He is able to interact with the public and answer basic questions about his

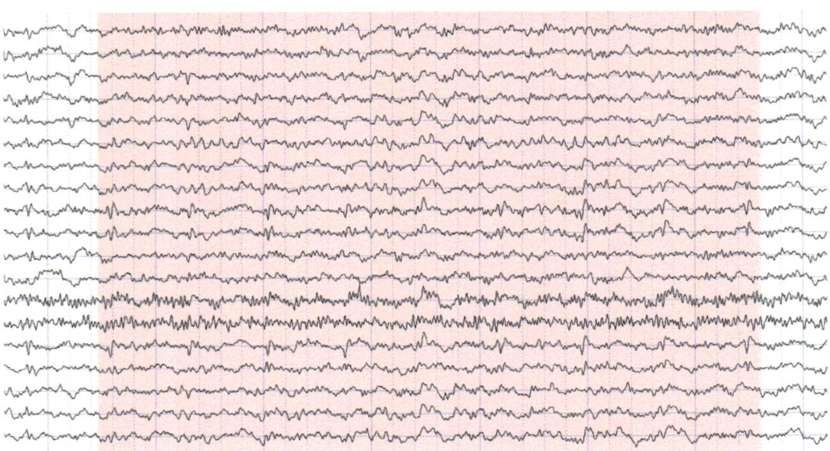

Figure 11.3. Eight-second EEG sample, 100 Hz, linked ears, 50 μV display amplitude from Case 1's EEG, 06/28/2017.

playing. He is enrolled in a college-level piano performance course at a local community college. Most significantly, he has begun to identify and express internal emotional states. For example, when I asked him how he felt when an audience applauded after his performance, he smiled and quickly said, "Happy!" He also has begun asking me how I feel and reminding me to keep cool on hot days. He graduated high school this year and attended some graduation parties; has been very much accepted by his neurotypical peers at his school, particularly the girls. He has become very talkative and outgoing, although he continues to talk about limited subjects in a fairly stilted way.

A 19 channel qEEG on 06/28/2017 (there were several others done over the course of treatment) revealed striking improvements from original recording (Figure 11.3).

Although some EMG artifact remains on the jaw (T3/T4 leads) there has been substantial normalization of the EEG. The summary z-score topographic maps demonstrate average to slightly below average absolute power across the spectrum (except for localized left temporal delta elevation), essentially no hypercoherence, and some lingering local frontal/central hypocoherence in alpha, beta and high beta; these are the current training targets (Figure 11.4).

Case 2

Upon intake in January 2015, Case 2 was living in a sheltered living facility connected with a post-secondary college for young adults with ASD. He had been diagnosed with Asperger's disorder, anxiety disorder, unspecified, obsessive-compulsive disorder, and auditory processing delay. He continues to live in this quasi-independent living facility. At intake he needed a moderate level of support in activities of daily

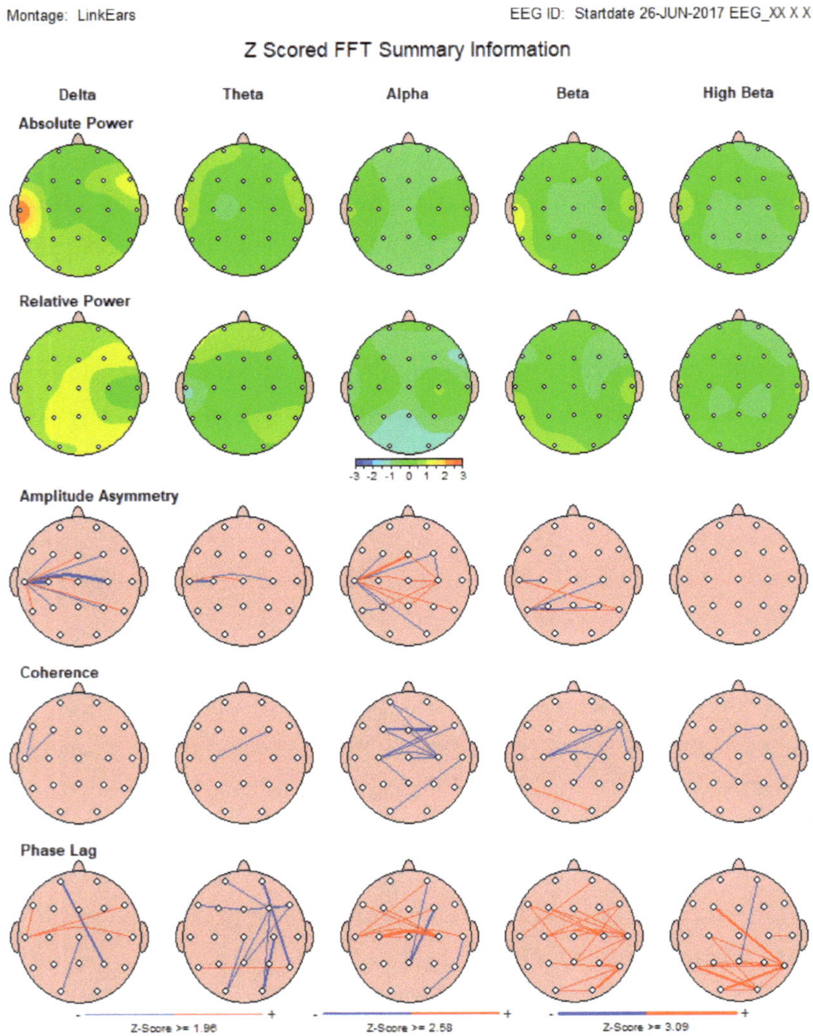

Figure 11.4. Summary z-score topographic maps from Case 1's EEG on 06/28/2017.

living and close supervision from staff and in DSM terms he met criteria for autism spectrum disorder, without intellectual impairment, Level 2, needs moderate support. He was obsessive about objects like pens and jackknives, as well as internet porn. He became irritated and annoyed very easily and was very impatient. He showed no social interest in others and mostly preferred playing videogames or watching movies by himself. He repeated himself and phrases others said incessantly, three or four times. He would respond to questions, but then would repeat what he or anyone said multiple times. He was holding a part-time job checking stock at an REI sport outlet store. His reading comprehension was low, but his memory for specific details was very strong. He had been tried on many different psychiatric medications. At intake he was taking Abilify 7.5 mg and Topamax 100 mg since a recent psychiatric hospitalization.

An initial qEEG recording on 02/04/2015 showed no excess power at the low frequencies, moderate and intermittent failures of alpha blocking, and somewhat excessive eye blinking and episodic EMG consistent with anxiety (Figure 11.5).

Statistical analysis showed average (delta, theta, alpha) to low average absolute power (in beta), with global

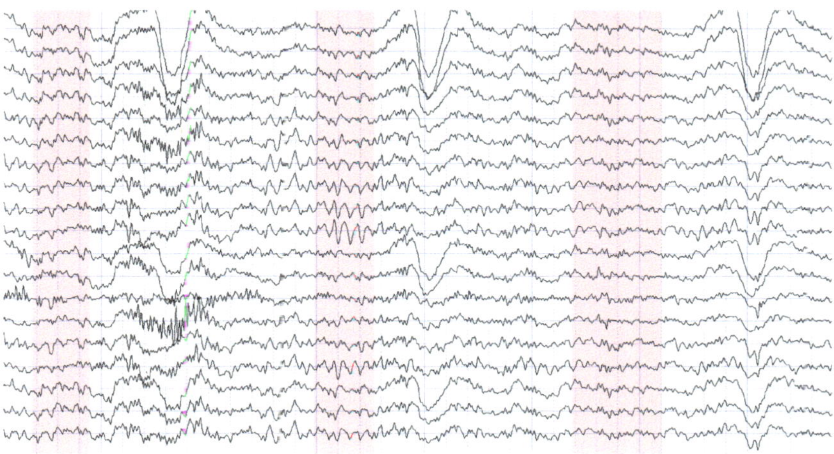

Figure 11.5. Eight-second EEG sample, 40 Hz bandpass, linked ears, 50 μV display amplitude from Case 2's EEG, 02/04/2015.

hypercoherence in high beta, frontal central to occipital delta hypercoherence and left temporal to occipital/right posterior temporal beta hypercoherence. There were scattered short phase lags in all bands but alpha (Figure 11.6).

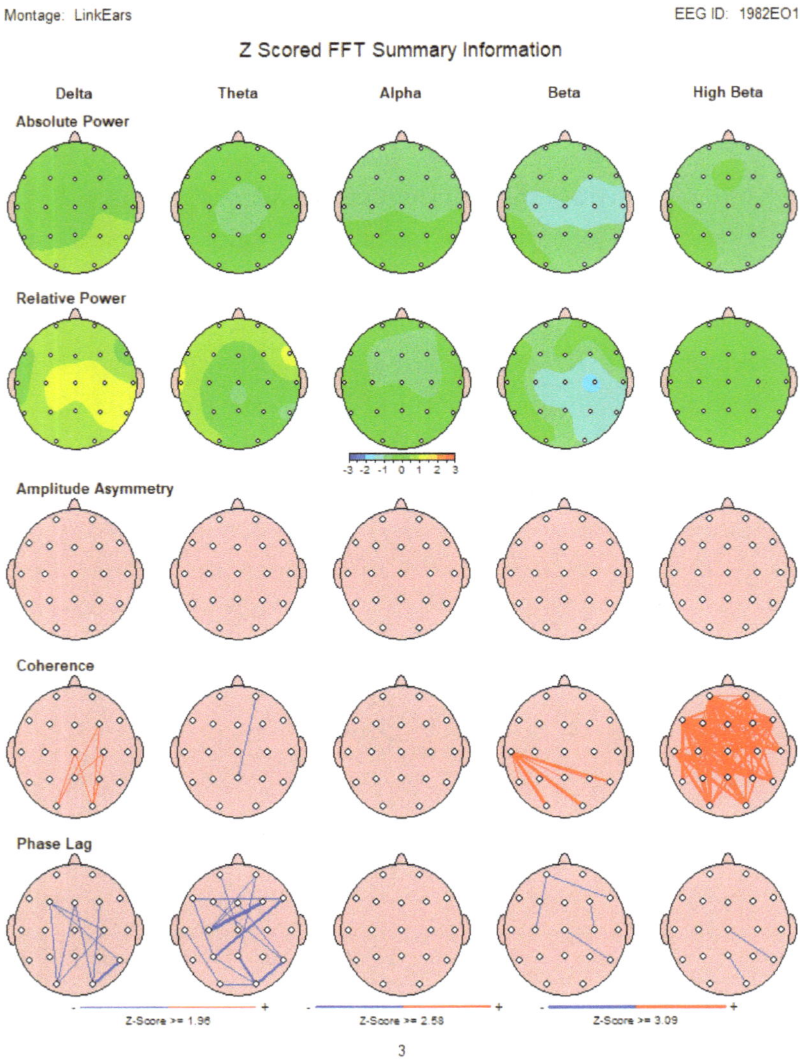

Figure 11.6. Summary z-score topographic maps from Case 2's EEG on 02/04/2015

Case 2 has had 120 sessions of neurofeedback, some of which included heart rate variability (HRV) biofeedback to promote a calmer emotional state. The neurofeedback targeted the hypercoherence in high beta and beta. He continues seeing a psychiatrist who prescribes Topomax, 50 mg (down from 150 mg some months ago), 1 mg Risperdal, 1000 mg Metformin bid, Clomipramine 100 mg qhs and an unspecified dose of Guanfacine qam.

Case 2 is working 4–5 days a week at a movie theater and enjoys this job, which he has now had for over a year. He is repeating himself/others much less often now and responds quickly to a hand signal his principal therapist at our clinic developed with him. His staff at Minnesota Life College also uses this. He appears to have lost his obsessions with pens, jackknives and internet porn.

Case 2 had a difficult series of incidents recently, involving going off-grounds at night to a friend's condo. He had been told not to do this because of staying out too late and the danger of walking home alone in the middle of the night. He is now banned from seeing this person, a former resident at MLC quasi-independent living facilities. He is able to discuss why this person is not good for him and has accepted not seeing his friend with minimal argument and upset.

Case 2 is more relaxed than at the beginning of treatment. His eye contact is much better and he is more self-aware and better at catching himself when he begins to repeat things. He is more communicative and social which has been noted by his staff and the staff of this clinic. Anecdotally, Case 2 asked me recently how my puppy is doing, indicating social interest an improved "theory of mind." In fact, this increased social interest and connection probably led to the misadventures with his friend who moved off-campus. Cognitive behavior therapy

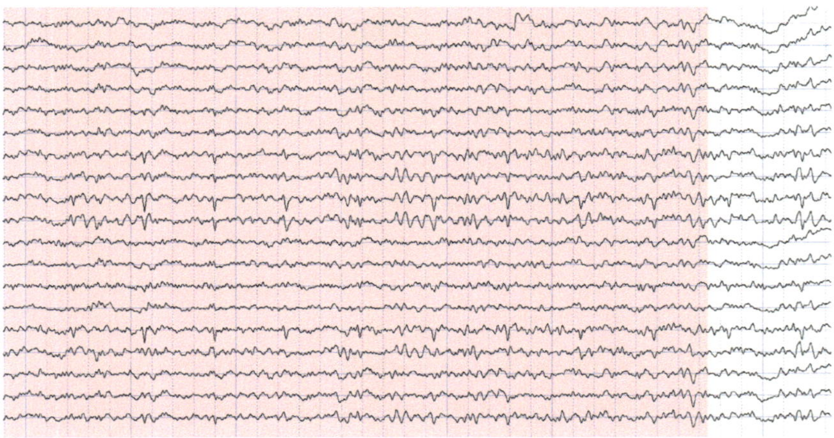

Figure 11.7. Eight-second EEG sample, 40 Hz bandpass, linked ears, 50 μV display amplitude from Case 2's EEG, 12/04/2017.

(CBT) is being done to help him be open to taking advice from people he trusts and to think constructively about his activities. He is successfully holding down a nearly full-time job in a normal workplace and reports indicate he is handling this well.

A repeat qEEG on 12/04/2017 revealed somewhat improved alpha blocking, much less blinking and less EMG, as seen in this sample (Figure 11.7).

Statistical analysis showed substantial normalization of the beta and high beta hypercoherence, with continued short phase lags in delta/theta and continued mild deficiency of frontal absolute power in beta. Further neurofeedback is aimed at these deficits (Figure 11.8).

Case 3

Case 3 was originally evaluated with qEEG on 05/19/2004 at the age of 7. Upon intake he had a diagnosis of autistic disorder. He was also diagnosed with immune-deficiency and an autoimmune disorder. He was very rigid, emotionally reactive and showed telegraphic, repetitive speech. He was very anxious and obsessive. He had poor control of his body movements and the EEG recording showed numerous body, head and eye movement artifacts. There were occasional runs of high amplitude theta waves in central, temporal, parietal and

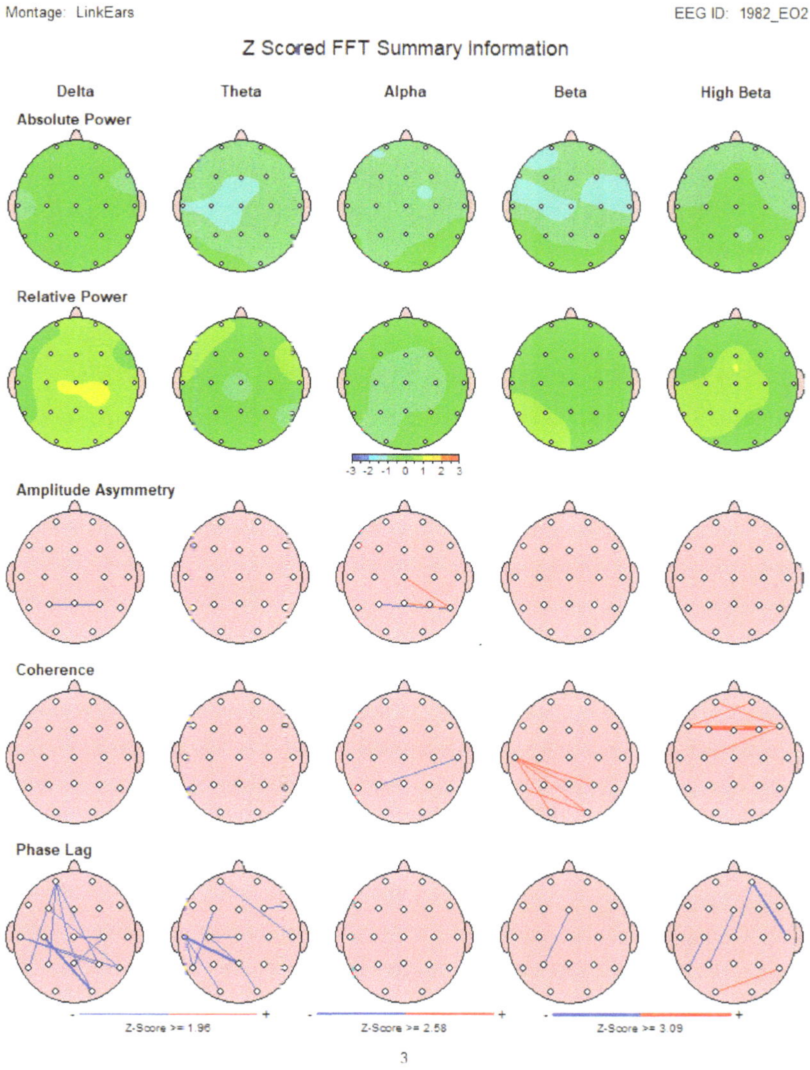

Figure 11.8. Summary z-score topographic maps from Case 2's EEG on 12/04/2017

occipital regions, although these were interspersed with normal levels of theta. There were high amplitude spindling beta waves over frontal and prefrontal and right central/parietal regions, as seen in Figure 11.9.

Statistical analysis showed strongly diminished left temporal alpha with globally low alpha power. The left frontal region showed elevated beta and high beta absolute power. High beta absolute power was very strongly elevated over left frontal, central and parietal cortex and also in a wide area of right hemisphere central, parietal and posterior temporal brain. Coherence was largely average, with only a few leads showing low coherence in delta and theta involving the right temporal to left and right central leads, and high beta hypercoherence between the right central temporal and the right posterior temporal, right parietal and right occipital leads (Figure 11.10).

The power abnormalities are better seen with single Hz topographic maps of the absolute power (Figure 11.11).

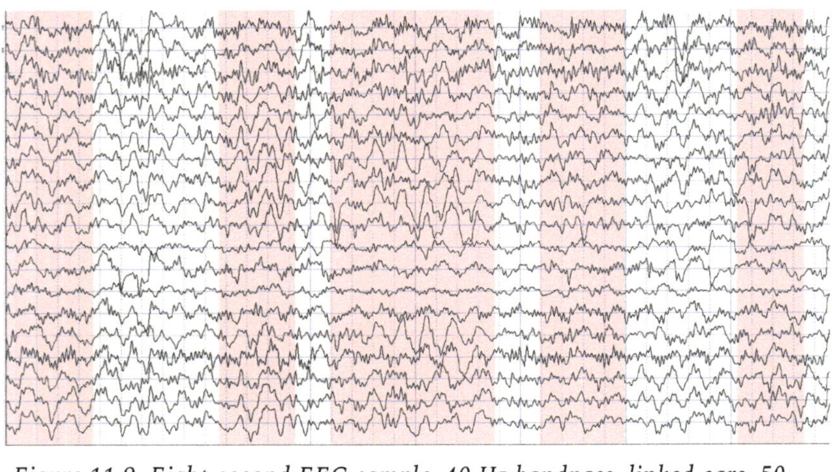

Figure 11.9. Eight-second EEG sample, 40 Hz bandpass, linked ears, 50 μV display amplitude from Case 3's EEG, 05/19/2004.

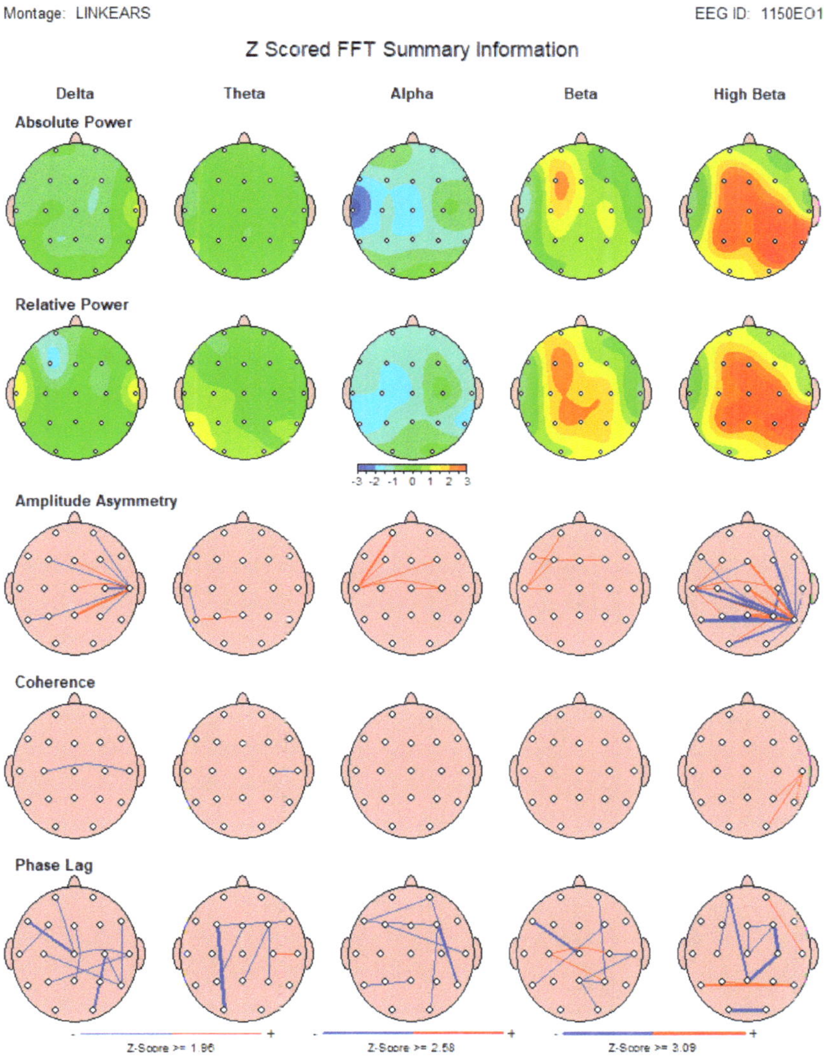

Figure 11.10. Summary z-score topographic maps from Case 3's EEG on 05/19/2004.

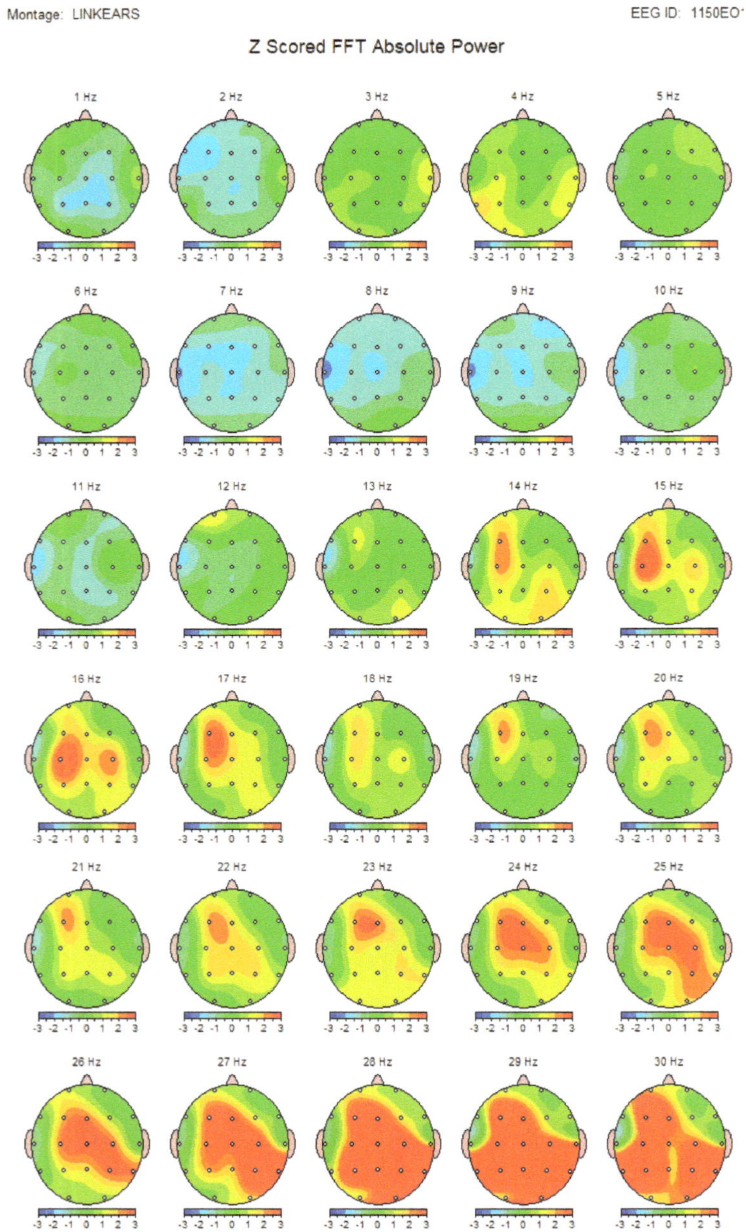

Figure 11.11. Z-score topographic maps of absolute power, 1–30 Hz from Case 3's EEG on 05/19/2004.

Neurofeedback initially aimed to increase left temporal power at 7–11 Hz and decrease 14–35 Hz power in the left frontal, frontal/central, central and right central to parietal regions. Approximately 60 sessions were conducted between 2004 and 2006. Symptoms of anxiety were gradually reduced and Case 3 became calmer and more interested in friendships. This patient returned for further treatment fully 10 years after the initial encounter. At that point he had made a good number of neurotypical friends, and was progressing through school, enjoying math and history. However, he was easily annoyed, with some strong temper outbursts. He had numerous symptoms of anxiety including restless sleep, headaches, dry mouth, twitches and fast heartbeat. A repeat qEEG on 10/01/2014 showed largely normal power, with little muscle tension, normal theta and normal alpha blocking, but continued high amplitude frontal beta spindles as seen in Figure 11.12.

Statistical analysis of the data showed elevated beta/high beta power in frontal/central and right frontal, central and

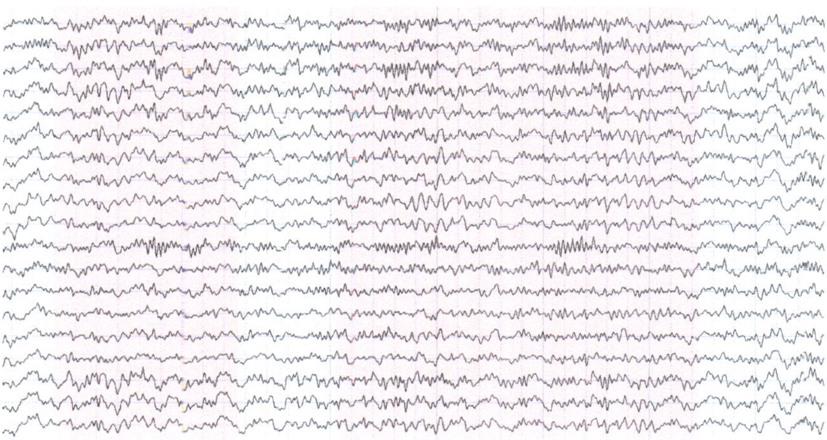

Figure 11.12. Eight-second EEG sample, 40 Hz bandpass, linked ears, 50 μV display amplitude from Case 3's EEG, 10/01/2014.

parietal, similar to what we saw in 2004. Coherence was again largely average and phase lags were mostly short, except with long phase delays in high beta (Figure 11.13).

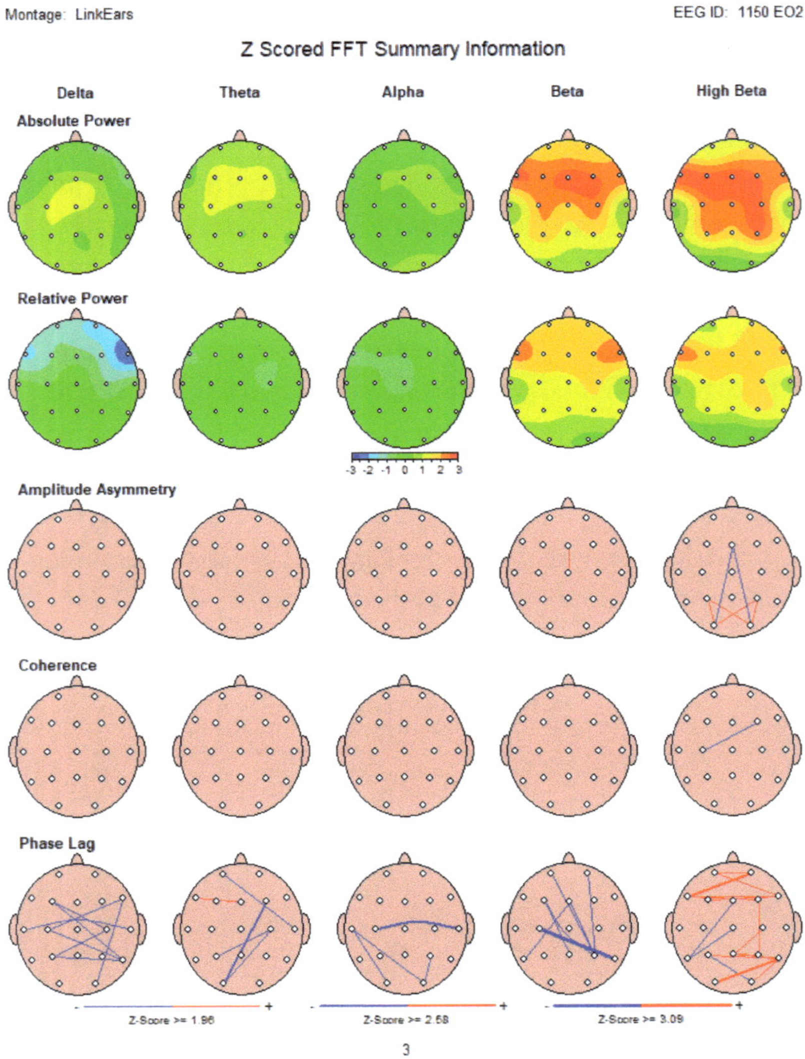

Figure 11.13. Z-score topographic maps of absolute power, 1–30 Hz from Case 3's EEG on 10/01/2014.

Further neurofeedback aimed to train down the high frequency power over frontal, central and right parietal regions. A third qEEG after 50 sessions showed diminished high beta power, but with emerging right frontal alpha and a variety of coherence abnormalities. There was hypercoherence between the medial temporal leads in alpha and beta, with central, parietal and occipital hypocoherence in alpha, beta and high beta frequencies. Phase lags remained short in scattered patterns except in high beta (Figure 11.14).

Behaviorally, Case 3 had become less emotionally reactive, and was doing well in school academically and socially. He was accepted and apparently enjoyed by his peers, his sister and her friends. Treatment continued at a rate of 4–6 times per month from late 2014 through July 2015. Case 3 returned to treatment in September 2016. He had developed increasing social awareness, making comments about not supporting Victoria's Secret because they don't cater to all sizes of women. He had also developed a great deal of anxiety and worry about the presidential election and has continued to be very worried about the ongoing issues surrounding the presidency, the state of our international relationships and how these current events may affect him and his family. We are currently addressing the anxiety with both neurofeedback aimed at improving executive control of the thought process and with cognitive therapy, to which he is now responsive.

Conclusions

The cases of autistic disorder we have seen have responded to neurofeedback with positive changes in social interaction, reductions in self-stimulation and expressions of anxiety, and with increased ability to sustain employment. Parents have been diligent in following up with appointments and have repeated told us they found neurofeedback to be the most beneficial treatment they have accessed for their children. Our experience is that a very large number of sessions are necessary for people with severe autistic disorder and it is probably best

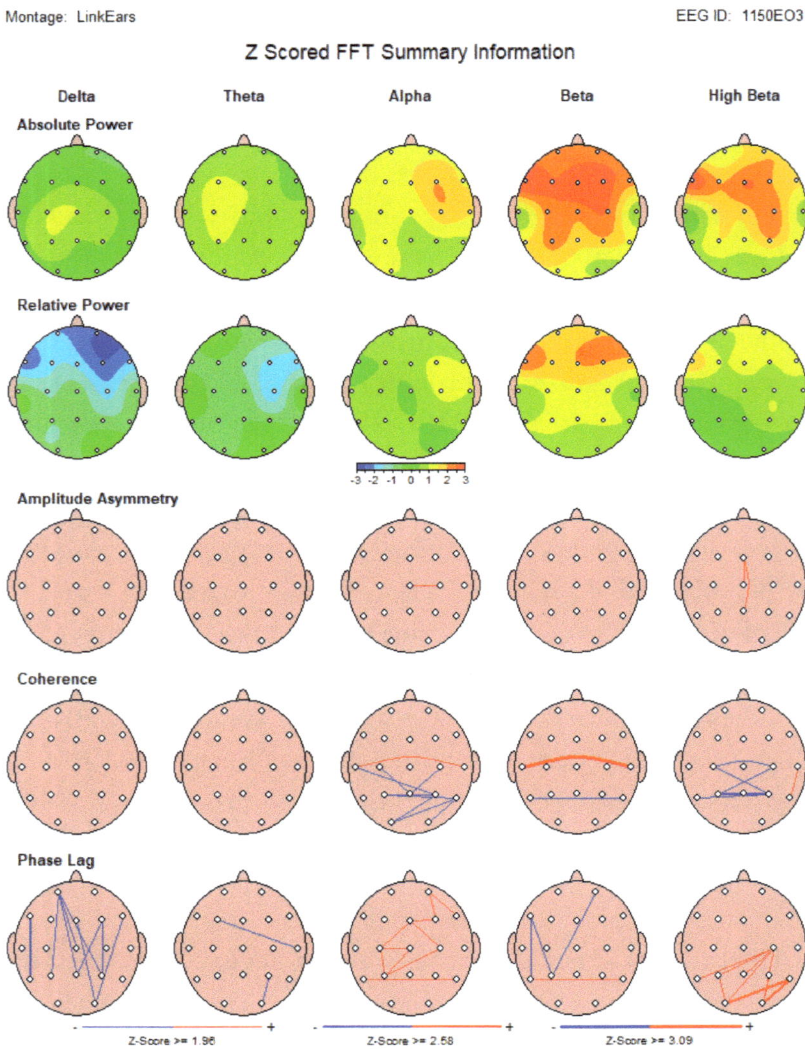

Figure 11.14. Z-score topographic maps of absolute power, 1–30 Hz from Case 3's EEG on 10/01/2014.

to arrange for home training to complement and extend training in the clinic. For more moderate severity it appears that treatments in the range of 60 sessions at twice weekly intervals are significantly beneficial, although across developmental time frames (1–3 years) repeated rounds of treatment may be called for. It should be noted that most of the parents we see have been using a wide range of treatments and accommodations for their children, including intensive applied behavior analysis, occupational therapy, supplements including methyl B-12 and a range of related treatments. As patients become higher functioning, calmer and more socially interactive they can benefit from traditional cognitive behavioral therapy. We strongly encourage such a multimodal approach to this difficult disorder.

References

Seltzer, M.M., Krauss, M.W., Shattuck, P.T., Orsmond G., Swe, A & Lord, C. (2003). The symptoms of autism spectrum disorders in adolescence and adulthood. *Journal of Autism & Developmental Disorders, 33*(6), 565–581.

Wang, J., Barstein, J., Ethridge, L.E., Mosconi, M.W., Takarae, Y. & Sweeney, J.A. (2013). Resting state EEG abnormalities in autism spectrum disorders. *Journal of Neurodevelopmental Disorders*, 5, 24. Retrieved from http://www.jneurodevdisorders.com/content/5/1/24.

12

Introduction to Sensory Integration Methods in Autism

Sarah A. Schoen,[1,2] Virginia Spielmann,[1] and Lucy Jane Miller,[1,2,3]

The ontogeny of sensory processing is heterogeneous and impacted by multiple complex factors including how genetic characteristics interact with environment and experience (Lickliter, 2008; Smith & Thelen, 2003). As the human organism develops, the eight cross-modal sensory systems (i.e. touch, proprioception, vestibular, vision, sound, taste, smell and interoception) mature and operate interdependently, develop asymmetrically and rely on environmental and relational experience for structural and functional organization (Ayres, 1963; Cunningham & Murphy, 1978; Spitzer, 1999; Thelen, 2005). In order for an individual to develop robust gross and fine motor control and skill; interpersonal competency; academic aptitude; and vocational capability, a foundation of intact sensory processing and integration is paramount (Ayres, 2011; Greenspan & Wieder, 2006a; Shanker, 2004).

The period of life that includes fetal development as well as the neonatal and infant periods was coined the "sensorimotor" years by Piaget (Young, 2011b), and it is during this period that the sensory systems dominate and work in concert to support development through the major milestones of the first years of life—including the ability to co-regulate and self-regulate

---

[1]STAR Institute for Sensory Processing Disorder, Greenwood Village, CO
[2]Rocky Mountain University of Health Professions, Provo, UT
[3]Department of Pediatrics, University of Colorado Denver, Denver, CP

(Browne & Talmi, 2015; Sameroff, 2009) —as well as other classic developmental milestones.

This chapter will explore atypical development of sensory processing in individuals on the autism spectrum and introduce the STAR PROCESS (Sensory Therapies and Research Play, Regulation/Relationships, Organization, Collaboration, Enjoyment, Sensory, Success), an evidence-based intervention that supports development of cohesive and organized sensory processing with an emphasis on the daily life functioning of individuals and their families.

Sensory Processing in Autism

Sensory processing challenges are extremely common in autism spectrum disorder and are reported in the literature with estimates ranging from 69% to 95% (Baranek, David, Poe, Stone, & Watson, 2006; Leekam, Nieto, Libby, Wing, & Gould, 2007; Tomchek & Dunn, 2007; Van Etten et al., 2017). A growing awareness exists of the importance of multisensory processing in neurotypical development and the impact of poor multisensory integration (MSI) on daily life activities and routines. Advocacy about the effects of sensory issues in autism led to the inclusion of sensory features in the latest version of the Diagnostic and Statistical Manual of Mental Disorders (DSM-5; American Psychiatric Association. Parents of children with autism often seek sensory-based intervention (Goin-Kochel, Myers, & Mackintosh, 2007; Green et al., 2006; Mandell, Novak, & Levy, 2005) as a method to remediate the challenges their children face. Sensory integration intervention is the most commonly implemented therapy by occupational therapists for children with autism spectrum disorder (ASD; Case-Smith & Miller, 1999) and is one of the most commonly requested types of occupational therapy treatments in general (Goin-Kochel et al., 2007).

History and Terminology

The field of sensory integration (SI) originated with the work of A. Jean Ayres, an occupational therapist and educational psychologist, over 50 years ago (Ayres, 1963). SI was originally conceptualized and applied to children with learning disabilities. In the late 1970s and early 1980s, Ayres expanded the study of SI to children with autism (Ayres, 1979; Ayres & Tickle, 1980).

Differences in use of terminology has made research into aspects of SI challenging. At the time of Ayres' conceptualization, "sensory integration" was the label given to the theory of SI, as well as to SI assessment, the intervention for SI issues and to the diagnostic category (which Ayres termed SI dysfunction). Meanwhile, a further confound developed because of a new neuroscience field called multisensory integration (Schroeder & Foxe, 2005; Stein, Stanford, & Rowland, 2014). These issues contributed to the reexamination of occupational therapy's terminology originally proposed by Ayres. In 2007, a paper was published reflecting an attempt to clarify the nosology of the disorder, to differentiate it from the theory, assessment, and intervention procedures (Miller, Anzalone, Lane, Cermak, & Osten, 2007). The suggestion was made to change the label for the clinical condition from sensory integration dysfunction to sensory processing disorder. Three other diagnostic classification systems were also already using this terminology: the Diagnostic Classification of Mental Health and Developmental Disorders of Infancy and Early Childhood, Revised (Zero to Three, 2005), the Diagnostic Manual for Infancy and Early Childhood of the Interdisciplinary Council on Developmental and Learning Disorders (ICDL; (The Interdisciplinary Council on Development and Learning, 2005a) and the Psychodynamic Diagnostic Manual (American

Psychoanalytic Association & Alliance of Psychoanalytic Organizations, 2006). The nosology was widely adopted to provide a common language for clinicians and researchers.

Another commonly referred to term is sensory processing and integration challenges (Watling, Patten Koenig, Davies, & Schaaf, 2011).

Patterns of Dysfunction

Three primary patterns of dysfunction were articulated in the proposed 2007 nosology: sensory modulation disorder, sensory-based motor disorder and sensory discrimination disorder. Sensory modulation refers to difficulties regulating and grading responses to sensory experiences. Modulation difficulties can be observed in any of an individual's eight sensory systems1 and include sensory over–responsivity (SOR; exaggerated, intense responses to non-noxious stimuli), sensory under responsivity (SUR; muted responses or slow detection) and/or sensory craving (SC; insatiable appetite for sensation). These three subtypes may be found alone or in combination, according to the different sensory subsystems impacted.

Sensory discrimination challenges can also occur in any sensory modality and are characterized by difficulties interpreting qualities of sensory stimuli. This may manifest in difficulties differentiating between textures, sounds, sights, or intensity and direction of movements.

Sensory-based motor difficulties include postural functions (difficulty with balance and equilibrium, coordination, movement against gravity and endurance in sustaining muscle activation for participation in daily life activities) and praxis challenge, also called dyspraxia and/or motor planning deficits (difficulties in conceptualizing, planning, organizing, sequencing and executing actions; Ayres, 2011). Praxis abilities are essential to completing new simple motor actions, as well as interacting within the environment, completing functional daily skills (Cermak, Gubbay, & Larkin, 2002) and dealing with novelty (May-Benson, 2001).

While the characteristics of the subtypes have been delineated, they continue to be refined in research studies of various clinical populations (Engel-Yeger, Hardal-Nasser, & Gal, 2011; Ghanizadeh, 2011; Lane, Young, Baker, & Angley, 2010). In the field of autism, research has largely focused on problems in sensory modulation (Ben-Sasson et al., 2009b; Lane, et al., 2010), but the DSM-5 criteria use different terminology than the 2007 nosology to describe these constructs. The DSM-5 labels include hyper-reactivity, hypo-reactivity and unusual sensory interests (American Psychiatric Association, 2013). Hyper-reactivity is analogous to sensory over-responsivity and is used to describe individuals who have an adverse, heightened response to specific sensory stimuli. Hypo-reactivity is synonymous with sensory under-responsivity or an apparent indifference to sensory experiences. "Unusual interests in sensory aspects of the environment" is comparable to sensory craving, reflecting an excessive seeking of, or fascination with, a sensory stimulus. Although sensory modulation issues are frequently reported in children with autism (Baranek et al., 2006), there is also an increasing awareness of the sensory-motor challenges in this population (Fournier et al., 2010; Lloyd, MacDonald, & Lord, 2013; Ming, Brimacombe, & Wagner, 2007; Whyatt & Craig, 2013). Posture and praxis issues are documented in the literature (Schaaf et al., 2015) as well as problems conceptualizing "what to do" (Bhat, Landa, & Galloway, 2011), which is fundamental to the play process. These challenges are often rooted in difficulty recognizing available affordances (Gibson, 1979; Jones, 2003) and/or generating an ideational response (May-Benson, 2001) both of which are fundamental to the development of praxis (Bodison, 2015; May-Benson & Cermak, 2007).

Sensory processing challenges are heterogeneous, wide spread and impact daily life along a continuum (Ausderau et al., 2016; Dunn, 2008b; Robertson & Baron-Cohen, 2017). The National Institute of Mental Health (NIMH) instituted a movement consistent with this thinking, in which the study of sensory processing and sensory dysfunction are now conceptualized multi dimensionally (National Institute of Mental Health, 2017). Therefore, deficits and challenges in sensory processing are viewed as dimensions that affect all individuals and are part of a wide range of clinical conditions to varying degrees (Brown, Shankar, & Smith, 2009; Dunn, 2008a; Engel-Yeger et al., 2016). Thus, the current perspective suggests substituting dimensional taxonomy for categorical classification ("disorder"; (Ruscio & Ruscio, 2008; Widakowich, Van Wettere, Jurysta, Linkowski, & Hubain, 2013).

Ayres Sensory Integration Intervention (ASI)

There are many empirical studies that claim to study the effectiveness of SI treatment. Many of the studies have outcomes demonstrating small or no effects of treatment (Barton, Reichow, Schnitz, Smith, & Sherlock, 2015; Devlin, Healy, Leader, & Hughes, 2011). However, upon close examination, it is clear that these studies usually do not adhere to the basic principles of sensory integration as conceptualized by Ayres (Pfeiffer, May-Benson, & Bodison, 2018; Schaaf et al., 2015b). Instead studies utilize interventions that employ single sensory strategies, often passively applied to the client, such as weighted vests (Stephenson & Carter, 2009), "deep pressure" brushing of the skin (Bhopti & Brown, 2013), and/or vestibular protocols (Van Rie & Heflin, 2009) in the absence of a full occupational therapy sensory integration program. Thus, in 2007, the Franklin B. Baker/A. Jean Ayres Baker Trust trademarked the name Ayres Sensory Integration (ASI; Roley, Mailloux, Miller-Kuhaneck, & Glennon, 2007) to reflect the intervention and preserve the original principles espoused by Ayres (1972). References to the Ayres Sensory Integration (ASI) fidelity measure (Parham et al., 2007) highlight key, well-defined principles of treatment using ASI along with therapist qualifications, physical space needed, and recommended equipment (Parham et al., 2007).

ASI is an individualized treatment approach based on the unique sensory processing and sensory motor needs of the individual (Schaaf & Mailloux, 2015). As described above it is not a protocol, a single sensory system strategy, or passively applied stimulation. Examples not considered ASI include sitting a child on a therapy ball for schoolwork, brushing the child's skin, spinning a child on a piece of mobile equipment, or using a weighted vest (Case-Smith, Weaver, & Fristad, 2015). ASI is a problem-solving approach that requires the clinician to link the underlying sensory issues to the child's challenges with participation in daily life. The approach relies on specific sensory motor equipment, most of which is dynamic (e.g. suspended from the ceiling or mounted on wheels and offering variations in intensity of movement experience). Activities and equipment are selected to meet the individual sensory and motor needs of the child.

Foundational to sensory integration treatment/ASI is the recognition of the importance of sensation to development. Development is characterized by multisensory experiences that allow for efficient completion of daily activities (Lickliter, 2008; Stein, Stanford, & Rowland, 2014). Speed of processing is enhanced when sensory experiences are combined; for example, speech perception is faster when you can both hear and see the mouth of the person you are talking to (Stevenson, Segers, Ferber, Barense, & Wallace, 2014). Ayres discussed the foundational nature of sensory input arising from the tactile, proprioceptive and vestibular systems due to their primal and pervasive influence (Ayres, 1972). These sensory domains are thought to be important to learning and behavior by building a child's sense of safety and security in the environment, as well as being central to development (e.g. body awareness and body scheme, ability to move against gravity; Ayres, 1972, 1979).

The child must be an active participant in the therapy process. Therapy is child directed, capitalizing on the child's unique interests and choice of play materials (Schaaf & Mailloux, 2015). Sometimes referred to as "tapping the child's inner drive," motivation to engage in activities is central to the approach (Schaaf & Mailloux, 2015). The therapist creates an atmosphere of safety and trust that supports the child's willingness to address their challenges in function. Ayres called this the "just right challenge.". In keeping with both this concept and the work of Vygotsky (Tudge, 1992), activities are designed within the child's zone of proximal development, hard enough that they require the assistance/support of the therapist to accomplish (e.g. bring the child to the next level) but achievable so as to ensure success.

Foundational Research

Physiological Findings

Early research related to the underlying mechanisms of sensory processing challenges implicates the role of the autonomic nervous system (ANS) particularly in sensory modulation. Miller and colleagues first studied electrodermal activity as a marker of the sympathetic nervous system in children with sensory over-responsivity (McIntosh, Miller, Shyu, &

Hagerman, 1999; Miller et al., 1999). Studies utilized a novel protocol called the sensory challenge protocol during which participants received 10 contiguous trials of stimulation across five sensory domains (tactile, visual, auditory, olfactory and vestibular). Individuals with over-responsivity showed higher magnitude responses, responded more frequently, and did not habituate well to the repeated stimulus (McIntosh et al., 1999; Miller et al., 1999). These findings were replicated in subsequent research focusing on children with ASD (Schoen, Miller, & Green, 2008; Schoen, Miller, Brett-Green, & Nielsen, 2009) suggesting that intervention should address symptoms of over-arousal initially and early in the treatment process. This finding contributed to the evolution of the STAR PROCESS described later in this chapter.

Data was collected to explore the nature of ANS involvement in various clinical populations including children with autism (Schoen et al., 2008) and children with ADHD (Lane, Reynolds, & Thacker, 2010). Findings related to children with autism first identified two groups of responders: one with low arousal, low reactivity, and faster habituation, and the other with high arousal, high reactivity, and slower habituation (Schoen, Miller, Brett-Green, & Hepburn, 2008). This is consistent with the behavioral subtypes of sensory under-responsivity and sensory over-responsivity reported in this population (Ben-Sasson, Carter, & Briggs-Gowan, 2009a). A follow-up study compared children with autism to children with idiopathic sensory processing challenges (Schoen et al., 2009). This study showed that children with autism had significantly lower arousal and lower reactivity than the children with idiopathic sensory processing issues without ASD, suggesting a relatively high number of children with under-responsivity in this sample. While all three modulation subtypes (SOR, SUR and

SC) are commonly observed in children with ASD, a meta-analysis of symptoms in ASD suggest several moderating factors such as autism severity, and chronological age (Ben-Sasson, Carter, & Briggs-Gowan, 2010). Taken together, this research helped validate that the subtypes described above were evident in ASD as well as inform the STAR PROCESS intervention described below.

Treatment Effectiveness

A small but growing body of literature supports the effectiveness of ASI. Three well-designed randomized trials offer preliminary support for the effectiveness of this intervention (Miller, Coll, & Schoen, 2007; Pfeiffer, Koenig, Kinnealey, Sheppard, & Henderson, 2011; Schaaf et al., 2014). The most sensitive outcome measure in all three studies was goal attainment scaling; a procedure that captures progress on parent centered individualized goals (Kiresuk, Smith, & Cardillo, 2014). Additionally, gains were reported on standardized measures of attention, cognition and social functions (Miller et al., 2007b), amount of caregiver assistance needed for daily living tasks (Schaaf et al., 2014) and a reduction in autism mannerisms (Pfeiffer et al., 2011). Several non-randomized studies also support the effectiveness of this approach (Case-Smith & Bryan, 1999; Iwanaga et al., 2014; Linderman & Stewart, 1999; Schaaf, Benevides, Kelly, & Mailloux-Maggio, 2012; Smith, Press, Koenig, & Kinnealey, 2005). These studies should be differentiated from much of the research claiming to study "sensory integration" that does not adhere to the principles of ASI (Devlin, Leader, & Healy, 2009; Devlin et al., 2011;), is not individualized (Devlin et al., 2009; Devlin et al., 2011), is not delivered by trained therapists (Lydon, Healy, & Grey, 2017) and/ or relies exclusively on sensory strategies or protocols which are in direct conflict with ASI practices (Quigley, Peterson, Frieder, & Peterson, 2011).

STAR PROCESS

In 2005, Miller and colleagues began to formalize the STAR PROCESS intervention. Building on the work of Ayres, the STAR PROCESS is a unique intervention that combines the foundational sensory integration principles and strategies described above (Ayres, 1979) with methods from Developmental, Individual-differences, Relationship-based (DIRFloortime®) therapy (Greenspan & Wieder, 1998) and clinical psychology. The STAR PROCESS is an intensive, multidisciplinary, intervention that addresses the child's challenges through individualized treatment sessions that incorporate parent participation and parent coaching.

The gold-standard for delivering occupational therapy for sensory processing challenges using the STAR PROCESS is an "intensive model" (Schoen, Miller, & Flanagan, 2018). Therapy takes place 3–5 times a week, each session lasting 50 minutes for a minimum of 30 sessions. Parents actively engage in all sessions with the occupational therapist and also collaborate in 5–6 parent only (no children) meetings. The STAR PROCESS addresses each child's unique sensory and social-emotional needs and each parent's priorities. Sessions can take place in the sensory integration gym (Parham et al., 2007), and in the child's natural environments, on playgrounds, at home, at school, or in the community when possible (Miller, Fuller, & Roetenberg, 2014). When necessary, which occurs frequently, mental health colleagues from the "Family Services" team contribute to parent education and provide support for children experiencing high levels of anxiety, stress-behaviors and challenges related to parental attunement and/or developmental trauma. Similarly, a STAR PROCESS trained speech and language pathologist supports the treatment process and may provide individualized treatment for children experiencing difficulties with communication and/or auditory processing.

The STAR PROCESS is based on the understanding that relationship and regulation underpin human development (Fonagy & Target, 2002; Lillas & Turnbull, 2009; Papoušek, 2016; Stern, 1995; Young, 2011a; Zeanah, Berlin, & Boris, 2011) and are therefore foundational to intervention (Greenspan & Wieder, 2006b). As seen in the sensory pyramid model (see Figure 12.1), arousal regulation, relationships/engagement and sensory processing are interdependent and intertwined in the treatment process. Outcomes related to early sensory-motor functions and later cognitive and language functioning are dependent on this solid foundation (Casenhiser, Shanker, & Stieben, 2013; Greenspan & Shanker, 2007; Shanker, 2004).

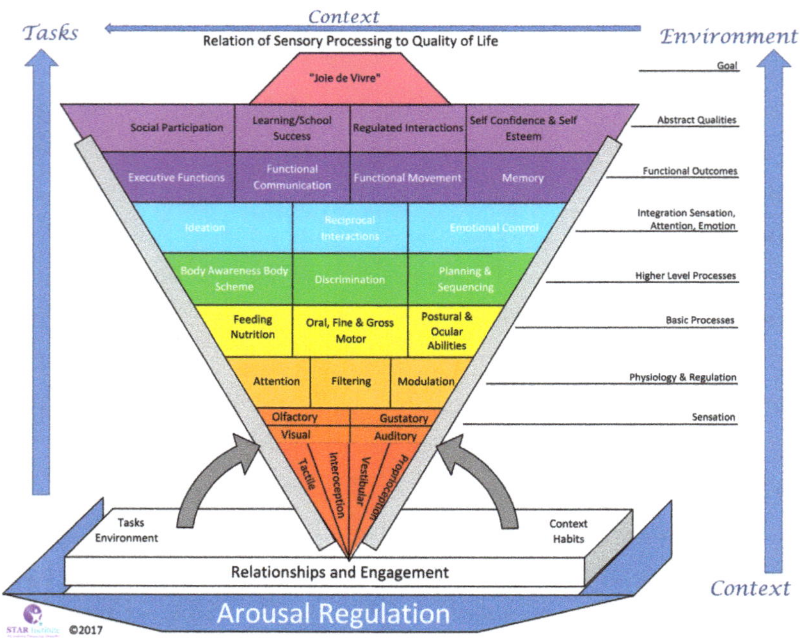

Figure 12.1. The sensory pyramid model.

Importantly, intervention is only indicated if the sensory processing issues negatively and significantly impact functioning in daily life (Miller et al., 2014).

Central to the STAR PROCESS is that therapy is process-based. This means that the therapeutic interactions that come from the process of relationship-based play supplant the accomplishment of discrete skill achievement. The therapist works in "flow" (Csíkszentmihályi, 1997) with the child and parent while they are all immersed in the interaction and the process of being play partners (Greenspan & Wieder, 2006a). The ultimate goal of intervention is "joie de vivre" (joy in life; Rogers, 1961, p. 432), not specifically what is achieved (Miller et al., 2014).

Principles of Intervention

Within the STAR PROCESS are three important relationships—the relationship between the therapist and the child, the relationship between the therapist and the parent and the relationship between the parent and the child (Fonagy, Gergely, & Jurist, 2004; Gergely et al., 1998; Lillas & Turnbull, 2009; Provenzi, Olson, Montirosso, & Tronick, 2015). Establishing trust and a focus on parent-therapist collaboration is key to the success of intervention (Als, Tronick, & Brazelton, 1980; Brazelton & Greenspan, 2009; Miller et al., 2014; Shonkoff & Phillips, 2000).

Therapy occurs within the context of play. Play provides that platform for interaction and learning, by engaging the child, creating motivation, and ensuring fun (Berk & Meyers, 2013; Hiles Howard, Lindaman, Copeland, & Cross, 2017; Porges, 2015; Wieder & Greenspan, 2003). Play schemes are designed to address concepts related not only to sensory processing and sensory-motor abilities, but also to emotions, emotional regulation, prosocial skills and socialization.

The therapist must attune to the child and connect by acknowledging their communicative intent, exchanging affective signals, reciprocal communication, and meeting them at their developmental play level. This support, and the sharing of ideas and interests, ensures a sense of safety and joy throughout the session.

Arousal regulation is monitored throughout and supported via modification of the sensory environment, grading expectations of emotional and sensory-motor demands as well as adaptation of the therapist's pace, affect and voice to the needs of the child. The STAR PROCESS focuses on the child's "just right success" (Bialer & Miller, 2011; Miller et al., 2014). Success, and an increasing sense of self, is reinforced by the child's use of positive self-talk (Nelson, 2015; Winsler, Abar, Feder, Schunn, & Rubio, 2007), and parental understanding of the principles that create success for the child.

Importance of Clinical Reasoning

Occupational therapy often uses clinical reasoning during the therapeutic process, rather than following a set protocol (Boyt Schell & Schell, 2008; Mattingly, 1991). Clinical reasoning is an ongoing process that takes place at every moment during every treatment session (Mattingly & Fleming, 1994). Clinical reasoning also helps the therapist decide what to change from session to session, from the start of treatment to the end of treatment, and when projecting treatment needs onto future contexts. Intervention is always dynamic, requiring the therapist to constantly monitor the needs of the child and family: moment to moment—day to day—week to week—and in follow up once the child returns home. Adjustments are made based on the therapist's ability to read subtle changes in the child or parent. These cues are often sensed intuitively

(Fonagy, 2015; Mattingly & Fleming, 1994; Taylor, 2008), rather than observed, and convey to the therapist a need to modify some aspect of what is going on in the session.

Assessment

Central to individualizing treatment and the development a comprehensive treatment plan is assessment (Fonagy, 1998; Greenspan, DeGangi, & Wieder, 2001; ICDL, 2005b, p. 249). This process begins with an in-depth history obtained from the family and a clinical interview that addresses the child's strengths and challenges (Greenspan & Greenspan, 2003). The focus is on collecting information about the family's primary concerns and the presenting problems relative to the child's functioning in daily life at home, at school, and in the community. Assessment includes direct observation of the child using a standardized test battery of sensory processing and sensory motor abilities, as well as administration of standardized caregiver report measures of sensory processing, social emotional functioning and adaptive behavior challenges.

We use a newly developed measure, the Sensory Processing Three Dimensions (SP3D) Scale (Miller, Schoen, & Mulligan, 2016). This scale contains three parts:

- the examiner administered performance measure called the SP3D Assessment which included an examiner completed Behavior During Testing component;
- the parent report scale called the SP3D Inventory; and
- the SP3D Occupational Performance scale, a screening of daily functional performance.

The scales rate sensory modulation and quantitatively assess sensory discrimination across five sensory domains (e.g.

tactile, visual, auditory, proprioception and vestibular) as well as rating and quantifying sensory-based motor abilities related to postural functioning and praxis.

The child is also observed during structured and unstructured play in the therapy gym while the therapist supports the child's optimal capacities, including emotional regulation, arousal and relationship/engagement. Formal and informal assessment of the child's functional emotional development and principal relationships is made during these clinical observations. Information gleaned from the assessment includes a determination of the role of interoception in relation to the child's emotional state (Murphy, Brewer, & Bird, 2017; Seth & Friston, 2016; Tsakiris & Critchley, 2016), emotional capacity, and emotional regulation.

Data from all sources is gathered in order to develop hypotheses about the child's underlying sensory processing and/or sensory-motor challenges that may be impacting the child's ability to function in daily life. These hypotheses are conveyed in the evaluation report in the form of "impact statements" that link sensory processing challenges to presenting problems. "The impact of sensory over-responsivity on ability to stay regulated during the school day;"; and/or "the impact of praxis abilities on the ability to have a successful play-date" are examples of impact statements. These findings are shared with the parents/caregivers during a 1-hour feedback session (without child present) that help parents understand their child's social, emotional, and behavioral concerns from the perspective of the sensory processing and/or sensory-motor challenges.

Goal setting

Once the evaluation is complete, the clinician meets with the family for the 1-hour goal setting session (no children present) during which goals are established based on the parents' priorities. Goals are specific, objective, measurable and attainable within the number of sessions recommended (usually about 30 sessions) utilizing the procedure recommended by Goal Attainment (GA) Scaling (Kiresuk et al., 2014). GA Scaling focuses on changes that are individualized to the child that usually cannot be captured by standardized scales (Steenbeek, Gorter, Ketelaar, Galama, & Lindeman, 2011). Setting goals with parents has the additional benefit of providing an opportunity to interweave parent and clinician information early in the relationship (Turner-Stokes, 2009). Goal attainment engages parents in the treatment process, expanding parental confidence and improving knowledge and motivation, and ensuring enjoyment of their child's successes (Øien, Fallang, & Østensjø, 2010). The process offers clinical utility because it is easily understood by families and relevant to their needs (McLaren & Rodger, 2003). Re-evaluation of goals is an important component at the end of treatment in order to acknowledge changes from intervention.

Qualitative analysis was conducted of GA scales collected on 33 families participating in the STAR PROCESS. Goals reflecting parent priorities for change were examined for common themes. The two most consistent priorities were emotional/self-regulation and improvement in self-care/activities of daily living.

Parent Collaboration

Parent collaboration includes parent-only educational meetings and parent coaching. Parent meetings are designed to empower parents with knowledge of their child's strengths and supports observed during treatment that can help promote optimal functioning in a wider range of settings (e.g. home, school, community). The key to achieving carryover into the home is knowledge of what is successful in treatment. The therapist extracts elements from treatment and problem-solves with the family to ensure they can be applied to situations outside of the therapeutic environment.

Parent coaching is designed to empower parents with self-confidence, skills for functioning at home and joy in relating to their child. Participation in therapeutic play with the therapist's guidance ensures competency at home. The parent becomes a critical part of the "magic moments" of therapy during which their child achieves a new level of mastery never previously experienced.

Carryover to Home

"A SECRET" problem solving approach (Attention, Sensation, Emotion Regulation, Culture, Relationship, Environment and Task; Bailer & Miller, 2011) is used to help families define what activities/strategies will be helpful for the child at home or in school. Each component of A SECRET represents an element that can contribute to a child's success in daily life, assisting the family and child to be more independent, and to think through a situation before it occurs. It is based on individual differences reflecting a family's unique sensory, social, and emotional profile and guiding parents and/or teachers to implement a sensory lifestyle to help the child all day long.

Therapist Qualifications

An important feature of the STAR PROCESS is the ongoing mentoring of the therapist. Weekly sessions utilize reflective supervision to examine feelings or thoughts about specific cases and to use this awareness to better serve the child and the family. Weekly video review or session observation by a mentor facilitates this process. Therapists bring cases to discussion at team meetings to encourage further problem solving and clinical reasoning by the entire team. Therapists are required to have a basic background in sensory integration theory and relationship-based therapy as well as participation in the STAR Institute mentorship program.

Research on the STAR PROCESS

Research on the STAR PROCESS was initiated with the first pilot randomized controlled trial completed by Miller and team (Miller et al., 2007b). While this study did not include all of the elements of the STAR PROCESS, many features were tested; intensity and duration of therapy, individualized goal setting, and adherence to principles of sensory integration.

Building on this research was a retrospective chart review of 179 clients who received treatment using the full program described as the STAR PROCESS (Schoen et al., 2018). Parents reported significant improvements in areas of daily life functioning such as functional communication, self-direction, self-care, home living, health, safety, leisure, and social skills (ES = .45–.55). They also reported a large (> 1 SD) reduction in problematic behaviors associated with externalizing, internalizing and other behavioral symptoms such as hyperactivity, aggression, anxiety, depression, withdrawal and inattention (ES = .41–.52) as well as a decrease in sensory symptoms (ES = .18–.52). In fact, those treated for sensory craving challenges had the most significant reduction in externalizing and behavior problems after intervention. Lastly, motor skills significantly improved in the areas of fine motor, gross motor and visual motor abilities. Thus, this study provides preliminary support for effectiveness of the STAR PROCESS intervention, although follow up with a randomized clinical trial is needed.

More recent efforts have been directed towards single subject research using a multiple baseline design. Data was collected from four participants during a baseline, no therapy condition, and then weekly following STAR PROCESS intervention. Play and social behavior with the parent (no therapist present) were coded on a sensory friendly playground as the measure of change. Common across all participants were gains in cooperative play and parent participation in the play scheme. Parents joined in the play and helped to raise the child's play level; one participant showed an increase in novel use of the playground equipment (Schoen, Miller, Camarata & Valdez, 2018).

Two additional sources of unpublished data from studies are available. Study one included 110 participants who completed the Draw a Person test pre and post STAR PROCESS intervention. Twenty-nine were female and 81 were male, ranging in age from 3 to 13 years of age. Results indicated a significant improvement in scores ($t = 6.76$; $p < .001$). No skill training in how to "draw a person" takes place during the STAR PROCESS. Quantitatively higher scores in various elements of the drawing showed an increased number of details and/or reflected improved motor ability. For example, if the drawing had two-dimensional elements (two-dimensional limbs, trunk and facial features), had hair and clothing, or hands and feet shown in perspective. Points were also awarded if lines were drawn with increased control (e.g. firmly and correctly joined). Qualitative changes were also noted and interpreted as improvements in body awareness and sense of self.

Study 2 was from a follow-up study that was conducted with 59 families whose child participated in a 20–30 session STAR program. This study queried parents 3 to 75 weeks post intervention to determine whether gains made immediately following intervention were sustained. Questions were about functioning at home and school, how long improvements lasted, how well what they learned worked, and in general how satisfied families were with the STAR PROCESS. Based on a visual analog scale (from 1 to 10), scores on 75% of the questions were above 7 (higher scores are better; only two questions scoring 6). The more recent a family had completed their program the higher the overall score especially for how satisfied they were with the services, how school life had been going, and how long improvements lasted.

Summary

In summary, the STAR PROCESS is a novel treatment approach that combines principles of ASI and DIRFloortime with parent collaboration, parent participation and parent coaching. This is designed to be a short-term, multidisciplinary program. The approach is based on years of research and clinical experience. Preliminary information regarding treatment effectiveness is promising. The goals of intervention include joie de vivre and improved quality of life the child and the family.

References

Als, H., Tronick, E. Z., & Brazelton, T. B. (1980). Affective reciprocity and the development of autonomy: The study of a blind Infant. *Journal of the American Academy of Child Psychiatry, 19*(1), 22–40.

American Psychiatric Association. (2013). *Diagnostic and statistical manual of mental disorders*, DSM-5 (5th ed.). Washington, DC: American Psychiatric Association.

American Psychoanalytic Association, & Alliance of Psychoanalytic Organizations. (2006). *Psychodynamic diagnostic manual*. Silver

Spring, MD: Alliance of Psychoanalytic Organizations.
Ausderau, K. K., Sideris, J., Little, L. M., Furlong, M., Bulluck, J. C., & Baranek, G. T. (2016). Sensory subtypes and associated outcomes in children with autism spectrum disorders. *Autism Research, 9*(12), 1316–1327.
Ayres, A. J. (1963). The development of perceptual - motor abilities: A theoretical basis for treatment of dysfunction. *American Journal of Occupational Therapy, 17*, 221–225.
Ayres, A. J. (1972). *Sensory integration and learning disabilities*. Los Angeles, CA: Western Psychological Services.
Ayres, A. J. (1979). *Sensory integration and the child* (1st ed.). Los Angeles, CA: Western Psychological Services.
Ayres, A. J. (2011). *Ayres dyspraxia monograph*. (Z. Mailloux, S. S. Roley, & G. Coleman, Eds.) (25th Anniv). Torrance, CA: Pediatric Therapy Network.
Ayres, A. J., & Tickle, L. S. (1980). Hyper-responsivity to touch and vestibular stimuli as a predictor of positive response to sensory integration procedures by autistic children. *American Journal of Occupational Therapy, 34*(6), 375–381.
Bailer, D., & Miller, L. J. (2011). *No longer a secret: Unique common sense strategies for children with sensory or motor challenges*. Arlington, TX: Sensory World.
Barton, E. E., Reichow, B., Schnitz, A., Smith, I. C., & Sherlock, D. (2015). A systematic review of sensory-based treatments for children with disabilities. *Research in Developmental Disabilities, 37*, 64–80.
Baranek, G. T., David, F. J., Poe, M. D., Stone, W. L., & Watson, L. R. (2006). Sensory experiences questionnaire: Discriminating sensory features in young children with autism, developmental delays, and typical development. *Journal of Child Psychology and Psychiatry, 47*(6), 591–601.
Ben-Sasson, A., Carter, A. S., & Briggs-Gowan, M. J. (2009a). Sensory over-responsivity in elementary school: Prevalence and social-emotional correlates. *Journal of Abnormal Child Psychology, 37*(5), 705–716.
Ben-Sasson, A., Hen, L., Fluss, R., Cermak, S. A., Engel-Yeger, B., & Gal, E. (2009b). A meta-analysis of sensory modulation symptoms in individuals with autism spectrum disorders. *Journal of Autism and Developmental Disorders, 39*(1), 1–11.
Ben-Sasson, A., Carter, A., & Briggs-Gowan, M. (2010). The development of sensory over-responsivity from infancy to elementary school. *Journal of Abnormal Child Psychology, 38*(8), 1193–1202.
Berk, L. E., & Meyers, A. B. (2013). The role of make-believe play in the development of executive function status of research and future directions. *American Journal of Play, 6*(1), 98–110.

Bhat, A. N., Landa, R. J., & Galloway, J. C. (2011). Current perspectives on motor functioning in infants, children, and adults with autism spectrum disorders. *Physical Therapy, 91*(7), 1116–1129.

Bhopti, A., & Brown, T. (2013). Examining the Wilbargers' deep pressure and proprioceptive technique for treating children with sensory defensiveness using a multiple-single-case study approach. *Journal of Occupational Therapy, Schools, & Early Intervention, 6*(2), 108–130.

Bodison, S. C. (2015). Developmental dyspraxia and the play skills of children with autism. *The American Journal of Occupational Therapy, 69*(5).

Boyt Schell, B. A., & Schell, J. W. (2008). *Clinical and professional reasoning in occupational therapy*. Wolters Kluwer Health.

Brazelton, T. B., & Greenspan, S. I. (2009). *The irreducible needs of children: What every child must have to grow, learn, and flourish.* Philadelphia, PA: De Capo Press/Lifelong Books.

Brown, S., Shankar, R., & Smith, K. (2009). Borderline personality disorder and sensory processing impairment. *Progress in Neurology and Psychiatry, 13*(4), 10–16.

Browne, J. V., & Talmi, A. (2015). The BABIES model: Training for community professionals who work with newborns and young infants with special needs and their families, (September).

Case-Smith, J., & Bryan, T. (1999). The effects of occupational therapy with sensory integration emphasis on preschool-age children with autism. *American Journal of Occupational Therapy, 53*(5), 489-497.

Case-Smith, J., & Miller, H. (1999). Occupational therapy with children with pervasive developmental disorders. *American Journal of Occupational Therapy, 53*(5), 506–513.

Case-Smith, J., Weaver, L. L., & Fristad, M. A. (2015). A systematic review of sensory processing interventions for children with autism spectrum disorders. *Autism, 19*(2), 133–148.

Casenhiser, D. M., Shanker, S. G., & Stieben, J. (2013). Learning through interaction in children with autism: preliminary data from asocial-communication-based intervention. *Autism, 17*(2), 220–241.

Cermak, S., Gubbay, S., Larkin, D. (2002). What is developmental coordination disorder? In S. Cermak & D. Larkin (Eds.), *Developmental coordination disorder* (pp. 2–21). New York, NY: Delmar Thompson.

Csíkszentmihályi, M. (1997). *Finding flow: The psychology of engagement with everyday life*. London: Basic Books.

Cunningham, T. J., & Murphy, E. H. (1978). Ontogeny of sensory systems. In R. B. Masterton (Ed.), *Handbook of behavioral neurobiology: Sensory integration*. New York, NY: Plenum Press.

Devlin, S., Healy, O., Leader, G., & Hughes, B. M. (2011). Comparison of behavioral intervention and sensory-integration therapy in the treatment of challenging behavior. *Journal of Autism and Developmental Disorders, 41*(10), 1303–1320.

Devlin, S., Leader, G., & Healy, O. (2009). Comparison of behavioral intervention and sensory-integration therapy in the treatment of self-injurious behavior. *Research in Autism Spectrum Disorders, 3*(1), 223–231.

Dunn, W. (2008a). *Living sensationally: Understanding your senses.* Philadelphia, PA: Thomson-Shore, Inc.

Dunn, W. (2008b). Sensory processing as an evidence-based practice at school. *Physical & Occupational Therapy in Pediatrics, 28*(2), 137–140.

Engel-Yeger, B., Hardal-Nasser, R., & Gal, E. (2011). Sensory processing dysfunctions as expressed among children with different severities of intellectual developmental disabilities. *Research in Developmental Disabilities, 32*(5), 1770–1775.

Engel-Yeger, B., Muzio, C., Rinosi, G., Solano, P., Geoffroy, P. A., Pompili, M., ... Serafini, G. (2016). Extreme sensory processing patterns and their relation with clinical conditions among individuals with major affective disorders. *Psychiatry Research, 236*, 112–118.

Fonagy, P. (1998). Prevention, the appropriate target of infant psychotherapy. *Infant Mental Health Journal, 19*(2), 124–150.

Fonagy, P. (2015). Mutual regulation, mentalization, and therapeutic action: A reflection on the contributions of Ed Tronick to developmental and psychotherapeutic thinking. *Psychoanalytic Inquiry, 35*(4), 355–369.

Fonagy, P., Gergely, G., & Jurist, E. (2004). *Affect regulation, mentalization and the development of the self* (new ed.). London: Karnac Books.

Fonagy, P., & Target, M. (2002). Early intervention and the development of self-regulation. *Psychoanalytic Inquiry, 22*(3), 307–335.

Fournier, K. A., Kimberg, C. I., Radonovich, K. J., Tillman, M. D., Chow, J. W., Lewis, M. H., . . . Hass, C. J. (2010). Decreased static and dynamic postural control in children with autism spectrum disorders. *Gait & Posture, 32*(1), 6–9.

Gergely, G., Koós, O., Frigyes, J., Lakatos, K., Ney, K., & Toth, I. (1998). Affect-mirroring as a mechanism of parental sensitivity. *Infant Behavior and Development, 21*(Suppl), 67.

Ghanizadeh, A. (2011). Sensory processing problems in children with ADHD, a systematic review. *Psychiatry Investigation, 8*(2), 89–94.

Gibson, J. J. (1979). Theory of affordances. In *The ecological approach to visual perception.* New York, NY: Psychology Press.

Goin-Kochel, R. P., Myers, B. J., & Mackintosh, V. H. (2007). Parental reports on the use of treatments and therapies for children with autism spectrum disorders. *Research in Autism Spectrum Disorders, 1*(3), 195–209.

Green, V. A., Pituch, K. A., Itchon, J., Choi, A., O'Reilly, M., & Sigafoos, J. (2006). Internet survey of treatments used by parents of children with autism. *Research in Developmental Disabilities, 27*(1), 70–84.

Greenspan, S. I., DeGangi, G., & Wieder, S. (2001). *The functional emotional assessment scale for infancy and early childhood: Clinical and research applications.* Bethesda, MD: Interdisciplinary Council on Developmental and Learning Disorders.

Greenspan, S. I., & Greenspan, N. T. (2003). *The clinical interview of the child* (3rd ed.). Arlington, VA: American Psychiatric Association.

Greenspan, S. I., & Shanker, S. G. (2007). The developmental pathways leading to pattern recognition, joint attention, language and cognition. *New Ideas in Psychology, 25*(2), 173–187.

Greenspan, S. I., & Wieder, S. (1998). *The child with special needs: Encouraging intellectual and emotional growth.* Reading, MA: Addison-Wesley/Addison Wesley Longman.

Greenspan, S. I., & Wieder, S. (2006a). *Engaging autism: Using the floortime approach help children, relate, communicate, and think.* Philadelphia, PA: De Capo Press/Lifelong Books.

Greenspan, S. I., & Wieder, S. (2006b). *Infant and early childhood mental health.* Arlington, VA: American Psychiatric Association.

Hiles Howard, A. R., Lindaman, S., Copeland, R., & Cross, D. R. (2017). Theraplay impact on parents and children with autism spectrum disorder: Improvements in affect, joint attention, and social cooperation. *International Journal of Play Therapy, 27*(1), 56–68.

Iwanaga, R., Honda, S., Nakane, H., Tanaka, K., Toeda, H., & Tanaka, G. (2014). Pilot study: Efficacy of sensory integration therapy for Japanese children with high-functioning autism spectrum disorder. *Occupational Therapy International, 21*(1), 4–11.

Jones, K. (2003). What is an affordance? *Ecological Psychology, 15*(2), 107–114.

Kiresuk, T. J., Smith, A., & Cardillo, J. E. (2014). *Goal attainment scaling: Applications, theory, and measurement.* New York, NY: Psychology Press.

Lane, S. J., Reynolds, S., & Thacker, L. (2010). Sensory over-responsivity and ADHD: Differentiating using electrodermal responses, cortisol, and anxiety. *Frontiers in Integrative Neuroscience, 4*, 8.

Lane, A. E., Young, R. L., Baker, A. E. Z., & Angley, M. T. (2010). Sensory processing subtypes in autism: Association with adaptive behavior. *Journal of Autism and Developmental Disorders, 40*(1), 112–122.

Leekam, S. R., Nieto, C., Libby, S. J., Wing, L., & Gould, J. (2007). Describing the sensory abnormalities of children and adults with autism. *Journal of Autism and Developmental Disorders, 37*(5), 894–910.

Lickliter, R. (2008). Developmental dynamics: the new view from the life sciences. In A. Fogel, S. Shanker, & B. J. King (Eds.), *Human development in the twenty-first century* (pp. 11–17). New York, NY: Cambridge University Press.
Lillas, C., & Turnbull, J. (2009). *Infant / child mental health, early intervention, and relationship-based therapies. Clinical Social Work Journal*. New York, NY: Norton.
Linderman, T. M., & Stewart, K. B. (1999). Sensory integrative-based occupational therapy and functional outcomes in young children with pervasive developmental disorders: A single-subject study. *American Journal of Occupational Therapy, 53*(2), 207–213.
Lloyd, M., MacDonald, M., & Lord, C. (2013). Motor skills of toddlers with autism spectrum disorders. *Autism, 17*(2), 133–146.
Lydon, H., Healy, O., & Grey, I. (2017). Comparison of behavioral intervention and sensory integration therapy on challenging behavior of children with autism. *Behavioral Interventions, 32*(4), 297–310.
Mandell, D., Novak, M., & Levy, S. (2005). Frequency and correlates of treatment use among a community sample of children with autism (presentation). Proceedings from*: The 4th International Meeting for Autism Research*. San Diego, CA.
Mattingly, C. (1991). What is clinical reasoning? *The American Journal of Occupational Therapy, 45*(11), 979–86.
Mattingly, C., & Fleming, M. H. (1994). *Clinical reasoning: Forms of inquiry in a therapeutic practice*. Philadelphia, PA: FA Davis.
May-Benson, T. A. (2001). A theoretical model of ideation in praxis. In S. S. Roley, E. I. Blanche, & R. C. Schaaf (Eds.), *Understanding the nature of sensory integration with diverse populations* (pp. 163–182). Austin, TX: Pro-ed.
May-Benson, T. A., & Cermak, S. A. (2007). Development of an assessment for ideational Praxis. *American Journal of Occupational Therapy, 61*(2), 148–153.
McIntosh, D. N., Miller, L. J., Shyu, V., & Hagerman, R. J. (1999). Sensory-modulation disruption, electrodermal responses, and functional behaviors. *Developmental Medicine and Child Neurology, 41*(9), 608–615.
McLaren, C., & Rodger, S. (2003). Goal attainment scaling: Clinical implications for paediatric occupational therapy practice. *Australian Occupational Therapy Journal, 50*(4), 216–224.
Miller, L. J., McIntosh, D., McGrath, J., Shyu, V., Lampe, M., Taylor, A., . . . Hagerman, R. (1999). Electrodermal responses to sensory stimuli in individuals with fragile X syndrome. *American Journal of Medical Genetics, 83*, 268–279.
Miller, L. J., Anzalone, M. E., Lane, S. J., Cermak, S. A., & Osten, E. T. (2007a). Concept evolution in sensory integration: A proposed nosology for diagnosis. *American Journal of Occupational Therapy,*

61(2), 135–140.
Miller, L. J., Coll, J. R., & Schoen, S. A. (2007b). A randomized controlled pilot study of the effectiveness of occupational therapy for children with sensory modulation disorder. *The American Journal of Occupational Therapy*, *61*(2), 228–238.
Miller, L. J., Fuller, D. A., & Roetenberg, J. (2014). *Sensational kids revised edition: Hope and help for children with sensory processing disorder (SPD)*. New York, NY: Penguin.
Miller, L. J., Schoen, S. A., & Mulligan, S. (2016). Sensory processing three dimensions (SP3D) scale. *Manuscript in Preparation.*
Ming, X., Brimacombe, M., & Wagner, G. C. (2007). Prevalence of motor impairment in autism spectrum disorders. *Brain & development, 29*(9), 565–570.
Murphy, J., Brewer, R., & Bird, G. (2017). Interoception and psychopathology: A developmental neuroscience perspective. *Developmental Cognitive Neuroscience*, *23*, 45–56.
National Institute of Mental Health. (2017). Research domain criteria (RDoC) construct: Perception. https://www.nimh.nih.gov/research-priorities/rdoc/constructs/perception.shtml
Nelson, K. (2015). Making sense with private speech. *Cognitive Development*, *36*, 171–179.
Øien, I., Fallang, B., & Østensjø, S. (2010). Goal-setting in paediatric rehabilitation: Perceptions of parents and professional. *Child: Care, Health and Development*, *36*(4), 558–565.
Papoušek, M. (2016). Disinterest in play in infancy: Problems in the regulation of attention and play. In M. Cierpka (Ed.), *Regulatory disorders in infants: Assessment, diagnosis, and treatment* (pp. 161–180). Cham: Springer International Publishing.
Parham, L. D., Cohn, S. E., Spitzer, S., Koomar, J. A., Miller, L. J., Burke, J. P., ... Summers, C. A. (2007). Fidelity in sensory integration intervention fidelity in sensory integration intervention research. *Department of Occupational Therapy Faculty Papers*, *25*(2), 216–227.
Pfeiffer, B., Koenig, K., Kinnealey, M., Sheppard, M., & Henderson, L. (2011). Effectiveness of sensory integration interventions in children with autism spectrum disorders: A pilot study. *American Journal of Occupational Therapy*, *65*(1), 76–85.
Pfeiffer, B., May-Benson, T. A., & Bodison, S. C. (2018). State of the science of sensory integration research with children and youth. *American Journal of Occupational Therapy*, *72*(1), 1–4.
Porges, S. W. (2015). Play as a neural exercise: Insights from the polyvagal theory. In D. Pearce-McCall (Ed.), *Power of play for mind/brain health* (pp. 3–7). https://mindgains.org/bonus/GAINS-The-Power-of-Play-for-Mind-Brain-Health.pdf.
Provenzi, L., Olson, K. L., Montirosso, R., & Tronick, E. Z. (2015). Infants, mothers, and dyadic contributions to stability and

prediction of social stress response at 6 months. *Developmental Psychology, 52*(1),1–8.

Quigley, S. P., Peterson, L., Frieder, J. E., & Peterson, S. (2011). Effects of a weighted vest on problem behaviors during functional analyses in children with pervasive developmental disorders. *Research in Autism Spectrum Disorders, 5*(1), 529–538.

Robertson, C. E., & Baron-Cohen, S. (2017). Sensory perception in autism. *Nature Reviews Neuroscience, 18*(11), 671–684.

Rogers, C. R. (1961). *On becoming a person: A therapist's view of psychotherapy*. Boston: Houghton Mifflin Company.

Roley, S. S., Mailloux, Z., Miller-Kuhaneck, H., & Glennon, T. (2007). Understanding Ayres' sensory integration. *AOTA Continuing Education, 12*(17), 1–8.

Ruscio, J., & Ruscio, A. M. (2008). Categories and dimensions advancing psychological science through the study of latent structure. *Current Directions in Psychological Science, 17*(3), 203–207.

Sameroff, A. J. (2009). The transactional model. In A. J. Sameroff (Ed.), *The transactional model of development: How children and contexts shape each other* (pp. 3–21). Washington, DC: American Psychological Association.

Schaaf, R. C., Benevides, T. W., Kelly, D., & Mailloux-Maggio, Z. (2012). Occupational therapy and sensory integration for children with autism: A feasibility, safety, acceptability and fidelity study. *Autism, 16*(3), 321–327.

Schaaf, R. C., Benevides, T., Mailloux, Z., Faller, P., Hunt, J., van Hooydonk, E., ... Kelly, D. (2014). An intervention for sensory difficulties in children with autism: A randomized trial. *Journal of Autism and Developmental Disorders, 44*(2014), 1493–1506.

Schaaf, R. C., & Mailloux, Z. (2015). *Clinician's guide for implementing Ayres sensory integration: Promoting participation for children with autism*. Bethesda, MD: American Occupational Therapy Association.

Schaaf, R. C., Roley, S. S., Mailloux, Z., Parham, L. D., Lane, C. J., & Cermak, S. (2015a). Sensory integration and praxis patterns in children with autism. *American Journal of Occupational Therapy, 69*(1), http://doi.org/10.5014/ajot.2015.012476.

Schaaf, R. C., Schoen, S. A., May-Benson, T. A., Parham, L. D., Lane, S. J., Roley, S. S., & Mailloux, Z. (2015b). State of the science: A roadmap for research in sensory integration. *American Journal of Occupational Therapy, 69*(4), http://doi.org/10.5014/ajot.2015.019539.

Schoen, S. A., Miller, L. J., Brett-Green, B., & Hepburn, S. L. (2008). Psychophysiology of children with autism spectrum disorder. *Research in Autism Spectrum Disorders, 2*(3), 417–429.

Schoen, S. A., Miller, L. J., Brett-Green, B. A., & Nielsen, D. M. (2009). Physiological and behavioral differences in sensory processing: A comparison of children with autism spectrum disorder and sensory modulation disorder. *Frontiers in Integrative Neuroscience, 3*, 29.

Schoen, S. A., Miller, L. J., & Flanagan, J. (2018). A retrospective pre-post treatment study of occupational therapy intervention for children with sensory processing challenges. *The Open Journal of Occupational Therapy, 6*(1), 4.

Schoen, S. A., Miller, L. J., & Green, K. E. (2008). Pilot study of the Sensory Over-Responsivity Scales: Assessment and inventory. *American Journal of Occupational Therapy, 62*(4), 393–406.

Schoen, S. A., Miller, L. J., Camarata, S., Valdez, A. (2018). Use of STAR PROCESS for children with SPD. Manuscript in Preparation.

Schroeder, C. E., & Foxe, J. (2005). Multisensory contributions to low-level, 'unisensory' processing. *Current opinion in neurobiology, 15*(4), 454–458.

Seth, A. K., & Friston, K. J. (2016). Active interoceptive inference and the emotional brain. *Philosophical Transactions of the Royal Society of London. Series B, Biological Sciences, 371*(1708), 20160007.

Shanker, S. (2004). Autism and the dynamic developmental model of emotions. *Philosophy, Psychiatry, & Psychology, 11*(3), 219–233.

Shonkoff, J. P., & Phillips, D. (Eds.) (2000). *From neurons to neighborhoods: The science of early childhood development.* Washington, DC: Committee on Integrating the Science of Early Childhood Development, Board on Children, Youth, and Families.

Smith, S. A., Press, B., Koenig, K. P., & Kinnealey, M. (2005). Effects of sensory integration intervention on self-stimulating and self-injurious behaviors. *American Journal of Occupational Therapy, 59*(4), 418–425.

Smith, L. B., & Thelen, E. (2003). Development as a dynamic system. *Trends in Cognitive Sciences, 7*(8), 343–348.

Spitzer, S. L. (1999). Dynamic systems theory: Relevance to the theory of sensory integration and the study of occupation. *Sensory Integration Special Interest Section Quarterly AOTA, 22*(2), 1–4.

Steenbeek, D., Gorter, J. W., Ketelaar, M., Galama, K., & Lindeman, E. (2011). Responsiveness of goal attainment scaling in comparison to two standardized measures in outcome evaluation of children with cerebral palsy. *Clinical Rehabilitation, 25*(12), 1128–1139.

Stein, B. E., Stanford, T. R., & Rowland, B. A. (2014). Development of multisensory integration from the perspective of the individual neuron. *Nature Reviews Neuroscience, 15*(8), 520–535.

Stephenson, J., & Carter, M. (2009). The use of weighted vests with children with autism spectrum disorders and other disabilities. *Journal of Autism and Developmental Disorders, 39*(1), 105.

Stern, D. N. (1995). *The motherhood constellation: A unified view of parent-infant psychotherapy*. London: Karnac Books.

Stevenson, R. A., Segers, M., Ferber, S., Barense, M. D., & Wallace,

M. T. (2014). The impact of multisensory integration deficits on speech perception in children with autism spectrum disorders. *Frontiers in Psychology, 5*, 379.
Taylor, R. R. (2008). Knowing ourselves as therapists: Introducing therapeutic modes. In *The intentional relationship* (pp. 67–86). Philadelphia, PA: F.A. Davis Company.
The Interdisciplinary Council on Development and Learning. (2005a). *Diagnostic manual for infancy and early childhood.* Bethesda, MD: The Interdisciplinary Council on Development and Learning, Inc.
The Interdisciplinary Council on Development and Learning, (2005b). A comprehensive approach to clinical evaluation (Appendix 1). In *Diagnostic manual for infancy and early childhood.* Bethesda, MD: The Interdisciplinary Council on Development and Learning, Inc.
Thelen, E. (2005). Dynamic systems theory and the complexity of change. *Psychoanalytic dialogues: The International Journal of Relational Perspectives, 15*(2), 255–283.
Tomchek, S. D., & Dunn, W. (2007). Sensory processing in children with and without autism: A comparative study using the short sensory profile. *American Journal of Occupational Therapy 61*(2), 190–200.
Tsakiris, M., & Critchley, H. (2016). Interoception beyond homeostasis: Affect, cognition and mental health. *Philosophical transactions of the Royal Society of London, Series B, Biological Sciences, 371*(1708), 20160002.
Tudge, J. (1992). Vygotsky, the zone of proximal development, and peer collaboration: Implications for classroom practice. In L. C. Moll (Ed.), *Vygotsky and education: Instructional implications and applications of sociohistorical psychology* (pp. 155–172). New York, NY: Cambridge University Press.
Turner-Stokes, L. (2009). Goal attainment scaling (GAS) in rehabilitation: A practical guide. *Clinical Rehabilitation, 23*(4), 362–370.
Van Etten, H. M., Kaur, M., Srinivasan, S. M., Cohen, S. J., Bhat, A., & Dobkins, K. R. (2017). Increased prevalence of unusual sensory behaviors in infants at risk for, and teens with, autism. *Journal of Autism and Developmental Disorders, 47*(11), 3431–3445.
Van Rie, G. L., & Heflin, L. J. (2009). The effect of sensory activities on correct responding for children with autism spectrum disorders. *Research in Autism Spectrum Disorders, 3*(3), 783–796.
Watling, R., Patten Koenig, K., Davies, P. L., & Schaaf, R. C. (2011). *Occupational therapy practice guidelines for children and adolescents with challenges in sensory processing and sensory integration.* Bethesda, MD: AOTA Press.
Whyatt, C., & Craig, C. (2013). Sensory-motor problems in autism. *Frontiers in Integrative Neuroscience, 7*(51), 12.
Widakowich, C., Van Wettere, L., Jurysta, F., Linkowski, P., & Hubain,

P. (2013). Dimensional approach vs. categorical approach in psychiatric diagnosis: Historical and epistemological aspects. *Annales Medico-Psychologiques, 171*(5), 300–305.
Wieder, S., & Greenspan, S. I. (2003). Climbing the symbolic ladder in the DIR model through floor time/interactive play. *Autism: The International Journal of Research and Practice*, *7*(4), 425–435.
Winsler, A., Abar, B., Feder, M. A., Schunn, C. D., & Rubio, D. A. (2007). Private speech and executive functioning among high-functioning children with autistic spectrum disorders. *Journal of Autism and Developmental Disorders*, *37*(9), 1617–1635.
Young, G. (2011a). Attachment basics. In *Development and causality* (pp. 523–547). New York, NY: Springer New York.
Young, G. (2011b). Piaget and development. In *Development and causality* (pp. 47–72). New York, NY: Springer New York.
Zeanah, C. H., Berlin, L. J., & Boris, N. W. (2011). Practitioner review: Clinical applications of attachment theory and research for infants and young children. *Journal of Child Psychology and Psychiatry*, *52*(8), 819–833.
Zero to Three. (2005). *Diagnostic classification of mental health and developmental disorders of infancy and early childhood: Revised edition* (DC: 0–3R). Washington, DC: Zero to Three Press.

13

Berard Auditory Integration Training

Sally Brockett
IDEA Training Center, North Haven, CT

Guy Berard, MD developed a method of using uniquely modulated music to stimulate the auditory system. His goal was to enhance auditory processing to be more efficient (Berard, 1993). Berard believed "everything happens as if human behavior were largely conditioned by the manner in which one hears" (Berard, 1993). Berard's work focused on the concept that *how* we hear plays a very significant role in *how* we behave and learn. He felt that when the auditory system functioned effectively, it would manifest in improved behaviors, as well as improvements in language, social, motor, and academic performance. Unfortunately, even today, there are professionals who are not aware that many individuals who are struggling with academics and behavioral problems have an inefficient auditory system. This interferes with effective listening and processing, which puts the individual at a great disadvantage in the classroom and workplace.

As an ear, nose, and throat (ENT) physician, Berard's primary focus during his earliest years of practice with AIT was on middle ear function and the cochlea. His AIT program was used primarily to assist in certain types of hearing impairment. However, he observed that learning-related skills and abilities, such as attentive listening, concentration, auditory discrimination, and memory skills, often improved following his AIT program. The Berard program is now noted for its use as an educationally-related intervention (Berard & Brockett, 2011). In recent years, as understanding of sensory processing has increased, it has become evident that Berard AIT also significantly impacts sensory modulation and the visual system (Brockett, Lawton-Shirley, & Kimball, 2014; Brockett, 2015).

Ayres identified the brain's processing of sound as an essential form of sensory integration and proposed that vestibular-auditory processing influences both survival and discriminative functions. The information provided through this system helps sort out what is safe versus not safe, an understanding that can be critical to survival. It also guides us about our position in space, and can stimulate movement responses. During early development, the system also helps direct the infant/toddler to caregivers for engagement that facilitates opportunities to thrive (Ayres, 1972).

Various theories gradually emerged to explain how AIT produced the observed results, including biochemical changes (Edelson, 1995), improved ability to shift attention and "tune in" (Edelson, 1996), and improved function in the middle ear (Edelson, 1994). The cerebellar-vestibular theory proposed that the results of Berard AIT were associated with the unique effect of the auditory vibrational stimulation produced by the specific type of modulation used for this method. The random modulation may create changes in the vibrational patterns perceived by the ear, which then, stimulates the vestibular connection to the cerebellum more intensely (Lawton-Shirley, N. personal communication, May 20, 2018). During Berard AIT, the average maximum listen volume is below 85 dB, a safe level for the 30-minute sessions (OSHA, 1981). Another aspect of the intensity is the frequency of the sessions, (2) 30-minute sessions each day for 10 days (Brockett, 1994). This unique vibrational stimulation could potentially impact auditory and vestibular-cerebellar connections, which could result in improvements in functions regulated by these structures (Brown, 1999; Frick & Hacker, 2001; Netter, 1986; Rimland & Edelson, 1994). Specific facilitation of auditory/vestibular processing has been associated with changes in sensory processing and modulation, arousal, attention and focus, postural control, social emotional development, auditory filtering, and visual-motor performance (Ayres, 1972; Frick & Hacker, 2001; Hall & Case-Smith, 2007; Rimland & Edelson, 2004).

Auditory Processing Deficits in Autism

One of the characteristics of autism is difficulty with communication and social interactions. An underlying cause may be the challenges with auditory processing experienced by those on the autism spectrum. Auditory processing must be efficient in order to communicate and engage in social interactions, but it is now recognized that the auditory system, and auditory processing, are often not working effectively for those on the spectrum (Grandin & Panek, 2013). There may be difficulties in various areas of the auditory system, all of which compound the significance of the challenge faced by those with autism.

Hypersensitivity to sound is one problem that is often easy to recognize. Sounds that are tolerat-ed comfortably by most people can be painful, irritating, and frightening when the auditory sys-tem is not functioning as it should. Behaviors such as covering the ears, startling to sounds that don't bother others, and hearing sounds, such as an approaching airplane, before others can hear it, are often signs of hypersensitive hearing. Those on the spectrum may be in constant fear of when the next assault from sound will occur. Sudden, loud sounds may be very troublesome, but even sounds at a low volume can be a problem depending upon the frequencies involved and how the individual hears those particular frequencies.

Receptive language or language input problems can also interfere with communication. One could ask, "Do you hear what I hear?" and for many on the spectrum, the answer is "no", they do not hear the same sounds as we hear them. For example, Temple Grandin explains that the fast transition consonants, such as /b/, /t/, /f/, etc., are pronounced very quickly and in a conso-nant/vowel combination such as *ball, tall, fall*; it may be difficult to distinguish the differences. When the words sound the same, the listener may need to rely on content to figure out what word was spoken (Grandin & Panek, 2013). By the time this is done, the speaker has often al-ready said another sentence, or more, causing even more confusion for an individual with autism. Other language input problems can occur if the listener does not hear the space between the words, causing all the words to run together as they do when we listen to a foreign language. Or, the listener may not be able to attach meaning to the words they hear, even when they hear them clearly and correctly, so the verbal information does not make sense to them.

Just as language input can be a problem, language output, or expressive language can also be dif-ficult for those on the spectrum. Some may never become verbal, while others may require in-tense therapy in order to develop spoken language. When auditory processing is faulty, it can take a lot of time to organize a thought and then verbalize it. When distractions occur, such as the person repeating the question, or someone else making a comment, it disrupts the processing and the person with autism may need to start over again. They often need quiet time, without inter-ruptions, to process their response.

Some individuals on the autism spectrum are able to become verbal with assistance from audio scripts such as TV commercials or video shows. When they listen and hear the words from the audio scripts, the pronunciation, intonation, rhythm, and timing, are always exactly the same. The accompanying video also provides meaning to what they hear. This may make it easier for them to eventually make sense out of the words. During life experiences, the video, or visual component, is often not a part of the activity, so the person with autism is dependent solely on the audi-tory message. Some memorize scripts and, over time, begin to use them to communicate. Provid-ing visual support for the auditory message can enhance processing, for both receptive and ex-pressive language.

Alfred Tomatis, Guy Berard, and Stephen Porges were interested in the function of the middle ear, and in particular, the parasympathetic nervous system's effect on the tensor tympani and sta-pedius muscles. When these muscles are working properly, the person can tune into the higher frequencies of human speech. However, stress, anxiety, and fear, trigger the fight-or-flight reac-tion, which shuts down the appropriate function of the tympani and stapedius muscles, limiting the individual's ability to process the human speech frequencies properly. The ability to listen, communicate, and connect to another person is reduced, until the situation resolves so the indi-vidual can feel safe. Feeling safe enables the parasympathetic system to switch off the stress re-action, and according to Porges, turns on a "social engagement system" and the middle ear mus-cles. Once the individual feels secure, he can connect better and listen to the human voice more efficiently because higher frequencies of human speech can now be processed more effectively (Doidge, 2015). This is one reason why talking to a person who is in a state of high stress and anxiety may have poor results. Using visual supports and other calming strategies to reduce the stress may be more productive than language.

Procedure

The standard protocol for Berard AIT provides two 30-minute sessions of listening each day for 10 days within a 12 day period. A break of at least 3 hours between the listening sessions allows for a rest from the auditory stimulation. Music for Berard AIT is typically a mixture of lively reggae, light rock, and jazz, with a wide range of frequencies from 20 Hz to 20 kHz. The music is processed, or modulated by the Berard AIT device, the Earducator/6F™ (Hollagen Designs CC, Western Cape, South Africa). The Audiokinetron is still in use by some Berard practitioners. The Earducator/6FTM alternately suppresses and emphasizes low and high frequencies on a random basis through the use of a broadband filter, and the music does not exceed an average output of 85 dB. Closed headphones (Beyerdynamic CT250-80) are recommended by Hollagen Designs CC (Brockett et al., 2014; Brockett, 2015).

According to Berard, narrow-band filters allow specific frequencies, that the listener hears too well, to be filtered, and is another feature in his method of processing the sounds (Berard, 1993). A listening test to show minimum hearing levels at 11 frequencies is administered to the individual. The tester repeats frequencies to establish reliability. The results are analyzed using a computer program, available to all Berard practitioners, based on Berard's protocol for selecting filters (Berard, Edelson, & Brockett, 2000). The protocol identifies the relative peaks in the listening profile and prioritizes the activation of narrow-band filters. No narrow-band filters are used when a reliable test is not available, or when the analysis indicates no filters are needed.

The protocol for Berard AIT recommends quiet listening without engagement in cognitive activities. Most participants are able to listen quietly, though some may require a passive sensory fidget toy to keep their hands away from the headphone cord and to help them cooperate with the listening process. Activities such as reading, assembling puzzles, writing, and other cognitively stimulating tasks are distracting and not recommended (Brockett et al., 2014).

After 10 half-hour listening sessions have been completed (the mid-point in training), some adjustments may be made in the use of narrow-band filters, depending on reassessment of the listening profile. The volume may also be reduced in the left ear if the individual has difficulties with speech-language development. The theory behind this is to stimulate language growth in the left hemisphere (Berard, 1993).

Studies

A variety of studies began in the early 1990s in order to learn more about how effective the AIT program could be, what types of changes resulted, and who might be good candidates. The first study was a placebo-controlled pilot study conducted by Rimland and Edelson with 19 individuals with autism. Results indicated statistically significant improvements in behaviors, sound sensitivity, and hyperactivity after AIT (Rimland & Edelson, 1995). Following the encouraging results of this pilot study, these researchers undertook a second, comprehensive study from 1991-1993 with 445 participants who were on the autism spectrum. This study involved an open-clinical research design which included several experimental control measures. After the 10 hours of listening sessions, sound sensitivity, a common finding with those on the autism spectrum, was significantly reduced. Hearing acuity improved slightly, and variability within the audiogram was reduced, indicating that the listener heard frequencies at a more consistent level across the frequency range. Behavior rating forms were used to measure changes in problem behaviors. Starting at 1 month after the AIT sessions, there was a sharp reduction in challenging behaviors and this reduction was maintained through the 9 months of monitoring. Contrary to expectations, lower functioning subjects with autism showed the most benefits. This method of intervention was found to be appropriate for a broad range of individuals, not just higher functioning people (Rimland & Edelson, 1994).

A placebo-controlled third study investigated electrophysiological and audiometric effects of AIT, including the auditory P300 event-related potential (ERP). The P300 is an important indicator of attention and working memory (Linden, 2005). It is most commonly elicited in an "oddball" paradigm when a subject detects an occasional "target" stimulus in a regular train of standard stimuli. The P300 wave only occurs if the subject is actively engaged in the task of detecting the targets. The P300 wave may represent the transfer of information to consciousness, a process that involves many different regions of the brain (Picton, 1992). Three months after the completion of AIT, the three subjects in the experimental group showed dramatic improvement in the auditory P300 ERP, while no changes were measured in the control group. The results of this AIT study showed normalization of brain wave activity, and behavioral changes were consistent with the previous two studies (Edelson et al., 1999).

Changes in Sensory Modulation and Behaviors

Most of the studies during the 1990s concentrated on monitoring behavioral changes and decreases in sound sensitivity. However, Berard practitioners gradually began to hear more and more reports from parents and therapists about improvements in sensory challenges after clients completed the Berard training program. This raised the consideration that perhaps AIT created changes in sensory modulation that facilitated the progress in behavioral changes, especially if the behaviors exhibited were compensations for faulty sensory experiences. It is recognized that sensory modulation helps the individual manage the changes that occur in their living environment throughout the day. When modulation is working efficiently, the individual is able to adjust to the changes and demands of their experiences in order to achieve success (Bundy, Lane, & Murry, 2002; McIntosh, Miller, Shyu, & Hagerman, 1999; Miller, 2006).

There are a variety of abilities that appear to be impacted by Berard AIT, including movement and gravity awareness (functions of the vestibular system), and hearing, which is critical for language development, attention, and learning (Oetter, 2009). When novel sound is provided with intensity and repetition, the neuroplasticity of the brain is stimulated, allowing growth and change to occur (Cool, 2004; Frick & Lawton-Shirley, 1994; Netter, 1986). The elements necessary for neuroplasticity to be activated are contained in the Berard AIT experience. The modulated music that shifts rapidly and randomly from treble to bass is novel stimulation to the brain because the musical frequencies are typically blended together. The schedule of the listening sessions also provides the intensity and repetition that is important.

Brockett, Lawton-Shirley, and Kimball (2014) completed a case review of 54 clients to identify changes in sensory modulation and behaviors after completing the Berard AIT program. The purpose of this case review was to determine if behaviors specifically related to sensory modulation showed positive changes following 10 hours of Berard AIT. Sensory modulation was identified, for the purposes of this study, as a neurophysiological process reflected in the individual's ability to regulate and organize behavioral, motor, emotional, and anticipatory reactions to sensory information and events (Brockett et al., 2014).

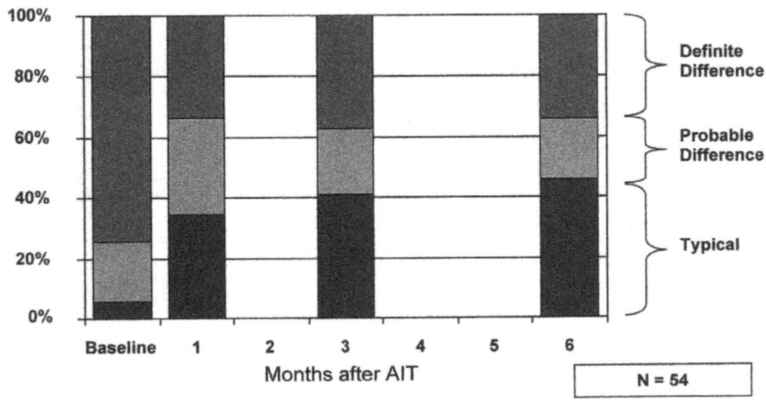

Figure 13.1. SSP-short form, changes during 6 months after AIT.

The Short Sensory Profile (SSP) measures behaviors reflecting sensory modulation during daily life activities. Brockett used the SSP to measure sensory modulation responses such as behaviors reflective of sensory defensiveness, vestibular processing, and behavior outcomes of sensory modulation before and after AIT. During the case review, the SSP total test scores and individual factor sections improved from pre-test to post-test ($p < 0.01$). As the SSP was designed to measure the components of sensory modulation, the statistical results appear to support clinical observations that Berard AIT can result in improved abilities in those sensory modulation components and these changes were maintained through the 1, 3 and 6 month post testing (Figure13.1; Brockett et al., 2014).

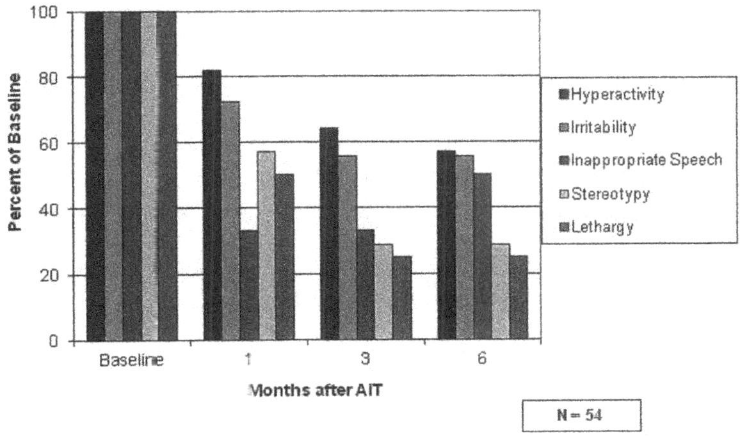

Figure 13.2. ABC-median change from baseline to six months post-Berard AIT.

The Aberrant Behavior Checklist (ABC) has been used to measure behavioral outcomes of AIT in studies looking at response to treatment for children with a diagnosis of autism or attention deficit disorder (Edelson et al., 1999; Rimland & Edelson, 1994). Behaviors assessed by the ABC (such as irritability, lethargy, stereotypy, and hyperactivity) have also been identified as behavioral reflections of poor sensory modulation (Aman & Singh, 1986; Dunn, 1999; Hall & Case-Smith, 2007). The case review study showed that behavioral difficulties reduced on all five factors of the ABC ($p < 0.01$). It is important to note that most changes occurred within 1 month of the intervention and maintained at three and six months (Figure. 13.2).

The case review included a correlational analysis between the ABC and SSP factors to help determine if sensory modulation, as measured by the SSP, is a significant contributor to the behavioral factors measured by the ABC (Brockett et al., 2014). Review of the data showed that correlations were significant for four of the five factors ($p<0.05$): Irritability (-0.531, $p < 0.01$),

Stereo¬typy (-0.410, $p < 0.01$), Hyperactivity (-0.399, $p < 0.01$), Inappropriate Speech (-0.288, $p < 0.05$). Sensory modulation appears to be a component of these behaviors. Data also indicated that the changes were not affected by the age of the subject.

Berard practitioners report that clinical, parental, and teacher observations often show the challenging behaviors reduce or resolve after the AIT program. If sensory modulation is more efficient for the individuals after AIT, the compensating behaviors, which are often be disruptive to daily living experiences, may not be needed.

Berard AIT Impacts Visual System

Berard practitioners, and parents of children who have received Berard AIT, have reported changes in various aspects of vision, including skills and abilities such as acuity, depth perception, spatial awareness, and so forth (Brockett, 2015). At first thought, it may seem unlikely that listening to processed music would cause a change in the visual system. However, if one considers the connections between the auditory system and the visual system, and also the functions of the cerebellar-vestibular system, it is easier to understand that specific, intense auditory stimulation could impact on visual functions.

Optometrists have a long history of interest in auditory and visual processing, and recognize the importance of integrating these systems in order for the struggling learner to achieve success. In the 1970s, Rosner introduced the Visual Analysis Test (VAT) and the Auditory Analysis Test (AAT) to be used in conjunction with his perceptual skills curriculum (Press, 2012a). Therapy activities that focus on processing within many domains, including visual and auditory, were introduced in *Thinking Goes to School* by Hans Furth and Harry Wachs (1975).

Dyslexia is often considered to be a visual disorder and is a concern for those involved with children who are struggling with academics, particularly reading. Intervention is often focused on treatments related to vision. However, Griffin and Walton suggest there are two forms of dyslexia. Dyseidetic is the visual form, while dysphonetic is the auditory form. Both forms involve visual and auditory processing difficulties (Walton & Griffin, 2006). Studies by both Solan and Birch found that weaknesses in auditory/visual integration are factors in reading disabilities (Solan, 2004; Birch, 1964).

When those who have participated in Berard AIT begin to read more efficiently, one or both forms of dyslexia may have been contributing factors to the reading problems. After completing Berard AIT, a client was asked why she was now able to read twice as long compared to before the training program. She replied that she no longer got tired when reading because she knew what the words were when she saw them, and she understood what they meant. She no longer needed to "sound out" the word and figure out what it meant in the context of the story. The AIT stimulation may have triggered reorganization and integration of the auditory/visual connections, allowing development of the skills needed to become a proficient reader.

The important relationship of auditory and visual processing through the vestibular system is noted by Solan and his colleagues to be a dominant factor in primary learning processes. They state "since vestibular responses are associated with eye movements and hearing, they contribute to visual and auditory processing" (Solan, Shelley-Tremblay, & Larson, 2007). These observations provide further support for the cerebellar-vestibular system theory about Berard AIT.

The book, *Parallels between Auditory and Visual Processing,* describes the similarities between the auditory and visual systems (Press, 2012b), which is supported by Holland. Holland states that every function in the visual system has an equivalent in the auditory system (Holland, 2006). Professionals in the field of special education are quite familiar with evaluations of figure-ground, discrimination, memory, closure, and sequencing in both the domain of audition as well as that of vision. Holland makes a significant point that there is a top-down and bottom-up interaction of auditory processing in the inferior colliculus for sound as there is in the superior colliculus for vision. In other words, auditory perception mirrors visual perception (Press, 2012b).

An important outcome of research at the Ruhr University-Bochum, in Germany, also supports the concept that neural pathways simultaneously process information from different senses. These researchers discovered that patients who are blind in one side of their visual field can benefit from listening to sounds on the affected side. After passively listening for an hour, the patients' ability to detect light stimuli in the blind half of their visual field improved significantly. Lewald states "there is increasing evidence that processing of incoming sensory information is not strictly separated in the brain" (Lewald, Tegenthoff, Peters, &Hausmann, 2012).

Lewald reports that nerve cells in the superior colliculus process auditory and visual information simultaneously, and this area is not usually affected by visual field defects. So there are some dormant capabilities in the blind half of the visual field. Because these same nerve cells also receive auditory information, the researchers tried acoustic stimuli to increase sensitivity to light stimuli, and it was successful, though the effect lasted 1.5 hours. The researchers are now focused on gaining more sustained improvement in visual abilities and use of sound stimulation for more complex visual functions (Lewald et al., 2012).

There have been some individual reports from parents and optometrists of enhancements in functional visual skills after participation in a Berard AIT program, though no clinical studies have been published. Wendy Garson, OD, presented a case study at the Berard Auditory Integration Training & Developmental Optometry Conference which was co-sponsored by the Optometric Extension Program Foundation and the Berard AIT International Society, on April, 2015 in Falls Church, VA. Garson reports that, after completing a visual evaluation, her patient, a young adult who experienced difficulty with functional visual skills, was immediately referred for Berard AIT. Upon completion of the 10-day AIT program, Garson re-assessed the patient's visual skills and found significant improvement in several areas, even without any type of visual intervention having been provided at that point. Similar reports have been made by parents, but no research is available at this time. Because AIT only requires a short time of listening, and some changes do seem to occur during that period, this is an area that could benefit from further study.

There is ample evidence of the connection or integration between the auditory and visual systems, and there is evidence that when the integration of these systems is faulty, there can be significant breakdowns in the learning process. Retraining the auditory system, which seems to carry over to retraining of at least some visual functions, may enhance the learning process (Brockett, 2015).

Case Studies

Two case studies will be presented here to demonstrate the process and results of the Berard AIT method. Names have been changed to respect confidentiality, but ages and other data are accurately presented. These cases represent typical responses to the Berard method, but it is important to recognize that each individual is unique and may respond differently. There is a range of results from highly successful to mildly responsive, and a few may not show noticeable change. Some individuals show obvious change quickly, while others may respond gradually. Many will demonstrate a mixture of positive behavioral changes with some challenging transition behaviors until the person adjusts and stabilizes, while others exhibit only positive progression.

Case 1

Background. Diego is a 5 year, 3 month old boy with a diagnosis of autism. His parents choose to provide Berard AIT due to his hypersensitivity to sound and his failure to develop any language. His mother states that he reacts with signs of distress and discomfort to loud speakers, screaming, music, hair dryer and the vacuum cleaner. She reports a history of some sinusitis which has been treated with antibiotics as needed, and a few ear infections.

Procedure. Diego participated in a standard program of Berard AIT with two 30-minute listening sessions each day for 10 days. Diego's mother was asked to complete the Aberrant Behavior Checklist (ABC) and The Sensory Profile (Short Form—SSP) to obtain baseline data that would be used to monitor his progress. He accepted the headphones for the sessions but needed some encouragement to cooperate for the 30 minutes.

Results. After his first 30-minute session of listening in the morning, Diego took a nap. This is very unusual for him to do and his mother felt he had to have been very tired to sleep in the morning. During the second day of training, Diego reportedly demonstrated increased pointing to objects while making verbal approximations, and increased his imitation of words. His mother noted that he was drinking with better oral motor control and continuous swallowing. Socially, Diego showed increased social initiation with his brother, and more awareness of his environment. On day 3, Diego was able to catch a ball six times and also threw the ball back to his mom. He continued to try to imitate speech and motor activities. On day 4, his mother reported that he was now able to chew gum and not swallow it. His constant jumping was also decreasing. On day 5, he was tolerating brushing his front teeth and was trying to dress himself. He also walked more independently with his mother without needing his hand held. On day 7, he called his mother "mama" for the first time ever. On day 8, he said "eat" spontaneously.

After the 10 days of listening were completed, Diego's progress was monitored by having his mother complete the rating forms at 1, 3, and 6 months post-AIT to show his behaviors at those intervals. The following data indicates the changes in his scores during this time period.

Table 13.1
Improvement on the Aberrant Behavior Checklist (ABC)

Category	% Improvement
Irritability	80
Lethargy	60
Stereotypy	60
Hyperactivity	60
Inappropriate speech	75

The ABC is designed to measure changes in behaviors due to interventions that may be implemented.

Table 13.2
Improvement on the Short Sensory Profile (SSP)

Baseline total score: 93/190	Range: Definite Difference
Post-AIT total score: 162/190	Range: Typical Range

Note. Higher scores indicate more typical behavior and performance.

The Sensory Profile measures a child's sensory processing abilities and its effect on daily functional performance. Typical performance indicates that the 84% of children meet or exceed this threshold. Probable difference indicates that 14% of the children fall within this category. Definite difference indicates that 2% of the children fall within this category.

Observations from parents and others involved with the child can be helpful when monitoring progress.

Comments from mother:

> *Diego's awareness has improved so much. When riding a merry-go-round, he became aware of the other rides and wanted to go on them. He did and enjoyed it. At a birthday party he would put his hands on his ears and get away when people sang "Happy Birthday". This time he came and joined the group, listened to the song, and at the end he clapped his hands and vocalized "ehhh."*
>
> *Diego is also much more independent. He now serves himself food and drinks more often. He wants to walk without me holding his hands. At the pool, he is aware of the depth and wants to get to the deeper area by himself. We supervise and he is trying to float now. Before he was really afraid (panicked) to get water up to his chest.*
>
> *Social relations with his brother are improved now. They share games and ride tricycles together. Diego is pedaling his bike a lot more. Diego pays attention to his cousins and what they are doing. I encourage him to join them and he does it with no problem. Now when we go to family reunions for picnics and birthdays, he stays with the group all the time. Before, he used to look for a way out after he spent a while with others.*

> *Diego's communication is getting better because he understands much more. When he gets mad about some things, I call it to his attention and he pays attention and I talk to him so he calms and waits. I am stimulating him to talk and he is willing and tries to repeat. His attention span is much longer.*
>
> *Diego tolerates the toothbrush, hair brush and nail cutting now. At the end of 6 months, Diego is no longer covering his ears due to noise. He does not cry or do anything that would show discomfort.*
>
> *Diego's improvement is noticeable, even my family members have noticed.*

Case 2

Background. Tim is a 3 year, 11 month old boy diagnosed with autism. His parents chose to do Berard AIT due to his hypersensitivity to sound, and significant delay in language. He is just beginning to speak a few single words. He has had a history of ear infections which were treated with amoxicillin, Augmentin, and Zithromax. Tim participates in a 30 hour/week applied behavior analysis program and a sensory diet is implemented. Medications include Zyrtec daily for allergies and Trazadone for sleep. Tim's auditory sensitivities interfere with daily activities. He hears sounds before others can hear them, is very stressed by sirens, fire alarms, and hair clippers. He could not tolerate haircuts or having his ears examined. He was not able to cooperate with the Berard audio test protocol. He did pass a prior sound field test that indicated his hearing was adequate for speech/language development.

Results. Tim accepted the headphones without difficulty and his cooperation with the process was excellent. After 4 days of AIT, his mother noted that he crossed the midline, demonstrating ability to reach across the middle of his body with his arm to pick up his cup. This was a first for him and represents important developmental progress. On day 5, Tim was very active, with lots of spinning and stimulatory activities. During the last 5 days, Tim was calmer. His mother reported that on day 6, Tim heard a seagull in the sky and looked up at it. This was the first time he had been seen observing a bird in the sky.

After the 10 days of listening were completed, Tim's progress was monitored by having his mother complete the rating forms at 1, 3, and 6 months post-AIT to show his behaviors at those intervals. The following data indicates the changes in his scores during this time period.

Table 13.3
Improvement on the Aberrant Behavior Checklist (ABC)

Category	% Improvement
Irritability	50
Lethargy	53
Stereotypy	no significant change
Hyperactivity	23
Inappropriate speech	not a problem

The ABC is designed to measure changes in behaviors due to interventions that may be implemented.

Table 13.4
Improvement on the Short Sensory Profile (SSP)

Baseline total score: 110/190	Range: Definite Difference
Post-AIT total score: 145/190	Range: Probable Range

Note. Higher scores indicate more typical behavior and performance.

Improvement was also seen in the Autism Treatment Effectiveness Checklist (ATEC), improving from a baseline total score of 73 to a 6-month total score of 60. The ATEC is designed to measure change in an individual due to various interventions. Areas scored include communication, sociability, sensory/cognitive awareness, and health/physical/behavior.

Written communication from Tim's mother included the following comments:

> *Tim is doing well. The first two weeks after AIT, Tim was doing a lot of spinning, hand flapping, and jumping off the furniture. He was also agitated and uncooperative during that time period. All these behaviors stopped the first month just as you said they would. Tim was also refusing to make eye contact with his teachers at school. This has also stopped.*
>
> *As you know, one of the major reasons for doing AIT with Tim was his extreme hearing sensitivity and sensory issues. We have seen excellent results in these areas. Two weeks after completing AIT, Tim had his first hair cut by someone other than myself, and he hardly put up a fuss! Even more amazing is the fact that Tim let the doctor check his ears when he did not feel well. He did not cry or fight. Until now, Tim would have to be physically restrained, including having his arms, legs, and head held down while he screamed hysterically.*
>
> *Tim also seems to be more aware of his environment. He is more interested in people and animals. He pets the dog for the first time and laughed. He is also very interested in other boys and men. He attempted to climb a tree with some other kids his age. He has also been able to play outside without a hat on. Usually the sun is too bright for him.*

Conclusion

This chapter provides information about auditory deficits in autism, an introduction to the Berard AIT method, its impact on sensory modulation including the visual system, and some cases studies as examples individual responses. More details are available at the official Berard AIT website at BerardAITwebsite.com, or on the Berard AIT Channel on YouTube. The book, *Hearing Equals Behavior: Updated and Expanded*, by Guy Berard and Sally Brockett offers more comprehensive information.

During the early 1990s, when Bernard Rimland, the late director of the Autism Research Institute, was asked if Berard AIT did work, he responded, "Yes"," I am reasonably certain that it does work." At that time, he reported in the preface to *Hearing Equals Behavior: Updated and Expanded*, that although there was still insufficient scientific evidence to permit categorical statements to be made, he felt that many, if not most, parents of autistic children who try the Berard method, will be justifiably pleased with the results (Berard & Brockett, 2011). Since that time, scientific study has been undertaken to examine more details about the impact of the training on the individual. The following chapter will present information about this newer research.

References

Aman, M. G., & Singh, N. N. (1986). *Aberrant behavior checklist: Manual.* Aurora, NY: Slosson Educational Publications.

Ayres, J. (1972). *Sensory integration and learning disorders.* Los Angeles, CA: Western Psychological Services.

Berard, G. (1993). *Hearing equals behavior.* New Canaan, CT: Keats.

Berard, G., & Brockett, S. (2011). *Hearing equals behavior: Updated and expanded.* Manchester Center, VT: Shires Press.

Berard, G., Edelson, S. M., Brockett, S. (2000). Filtering auditory peaks using the Berard Method of AIT. *Society for Auditory Intervention Techniques, Sound Connect, 8*(1), 1.

Birch, H. G., Belmont, L. (1964). Auditory-visual integration in normal and retarded readers. *American Journal of Orthopsychiatry, 34*, 852-861.

Brockett, S. (1994). Theories of auditory integration training: Cerebellar-vestibular system. *Society for Auditory Intervention Techniques, Sound Connection, 2*(2), 6.

Brockett, S. (2015). Integration of auditory and visual systems. Retrieved from http://berardaitwebsite.com/wp-content/uploads/IntegratAudVisSyst-1.pdf.

Brockett, S., Lawton-Shirley, N. K., & Kimball, J. G. (2014). Berard auditory integration training: Behavior changes related to sensory modulation. Retrieved from http://berardaitwebsite.com/wp-content/uploads/Berard-AIT-Behavior-Sensory-Changes-2-2014-1.pdf.

Brown, M. M. (1999). Auditory integration training and autism: Two case studies. *British Journal of Occupational Therapy, 62*(1), 13-18.

Bundy, A., Lane, S., & Murray, E. (2002). *Sensory integration theory and practice.* Philadelphia, PA: F. A. Davis Company.

Cool, S. (2004). Listening with the whole body: A neurobiological and neurochemical perspective. *Professional Development Programs.* Minneapolis, MN, April 4.

Doidge, N. (2015). *The brain's way of healing.* New York, NY: Viking.

Dunn, W. (1999). *The sensory profile.* San Antonio, TX: Psychological Corporation.

Edelson, S. M. (1994). Theories of auditory integration training: Middle ear. *Society for Auditory Intervention Techniques, Sound Connection, 2*(1), 6.

Edelson, S. M. (1995). Theories of auditory integration training: Biochemical changes. *Society for Auditory Intervention Techniques, Sound Connection, 3*(2), 6.

Edelson, S. M. (1996). Theories of auditory integration training: "Tune In/Tune Out" & shifting attention. Retrieved from http://berardaitwebsite.com/2015/10/03/volume-4-number-2-1996-2/.

Edelson, S. M., Arin, D., Bauman, M., Lukas, S. E., Rudy, J. H., Sholar, M., & Rimland, B. (1999). Auditory integration training: A double-blind study of behavioral and electrophysiological effects in people with autism. *Focus on Autism and Other Developmental Disabilities 14*(2), 73-81.

Frick, S., & Lawton-Shirley, N. (1994). Auditory integration training from a sensory integration perspective. *Sensory Integration Special Interest Section Newsletter, 17*(4), 1-3.

Frick, S., & Hacker C. (2001). *Listening with the whole body.* Madison, WI: Vital Sounds.

Furth, H. G., & Wachs, H. (1975). *Thinking goes to school: Piaget's theory in practice.* New York: Oxford University Press.

Grandin, T., & Panek, R. (2013). *The autistic brain: Thinking across the spectrum.* Boston, MA: Houghton Mifflin Harcourt.

Hall, L., & Case-Smith, J. (2007). The effect of sound-based intervention on children with sensory processing disorders and visual-motor delays. *American Journal of Occupational Therapy, 61*(2), 209-215.

Holland, K. (2006). *Auditory processing.* Presented at BABO Annual Meeting, Nottingham, UK. Last Accessed August 8, 2012.

Lewald, J., Tegenthoff, M., Peters, S., & Hausmann, M. (2012). Passive auditory stimulation improves vision in hemianopia. *PLoS ONE*, 7(5), e31603.

Linden, D. (2005). The P300: Where in the brain is it produced and what does it tell us? Retrieved from http://journals.sagepub.com/doi/abs/10.1177/1073858405280524.

McIntosh, D. N., Miller, L. J., Shyu, V., & Hagerman, R. J. (1999). Sensory-modulation disruption, electrodermal responses, and functional behaviors. *Developmental Medicine and Child Neurology, 41*(9), 608-615.

Miller, J. (2006). *Sensational kids*. London, England: C. B. Putnam Publishing.

Netter, F. H. (1986). *Nervous system, Part I: Anatomy and physiology* (Ciba collection of medical illustrations, 1). Ciba Pharmaceutical, Inc.

Occupational Safety and Health Administration (1981). "How loud is too loud?" Retrieved from https://www.osha.gov/SLTC/noisehearingconservation/loud.html. Last accessed May 21, 2018.

Oetter, P. (2009). *Power tools workshop. Professional development program.* Camarillo, CA, December 5.

Picton, T. W. (1992). The P300 wave of the human event-related potential. Retrieved from https://www.researchgate.net/publication/21690394

Press, L. J. (2012a). Historical perspectives on auditory and visual processing. *Journal of Behavioral Optometry, 23*(4), 99-105.

Press, L. J. (2012b). *Parallels between auditory and visual processing*. Santa Ana, CA: Optometric Extension Program Foundation.

Rimland, B., & Edelson, S. (1994). The effects of auditory integration training on autism. *American Journal of Speech-Language Pathology, 3*, 16-24.

Rimland, B., & Edelson, S. (1995). Auditory integration training: A pilot study. *Journal of Autism and Developmental Disorders, 25*(1), 61-70.

Rimland, B., & Edelson, S. (2004). *The efficacy of auditory integration training: Summaries and critiques of 28 reports.* San Diego, CA: Autism Research Institute.

Solan, H. A. (2004). Visual and auditory processing in reading disability: A matter of cognitive dissonance. *Optometric Vision Development, 35*, 16-21.

Solan, H. A., Shelley-Tremblay, J., Larson, S. (2007). Vestibular function, sensory integration, and balance anomalies: A brief literature review. *Optometric Vision Development, 38*, 1-5.

Walton, H. N., & Griffin, J. F. (2006). Viewpoint: The vision-audition-cortical vocalization connection in reading. *Journal of Behavioral Optometry, 35*, 16-21.

14

Visual-Spatial Integration Using Spatial Lenses in Autism

Melvin Kaplan and Barbara Kotsamanidis-Burg
The Center for Visual Management, Tarrytown NY

It is astonishing what the human eye can see—and as strange as it sounds, what we are equally skilled at *not* seeing. When the software of the visual system is intact, our brain unconsciously collects and organizes the visual information we need, while filtering out distracting or irrelevant sights. In other words, we view a subjective illusion—not reality.

Our biology is not designed to make us see everything perfectly at all times. Instead, it is designed for visually-guided problem solving. By rapidly scanning our world and focusing our attention on its most crucial aspects, we take charge of our environment rather than being at its mercy. Seeing nothing makes life difficult for people who are blind—but seeing everything, or sensory overload, without being able to control or make sense of this input can be just as disabling.

Harvard psychologists Simons & Chabris (Simons & Chabris, 1999) asked participants to watch a basketball film and to count how many times the ball was passed between players. A person disguised in a gorilla costume sauntered through the middle of the court and yet half of the participants did not notice. "At some level, I think every serious person in psychology has always believed that we do not consciously perceive everything that happens to us," Chabris commented (as cited in Carpenter, 2001). "The shocking thing that you could show was that so little was being perceived."

Selective seeing is a critical a skill that we exhibit from the moment we are born. Pediatrician T. Berry Brazelton comments on the newborns "marvelous capacity to control levels of stimulation," noting how babies can zero in on some stimuli while tuning others out completely. (Brazelton & Nugent, 1995). As we grow into adulthood, we fine tune this ability to control the amount of stimulation we perceive. We are rarely conscious of the fast and fluid scanning movements our eyes make, yet this rapid scanning constantly edits the messages we receive from our world, shapes the way in which we act on these messages and defines how we learn to move in space and time.

This inability to integrate figure with background, or as we will refer to throughout this chapter, *focal* and *spatial* vision, may appear to be a serious biological flaw, but for some, it is simply a matter of survival. Individuals who have visual-spatial integration delays, including many individuals on the spectrum, cannot adapt to living in a highly complex world without limiting or organizing the amount of information that is being perceived. Therefore, the world is reduced to what they can control. Similarly, the participants watching the famous "gorilla video" achieve their goal of counting basketball passes, because they are in effect blind to extraneous details (even large and furry ones).

Biology gives us a brain, but the information we receive via each sense—and particularly through vision, arguably the most important of our senses—empowers that brain to develop into a thinking mind. The eyes lead the mind in this interaction of mind, body and world. The model of visual processing we discuss in this chapter primarily relates to a brain system that perceives form, color, movement and depth. To allow us to effectively perform visual-problem solving, these mutually dependent elements must work in a coordinated manner. If the mind is unable to orchestrate the interaction, people are forced to learn to live in a compartmentalized world, lacking the ability to integrate vision in a higher order.

To put it another way, when the visual process is well organized, we live and learn. When it is disorganized, we need to learn to live.

Case Study: Jay

Jay, a patient just over 50 years old, visited our center in 2006. Diagnosed as brain-damaged in childhood, Jay exhibits many of the symptoms of high functioning autism, or Asperger's syndrome. He had benefited from many sensory interventions in the past, but he still had tremendous difficulty making eye contact, experienced episodes of "blindness" (at some point in his life he would only look through binoculars) and had a crippling obsession that forced him to compulsively retrace routes in his daily routine. We prescribed prism lenses for Jay, and he learned a series of visual exercises to alter his deficits.

Several months into his therapy program, Jay was interviewed for the Alabama Council for Developmental Disabilities' newsletter, the *Advocate*. He told the interviewer that these interventions "changed my life many times over." He went on to say, "I never really knew I saw things distorted until I got the prism glasses. I think the distortion is what made me do all the things I did, like the blindness and the retracing. But now I can go anywhere and do anything. I can go to weddings and graduations, and can handle more responsibilities in my job at the library. This has really opened my life. I am like a new person."

It is important to note that vision training does not cure patients like Jay, because disorders like autism have multiple causes. In cases like his, however, prism lenses and visual management can alleviate enough symptoms to make life vastly more rewarding, productive and enjoyable. In other cases where patients' symptoms stem solely from visual dysfunction, these individuals often improve to the degree that complete cure is possible.

Over many decades, we have been champions of yoked prisms, which are also referred to as spatial lenses, prescribing them for individuals with learning differences, emotional difficulties, autistic spectrum disorders, or various traumatic brain injuries.

Yoked Prisms—A Tool for Perceptual Adaptation

Yoked prisms have proven to be an exceptional tool for investigating how humans acquire perceptual knowledge, and for clinically training consistent perception and competent actions in individuals with learning difficulties in autism, and with emotional and postural impairment.

(Carmody, Kaplan, & Gaydos, 2001; Kaplan, Carmody, & Gaydos, 1996; E. Sokhadze et al., 2012). Hubert Dolezal (1982) said, "not until the nineteenth century was there an explicit realization that the retinal and past retinal neuron transforms of information reaching the brain were more important by far in understanding the basic phenomena of perceptual learning, remembering, cognition and language than the transformation of the optical image by the lens system of the eye."

All optical lenses are light transformers. Conventional optical lenses are designed to correct errors in refraction and positional displacement. Structural problems, such as myopia, hyperopia and astigmatism are inherited or acquired problems of visual clarity. The refractive plus or minus and

Table 14.1
Various Applications of Yoked Prism Lenses

Base Down	Base down prisms affect rotation about the horizontal axis in space, rotating the visual level of attention higher and further away. This leads to a slight upward expansion of one's field of vision. There is a corresponding effect on vergence movements, improving spatial organization, sense of timing and awareness of depth.
Base Left	Base left prisms rotate the energy input about the vertical axis, moving attention towards the right field of view. This affects orientation, influencing posture, transport (walking) and vergence eye movements.
Base Right	Base right prisms rotate the energy input about the vertical axis, moving attention towards the left field of view. This affects orientation, influencing posture, transport (walking) and vergence eye movements.
Base Up	Base up prisms affect rotation about the horizontal axis in space, rotating the visual level of attention to a lower closer field of view. This leads to a slight downward tunneling or focusing of one's field of vision. There is a corresponding effect on vergence movements (in which the eyes move inward, as in reading), improving spatial organization, sense of timing and awareness of depth.

the astigmatic correction alter the flow of information into the central nervous system. *Single Prism* lenses are three-sided transparent pyramids, rather than traditional refractive lenses, positioned to displace light and affect the perception of depth and space, and are used to correct displacement by establishing fusion of the patient's visual field. Prism lenses can differ in strength (diopter). Single prisms are usually prescribed in cases of double vision to achieve single vision. These prisms affect the frontal reference place, which is perpendicular to the ground and divides the body into dorsal (posterior) and frontal (anterior), supplying two dimensions of information.

Yoked Prisms are binocular prim lenses of equal strength and whose bases are oriented in the same direction. They affect the sagittal plane, which is perpendicular to the ground and divides the body into right and left halves. The sagittal axis passes from posterior to anterior, while the frontal axis passes from left to right. Yoked prisms affect degrees of freedom, and motor equivalence in motor control for how we organize movement and orient the interaction of mind, body and world. Low magnitude yoked prisms are designed to lead eye movements preconsciously until perceptual adaptation occurs. Success is "captured immediately." Performance adaptation precedes perceptual adaptation which can be both measured and observed in the actions on eyes and body movements.

Large magnitude yoked prisms are a necessary tool for the empirical method for perceptual reformatory competence. The purpose of the visual intervention is related to the mind's control system. When the transformed light encounters delays in the processing of information, it negates the control system's feedback, performance, and perception, and deviates from the expected initiated action. The deviations we may see result in either compression or suppression of visual fields. The goal of a behavioral or developmental vision specialist is to restore homeostatic control—biologically, emotionally and socially.

In much of the literature on prisms, it is the focal aspect of vision that is emphasized. Prism lenses are prescribed to displace the image on the retina and align the fovea, producing single binocular vision. When an image enters a prism, it is compressed toward the prism base and expanded toward the apex. If prisms are applied in a yoked configuration with binocular prisms oriented in the same direction, they induce spatial reorganization about the axes and planes of space. There is then a comparable shift in organization and orientation of the body, as directed by incoming light.

Research Evidence for Efficacy of Yoked Prisms

In 2011, researchers with the University of Louisville, the Autism Research Institute, and The Center for Visual Management (Dombrowski et al., 2014; G. Sokhadze et al., 2012) investigated modulatory effects of spatial prism lenses on spatial attention in autism. These studies investigated the efficacy of spatial prism lenses used to correct deficits in spatial vision present in autism. In addition, the study sought to understand the abnormal neural and functional mechanisms underlying visual distortion in autism by incorporating neurophysiologic studies, behavioral studies, and event-potential (ERP) measurements of spatial attention.

When comparing reaction time and accuracy of responses, prism lens conditions tended to be faster than that of placebo lens conditions. The effects of wearing spatial prism lenses is indicative of more effective special attentional processing, especially in more complex diagonal incongruent trials (G. Sokhadze et al., 2011). What testing further determined was a significant decrease in average heart rate, reflecting improved autonomic balance. Behavioral measures reflected improvements in hyperactivity, ADHD symptoms and repetitive behaviors. The Autism Behavior Checklist (ABC checklist) showed three of the five scaled scores were reduced. Lethargy and inappropriate speech were reduced, while hyperactivity was significantly reduced when compared to baselines. Using the Repetitive Behavioral Scale, significant differences in stereotypical behaviors and compulsive behaviors were found. Using the Achenbach System of Empirically Based Assessment (ASEBA), we found a significant decrease in rule breaking and in ADHD symptoms (Dombrowski et al., 2014).

These studies support the utility of wearing prism lenses to correct spatial vision in autism and the sensitivity of ERPs to detect visuo-spatial attention improvement. We have found that comparing the autistic patient's performance and ERPs with and without prism lenses can be a very informative approach to understanding the mechanisms of visual deficits and spatial attention orienting impairments typical of autism.

Vision is More Than a Skill—It is a Process

A conventional visual examination is a *focal* examination, which is static in nature. Comprehensive eye and vision examinations generally include patient history, visual acuity refraction, and testing of ocular health. These examinations primarily address the biological "hardware" of the visual system at the level of the eyes, rather than the "software" of the visual system at the level of the central and peripheral nervous systems. The hardware examination measures and evaluates "what" the patient sees. The goal is to make vision clearer using lenses to correct errors in refraction related to the lens or the shape of the eyeball.

In contrast, the Kaplan Battery (Kaplan, 2006) includes a "software" examination in which the practitioner observes how the patient's brain and body process, how the individual responds and adapts behaviorally to, the questions of "where am I?" and "where is it?" in space. While evaluating the focal aspects and attending to the global percepts, those of us in behavioral optometry are evaluating focusing, eye teaming and eye movements, without neglecting the implications of poor visual processing skills on posture, attention, and disposition. Rather than viewing vision in isolation, the scientist in us views and treats the influence of visual processing on the child as a whole.

The level of efficiency each of us achieves in orienting to and organizing our spatial world dictates our successes (or failures) in achieving a normal relationship, both biologically and psychologically, with our world. Here is a look at each crucial function.

Spatial Orientation

Are you sitting upright right now or lying down? Is your head (or your hand, or foot) moving? If so, how fast is it moving and in what direction? Your mind can answer these questions because you have the ability to orient yourself in space—that is, to constantly monitor your own position and movements. Most people assume that we are born with this ability, but, it develops as we interact with our environment.

Table 14.2
Comparison of Spatial and Focal Vision

Spatial Vision	Focal Vision
"Where am I?" in space? / "Where is it?" in space	"What is it?" (object recognition) function
Dynamic (kinetic)—identifies movement, change	Static—identifies stable features of surroundings
Low-resolution non-color vision (rods)	High resolution color vision (cones)
Involves entire visual field	Involves only central vision—limited to central two degrees of visual field (fovea)
Not degraded at night	Degraded at night
Largely non-conscious	Largely conscious
Integrates with other sensory systems	Works in isolation
Is largely learned, and thus can be greatly enhanced through a visual management program	Is innate rather than learned

To orient ourselves in space, we need to develop a "body schema"—a mental model of our body that allows us to organize the information we get from our senses so we can constantly reorganize. The antithesis, not forming an adequate body schema, leads to developmental delays.

Spatial Organization

While spatial orientation refers to our internal development of a body schema, spatial organization refers to our ability to organize the objects and events in our world in relationship to each other, ourselves and other people. For example, good spatial organization allows us to hit a baseball (because we know our location and can swing accurately towards the location of the ball) or to drive safely in traffic.

Spatial organization originates with the body schema, which provides a three-dimensional reference point of "self." Once we know where we are in space, we can begin to tell left from right and understand what is above or below us. We can tell which direction a dog or a car is moving in, and how quickly it is moving towards or away from us. And we can learn how to identify the letters of the alphabet and how to read sentences from left to right.

Vision is a dual neural system between focal and global systems and one major limitation of traditional eye examinations is that they concern themselves almost exclusively with perfecting the patient's visual identification ability. Whereas, the spatial system visual analysis involves both motor and sensory, attention is paid to the integration of visual perspective with actual motor performance.

The difference between a traditional and a performance-based vision evaluation becomes clear when a parent brings an autistic child for a traditional exam. Unlike other special needs, such as Down syndrome or cerebral palsy, studies suggest that refractive error is only prevalent in about 10 to 30 percent of children on the spectrum (and in such cases, usually of genetic etiology; Anketell, Saunders, Gallagher, Bailey, & Little, 2016; Black, McCarus, Collins, & Jensen, 2013), therefore in 70 to 90 percent of cases patients with autism see clearly and have no eye health issues. The parent is told that "vision is not the problem." The doctor is signing off on the *focal* pathway.

Autistic Behavior as a Disorder of Neural Information Processing

The broad variation in function and severities within the autism spectrum disorder (ASD) suggest the involvement of multiple factors interacting in complex ways with normal developmental factors. Identification of these factors and the common developmental paths into which they feed was formulated in the motor equivalence problem (Bernstein, 1967).

In Bernstein's formulation, the problem results from infinite redundancy, yet flexibility between movements. Thus, the nervous system apparently must choose a particular motor solution every time it acts. In Bernstein's formulation, a single muscle never acts in isolation, Rather, large numbers of "nervous centers" cooperate in order to make a whole movement possible. Nervous impulses from different parts of the brain may converge on the periphery in combination to produce a movement. However, there is a great difficulty for scientists in understanding and coordinating the facts linking impulses to a movement. Bernstein's rational understanding of movement and prediction of motor learning via what we now call "plasticity" was revolutionary for his time.

The very breath of autism's anatomical and functional abnormalities admits the possibility that its core dysfunctions may involve some pervasive alteration of neural processing.

A Qualitative Exam Begins When the Quantitative Exam Ends

The Kaplan Nonverbal Battery goes beyond the seeking of 20/20 acuity and seeks to understand neural information processing. Our biology is not designed to make us see everything perfectly at all times. Instead, it is designed for visually-guided problem solving. Seeing nothing makes life difficult for people who are blind—but seeing everything, without being able to filter, control or make sense of this input, can be just as disabling.

The tasks in the Kaplan Nonverbal Battery are arranged logically in a hierarchy that allows an observer to assess how the child adapts with increasing demands of mind, body and world. The initial tasks focus on visual perception in isolation, while succeeding tasks require the patient to coordinate visual, vestibular, proprioceptive, auditory, and gravitational input.

In each step, the clinician assesses the patient's posture, attention, and disposition in response to a visual demand, both before and after applying spatial prism lenses. To record the results, we recommend using a scoring sheet, such as the one provided in *Seeing Through New Eyes* (Kaplan, 2006). The level of efficiency each of us achieves in orienting to and organizing space dictates our success in achieving a normal relationship, both biologically and psychologically with our world.

The evaluator will be able to pick up many clues before formal testing begins, simply by observing the patient when they arrive. The vision problems of developmentally disabled children, and autistic children in particular, will manifest themselves in a variety of ways. Head tilts, body warps, stimming, toe-walking, grazing walls—these are all manifestations of spatial vision distortions to one's world. Many patients will toe walk, toe in, or touch the walls when they walk. These patients are unable to handle the integration of both self and space simultaneously. They will flap their hands to achieve balance, run their hands along the wall for tactile guidance, or toe in for orientation. They will walk on their toes because they do not trust themselves in space, and thus try to hold onto the ground for as long as possible. They often take shorter steps, which is also an attempt to maintain contact with the ground. Rather than sitting smoothly, some will need to feel for the chair and will sit awkwardly.

Your initial observation can also reveal signs of functional scoliosis that often occurs in response to visual processing delays. This is important, because this disorganized behavior can frequently be reversed with therapy. Case in point: Casey, a 7-year-old was referred to our office with multiple diagnoses, one of which was toe-walking, with an orthopedic diagnosis of spasticity of the muscles of the lower extremities. He was wearing an ankle foot to knee orthosis (brace) and was told if this does not prevent toe-walking, the next step would be surgery, since the etiology was a paralytic muscular disease. Other diagnoses included nonverbal autistic spectrum disorder and esotropia, an alternate turning in of his eyes.

By applying yoked prism lenses, 20 diopters base down, on Casey, he immediately and instinctively walked flat-footed without any prompting or cues. Casey's mother, naturally, was amazed. She asked if it would last. I explained to her that A.M. Skeffington, known as the father of behavioral optometry, taught us that "the fastest way to change a person is through a lens." However, what she was seeing is "visual capture," short lived performance that was not yet a completed perceptual adaptation. With proper visual management the change in behavior she just witnessed which is a change in the organization of brain matter, is subject to consolidation of new habits.

What it means for toe-walking individuals, especially those on the spectrum, is that survival depends on proprioceptive control. Therefore, the excessive reliance on tactile information, such as running one's hands along a wall or hand-flapping, is the result of not being grounded when orienting the body through their visual space world. These behavioral solutions can disappear when visual perception leads the mind, rather than the mind leading the visual system, through thought and memorization of the environment.

In Casey's story, we see a case of disorder in orientation and processing of spatial information. Transformation of light with disruptive yoked prism lenses (20 D) elicited an immediate effect. In Philip's case, pursuing the tasks of ball play in the Kaplan Battery, his response to a ball on the string being tossed to him was to step to his right and reach out his arms as hard to the left and catch the ball. It was a substitution of performance developed to keep up with his brothers when playing ball. Phil was not happy to be in our office. I asked him how would he like to reach out with two hands and catch like his brothers? I then placed 2 diopter base up yoked prisms on him and his performance changed immediately, where he reached out his arms and hands in front and caught the ball. His excitement was immediate and he asked to get started on vision training.

In both cases, Casey and Philip were observed to make instant changes (visual capture) —Casey by disruption, which makes the system consciously aware of change—and Philip by directing the reorganization of information processing unconsciously.

Visual Management Therapy

Visual management therapy is a global processing program, directed towards establishing the relationship between figure and ground, and further providing context within perceptual processing.

In clinically managing ASD children, I subscribe to the controlled and automatic processing behavior theory (Schneider & Chein, 2003) with a large caveat. I believe automatic processing develops in the action-oriented child prior to cognitive control. "In general, automatic processing operates through a relatively permanent set of associative connections and requires an appreciable amount of consistent training to develop fully" (Schneider & Shiffrin, 1977). An automatic attention response is a special type of autonomic process that directs attention automatically to a target stimulus. However, what one learns by experience can be changed by experience.

Therapy sessions are necessary to stabilize the gains. The changes are tied to movements of the eyes and body parts, the interaction of mind, body and world. Visual, clinical intervention involves three steps: awareness, attention, and automaticity. Specific interventions make the patient consciously aware of visual processing problems. Yoked prisms and visual therapy can reduce the amount of forced or effortful attention a task requires such that attention is commensurate to the task. New developments in visual processing with properly adjusted prisms, over time and with training, replace the previous dysfunctional processes such that self-organization at a higher level of control becomes automatic.

Practice in shifting attention by expanding the visual field of view while maintaining awareness of central field information increases the ability to rapidly process more information and with relaxed attention. These changes are accompanied by a feeling of well-being, improved short term memory and conscious empathy.

The goal of visual management therapy is to enable individuals to accurately process more information about the environment more rapidly, reduce stress, enrich perceptual awareness and enhance performance.

In one final case illustrates: Madison was referred to our office with a diagnosis of autism. She could best be described as a "screamer." She screamed throughout the evaluation. In addition, she was controlling, an avoider and a spitter. Madison's behaviors were defensive in nature. Kent Bach (Bach, 1994) eloquently states "defenses may be understood as unconscious devices or strategies for managing one's attention."

When Madison was assessed using The Kaplan Nonverbal Battery, she exhibited postural warps, attention deficits, movement problems, and an overall disposition that reflected fears and anxiety. Her vision was dysfunctional in that her eyes altered, back and forth, from left to the right, in a rapid pattern. As a result, she relied primarily on audition and touch to interpret her world.

During the evaluation when objects were stationary, base down (wide angle) spatial prisms increased Madison's attention. In contrast, when objects were moving, base up (telescopic) spatial prisms were preferred. However, her attention span was relatively short while wearing both sets of prisms.

Madison's treatment plan involved a developmental, "bottom-up" approach which began with wide-angle prisms and a program of disruption-—or large magnitude prism procedures to disassociate Madison from her present adaptive habituation, including defensive behaviors, and to stimulate increased visual attention. Six weeks later, in a follow-up exam, she again started with screaming and spitting, but at the same time, she was able to attentively watch a video—which she was unable to do during her initial visit. I then placed base-up prisms on her, and she calmed down, stopped spitting, and became more attentive. This dramatic change should lead to better conscious processing, resulting in a reduction in her fears and anxiety.

Madison is a typical example of many action-specific children who are on the autistic spectrum and/or have developmental delays. Spatial prism lenses often allow them to "let go," and their problem-solving abilities are once again developing in a "normal" manner to visual stimuli and without the need for adaptive behaviors that impact emotions.

Conclusion

In the chapter we sought to introduce a clinical tool, yoked prisms, which influences adaptive interactions in visual perception and performance with our complex environment.

We recognize that there are lenses designed to help identify "what" we see, but equally important, the need exists to identify "where" we are and "where" things are in reference to ourselves and our space-world. Yoked prisms are such lenses, as they influence how we observe the environment and organize spatial information as it pertains to the world we live in. It is a tool that can be used to identify and create changes in autism and other learning disabilities such as dyslexia and psychiatric individuals.

References

Anketell, P. M., Saunders, K. J., Gallagher, S., Bailey, C., & Little, J. A. (2016). Profile of refractive errors in European Caucasian children with autistic spectrum disorder: Increased prevalence and magnitude of astigmatism. *Ophthalmic & Physiological Optics, 36*(4), 395–403.

Bach, K. (1994). *Philosophical psychopathology*. London, UK: MIT Press.

Bernstein, N. A. (1967). *The coordination and regulation of movements.* Oxford: Pergamon Press.

Black, K., McCarus, C., Collins, M. L., & Jensen, A. (2013). Ocular manifestations of autism in ophthalmology. *Strabismus, 21*(2), 98–102.

Brazelton, T. B., & Nugent, J. K. (1995). *Neonatal behavioral assessment scale (*3rd ed.). London, UK: Mac Keith Press.

Carmody, D. P., Kaplan, M., & Gaydos, A. M. (2001). Spatial orientation adjustments in children with autism in Hong Kong. *Child Psychiatry and Human Development, 31*(3), 233–247.

Carpenter, S. (2001). Sights unseen. *Monitor on Psychology, 32*(4), 54.

Dolezal, H. (1982). *Living in a world transformed: Perceptual and performatory adaptation to visual distortion.* The Blackburn Press.

Dombrowski, B., Kaplan, M., Kotsamanidis-Burg, B., Edelson, S. M., Hensley, M. K., Sokhadze, E. M. & Casanova, M. F. (2014). Effects of spatial prism lenses and visual-motor training on heart rate variability and behavioral outcomes in autism. In K. Siri & T. Lyons (Eds.), *Cutting edge therapies for autism* (4th ed.), (pp. 138–150). New York, NY: Skyhorse Publishing.

Kaplan, M., Carmody, D. P., & Gaydos A. M. (1996). Postural orientation modifications in autism in response to spatial lenses. *Child Psychiatry and Human Development, 27*(2), 81–91.

Kaplan, M. (2006). *Seeing through new eyes: Changing the lives of children with autism.* London, UK: Jessica Kingsley Publishers.

Marr, D. (1982). *A computational investigation into the human representation and processing of visual information.* New York: Freeman.

Schneider, W., & Shiffrin, R. M. (1977). Controlled and automatic human information processing. I. Detection, search and attention. *Psychological Review, 84*(1), 1–66.

Schneider, W., & Chein, J.M. (2003) Controlled & automatic processing: Behavior, theory, and biological mechanisms, Cognitive Science, 27, 525–559

Simons, D. J., & Chabris, C. F. (1999). Gorillas in our midst: Sustained inattentional blindness for dynamic events. *Perception*, 28, 1059–1074.

Sokhadze, G. E., Kaplan, M., Edelson, S. M., Sokhadze, E. M., Baruth, J., El-Baz, A. S., Hensley, M., & Casanova, M. F. (2011). Modulatory effects of spatial prism lenses on spatial attention in autism: An event-related potential study. *Journal of Neurotherapy*, 15, 413–415.

Sokhadze, E. M., Kaplan, M., Edelson, S. M., Kotsamanidis, B., Hensley, M., Sokhadze, G. E., Dombroski, B., & Casanova, M.

F. (2012). Ambient prism lenses affect autonomic reactivity and attention to audio-visual stimuli in autism. *Psychophysiology*, 49, S40.

Sokhadze, G., Kaplan, M., Edelson, S.M., Sokhadze, E., El-Baz, A., Hensley, M., & Casanova, M. F. (2012). Effects of ambient prism lenses on autonomic reactivity to emotional stimuli in autism. *Applied Psychophysiology and Biofeedback*, 37, 303.

15

Effects of Wearing Ambient Prism Lenses and Visuo-motor Training on Aberrant and Repetitive Behaviors and Psychophysiological Reactivity in Children With Autism

Estate M. Sokhadze,[1,2] Melvin Kaplan,[3] Barbara Kotsamanidis-Burg,[3] Stephen M. Edelson,[4] Brynn Dombroski,[1] and Manuel F. Casanova[1,2]

The sense of vision is one of the most important sensory inputs of information for human beings, and dysfunction of vison may have numerous consequences (Kaplan, 2006). Vision can be classified into two main types. The first, focal, is conscious and allows us to see objects in high-resolution color. At the doctor's office, it is focal vision that is tested and given a score, sometimes resulting in the prescription of corrective lenses for near- or farsightedness. The other type of vision is known as ambient vision, which is largely non-conscious and is used in spatial orientation and depth perception. Unlike focal vision, which is restricted to 2 degrees of visual field, ambient vision involves the entire visual field and integrates with other sensory systems to determine one's position in space. Deficits in this ambient vision system can cause confusion, disorientation, and stress. In fact, such deficits have been

[1]Department of Psychiatry & Behavioral Sciences, University of Louisville, Louisville, KY
[2]University of South Carolina School of Medicine-Greenville, Greenville Health System, Greenville, SC
[3]Center for Visual Management, Tarrytown, NY
[4]Autism Research Institute, San Diego, CA

linked to autism spectrum disorder (ASD), attention deficit hyperactivity disorder (ADHD), and other developmental disorders by previous studies.

Autism spectrum disorder is a pervasive developmental disorder of childhood characterized by deficits in social interaction, language, and stereotyped behaviors along with a restricted range of interests. It is further marked by an innate inability to perceive and respond to social and emotional signals in a typical manner. This is due to the functional disconnectedness of networks important for specific aspects of social cognition and behavioral control. The underlying neural deficits are related to developmental abnormalities of functional connectivity of the associative frontal cortical areas with posterior neocortical areas which leads to abnormal global processing in autism, and contributes to an inability to integrate incoming individual parts and perceive them as a whole. According to several recent theories sensory processing abnormalities may play important role in impairments of perception, cognition, and behavior in individuals with autism. Among these sensory abnormalities, visual distortion may contribute to such typical symptoms of autism as relying on peripheral vision, strabismus, and manifestation of stereotypic behaviors. Reviews of visual dysfunctions typical of autism can be found in several publications (Behrmann, Thomas, & Humphreys, 2006; Dakin & Frith, 2005; Edgin & Pennington, 2005; Simmons et al., 2009).

Also frequently observed in ASD is an imbalance between the two branches of the autonomic nervous system (ANS), specifically, increased sympathetic tone and decreased parasympathetic tone. Several types of autonomic dysfunctions have been reported in autism, including increased basal sympathetic tone, as well as reduced baseline parasympathetic activity in association with increased baseline sympathetic tone (Ming et al., 2011; Porges, 2001). The sympathetic nervous system is activated during times of stress, increasing heart rate and blood pressure while slowing digestion. Activation of the parasympathetic nervous system has the opposite effect, decreasing heart rate and blood pressure and allowing for normal digestion. Thus, deviations from typical ANS function, as seen in ASD, can result in gastrointestinal or cardiovascular symptoms. As heart rate (HR) is determined by sympathetic and parasympathetic signals, we chose to use heart rate variability (HRV) as a useful indicator of autonomic balance. Heart rate variability (HRV) measures are widely used in psychopathology research for assessment of phasic and tonic cardiac autonomic control. Reduced HRV, specifically the attenuated power of high frequency (HF) component of the HRV (often referred to as respiratory sinus arrhythmia) along with high power of low frequency (LF) component of HRV is an indicator of limited psychophysiological flexibility. Several studies have shown that typical children suppressed the HF in HRV more than autistic children, and autistic children have unusually small deceleratory HR phasic responses to stimuli. Therefore, analysis of the HRV, the HF and phasic HR responses associated with dynamic parasympathetic activity, may provide very important information regarding the autonomic dysfunctions in autism. Studies have demonstrated several manifestations of abnormal sympathetic functions in measures other than HRV. For example, skin conductance response (SCR) studies in autistic children have shown a lack of the normal SCR habituation to the same stimulus over time (Toichi & Kamio, 2003). It is often reported that the autistic group had a higher baseline skin conductance level (SCL). It has been reported that children with autism had blunted autonomic responses to social stimuli. Furthermore, our own pilot studies also support excessive but less differentiated SCR to affective sounds, visual, and audio-visual stimuli. Since SCL is controlled solely by the sympathetic inputs (Boucsein, 2012), above effects indicate high sympathetic tone and low selectivity in autism.

Proposed courses of treatment to correct ambient vision have been tested by using ambient prism lenses both without exercises (Kaplan, Carmody, & Gaydos, 1996; Kaplan, Edelson, & Seip, 1998) and with daily exercises aimed at visual-motor coordination (Kaplan, 2006; Carmody, Kaplan, & Gaydos, 2001). Some early case studies did not report significant changes when ambient lenses were used without any accompanied training (Chok, Reed, Kennedy, & Bird, 2010) or reported relatively transient change (Kaplan et al., 1998). It was an important goal to evaluate outcomes of behavioral vision treatment based on wearing ambient prism lenses with daily visuo-motor exercises intended for 6 stage-based visual therapy. Each stage of the treatment was conducted for 1 month (or 4 weeks) and behavioral test outcomes and video recordings of tests were taken between the stages.

Therefore, the main objective of this study was to evaluate the effect of improving ambient vision with prism lenses in children with autism, on parent/caregiver ratings of behavior, and on measures of psychophysiological reactivity and overall autonomic function. To test the effectiveness of prism lenses in improving autonomic balance, a protocol was set in place which involved visual-motor exercises while wearing prism lenses. Then during each office visit, the patient's HR was recorded while he or she watched selected emotional scenes from the Disney movie, “The Lion King.” Participants were evaluated at baseline, and post-6-month-long visuo-motor training, while wearing ambient lenses using following questionnaires: Aberrant Behavior Checklist (ABC), Achenbach’s Child Behavioral Checklist (ASEBA), and Repetitive Behavior Scale–R (RBS-R).

Method

Participants

Fourteen out of 30 children enrolled in the study completed a whole course of ambient lenses treatment and visuo-motor training, along with baseline and post-treatment assessments. Mean age of participants was 12.8 years (SD = 3.82 years), range varied within 7–19 years, and four of them were girls. Three subjects from the initially recruited pool withdrew because of family circumstances (e.g., divorce, illness of primary caregiver etc.), three subjects moved out of city, two pairs of twins could not comply with visuo-motor training program’s daily training requirements, while remaining six dropped-out subjects either completed only part of the program or missed several mandatory evaluations and/or reporting behavioral data. Two of them were from neighboring states (Ohio and Tennessee) and had technical difficulties showing at the lab for monthly evaluations after completion of each stage of the study. Retention of subjects in this study was therefore estimated as 46.6%.

All participants’ autism spectrum disorder (ASD) diagnosis was made according to the DSM-IV-TR (APA, 2000) and further ascertained with the Autism Diagnostic Interview, Revised (ADI-R; Le Couteur, Lord, & Rutter, 2003). They also had a medical evaluation by a developmental pediatrician. All subjects had normal hearing based on past hearing screens. All autistic participants were high-functioning persons with

ASD with full scale IQ > 80 assessed using the Wechsler Intelligence Scale for Children (WISC-IV; Wechsler, 2004). Four out of 14 participants had a diagnosis of Asperger's Disorder. Study participants were recruited with an advertisement posted at local autism advocacy organizations (e.g., Louisville Chapter of Families for Effective Autism Treatment; FEAT) and some were recruited from existing pool of children with ASD seeking treatment at the Weisskopf Child Evaluation Center at University of Louisville.

The study complied with all relevant national regulations and institutional policies and has been approved by the local institutional review board (IRB). Participating subjects and their parents (or legal guardians) were provided with full information about the study including the purpose, requirements, responsibilities, reimbursement, risks, benefits, alternatives, and role of the local IRB. The subjects were not reimbursed for participation, but the study also did not incur them any costs. The consent and assent forms approved by the IRB were reviewed and explained to all subjects and family members who expressed interest to participate. All questions were answered before consent signature was requested. If the individual agreed to participate, both she/he and parent/guardian signed and dated the consent or assent form and received a copy countersigned by the investigator who obtained consent.

Determining Each Subject's Prism Lenses Prescription

Dr. Kaplan from the Center for Visual Management (Tarrytown, NY) visited University of Louisville twice and observed on-site each patient's head tilt, body posture, facial expressions, and breathing during visual pursuits, ball catching, and watching TV in seated and standing positions to determine which base direction of ambient lenses should be prescribed for each patient. Prism lenses were manufactured at the optic center in the state of New York following Dr. Kaplan's prescription to each participant (Figure 15.1). Three participants had their corrective glasses prescription incorporated in the ordered ambient prism lenses.

Daily Vision Exercises

At the beginning of each month, each study participant received, along with prescribed lenses, a packet of visuo-motor exercises program that were to be done for Week 1, Week 2, Week 3 and Week 4. Each week's exercises were designed to build neurosensory and neuromuscular skills from one week to the next. A description of the materials, lenses, setup, procedure, observations and time expected to be spent on each exercise were all included in the instructions. Additionally, graduate research students filmed a demonstration of each procedure in the lab and transferred the video demonstrations onto DVDs that were disseminated to each study participant along with printed instructions and training worksheet logs. The prescription prism lenses, the disruptive lenses and the red/green lenses were all provided by the Center for Visual Management. The materials needed involved a combination of household items and a few items that were relatively inexpensive to buy or build, such as a balance board and a chalk board. At the end of each month, patients came into the Cognitive Neuroscience Lab at the University of Louisville for a post-assessment evaluation and video recording of selected procedures chosen by the Center for Visual Management. The graduate researcher instructed the patient on which exercises to demonstrate in the lab and evaluated the patient's performance as either "efficient," "satisfactory," or "needs improvement" and wrote additional notes regarding the patient's

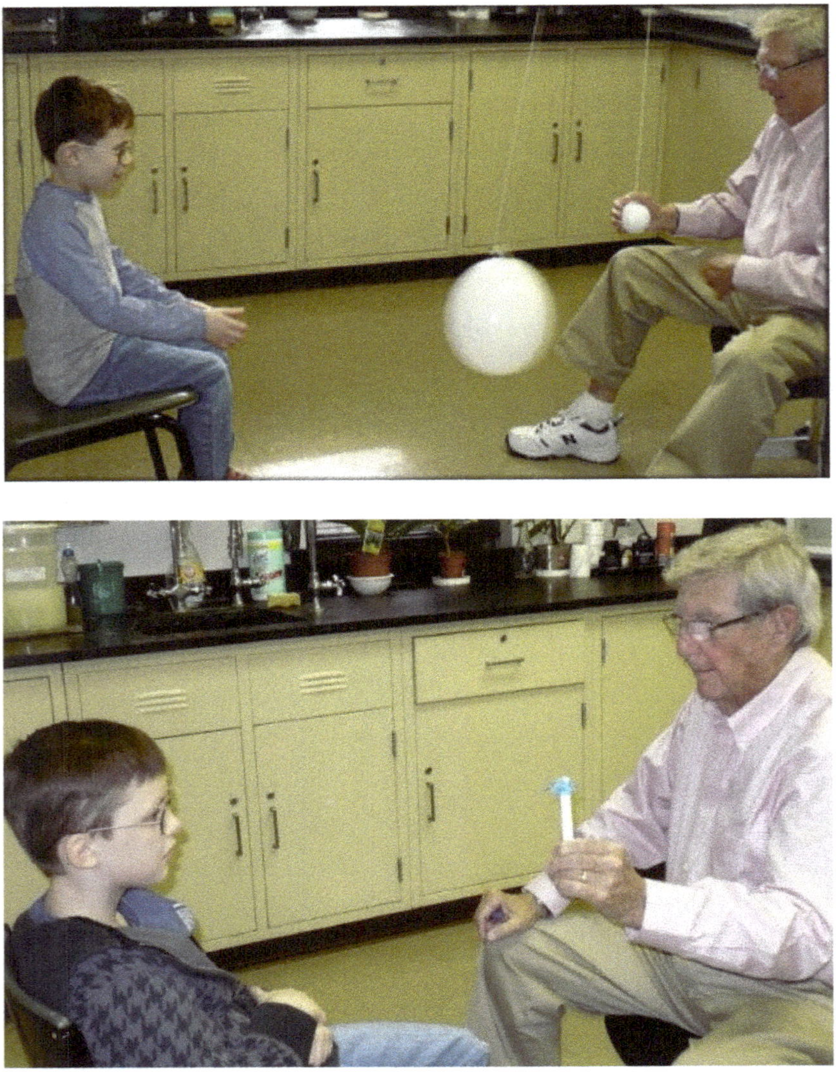

Figure 15.1ab. *Dr. Kaplan is conducting evaluations to prescribe prism lenses.*

posture, breathing, or other involuntary movements to be reviewed by the Center for Visual Management group. The video recordings were mailed to the Center for Visual Management for oversight in determining each patient's progress throughout the study.

Month 1. The purpose behind the exercises assigned for Month 1 was to disrupt and reintegrate the visual system. Observational changes could be seen in the patient's stress level, ease or difficulty in reorganizing visual perception and balance to the base direction, level of comfort or discomfort in completing the exercise, sustained visual attention, awareness of double vision, visual tracking, hand-eye coordination, smooth or uncoordinated movements, visual convergence, proper posture, as well as improved perception of distance and speed. In addition to wearing prescription prism lenses, disruptive lenses and/or red/green lenses as described, some of the equipment used in these exercises included a balance board, a trampoline and a yoga mat.

Month 2. The visuo-motor exercises assigned for the second month utilized a visual-vestibular technique to enhance body schema and self-awareness, develop visual-vestibular integration, coordinate balance and visual attention to self, and engage binocular fusion. Additionally, patients practiced sustaining visual feedback to a focal target, while increasing ambient awareness and reorganizing current visual perceptual patterns and visual fields which may have been previously compressed prior to wearing prism lenses and visuo-motor therapy. Additional equipment used in some of these exercises included a full-length mirror, a "Star" chart, and a chalkboard.

Month 3. The purpose of this month's exercises was to engage bilateral movements and visual-auditory integration as well as increase visual attention and eye movement skills including tracking and coordination. Other objectives included the introduction of fixation jumps to expand the visual eye field while incorporating proprioception of body movement and auditory input to reorganize the patient's current visual perceptual patterns as well as promote smooth tracking and breathing skills. New equipment introduced during this month's exercises included a metronome, bongos, a checkerboard, a circle and square chart, and a Hart chart for vison therapy.

Month 4. During Month 4 exercises, patients were asked to read before and after visuo-motor therapy and trainers were instructed to observe differences in speed, reading fluency and comprehension as well as changes in breathing and posture, including whether or not the patient appeared relaxed or tense. The primary goal of this month's exercises was to integrate two visual tracts, both focal and ambient vision while also creating depth perception, increasing smooth eye movements, and increasing visual attention and tracking ability. Additional equipment during this month's exercises included a pie tin, a slinky on a dowel, two matchbox cars or tennis balls, and bubble blowing solution with a wand.

Month 5. A constant theme throughout visuo-motor therapy was to increase visual attention, eye movements and tracking ability. For this month's exercises, several previously learned procedures were repeated, but now combined with other procedures to create depth perception, increase smooth eye movements, develop visual-vestibular integration and increase visual processing ability. Much of the same equipment was reused during this month's exercises; however, a walking rail was added to incorporate balance and depth perception with an exercise that was previous done standing or sitting in a stationary position.

Month 6. The final month's exercises for this study highlighted the fusion of vision and auditory integration with controlled breathing, increased proprioceptive input, visual attention, convergence skills and depth perception. This study concluded with the integration of visual-verbal sequences in which the patient was directed to name items such as animals or fruits in alphabetical order or simply count or recite the alphabet while bunting the ball. The ability to provide a correct verbal response while visually attending to and physically making contact with the ball is the direct result of cortical reorganization of the vision system. The patients in this study were successful in integrating their visual, auditory and proprioceptive systems through the daily use of prescription prism lenses in combination with visuo-motor exercises for a period of 6 months (Figure 15.2ab). A more detailed explanation of the types of vision lenses, visuo-motor exercises and equipment used in this study can be found in Dr. Kaplan's previously published book, Seeing Through New Eyes (Kaplan, 2006) and in a paper by Dombroski et al. (2014).

Behavioral Evaluations

Social and behavioral functioning of participants were evaluated using caregiver report and ratings. Participants in the study were evaluated prior to treatment, and following treatment. Behavioral functioning measures included several instruments. Aberrant Behavior Checklist (ABC; Aman & Singh, 1994) is a clinician administered rating scale assessing five problem areas: Irritability, Lethargy/Social Withdrawal, Stereotypy, Hyperactivity, and Inappropriate Speech. The

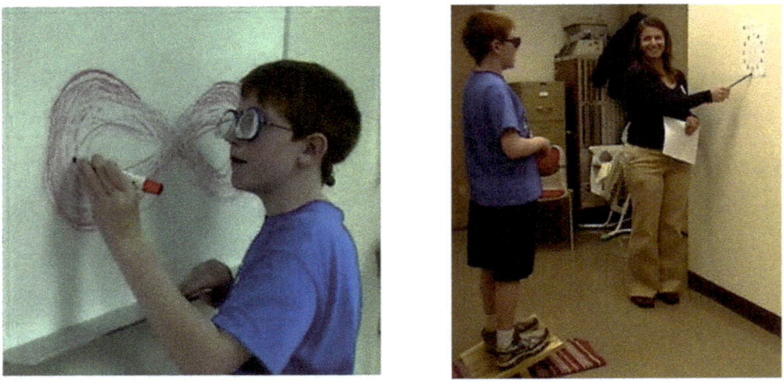

Figure 15.2ab. *Child with autism is performing visuo-motor tasks with disruptive prism lenses during midterm assessment in the lab.*

Repetitive Behavior Scale – R (RBS; Bodfish, Symons, Lewis, 1999) is a caregiver completed rating scale assessing repetitive and restricted behavior patterns in ASD. The Achenbach System of Empirically Based Assessment (ASEBA, Achenbach, 2001) checklist was used for assessing adaptive and maladaptive functioning. The school-age assessment form used was the CBCL/6–18, completed by parents.

Psychophysiological Reactivity Tests

Our interest was also in evaluating the effects of corrective ambient prism lenses on autonomic nervous system activity, as well as contributing to the understanding of abnormal autonomic reactivity to emotional stimuli present in autism. The study used emotionally arousing video excerpts taken from the classic Disney film "The Lion King.". Each episode (high and low emotional context block) was 2 min long, while totally four episodes were used, thus making the period of watching video up to 10 min. The order of movie episodes was counterbalanced across all subjects. Electrocardiographic (ECG) recording was used for heart rate (HR) monitoring and collection during the session. Electrodermal activity was recorded from the fingers for the monitoring of skin conductance level (SCL). Physiological activity was recorded using C-2 J&J Engineering Inc. (Poulsbo, WA) real-time physiological monitor with USE-2 Physiodata software. Analysis of more advanced heart rate variability (HRV) was enhanced using Kubios HRV software (Helsinki, Finland). The test was conducted twice, at the baseline (before treatment) and after completion of prism lenses treatment course.

Autonomic measures of interest were overall mean HR, low frequency (LF) power of HRV, high frequency (HF) power of HRV, and the ratio of the two (LF/HF). Mean HR, the standard deviation of the HR (SDHR), power and percentage of high frequency (HF), low frequency (LF), very low frequency (VLF) HRV components, and the ratio of the LF over the HF (LF/HF ratio) of HRV were calculated using Kubios software (Finland). The LF power of HRV is mostly indicative of sympathetic nervous system activity, while HF power is indicative of parasympathetic nervous system activity, in particular n. vagus effects on cardiac chronotropic functions. Our expectation was that wearing prism lenses and performing the visuo-motor exercises on daily basis would enhance the patient's ambient vision, thus reducing the confusion and stress caused by deficits in this type of vision. Expected outcomes were a decrease in HR, increase in high frequency (HF) power and decrease in low frequency (LF) power, indicative of enhanced parasympathetic nervous system activity and/or decreased sympathetic activity, and a decreased LF/HF ratio, which is considered as an indirect cardiac autonomic balance index. Lower LF/HF ratio of HRV is considered as an indication of better cardiac autonomic balance and improved psychophysiological flexibility in autism.

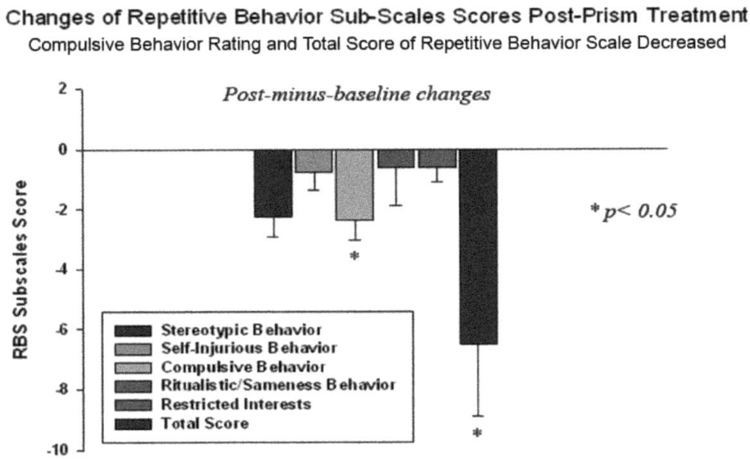

Figure 15.3. *Outcomes of Repetitive Behavioral Scale questionnaires (RBS-R) showing decreased Compulsive Behaviors Score and Total Score post prism lenses treatment.*

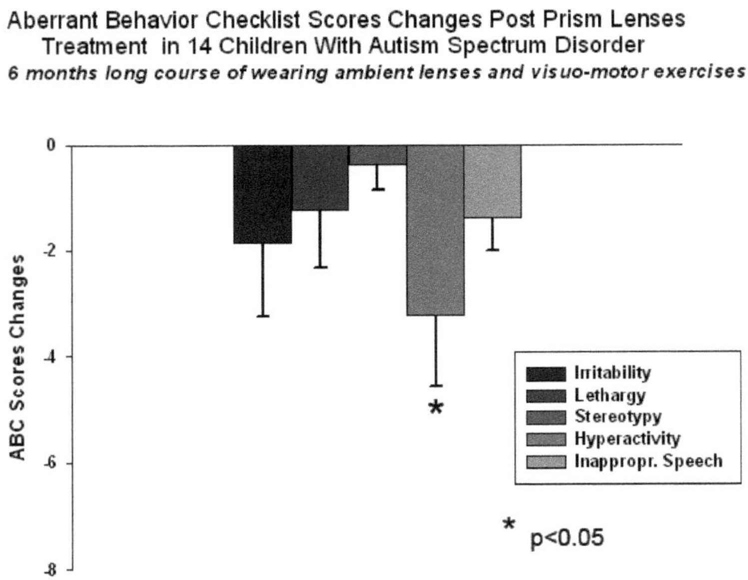

Figure 15.4. *Outcomes of Aberrant Behavior Checklist questionnaires (ABC) showing decreased Hyperactivity score post prism lenses treatment.*

Results

Behavioral Ratings Results

Empirical behavioral data outcomes were reported using the Autism Behavior Checklist (ABC), Repetitive Behavior Scale (RBS; Figures 15.3–15.4) and Achenbach's ASEBA (Figure 15.5). In the ABC, three out of five scaled scores were reduced. In particular, scores decreased in Lethargy/Social Withdrawal (-2.57± 3.56, t = 2.69; df = 13, p = 0.018), Inappropriate Speech (-1.42 ± 2.24, t = 2.38, df = 13, p = 0.033), and in Hyperactivity (-3.00 ± 4.57, t = 2.36; df = 13, p = 0.035) ratings compared to baseline scores. According to the Repetitive Behavior Scale (RBS), two out of six subscale scores post-treatment were significantly different from baseline level. These subscale scores included: Compulsive Behavior (-1.61 ± 2.25, t = 2.59; df = 13, p = 0.024) and overall Total Score (-5.61± 8.67, t = 2.33; df = 13, p = 0.038) compared to baseline scores. Achenbach's ASEBA (Figure 15.5) showed significant decrease on Rule-Breaking Behavior (mean= -1.41 ± 1.92, t = 2.54, df = 13, p = 0.027), Social Problems (-3.16 ± 4.26, t = 2.57, df = 13, p = 0.026), and ADHD symptom scores (mean = -3.58 ± 4.23, t = 2.93, df = 13, p = 0.014).

Heart Rate Variability and Skin Conductance Level Outcomes

Post treatment during watching the same "Lion King" video without prism lenses, a significant decrease in average heart rate was observed among the participants from the baseline pre-treatment 94.6 ± 2.99 beats/min to post-sessions 89.6 ±3.65 beats/min, with paired-sample t-test showing significant change (t = -2.52, df =13, p = 0.025). There was a decrease in LF power (index of sympathetic cardiac influences) from 60.2 ± 2.81 power units to 48.6 ± 3.57 units (t = -2.38, df = 13, p = 0.033) with peak of LF spectral power changing from 0.83 ± 0.03 to 0.11 ± 0.02 Hz, t = 2.29, df = 13, p = 0.039. At the same time, we

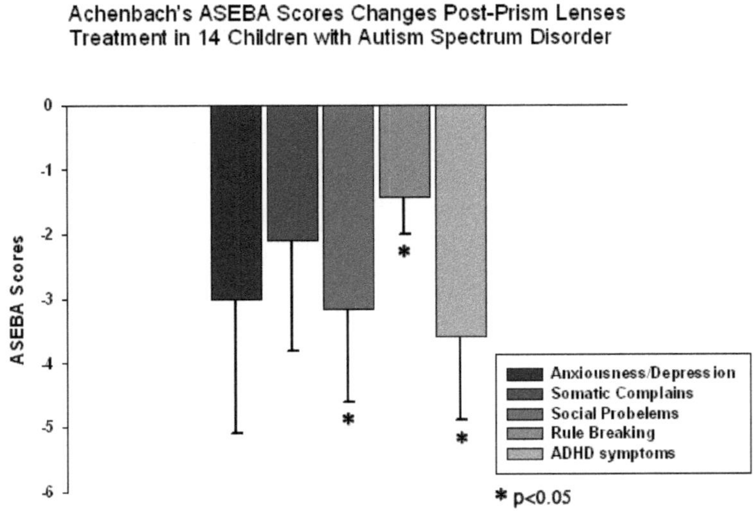

Figure 15.5. *Outcomes of Achenbach's ASEBA questionnaire showing decreased Rule Breaking and ADHD symptom scores post prism lenses treatment.*

found an increase in respiratory sinus arrhythmia reflected by an increase in the percentage of HF power of HRV (cardiac vagal control index) from 24.8 ± 2.16% to 37.6 ± 4.61% (t = 2.42, df = 13, p = 0.03) along with the increase of the power of HF in HRV spectrum from 39.81 ± 10.53 units to 51.41 ± 13.38 units (t = 2.38, df = 13, p = 0.033; Figure 15.6). VLF component of HRV (another measure of sympathetic activity) tended to decrease from 37.8% down to 29.7%, but the change did not reach statistical significance (t = -1.69, df = 13, p = 0.11). Lastly, the LF/HF power ratio (i.e., cardiac autonomic balance index) decreased from 1.70 ± 0.22 to 1.06 ± 0.13 (t = -2.52, df = 13, p = 0.025).

Skin conductance level (SCL) during the post-treatment measurement during watching "Lion King" movie decreased from 10.75 ± 7.05 μS down to 4.51 ± 2.89 μS, t = 3.26, df = 13, p = 0.008.

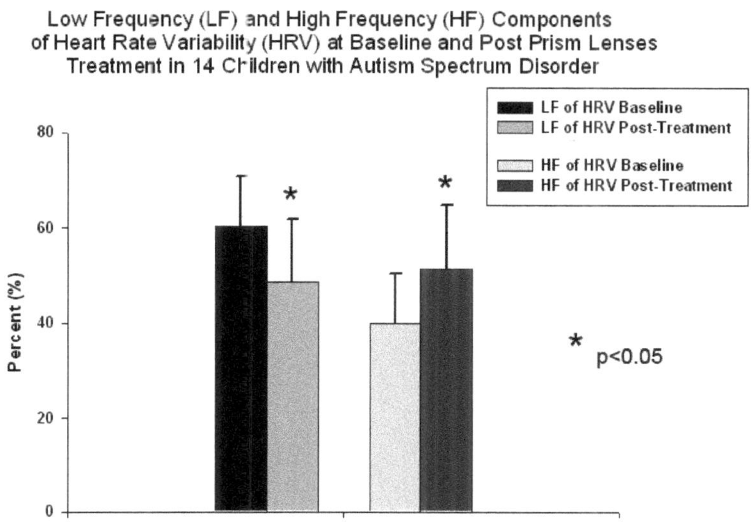

Figure 15.6. *Low frequency (LF) and High frequency (HF) components of HRV showed post prism lenses and visuo-motor training exercises changes indicative of decreased sympathetic and increased parasympathetic cardiac activity. Proportion of the LF component of HRV decreased, while proportion of HF of HRV increased indicating improved cardiac autonomic balance during exposure to emotional video clips from "Lion King" movie.*

Discussion

Behavioral measures reflect improvements in in multiple scores of aberrant behavior, in particular decreased rating of Lethargy and Social Withdrawal, Hyperactivity and Inappropriate Speech. Repetitive behaviors evaluations post-treatment also showed decreased Compulsive behavior rating and lower Total Repetitive and Stereotype behavior score. The ASEBA questionnaire showed a decrease of Rule-Breaking behavior, lower score on Social Problems and decreased score on ADHD symptoms.

The psychophysiological reactivity results are very encouraging in that they support the hypotheses that wearing ambient prism lenses in combination with vision exercises had the desired effect on HRV variables reflecting improved autonomic balance in children with ASD. First, the decrease in average heart rate suggests the participants were in a more relaxed state after treatment with corrective prism lenses. Second, the decrease in LF power and the increase in HF power were changes in the desired direction toward improved autonomic balance. This is also seen in the decreased LF/HF power ratio. Skin conductance decrease is a biomarker of reduced sympathetic arousal. These results are consistent with increased parasympathetic and decreased sympathetic tone, a significant improvement from initial cardiac autonomic activity in autism.

Children diagnosed with autism spectrum disorder (ASD) are characterized by impairments in communication, social interaction, and repetitive behavior. Ambient vision deficiency is a common comorbid condition in autism that negatively affects peripheral vision, attention, hand-eye coordination, balance, and gross motor movement. Ambient vision is necessary for control of anatomical movement involved in spatial orientation and proprioception. Dysfunction of this system impairs the ability to process environmental cues used to control gait, posture, movement, and speech. Loss of spatial orientation negatively affects the vestibular system, which leads to the development of adaptive responses that are consistent with the behavioral symptoms observed in autism.

Investigation of the abnormalities of the perception of depth in ASD and development of visuo-motor training and ambient vision corrective methods merits further attention. There are numerous clinical observations and case reports about depth perception being atypical in ASD (Simmons et al., 2009). Kaplan (2006) reported his observations that individuals with ASD often misjudge interpersonal distance during social communication and have difficulties with tasks such as ball-catching and other tasks requiring coordination of visual input with motor acts. Some of the above deficits are explained by a deficiency in ambient vision. Accurate depth perception and orientation in the surrounding space requires a precise processing and coordination of information from each eye, and it might be affected in neurodevelopmental disorders such as autism. According to Simmons et al. (2009) depth perception and stereopsis in ASD would seem to be an area that warrants more research. Spencer et al. (2000) examined the possibility of a neural basis for the perceptual and motor related abnormalities frequently cited in autism (de Jonge et al., 2007). They tested children diagnosed with ASD on two tasks specific to dorsal and ventral cortical stream functions. The results supported evidence that autistic individuals have a specific impairment in dorsal stream functioning. It was concluded that autism as a developmental disorder may have a greater vulnerability of the dorsal system (Goodale & Milner, 1992; Mishkin, Ungerleider, & Macko,1983). Other authors also support the view that an impairment might be present in the dorsal visual pathway in autism, and furthermore, that this might account for so called "weak central coherence" (Frith & Happé, 1994) at the visuospatial level (Pellicano et al., 2005).

Summary

In this study, thirty autistic children were recruited, evaluated, and individually prescribed corrective ambient prism lenses. Next, a 6-month daily vision therapy protocol was implemented in an attempt to ameliorate ambient vision deficiencies and abate autistic behaviors. Patients were instructed to wear the corrective ambient lenses all day, except when vision therapy procedures instructed otherwise. Daily vision therapy procedures included exercises that required the patients to wear disruptive prism lenses and occasionally red/green lenses. The combination of the lenses and tasks were used to address problems involved in balance, visual organization, and depth perception. Empirical behavioral data was reported using the Autism Behavior Checklist (ABC), Repetitive Behavior Scale (RBS), and Achenbach (ASEBA) questionnaires. Autonomic reactivity recordings at the baseline and post-treatment included heart rate (HR) and heart rate variability (HRV), which were taken while the subject was watching scenes from the classic Disney film, "The Lion King," to evoke emotional responses. Fourteen out of 30 initially enrolled patients completed the six-stage course and all required assessments and evaluations.

Results of this study showed that corrective ambient prism lenses combined with daily vision therapy both reduced autistic behaviors (according to ABC, ASEBA, and RBS rating scores) and enhanced autonomic cardiac balance during exposure to emotional stimuli in autism. Prism lenses address an important issue of ambient vision in ASD and possibly other developmental disorders as well. Our study with prism lenses and HR suggests improved ambient vision has a positive impact on autonomic function and behavior rating in children with autism, with the potential to ameliorate autistic behaviors and improve communication. We look forward to the future of prism lenses and their use in treating developmental disorders such as autism.

Acknowledgement

The study was support by a pilot research grant from the Autism Research Institute (ARI, San Diego, CA).

References

Achenbach, T. (2001). *ASEBA, Achenbach child behavior checklist (Parent checklist).* Burlington, VT: University of Vermont.

American Psychiatric Association (2000). *Diagnostic and statistical*

manual of mental disorders, (4th ed., text revision). Washington, DC.
Aman, M. G., & Singh, N. N. (1994). *Aberrant behavior checklist - community. Supplementary manual.* East Aurora, NY: Slosson Educational Publications.
Behrmann, M., Thomas, C., & Humphreys, K. (2006). Seeing it differently: Visual processing in autism. *Trends in Cognitive Sciences, 10*(6), 258–263.
Bodfish, J. W., Symons, F. J., & Lewis, J. (1999). *Repetitive behavior scale.* Western Carolina Center Research Reports.
Boucsein, W. (2012). *Electrodermal activity* (2nd ed.). New York: Springer.
Carmody, D. P., Kaplan, M., & Gaydos, A. M. (2001). Spatial orientation adjustments in children with autism in Hong Kong. *Child Psychiatry and Human Development, 31*(3), 233– 247.
Chok, J. T., Reed, D. D., Kennedy, A., & Bird, F. L., (2010). A single-case experimental analysis of the effects of ambient prism lenses for an adolescent with developmental disabilities. *Behavior Analysis in Practice, 3*(2), 42–51.
Dakin, S., & Frith, U. (2005). Vagaries of visual perception in autism. *Neuron, 48*(3), 497–507.
de Jonge, M. V., Kemner, C., de Haan, E. H., Coppens, J. E., van den Berg, J. T. P., & van Engeland, H. (2007). Visual information processing in high-functioning individuals with autism spectrum disorders and their parents. *Neuropsychology, 21*(1), 65–73.
Dombroski, B., Kaplan, M., Kotsamanidis-Burg, B., Edelson, S. M., Hensley, M. K., Sokhadze, E. M., & Casanova, M. F. (2014). Effects of ambient prism lenses and visual-motor training on heart rate variability and behavioral outcomes in autism. In K. Siri, &T. Lyons, (Eds.), *Cutting-edge therapies for autism* (4the d.; pp. 138–150). New York, NY: Skyhorse Publishing.
Edgin, J. O., & Pennington, B. F. (2005). Spatial cognition in autism spectrum disorders: Superior, impaired or just intact? *Journal of Autism and Developmental Disorders, 35*(6), 729–745.
Frith, U., & Happé, F. (1994). Autism: Beyond "theory of mind". *Cognition, 50*(1–3), 115–132.
Goodale, M. A., & Milner, A. D. (1992). Separate visual pathways for perception and action. *Trends in Neurosciences, 15*(1), 20–25.
Kaplan, M., Carmody, D. P., & Gaydos, A. M. (1996). Postural orientation modifications in autism in response to ambient lenses. *Child Psychiatry and Human Development, 27*(2), 81–91.
Kaplan, M., Edelson, S. M., & Seip, J. L. (1998). Behavioral changes in autistic individuals as a result of wearing ambient transitional

prism lenses. *Child Psychiatry and Human Development, 29*(1), 65–76.
Kaplan. M. (2006). *Seeing through new eyes.* Philadelphia, PA: J. Kingsley Publ.
Le Couteur, A., Lord, C., & Rutter, M. (2003). *The autism diagnostic interview – revised (ADI-R).* Los Angeles, CA: Western Psychological Services.
Ming, X., Bain, J. M., Smith, D., Brimacombe, M., Gold von-Simson, G., & Axelrod, F. B. (2011). Assessing autonomic dysfunction symptoms in children: A pilot study. *Journal of Child Neurology, 26*(4), 420–427.
Mishkin, M., Ungerleider, L. G., & Macko, K. A. (1983). Object vision and spatial vision: Two cortical pathways. *Trends in Neurosciences, 6,* 414–417.
Pellicano, E., Gibson, L., Maybery, M., Durkin, K., & Badcock, D. R. (2005). Abnormal global processing along the dorsal visual pathway in autism: A possible mechanism for weak visuospatial coherence? *Neuropsychologia, 43*(7), 1044–1053.
Porges, S. W. (2001). The polyvagal theory: Phylogenetic substrates of a social nervous system. *International Journal of Psychophysiology, 42*(2), 123–146.
Simmons, D. R., Robertson, A. E., McKay, L. S., Toal, E., McAleer, P., & Pollick, F. E. (2009). Vision in autism spectrum disorders. *Vision Research, 49*(22), 2705–2739.
Spencer, J., O'Brien, J., Riggs, K., Braddick, O., Atkinson, J., & Wattam-Bell, J. (2000). Motion processing in autism: Evidence for a dorsal stream deficiency. *Neuroreport, 11*(12), 2765–2767.
Toichi, M., & Kamio, Y. (2003). Paradoxical autonomic response to mental tasks in autism. *Journal of Autism and Developmental Disorders, 33*(4), 417–426.
Wechsler, D. (2004). *Wechsler intelligence scale for children - fourth edition integrated (WISC-IV Integrated).* San Antonio, TX: Harcourt.

16

Combined rTMS, Neurofeedback and Auditory Integration Therapy in Children With Autism: Two Case Studies

Estate M. Sokhadze,[1,3] Yao Wang,[2,3] Eva Lamina,[1]
Ayman S. El-Baz,[3] and Manuel F. Casanova[1,3]

Our research group proposed that low frequency transcranial magnetic stimulation (rTMS) may affect lateral inhibition in minicolumns and improve executive functions and behavioral symptoms of autism spectrum disorder (ASD). This hypothesis was based on Casanova's "minicolumnopathy" theory of autism (Casanova 2005, 2007; Casanova et al., 2003) and its rationale is described in more detail in a recent publication (Casanova et al., 2015) and several chapters (Casanova & Sokhadze, 2014; Sokhadze, Casanova, & Baruth, 2013). Our proposal aimed at establishing an early stage trial of rTMS in children with autism was awarded a NIH Eureka R01 grant and the study resulted in numerous publications reporting positive outcomes for this neuromodulation approach (Baruth et al., 2010; Casanova et al., 2012; Sokhadze et al., 2009, 2010, 2012, 2014b, 2016a, 2017; Wang et al., 2016a). The main positive outcomes were documented by reduced scores of parental questionnaires and checklists rating behavioral symptoms, improved performance in cognitive tests, and improved balance of autonomic

[1]University of South Carolina School of Medicine, Greenville Campus, Greenville, SC
[2]Beijing Language and Culture University, Beijing, China
[3]University of Louisville, Louisville, KY

nervous system activity (Casanova et al., 2014; Wang et al., 2016a). More detailed description of rTMS course length effects can be found in a recent study (Sokhadze et al., 2018) where we reported outcomes of 6, 12, and 18 sessions of weekly neuromodulation focusing mostly on behavioral measures and event-related potential (ERP) findings. Outcomes of evoked and induced electroencephalographic (EEG) gamma oscillation modulation by rTMS treatment were described in several other publications (Baruth et al., 2010; Sokhadze et al., 2009, 2016a).

In parallel to the above reported studies, we started a neurofeedback (NFB) training trial in children with autism. The initial pilot study using only 12 sessions of NFB using "inhibit all" (i.e., "squash") and 40 Hz gamma upregulation protocol in eight children with ASD did not yield significant results, making us extend the course length to 18 weekly sessions. Results of the trial in 18 patients with ASD were recently published (Wang et al., 2016b). At the same time, we decided to combine rTMS and neurofeedback, and administer NFB training immediately after each rTMS session. This decision was based on several considerations that we described in detail in our report of outcomes of integrated rTMS and NFB therapy (Sokhadze et al., 2014a). At the same time, we started a pilot study that addressed sensory issues in autism and implemented Berard Auditory Integration Training (AIT) with the help of a certified Berard AIT instructor. Preliminary results of this trial were reported in Sokhadze et al. (2016b) with main findings focusing on behavioral symptom outcomes, mismatch negativity (MMN) and exogenous ERP measures.

Our studies were widely publicized in the media and in the scientific-popular literature and it attracted the interest of out-of-city families with children affected by autism, who were willing to come for a course of daily treatment (as compared to local patients who were treated on weekly basis). Most of them were planning to come, stay at hotel for 2 weeks to be able to receive a 12-session course of rTMS combined with neurofeedback. The families who were visiting our lab for treatment, during the period when we had the AIT study in progress, expressed intention to sign for a combined course of rTMS, neurofeedback and AIT. We amended our institutional review board (IRB) approved protocol to accommodate this particular version of integrated neuromodulation therapy and started offering it not only to out-of-city patients but also to local patients.

Several families who participated in this particular three-arm neurotherapy decided to continue treatment on annual basis. As a result, we collected several case studies with multiple courses (i.e., at least three) of this combined treatment. In this chapter, we report results of two such cases. In both of them, patients participated three times in 2-week long courses of rTMS combined with neurofeedback training and Berard AIT. Each course was comprised of 12 sessions of 1.0 Hz rTMS over the dorsolateral prefrontal cortex (DLPFC) administered bilaterally and followed by the same number of neurofeedback training sessions (downregulation of high amplitude rhythms such as delta and theta and upregulation of relative power of 40 Hz-centered gamma). In addition, patients had AIT administered twice a day according to a classic Berard AIT protocol. During the morning session, rTMS was followed by a neurofeedback session and the first daily AIT session. The second AIT session was conducted after at least a 3-hour break. The measures used as dependent variables and behavioral and electrophysiological outcomes of these two cases were similar to those described in our prior studies using rTMS and neurofeedback combination and AIT (Sokhadze et al., 2014a, 2016b).

Method

Transcranial Magnetic Stimulation

For repetitive TMS administration we used a Magstim Rapid device (Magstim Co., Sheffield, UK) with a 70-mm wing span figure-eight coil. To identify resting motor threshold (MT) for each hemisphere the output of the magnetic stimulator was increased by 5% steps until a 50 µV deflection of electromyogram (EMG) or a visible twitch in the first dorsal interosseous (FDI) muscle was detected in at least two or three trials of TMS delivered over the motor cortex controlling the contralateral FDI. Electromyogram was recorded with a portable C-2 J&J Engineering Inc. physiological monitor with USE-3 software and Physiodata applications (J&J Engineering, Inc., Seattle, WA). In both cases the rTMS was administered daily (six sessions per week) with the following stimulation parameters: 1.0 Hz frequency, 90% MT, 180 pulses per session with nine trains of 20 pulses each with 20–30 s intervals between the trains

Berard Auditory Integration Training (AIT) Procedure

Both patients participated in a standard protocol of Berard AIT following exactly the same procedure provided by the same experimenter trained by a certified Berard instructor. In our study, subjects were trained during a 2 weeklong course consisting of 10 sessions in the first week (two per day) and another 10 sessions on the second week, that is, two 5-day sets. The listening sessions were separated by a mandatory 3-hour interval to allow a break from the auditory stimulation. Music for Berard AIT represented a variety of light rock, reggae, and jazz, selected specifically to assure that it contains a wide range of frequencies from 20 Hz to 20 kHz. A Sony CD changer (Model CDP-CE500) was used to program the sequence of preselected music pieces. Music was modulated by an electronic device called the Earducator™/6F (Hollagen Designs

CC, Western Cape, South Africa). The processed music did not exceed an average output of 85 dB. The Earducator/6F intermittently emphasized low and high sound frequencies in the music (called gating or modulation). Children listen to the music through closed, high fidelity headphones (Beyerdynamic DT250-80). The protocol for Berard AIT recommends quiet listening without engagement in cognitive activities.

Neurofeedback Procedure

Immediately after the rTMS session, subjects completed approximately 25 min long neurofeedback sessions using a "Focus/Neureka!" protocol designed to train so-called "focused attention" index (FA index) and "40 Hz-centered gamma" index (40 Hz index) measures according to the specification of the Peak BrainHappiness Trainer (PBHT) system (NeuroTek, Goshen, KY, USA). The goal of each subject was to enhance the" FA index" measure throughout the session while maintaining an adequate level of so called "Neureka!" measure (i.e., 40 Hz index) within a certain range. All sessions were completed using different fragments of documentary films depicting nature scenes from the BBC "Planet Earth" and "Life" series, and National Geographic DVDs (e.g., "Africa's Wildlife," "America's Greatest Animals," "Birds of Paradise"). Different scenes were utilized to maintain the engagement among the participants. Based on the thresholds set, the subject would receive biofeedback both in the visual and auditory modalities. Visual feedback was provided as changes in brightness, size, and continuation of the video controlled by the FA index and 40 Hz index measures. Auditory feedback was used to inform subjects when these measures were under the threshold level, in the case of FA index, or outside the acceptable range, in the case of 40 Hz index. All EEG signals and training parameters were measured using three electrodes, one active electrode at the prefrontal EEG (Fpz) site, the second being a reference on the left ear, and a third sensor serving as a ground and located between the other two electrodes. The sensors were soaked in a potassium chloride solution to enhance conduction. Each subject completed a minimum of 12 daily neurofeedback sessions, training to increase the FA index and 40 Hz Gamma index using the "Focus/Neureka" protocol. The threshold for both indices was adjusted 4–5 times by experimenter during each session to maintain moderate difficulty. The target length of each session recorded was 20–30 min, with most sessions (85 %) reaching the length goal of a 25-min minimum recording of usable EEG data. Eye blink artifacts removal was implemented using a custom made BioExplorer (BioExplorer 1.5, CyberEvolution, WA, USA) application.

Pre-, Post-treatment, and Follow-up Behavioral Measures

Social and behavioral functioning of participants were evaluated using caregiver reports and clinician ratings of improvement. Participants were evaluated prior to treatment and following treatment. Selected tests that have been shown to be sensitive to behavioral and social changes expected to occur with treatment and included following: The Aberrant Behavior Checklist (ABC, Aman & Singh, 1994), the Social Responsiveness Scale (SRS, Constantino & Gruber, 2005), and the Repetitive Behavior Scale - R (RBS, Bodfish et al., 1999). The ABC is a caregiver completed rating scale assessing five problem areas: Irritability, Lethargy/Social Withdrawal, Stereotypy, Hyperactivity, and Inappropriate Speech based on caregiver report. The SRS is a caregiver completed rating scale assessing social interest and interaction which provides a dimensional measure of social interaction allowing the rating of social skills in autism. The RBS is a caregiver completed rating scale assessing repetitive and restricted behavior patterns, including measures of stereotyped, self-injurious, compulsive, ritualistic, sameness behavior, and restricted behavior in ASD. In addition, we used the Achenbach System of Empirically Based Assessment (ASEBA) questionnaire (Achenbach, & Rescorla, 2012).

Visual oddball test with ERP recording.

In the Kanizsa illusory figure (Kanizsa, 1976), test subjects have to respond with a button-press to rare (25% probability) Kanizsa squares (targets) among Kanizsa triangles (rare distracters, 25%) and non-Kanizsa figures (standards). The stimuli were presented for 250 ms with inter-trial intervals (ITI) varying in the range of 1100–1300 ms. Subjects were instructed to press a button on a keypad with their right index finger when a target appeared, and not to respond to any of the three standard stimuli appeared (75%). Therefore, this task required the processing of both stimulus features (shape and collinearity) for discrimination of targets. Task had two blocks and took 15 minutes to complete.

Dependent measures and data analysis in ERP tasks.

Behavioral. Mean reaction time (RT), and accuracy (total error rate).

Electrophysiological. Mean amplitude and latency of ERP peak (e.g., P300) within a temporal window across a region-of-interest (ROI) channel group. A list of ERP dependent variables included stimulus-averaged amplitude and latency of the anterior N100 (80–140 ms), N200 (180–320 ms), posterior (centro-parietal, parietal, parieto-occipital etc.) N100 (80–160 ms), posterior N200 (240–320 ms), anterior P300 (P3a), and posterior P3b (400–600 ms). We also analyzed response-locked error-related negativity (ERN) occurring 40–160 ms post committed error. Only a portion of the above ERP measures are reported in this case studies chapter.

Autonomic activity recorded during rTMS procedures and in Berard AIT sessions.

Cardiovascular activity. Average heart rate (HR), the standard deviation of the HR (SDHR), power of high frequency (HF), low frequency (LF), very low frequency (VLF) components of heart rate variability (HRV), % power of LF (%LF [of LF + HF]) and HF (%) and the ratio of the LF over the HF (LF/HF ratio was used as an indirect cardiac autonomic balance index) of HRV were calculated as cardiac chronotropic activity measures. Artifact-corrected 5–8 min long recording epochs were analyzed with fast Fourier transformation (FFT) to assess HRV. Integrals of the spectrum in 0.04–0.15 Hz (LF of HRV) and 0.15–0.40 Hz (HF of HRV) bands were measured (in ms2) using Kubios HRV software.

Respiratory activity. Respiration rate (RESP), on per minute basis, and inspiration wave amplitude (IA) were calculated. These measures were used to control HF peak related to respiratory frequencies in HRV.

Electrodermal activity. Skin conductance level (SCL, in μS) and amplitude of the skin conductance response (SCR), defined as fluctuation with more than 0.02 μS increment, NS.SCR, the number of non-specific SCR (per min). Only a part of the autonomic responses is reported in this chapter focusing on two single cases.

Results

The current chapter reviews cases of two high-functioning boys with established autism spectrum disorder diagnosis who enrolled three times in two weeks-long integrated rTMS, neurofeedback and AIT treatment courses.

Case 1: MN

Intake. MN was a Caucasian 12-year-old boy when he was enrolled in the first course of integrated neurotherapy. MN was diagnosed with autism when he was two and a half years old. Among the most notable symptoms at that time were speech delays as well as fine and gross motor delays. He had in the past some comorbidities such as asthma and allergies. Among his restricted interest list there should be mentioned his fascination with elevators. Evaluation based on SRS-2 at the intake showed 84 T-score that indicated deficiencies in reciprocal social behavior that were clinically significant and led to severe interference with everyday social interactions. Such scores are strongly associated with clinical diagnosis of an autism spectrum disorder. On the ASEBA DSM--Oriented scales (APA, 2013), MN's score on the Somatic Problems scale was in the normal range. However, MN's scores on the Depressive Problems, Anxiety Problems, Attention DeficitIHyperactivity Problems and Oppositional Defiant Problems scales were in the clinical range above the 97th percentile. MN's score on the Conduct Problems scale was in the borderline clinical range (93rd to 97th percentile). His ABC Irritability rating score was moderate (21), while Hyperactivity score was high (37). Total score (score/items [S/I]) on RBS-R was also high (1.59).

MN's autonomic measures at the baseline showed accelerated heart rate (115 beats/per min [bpm]) along with elevated SCL (14.4 μV). The LF/HF index of HRV was 1.55. At the time of intake his medication included: Namenda (10 mg), Leucovorin (15 mg, 3/day), and clonidine (0.2 mg). During the last course of treatment, he started taking propranolol (40 mg) and an increased dosage of clonidine (0.3 mg). Reaction time in the oddball task was relatively fast (485 ms) and total error rate was low (5.4 %). Post-error slowing was positive but quite low (3.96 ms). His ERP measures were more or less within normative levels and will be discussed below during the overview of post-treatment oddball test outcomes. Audiometry before the AIT showed that he needed filtering at 4 kHz for Berard AIT procedures. MN completed 2 weeks of the initial course, had the second course after a 1-year break, and enrolled in the third course after 2 years, thus staying in the treatment for 4 years.

Post-treatment evaluations in MN case. The T-score of the SRS-2 test after the end of the 3rd course of treatment remained in the severe range (79 T), although it showed a

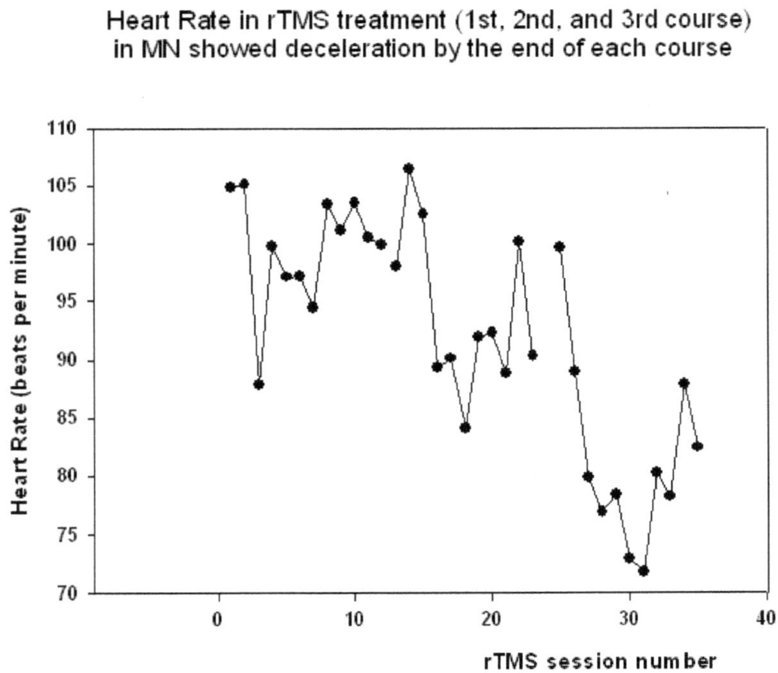

Figure 16. 1. Heart rate (HR) in t rTMS treatment during first, second, and third course in patient MN. The general trend of the cardiac rhythm is deceleration of HR during each course and across the whole 36 sessions of rTMS-based neuromodulation.

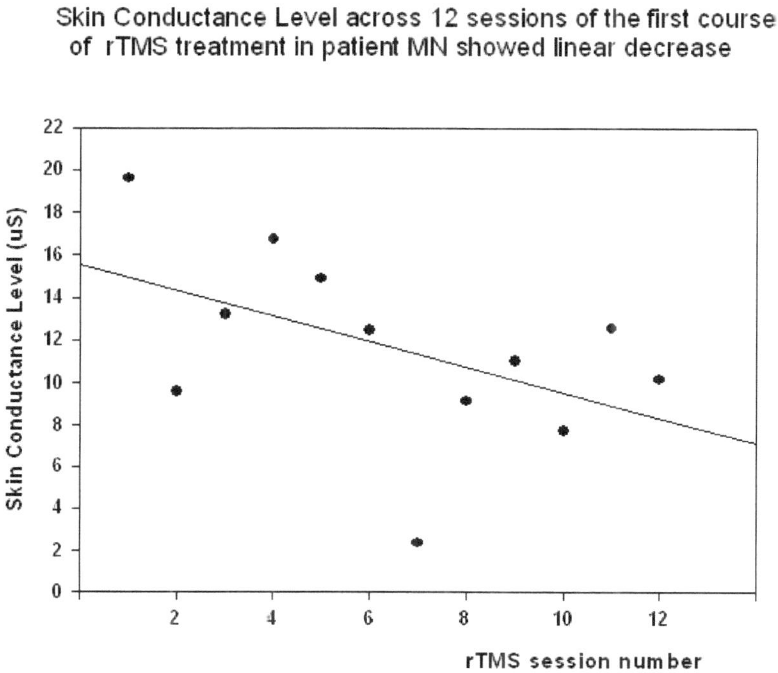

Figure 16. 2. Skin conductance level (SCL) across 12 sessions of the first course of rTMS treatment in patient MN. There is a linear trend to decrease of the SCL with increased number of rTMS sessions.

10.2 % decrease from the baseline. Evaluation based on ASEBA DSM-Oriented scales, showed that MN's scores on the Depressive Problems (20.7% decrease), Somatic Problems, Oppositional Defiant Problems and Conduct Problems (18.8% decrease) scales were now in the normal range. MN's score on the Anxiety Problems scale decreased (from 91 to 70, 23.1% decrease), but was still in the clinical range above the 97th percentile. MN's score on the Attention Deficit/Hyperactivity Problems scale was in the borderline clinical range (from 80 down to 65, i.e., 18.5% decrease). Decrease in scores of Oppositional Defiant Behavior was also substantial (from 80 down to 58, 27.5 %). ABC based evaluations showed post-treatment decrease of Irritability (by 61.9 %) and Hyperactivity (70.2%) rating scores. Evaluation of repetitive and stereotype behavior score (RBS-R Total S/I score) showed minimal decrease (5.5%). Patient MN showed a trend towards a decrease in heart rate (HR) during rTMS treatment. Figure 16. 1 shows a gradual decrease of mean HR across three courses of integrated neurotherapy. The autonomic balance index (LF/HR of HRV) showed a decrease from intake 1.54 down to post-treatment of 1.08. MN also showed a dramatic decrease of SCL during the first 12 sessions of rTMS (from 19.61 μV down to 10.18 μV, Fig 2). Changes of HR and HRV measures during AIT procedures were not significant, especially during the third course of integrated neurotherapy.

In a cognitive test (visual oddball task with Kanizsa illusory figures) MN did not show changes in reaction time (RT) but did improve accuracy (error rate from 5.42 % decreased down to 1.25%) and was accompanied by change in normative post-error RT slowing (from 3.98 ms up to 59.1 ms). Improved accuracy of responses was corroborated as well by increased negativity and shorter latency of error-related negativity (ERN) depicted in Figure 16. 3. Analysis of post- treatment test ERPs showed increased latency to target stimuli, specifically fronto-central N100 and P3a components, along with decreased amplitude of parietal P3b to non-target stimuli (from 3.97 down to 2.14 μV at the midline region of interest) and increased amplitude (e.g., at Pz from 1.69 up to 9.14 μV) and prolonged latency (from 292 up to 356 ms) of parietal P3b cognitive component in response to target stimuli (Fig. 4).

The patient has signed for a fourth course of combined rTMS, neurofeedback and AIT treatment. We plan to continue treating this subject and report his outcomes using classical singe case study design in the future.

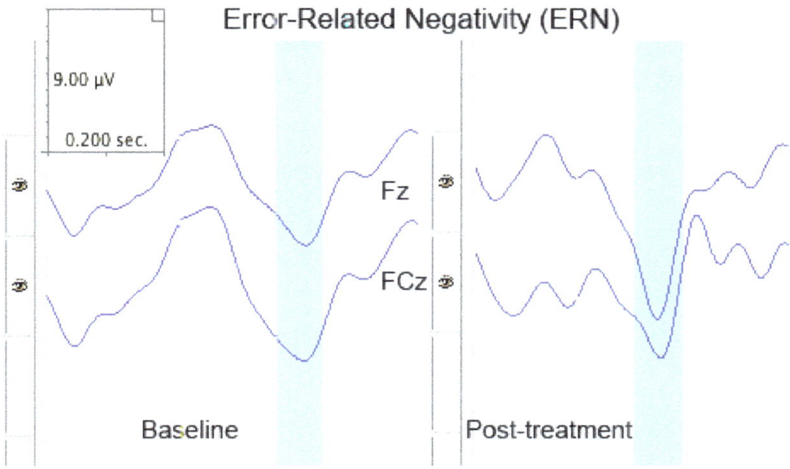

Figure 16. 3. Response-locked error-related negativity (ERN) in patient MN at intake baseline test and following combined TMS, neurofeedback and AIT treatment. Amplitude of the frontal and fronto-central ERN became more negative with shorter latency. These ERN changes reflect improvements in error monitoring function.

Case 2: JM

Intake. JM was a biracial (Asian/Caucasian) boy 10-year-old when he enrolled in the first integrated treatment course. He was diagnosed with autism spectrum disorder when he was 7 years old. His Full Intelligence Quotient (IQ) was 89 (low average), Verbal IQ was 99 on Wechsler Abbreviated Scale of Intelligence (WASI, Wechsler, 1999). Childhood Autism Rating Scale (CARS, Schopler et al., 1980) results placed JM in the mild to moderate range of autism. His SRS-2 T-score was 78 T, indicating deficiencies in reciprocal social behavior that were clinically significant and lead to severe interference with everyday social interactions. Such scores are strongly associated with clinical diagnosis of an ASD. On the ASEBA DSM-Oriented scales, JM's scores on the Anxiety Problems and Somatic Problems scales were in the normal range, but JM's scores on the Depressive Problems, Attention Deficit/

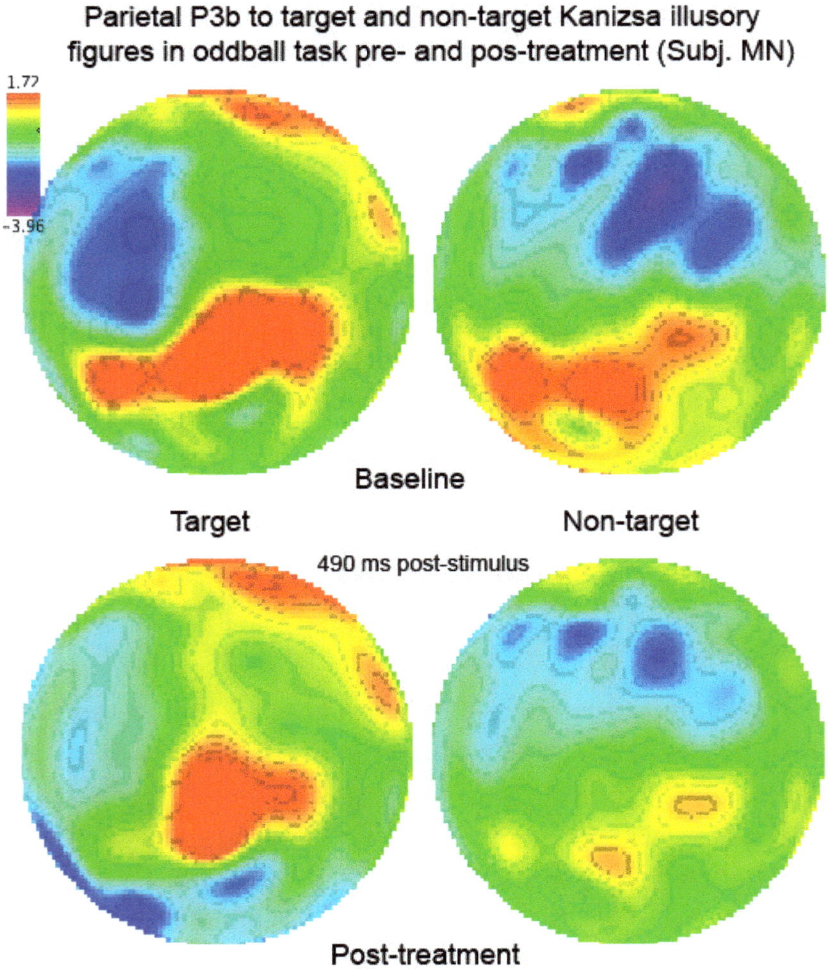

Figure 16. 4. Parietal P300 (P3b, 490 ms post-stimulus) to target and non-target Kanizsa illusory figures in a three-stimulus visual oddball task at the intake baseline and after combined treatment in patient MN. Post-treatment maps show decreased response to task-irrelevant non-target items and more centro-parietally distributed P3b to targets.

Hyperactivity Problems and Oppositional Defiant Problems scales were in the clinical range above the 97th percentile. JM's score on the Conduct Problems scale was in the borderline clinical range (93rd to 97th percentile). Medications taken by JM during intake included: Allegra (60 mg), Flonase, and Singulair (10 mg/day). Audiogram at the intake revealed almost 40% hearing loss in the left ear. After the initial course, the parent arranged additional testing and JM started using a hearing device. JM's ABC Irritability rating score mild (18), but Hyperactivity score was high (41). Total score (score/items) on RBS-R was relatively high (1.43). His autonomic measures showed elevated high heart rate (92 beats/per min) and his SCL was 6.04 μV. Autonomic cardiac balance index (i.e., LF/HF of HRV) was 1.16. Reaction time in the oddball task at baseline test was slow (644 ms) and accuracy very low (20.8% of total errors). ERP profile was featured by high magnitude of early negativities (i.e., fronto-central N100) to all types of stimuli, and less differentiated amplitude of frontal P300 (P3a) to target and non-target items. After enrollment, JM completed 2 weeks of the initial course, had the second course approximately 1 year after that, and came for the third course after a 2-year break, thus staying in the treatment for almost 4.5 years.

Post-treatment evaluations in JM case. Post-treatment evaluations after the second course using SRS-2 showed decrease of the T-score to 65 T (mild range) but returned to severe range after the third course (82 T). Scores in this range indicate deficiencies in reciprocal social behavior that are clinically significant and lead to severe interference with everyday social interactions. Such scores are strongly associated with clinical diagnosis of an ASD. Behavioral screening noted a decrease in the Repetitive Behavior Rating (RBS) from 82 to

71, i.e., 13.4% decrease of symptom severity. The ASEBA based evaluation after the third course of treatment showed that on DSM-Oriented scales, JM's scores on the Depressive Problems, Anxiety Problems, Somatic Problems and Conduct Problems scales (e.g., Conduct Problems, from 67 down to 56, 16.4 % decrease) were in the normal range. However, JM's score on the Attention Deficit/Hyperactivity Problems scale was still in the clinical range above the 97th percentile. His IVA-2 standard scale analysis also showed several quotient scores in the ranges close to those that reflect ADHD type deficits (e.g., Focus, Speed, Prudence and Consistency quotients were all in 67–75 range). At the same time, JM's post-treatment score on the Oppositional Defiant Problems scale was in the borderline clinical range (93rd to 97th percentile but changed from the initial 80 down to 66 after the third course, a 17.5% decrease). Thus, the ASEBA showed improvements in several domains. The ABC-based evaluations showed post-treatment decrease of Irritability (by 27.7 %) rating scores. Evaluation of repetitive and stereotype behavior score (RBS-R Total S/I score) showed a substantial decrease (20.1%).

Patient JM showed a trend towards a decrease heart rate (HR) during rTMS treatment (from intake 91 bpm to 83.2 bpm without any notable LF/HF index changes by the end of the treatment). JM showed a moderate decrease of SCL during rTMS sessions (from 6.06 μS down to 3.36 μS). Behavior of his cardiac activity measures were in line with those reported in our recent study (Sokhadze et al., 2016b), and was expressed as a gradual increase of HR across session numbers (see Fig. 5 for HR dynamics during second and third course of integrated treatment). The LF/HF index also showed a gradual increase from 0.85 up to 1.48.

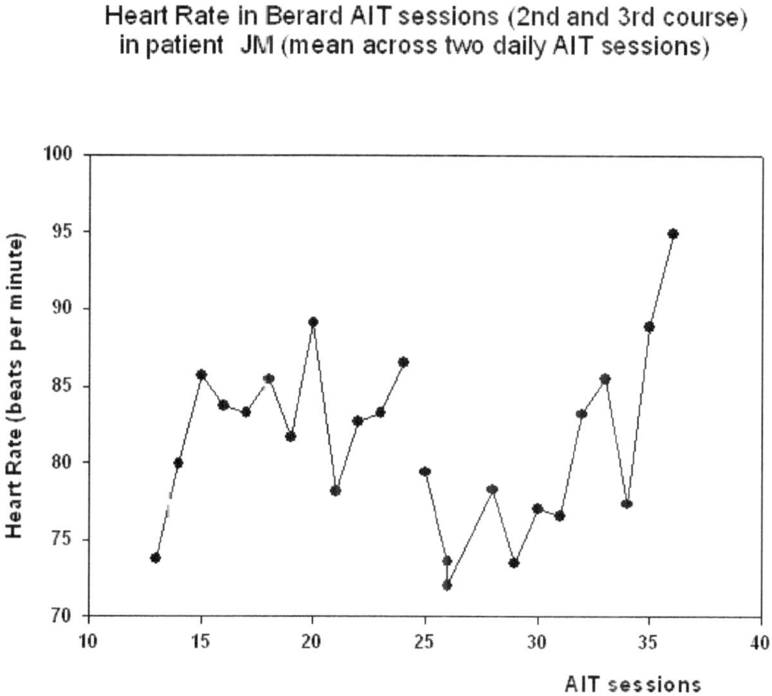

Figure 16. 5. Heart rate (HR) during Berard Auditory Integration Training (AIT) sessions during the second and third courses in patient JM. HR showed gradual increase across each course of Berard AIT. This trend is in accord with our prior results in children with ASD during AIT (Sokhadze et al., 2016b).

In a visual oddball test with Kanizsa illusory figures JM did not show changes in reaction time (RT, 644 ms vs. 660 ms) but improved accuracy (e.g., error rate from 20.1% decreased down to 4.58%). Analysis of post-treatment test ERPs showed at frontal and fronto-central sites a lower negativity of N100 to all stimuli (e.g., at midline from -4.75 μV to -2.85 μV to standard frequent stimuli) and decreased amplitude of novelty P3a component to non-target illusory figures (Fig. 16.6). Centro-parietal and parietal N200 showed increased negativity and

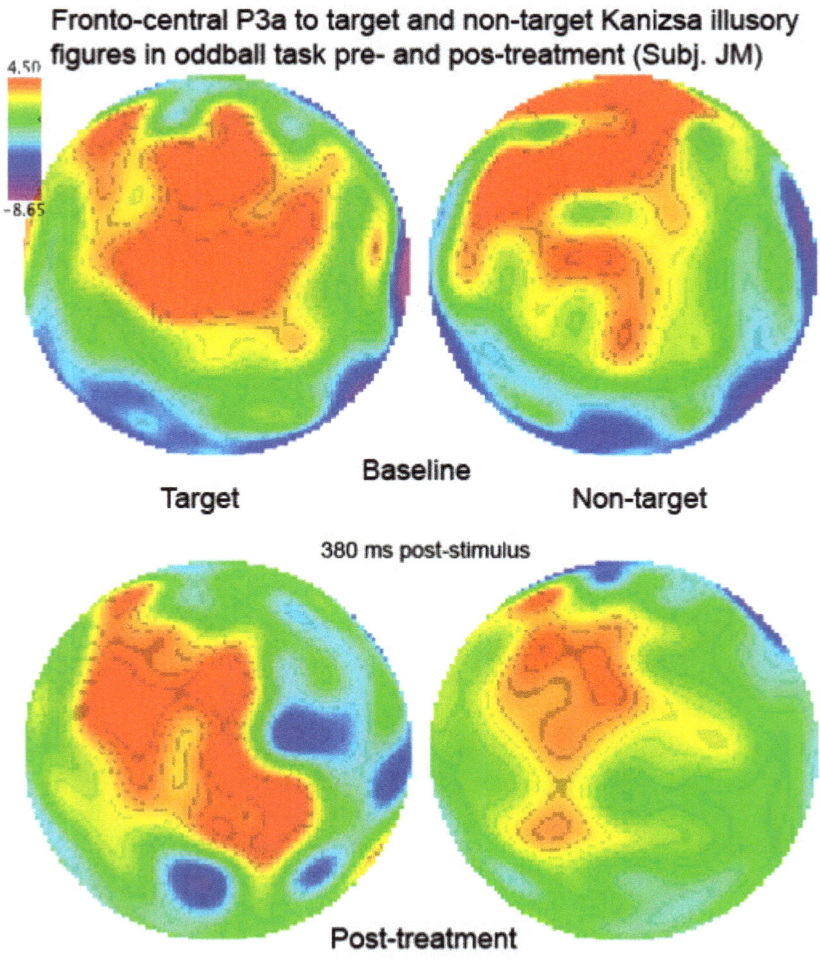

Figure 16. 6. Front-central (P3a, 380 ms post-stimulus) to target and non-target Kanizsa illusory figures in a three-stimulus visual oddball task at the intake baseline and after combined treatment in patient JM. Post-treatment maps show decreased response to task-irrelevant non-target items and more centrally distributed P3a to task-relevant targets.

prolonged latencies across all stimuli, but amplitude of P3b decreased to both non-target and target illusory figures (at midline, non-targets, from 4.75 μV down to 1.07μV, targets, from 9.25μV down to 2.94μV).

Conclusions

Results of the integrated neuromodulation intervention that combined rTMS, neurofeedback and sensory integration training in both cases resulted in improvements in behavioral ratings of autism symptoms (caregivers reports using ABC, RBS-R, SRS-2 and ASEBA questionnaires and checklists), improved accuracy of performance in visual oddball task, reduced reactivity (lower ERP amplitude, shorter latency) to task-irrelevant non-target stimuli along with improved reactivity to attended task-relevant stimuli. These results as well as reported autonomic activity changes are in many aspects concordant with our earlier studies where we used rTMS only, or a combination of rTMS with neurofeedback, neurofeedback-only, and AIT-only arms reviewed earlier, but of course, for single cases statistical comparisons with those studies are not possible. The chapter is intended to consider the advantages of combining rTMS with neurofeedback training and AIT in children with autism and the potential positive role of magnetic neuromodulation that enhances combined (neurofeedback and AIT) treatment effects.

The proposed methodology is especially important because it may lower the need for additional "booster" rTMS sessions after completion of the initial course of magnetic neuromodulation as post-TMS changes are operantly conditioned with the aid of NFB training. Furthermore, modern technologies allow the use of portable inexpensive neurofeedback systems (including home-use mobile applications for smart phones like

Android) and digital sound equalizers thus lowering the cost of NFB and AIT to help achieve longer lasting clinical effects. In general, combining rTMS treatment with neurofeedback-based operant conditioning and concurrently using sensory integration programs such as Berard AIT for children with ASD presenting sensory symptoms may advance neuromodulation approaches addressing several symptoms, deficits and other issues typical for autism.

References

Achenbach, T. M., & Rescorla, L. A. (2012). *Multicultural guide for the ASEBA forms and profiles for ages 1½–18* (2nd ed.). Burlington, VT: University of Vermont.

Aman, M. G., & Singh, N. N. (1994). *Aberrant behavior checklist - community. Supplementary manual.* East Aurora, NY: Slosson Educational Publications.

American Psychiatric Association (APA; 2013). *Diagnostic and statistical manual of mental disorders (DSM-V,* 5th ed.). American Psychiatric Publishing.

Baruth, J., Casanova, M. F., El-Baz, A., Horrell, T., Mathai, G., Sears, L., & Sokhadze, E. (2010). Low-frequency repetitive transcranial magnetic stimulation modulates evoked-gamma frequency oscillations in autism spectrum disorders. *Journal of Neurotherapy, 14*(3), 179–194.

Bodfish, J. W., Symons, F. J., & Lewis, M. H. (1999). *Repetitive behavior scale.* Morganton, NC: Western Carolina Center Research Reports.

Casanova, M. F. (2005). Minicolumnar pathology in autism. In M. F. Casanova (Ed.), *Recent developments in autism research* (pp. 133–144). New York: Nova Biomedical Books.

Casanova, M. F. (2007). The neuropathology of autism. *Brain Pathology, 17*(4), 422–433.

Casanova, M. F., Buxhoeveden, D., & Gomez, J. (2003). Disruption in the inhibitory architecture of the cell minicolumns: Implications for autism. *Neuroscientist, 9*(6), 496–507.

Casanova, M. F., Baruth, J. M., El-Baz, A., Tasman, A., Sears, L., & Sokhadze, E. (2012). Repetitive transcranial magnetic stimulation (rTMS) modulates event-related potential (ERP) indices of attention in autism. *Translational Neuroscience, 3*(2), 170–180.

Casanova, M. F., Hensley, M. K., Sokhadze, E. M., El-Baz, A. S., Wang, Y., Li, X., & Sears, L. (2014). Effects of weekly low-frequency rTMS on autonomic measures in children with autism spectrum disorders. *Frontiers in Human Neuroscience, 8*, 851.

Casanova, M. F., Sokhadze, E., Opris, I., Wang, Y., & Li, X. (2015). Autism spectrum disorders: Linking neuropathological findings to treatment with transcranial magnetic stimulation. *Acta Paediatrica, 104*(4), 346–355.

Casanova, M. F., & Sokhadze, E. M. (2014). Transcranial magnetic stimulation: Application in autism treatment. In V. W. Hu (Ed.), *Frontiers in autism research: New horizons for diagnosis and treatment* (pp. 583–606). Hackensack, NJ: World Scientific Publishing Co.

Constantino, J. N., & Gruber, C. P. (2005). *The social responsiveness scale (SRS) manual.* Los Angeles CA: Western Psychological Services.

Kanizsa, G. (1976). Subjective contours. *Scientific American, 234*(4), 48–52.

Schopler, E., Reichler, R. J., DeVellis, R. F., & Daly, K. (1980). Toward objective classification of childhood autism: Childhood Autism Rating Scale (CARS). *Journal of Autism and Developmental Disorders, 10*, 91–103.

Sokhadze, E., El-Baz, A., Baruth, J., Mathai, G., Sears, L., & Casanova M. F. (2009). Effects of low-frequency repetitive transcranial magnetic stimulation (rTMS) on gamma frequency oscillations and event-related potentials during processing of illusory figures in autism spectrum disorders. *Journal of Autism and Developmental Disorders, 39*(4), 619–634.

Sokhadze, E., Baruth, J., Tasman, A., Mansoor, M., Ramaswamy, R., Sears, L., ... Casanova, M. F. (2010). Low-frequency repetitive transcranial magnetic stimulation (rTMS) affects event-related potential measures of novelty processing in autism. *Applied Psychophysiology and Biofeedback, 35*(2), 147–161.

Sokhadze, E. M., Baruth, J. M., Sears, L., Sokhadze, G. E., El-Baz, A. S., & Casanova, M. F. (2012). Prefrontal neuromodulation using rTMS improves error monitoring and correction function in autism. *Applied Psychophysiology and Biofeedback, 37*(2), 91–102.

Sokhadze, E. M., Casanova, M. F., & Baruth, J. (2013). Transcranial magnetic stimulation in autism spectrum disorders. In L. Alba-Ferrara (Ed.), *Transcranial magnetic stimulation: Methods, clinical uses and effect on the brain* (pp. 219–231). New York: NOVA Publishers.

Sokhadze, E. M., El-Baz, A. S., Tasman, A., Sears, L. L., Wang, Y., Lamina, E. V., & Casanova, M. F. (2014a). Neuromodulation integrating rTMS and neurofeedback for the treatment of autism spectrum disorder: An exploratory study. *Applied Psychophysiology and Biofeedback, 39*(3–4), 237–257.

Sokhadze, E. M., El-Baz, A. S., Sears, L. L., Opris, I., & Casanova, M. F. (2014b). rTMS neuromodulation improves electrocortical functional measures of information processing and behavioral responses in autism. *Frontiers in Systems Neuroscience, 8*, 134

Sokhadze, E. M., Casanova, M. F., El-Baez, A. S., Farag, H. E., Li, X., & Wang, Y. (2016a). TMS-based neuromodulation of evoked

and induced gamma oscillations and event-related potentials in children with autism. *NeuroRegulation, 3*(3), 101–126.
Sokhadze, E., Casanova, M., Tasman, M., & Brockett, S. (2016b). Electrophysiological and behavioral outcomes of Berard auditory integration training (AIT) in children with autism spectrum disorder. *Applied Psychophysiology and Biofeedback 41*(4), 405–420.
Sokhadze, E. M., Casanova M. F., Casanova, E., Kelly, D. P., Khachidze, I., Wang, Y., Li, X. (2017). Applications of ERPs in autism research and as functional outcomes of neuromodulation treatment. In S. R Harris (Ed.), *Event-related potential (ERP): Methods, outcomes and research insights* (pp. 27–88). New York, NY: NOVA Science Publishers.
Sokhadze, E. M., Lamina, E. V., Casanova, E. L., Kelly, D. P., Opris, I., Tasman, A., & Casanova, M. F. (2018). Exploratory study of rTMS neuromodulation effects on electrocortical functional measures of performance in an oddball test and behavioral symptoms in autism. *Frontiers in Systems Neuroscience, 12*, 20.
Wang, Y., Hensley, M. K., Tasman, A., Sears, L., Casanova, M. F., & Sokhadze, E. M. (2016a). Heart rate variability and skin conductance during repetitive TMS course in children with autism. *Applied Psychophysiology and Biofeedback, 41*(1), 47–60,
Wang, Y., Sokhadze, E.M., El-Baz, A.S., Li, X., Sears, L., Casanova, M. F., & Tasman, A. (2016b). Relative power of specific EEG bands and their ratios during neurofeedback training in children with autism spectrum disorder. *Frontiers in Human Neuroscience, 9*, 723.
Wechsler, D. (1999). *Wechsler abbreviated scale of intelligence*. San Antonio, TX: Harcourt Assessment, Inc.

www.ingramcontent.com/pod-product-compliance
Lightning Source LLC
LaVergne TN
LVHW050907210926
848482LV00012B/370
* 9 7 8 0 9 9 7 8 1 9 4 4 1 *